The N H L All—Star Game

Andrew Podnieks

The NHL
All–Star Game

50 Years of the Great Tradition

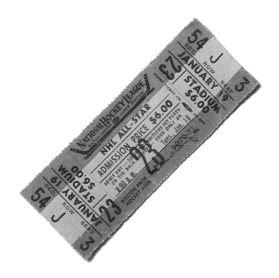

HarperCollins*PublishersLtd*

First HarperCollins hardcover ed.
ISBN 0-00-200058-X
First HarperCollins trade paper ed.
ISBN 0-00-639102-8

Canadian Cataloguing in Publication Data

Podnieks, Andrew
The NHL all–star game :
50 years of the great tradition

ISBN 0-00-200058-X

1. Hockey – Miscellanea.
2. National Hockey League –
   Miscellanea.
I. Title

GV847.8.N3P618 2000   796.962'64
C00-931180-7

00 01 02 03 04 RRD 5 4 3 2 1

Printed and bound in the United States
Set in Monotype Joanna and Gill Sans

For the families of Conn Smythe, Frank Selke,
Foster Hewitt, and Ace Bailey

Contents

Hod Stuart
Memorial Game

Montreal Arena, Thursday, January 2, 1908

Hod Stuart drowned in the Bay of Quinte on June 23, 1907, at the age of 28, just three months after helping his Montreal Wanderers of the Eastern Canadian Amateur Hockey Association (ECAHA) beat the Kenora Thistles to win the Stanley Cup. A cover-point, he was considered the finest defensive player of his time. Diving from a platform about six feet above ground at a lighthouse, Stuart was unaware of the shallowness of the waters and landed head-first in two feet of rocky water. He was found submerged, his head badly gashed and his neck broken.

Stuart began playing hockey with the Ottawa Senators in the Senior leagues, but through his business associations with his father, a contractor, he made his way to Quebec where he joined the Bulldogs. In 1902, he was offered a pro contract by the Pittsburgh entry in the International League, and the following winter his brother, Bruce, joined him there. After a year in Houghton and Portage Lake in Michigan, Stuart returned to Pittsburgh and started the 1906–07 season there. But he became disenchanted with the rough stickwork prevalent in the league and in December accepted an offer from the Wanderers at a then-record salary for a hockey player.

His reputation in Montreal quickly reached mythic proportions, and the appreciation accorded him upon news of his death was extraordinary. One such report came from an obituary in the *Montreal Gazette*:

"Stuart's work throughout the winter is well known here and requires little comment. He was the backbone of the team, and without him Wanderers would have been lost. He was a real general of the game, he knew it thoroughly himself, and could

play any position from forward to point, and he had the ability to impart what he knew to others. One feature won Stuart hosts of friends here in Montreal, and that was that in all the many hard games he took part in during the winter he played clean, gentlemanly hockey all the way through. In the famous Ottawa match which later led to the summoning of two of the players to a police court,

Hod Stuart during his
Portage Lake days.

Goalie Percy LeSueur.

Stuart bore the brunt of the rough work without flinching, and at the same time without retaliating."

In the wake of Stuart's death, the Wanderers and the other five teams in the ECAHA set up a Hod Stuart Memorial Match Committee so that a game could be arranged, the proceeds from which would go to Stuart's widow and two children. The format of the game likely represented the first-ever all–star format contest played in any sport, the Wanderers team playing a group of all–stars from around the league.

The All–Star team selections were being made literally up to game day. While it had long been assumed that Percy LeSueur would be in the All–Stars' net, two other notable goaltending stars—Paddy Moran of Quebec and Billy Nicholson of the Montreal Shamrocks—both petitioned the Committee to play. Interestingly, Ottawa and the Shamrocks were less forthcoming with their players. With the opening of the season just two days away, they were fearful of losing one of their stars to injury. Quebec offered Herb Jordan and brothers Joe and Charles "Chubby" Power for the game, though only Joe Power participated; the Shamrocks gave permission to Nicholson, Jack Laviolette, Johnny Brennan, and Jimmy Gardner;

and Billy Gilmour of Victorias, a former teammate of Stuart's, also put his name in the hat. In the end, however, only seven men could be chosen.

The game was played before a packed house at the Montreal Arena, some 3,800 spectators contributing more than $2,000 for the Stuart family. Younger brother, Bruce, who was supposed to play, had to withdraw because of injury. Jack Laviolette, too, had an eye problem that prevented him from playing, so Victorias captain Frank Patrick filled in admirably at the last minute.

Stuart's two linemates, Joe Power and Eddie Hogan, played, and the best feature of the game was that each of the teams in the league had at least one player in uniform. On the Wanderers' defence, replacing Stuart, was young Art Ross who was exhausted from the team's Western road trip and whose skates gave him problems all night long. "In flashes," however, according to reports, "he showed his best form, and fast skating and clever stick-handling won him rounds of applause."

The first half reflected only too well the team cohesion needed to succeed, with the Stars entirely unused to each others' play and passing too often unselfishly, and the Wanderers in mid-season form and building

a huge 7–1 lead. In the second half, though, the
All–Stars became more familiar with each other and
at one point reeled off five straight goals of their own.
It was a fast, clean, and entertaining game which the
fans applauded frequently.

*Details of Percy LeSueur's goal stick, with carvings to commemorate his participation
in the Hod Stuart Game. The Latin word PALMAMQUODMERUITFERAT
means "the hand that turns away the blow."*

Montreal Wanderers 10   All–Stars 7

Wanderers	All–Stars
Riley Hern, goal	Percy LeSueur, goal (Ottawa)
Art Ross, point	Rod Kennedy, point (Victorias)
Walter Smaill, cover-point	Frank Patrick, cover point (Victorias)
Frank Glass, rover	Joe Power, rover (Quebec)
Ernie Russell, centre	Grover Sargent, centre (Montreal)
Cecil Blachford, right wing	Eddie Hogan, right wing (Quebec)
Ernie Johnson, left wing	Jack Marshall, left wing (Shamrocks)

First Half
1. All–Stars, Patrick 5:00
2. Wanderers, Johnson 6:00
3. Wanderers, Russell 8:00
4. Wanderers, Glass 9:00
5. Wanderers, Russell 17:00
6. Wanderers, Russell 20:00
7. Wanderers, Blachford 21:00
8. Wanderers, Russell 23:00

Penalties: Glass (W), Patrick (AS)

Second Half
9. All–Stars, Kennedy 2:00
10. All–Stars, Patrick 8:00
11. All–Stars, Power 10:00
12. All–Stars, Power 13:00
13. All–Stars, Marshall 16:00
14. Wanderers, Blachford 19:00
15. Wanderers, Blachford 20:00
16. All–Stars, Sargent 21:00
17. Wanderers, Russell 22:00

Penalties: None
(no assists were awarded; time of goals rounded off to nearest minute; halves were thirty minutes each)

In Goal
Montreal—Hern
All–Stars—LeSueur

Referee Bob Meldrum

Judge of Play Tom Melville

Goal Umpires Charlie Cameron and D. Campbell

Attendance 3,800

Ace Bailey
Benefit Game

Maple Leaf Gardens, Wednesday, February 14, 1934

The Incident

After a violent episode in the second period of a Leafs-Bruins game at the Boston Garden on December 13, 1933, two players had to be carried off the ice. In the play that triggered the incident, Leafs defenceman King Clancy checked Eddie Shore hard as Shore was rushing the puck into the Leafs end. Dazed but bent on vengeance—and thinking he was hot in pursuit of King Clancy—Shore skated wildly at Ace Bailey as the play moved back into Boston territory. Tripped heavily from behind, Bailey fell to the ice with what Red Horner later called a sickening thud. Skating over to his stricken teammate, Horner found Bailey badly hurt, unconscious and bleeding from the head, and called Shore to account. Shore just smiled. Furious, Horner decked Shore with one punch and knocked him to the ice. Now two players were out cold on the ice.

As the Leafs gathered around Bailey, Bruins trainers attended to Shore. Anxious teammates had to carry them both off the ice. Shore had a three-inch gash to his head but Bailey's injury was far more serious, although both players soon regained consciousness. Bailey was still lying in the Bruins dressing-room when Shore came over to apologize. "It's all part of the game," Bailey graciously said. Then he passed out again and lapsed into convulsions and was rushed to nearby Audobon Hospital with what appeared to be a fractured skull.

Leafs owner Conn Smythe saw the whole play evolve from his seat and rushed to the dressing room to inquire about Bailey's condition, but he was jostled on the way by irate Bruins fans. One of them, Leonard Kenworthy of Everett, Massachusetts, sought out the nearest policeman and claimed Smythe had punched him and broken his glasses. (A piece of glass

The aftermath of the Bailey-Shore incident, December 13, 1933.

Howie Morenz

had indeed left a cut around the eye that would take three stitches to close.) Smythe was taken into custody while he was still in the dressing room with Bailey but was quickly released on a minimal bail charge of $100 and ordered to appear in court the next time his team was in Boston. Meanwhile, his distraught team had to finish the game and leave immediately after it to catch a train to Montreal.

By the following morning, Bailey's condition was grave and his death a distinct possibility, in fact all but a certainty, after a night during which he had suffered severe cerebral hemorrhaging. At noon, Dr. Donald Munro, a brain specialist, consulted with Ace's wife, Mabel, about an essential but high-risk procedure. At the same time, Boston homicide detectives were interviewing Shore and others about the incident and it became known that if Bailey should die, the charge against Shore would be manslaughter.

Bailey was transferred to City Hospital, where Dr. Munro performed two operations to relieve the pressure on his brain. After the second, on December 18, Munro bluntly stated, "His chances of living are very slim," and a priest was called in to read the last rites. Bailey's pulse was 160, his temperature was close to 106°, and the doctors felt that his life could not even be measured in minutes.

By the very next morning, however, Bailey somehow had fought off death and in the next days grew stronger and stronger. By Christmas, his life no longer hung in the balance. By mid-January, it was clear he would recover. On January 18, 1934, he was transferred to Toronto with explicit instructions that he not do any exercise at all. He was alive, he was home, but his health was still fragile. And he would never play hockey again.

Predictable blame and wild accusations ensued after the incident. Horner blamed Shore, but Shore said that he wasn't conscious of what he was doing once he had been dazed by King Clancy's hard check. Smythe blamed the Boston media for generating malicious hype leading up to the game, claiming the writers had incited the Boston players to violence. Meanwhile, league president Frank Calder absolved the two referees (Odie Cleghorn and Eusebe Daignault) of any irresponsibility in their handling of the game but suspended both Shore and Horner, the former indefinitely, the latter until January 1, 1934.

When Ace Bailey's father was informed of the accident at his home in Toronto, he flew into a rage. He boarded the first train to Boston carrying a loaded gun and telling anyone who would listen that he was going to kill Eddie Shore. Conn Smythe had gone back to Boston to keep watch over Ace. When he got wind of this added disaster approaching, he called Frank Selke back in Toronto for help. Selke could come up with only one possible answer and in turn phoned a friend in Boston, Bob Huddy, who was, like him, a chicken fancier. Fortunately, Huddy was also a member of the Boston police. Selke explained the situation to Huddy, who went straight to the bar of the hotel where Ace's father was staying. Sure

enough, Ace's father was expounding to one and all what he'd do to that so-and-so Shore when he met him face to face. Huddy managed to calm him down enough to see reason, got him to hand over the revolver, and put him on the next train back to Toronto with strict instructions to the conductor not to let him off before Union Station.

Though he repeatedly tried, Shore was not permitted to visit Bailey while Ace was still in the hospital. "I am afraid the excitement of the meeting would be too much at this time," explained Dr. Munro. When Bruins manager Art Ross managed to get in to see Ace, however, Bailey again absolved Shore of any wilful wrongdoing. Exhausted and himself near collapse, both from his own injury and worry over Bailey's condition, Shore went to Bermuda for three weeks to convalesce. When he knew Bailey would live but would not play again, Calder announced that Shore would not be allowed back to the NHL until January 28, a suspension that would last 16 games. Shore's remarkable popularity was such that when he was in uniform, the Boston Garden was routinely sold out. During his absence, attendance plummeted to about 6,000 a game.

The sports editor of the Journal in Montreal, Walter Gilhooley, first proposed a benefit game for Ace in the form of an open letter. On January 24, 1934, the NHL board of governors met in New York and decided that a special game would be staged in Toronto featuring the Leafs against the best of the rest of the league and the proceeds would go to Ace Bailey and family. The "All-Star" team would be selected by a committee consisting of Calder, Rangers owner Frank Patrick and Thomas Arnold, a league director.

Pre-Game Ceremonies

Prior to the game on Valentine's Day, 1934, the all-star players skated onto the ice in their club sweaters and had a group picture taken. They were then presented with their all-star garb by president Calder, Lester Patrick and Leafs club officials, among whom was Bailey. Goalie Charlie Gardiner came out

All-Stars' goalie Charlie Gardiner.

Ace Bailey performs the ceremonial opening faceoff between the Leafs' Joe Primeau and the Stars' Howie Morenz.

first to receive his number 1, and next in line was Eddie Shore to get his number 2. An apprehensive silence gripped the Gardens as Shore skated to centre ice. But when Bailey extended his hand to the Bruin, the crowd went wild as his sporting gesture made clear Bailey had forgiven his former opponent.

Another team picture was taken when the players were outfitted in their new sweaters. Then Ace Bailey presented the All-Stars with commemorative windbreakers donated by Conn Smythe and Colonel McGee of the T. Eaton Company. After that, he gave the two referees and all the players on both teams special medals donated by Leo Dandurand. (A medal was also given to trainer Bill O'Brien of the Maroons, who was "oil-man" for the All-Stars that night). Last, the players were presented with specially made sticks.

The ceremonies culminated with an historic presentation when Conn Smythe handed Bailey his number 6 and said:

"Allow me to present this sweater that you have worn so long and nobly for the Maple Leafs. No other player will ever use this number on the Maple Leaf hockey team."

Numbers had been retired in other sports (the number 1 of Jeff Russell of Montreal was listed in all Big Four programs for many years, the Hamilton Tigers had retired David Tope's number, and the University of Toronto had retired Johnny Copp's number 6 for Varsity rugby), but this was the first time in hockey.

During the warmup, seven-year-old Howie Morenz Jr. skated with the All-Stars wearing a sweater bearing the number ½. And before facing off the puck, Ace presented president Calder with a special trophy bearing Bailey's own name that had been produced by the Leafs in the hope that it would go to the winner of an annual game among All-Stars to set up a fund for injured players.

The Game

Charlie Conacher played the first two minutes of the game but he didn't come back after taking some punishment. Hooley Smith's bad knee also caught up with him; he played briefly but wasn't very effective. Frank Finnigan was cut over the eye and King Clancy was also hurt briefly, but for the most part there was remarkably little bodychecking and physical play. Sportsmanship was the order of the night, as testified by the fact that Eddie Upthegrove (the Leafs' penalty timekeeper) did not have a single visitor to his box. And this would become an All-Star Game tradition. As King Clancy appropriately said to coach Dick Irvin on the bench during the second period, "Gee, Dick, it's hell to watch all that speed coming in and no bodychecking." At another point in play, Red Horner said a brief, "Hello, Eddie," to Shore and Shore said, "Hello, Red," back.

Much like today, intermissions during the 1930s were full of on-ice entertainment, and the Ace Bailey Benefit Game was no exception. Courtesy of the Toronto Skating Club, fans were treated to a series of "fancy skating" and clown acts. In the first intermission, Junior City champion pair Helen Hobbs and Lorraine Hopkins performed, as did Edward Gooderham and Maude Smith and Jack Eastwood and Osburn Colson, runners-up in the Dominion fours. In the second intermission, Canadian and North American singles champion Constance Wilson Samuels was the feature attraction along with Adolph Windsperger, a renowned barrel jumper.

Paid attendance at the Gardens that night produced $20,909.40 for Ace Bailey and his family.

The pre-game ceremonies, featuring the presentation of All-Star sweaters to the players.

A stick used in the game (top) and the puck (bottom) from the Ace Bailey Benefit Game.

Toronto Maple Leafs 7   All–Stars 3

<table>
<tr><td colspan="2">Toronto Maple Leafs
Dick Irvin, coach</td><td colspan="2">All–Stars
Lester Patrick, coach (N.Y. Rangers)</td></tr>
</table>

		Toronto Maple Leafs			All–Stars
1	G	George Hainsworth	1	G	Charlie Gardiner (Chicago)
2	D	Red Horner	2	D	Eddie Shore (Boston)
3	D	Alex Levinsky	3	RW	Frank Finnigan (Ottawa)
4	D	Hap Day	4	LW	Aurel Joliat (Montreal Canadiens)
5	C	Andy Blair	5	LW	Herbie Lewis (Detroit)
7	D	King Clancy	6	D	Ching Johnson (N.Y. Rangers)
8	LW	Baldy Cotton	7	D	Lionel Conacher (Chicago)
9	RW	Charlie Conacher	9	C	Nels Stewart (Boston)
10	C	Joe Primeau	10	C	Hooley Smith (Montreal Maroons)
11	LW	Harvey Jackson	11	C	Normie Himes (N.Y. Americans)
12	LW	Hec Kilrea	12	D	Red Dutton (N.Y. Americans)
14	C	Bill Thoms	14	RW	Larry Aurie (Detroit)
15	RW	Ken Doraty	15	RW	Bill Cook (N.Y. Rangers)
16	RW	Charlie Sands	16	C	Howie Morenz (Montreal Canadiens)
17	LW	Buzz Boll	17	D	Al Shields (Ottawa)
			18	RW	Jimmy Ward (Montreal Maroons)

First Period

1. Toronto: Cotton (Blair, Doraty) 4:00
2. Toronto: Jackson (Kilrea, Primeau) 7:11
3. All–Stars: Stewart (Ward) 14:15

Penalties: None

Second Period

4. Toronto: Jackson (Thoms) 1:33
5. All–Stars: Morenz (Joliat) 8:24
6. All–Stars: Finnigan (Stewart). 9:15
7. Toronto: Day (unassisted) 11:13

Penalties: None

Third Period

8. Toronto: Kilrea (Jackson) 4:05
9. Toronto: Doraty (Blair) 18:26
10. Toronto: Blair (unassisted) 18:41

Penalties: None

In Goal

Toronto—Hainsworth
All–Stars—Gardiner

Referees Bobby Hewitson and Mike Rodden

Attendance 14,074

Howie Morenz Memorial Game

Montreal Forum, Wednesday, November 3, 1937

Over the years, Howarth (Howie) Morenz became known by a series of nicknames that celebrated his speed. Starting from his home town, the Mitchell (Ontario) Meteor went on to become the Stratford Streak during his intermediate years and then the Canadian Comet and the Hurtling Habitant. He played for the Canadiens for 11 seasons and scored as many as 40 goals in 1929–30 before being traded to Chicago and then to the Rangers, which took him away from Montreal for two unhappy years. When Cecil Hart took over the Habs as general manager in 1936, his first order of business was to re-acquire Morenz, and Howie was overjoyed to return to the land of the *bleu, blanc et rouge* for what would be his last year in the league, 1936–37. His career, and ultimately his life, would come to an end at the Montreal Forum on January 28, 1937, in what seemed an innocuous game against the Chicago Blackhawks.

Morenz was skating along the boards behind the Chicago net when he was checked by Earl Seibert. He fell hard and his skate blade got caught in a gap in the boards, which were then made of wood. As Seibert followed through on his check, Howie's body went one way while his leg stayed in place, shattering it in five separate locations just above the ankle. He was taken off the ice on a stretcher and rushed to St. Luke's Hospital with a career-threatening injury.

But it wasn't his leg wounds that caused his demise so much as his friends and a legion of fans. In St. Luke's, Morenz was besieged by well-wishers, all of whom were concerned about the distress they imagined this kind of injury would engender in a player who seemed born to skate but might not play again. Howie's hospital room was soon hosting a long and

Aurel Joliat pays respect to his teammate at the stall of Howie Morenz.

continuous party, and it wasn't a dry one. One visitor noted, "The whiskey was on the dresser and the beer was under the bed." Eventually, doctors had to restrict visits to family. Morenz had a mental breakdown and then, on March 7, a heart attack. He died the next day of a coronary embolism, never having left the hospital he was admitted to with a broken leg. Long-time teammate Aurel Joliat had another take on the tragedy: "When he realized that he would never play again, he couldn't live with it. I think Howie died of a broken heart." He was 34.

His number 7 sweater had hung in his usual stall in the Canadiens dressing room for the two years that he'd been away, which was the club's way of saying they missed him but he was still with them in spirit. When his leg had been broken, the sweater again hung in his stall, empty, limp, and unclaimed. Now it was immediately and officially retired by the club for the last time.

On March 11, 1937, centre ice at the Forum was reserved for Howie Morenz for one final celebration. There his body lay in state from 11 a.m. to 2:30 p.m., when funeral services were conducted—entirely in English—that began with "Nearer My God to Thee" and ended with "Abide with Me." Tens of thousands of fans had by then passed his coffin, and many more attended his funeral at the Mount Royal Cemetery. Radio station CFCF broadcast the proceedings and floral arrangements in the shape of the number seven seemed to be everywhere in the city. Seated around the rink were members of management and all the members of the Maple Leafs and Maroons, who that night played a game on the same sheet of ice.

Right after Morenz broke his leg, planning had begun for a testimonial game in the fall with the proceeds going to Howie. Now it would be a memorial game and his widow would receive all the funds.

This was not the second benefit, after the Ace Bailey Game in 1934, though it was much better known than the previous contest for Nels Crutchfield. "Crutch" had played for the Canadiens during his rookie season of 1934–35, but on September 28, 1935, he was involved in a serious car accident that ended his career and nearly cost him his life. The Canadiens organized a benefit night-not a true All-Star Game-in his honour, to be held January 31, 1936, at the Forum. The night was a series of entertainments and featured "fancy skating," a race between goalies Wilf Cude and Bill Beveridge, a women's game between the Canadiennes and Maroons, and two

"mini" All–Star games featuring numerous future Hall of Famers, notably Mike Grant, Newsy Lalonde, Art Ross, King Clancy, and Charlie Conacher. In all, the evening raised $7,000 and was attended by 11,000 fans. Although many All-Stars played in the games for Crutchfield, the evening has not endured in the minds of hockey historians as a true All–Star Game.

Perhaps because it was played so long after his death, or perhaps because (unlike Ace Bailey) he didn't survive his accident, the Howie Morenz Memorial Game was not hugely successful. Only 8,683 fans attended, raising $11,447. (During the game, Morenz's sweater and full uniform were auctioned off for another $500. Bought by Joe Catarinich, a former owner of the Habs, they were promptly returned between periods to Howie Morenz Jr. In fact, little Howie stole the show that night, skating in the warmup with both the NHL and Montreal All–Stars, shooting on the goalies and earning the loudest applause of the evening. Indeed, many of the players remarked how much Junior looked like his father.) Proceeds from the sale of programs for 25 cents each were also donated to the family. The Canadiens administration added $2,000 and the players another $900, and a few other gifts boosted Mary Morenz's hockey legacy to close to $20,000.

Pre-game ceremonies saw the presentation of league trophies to the winners from the previous year, namely, the Vezina to Normie Smith (Detroit), the Lady Byng to Marty Barry (Detroit), and the Hart Trophy to Babe Siebert (Canadiens). The ceremonies were augmented by the participation of the Honourable E.L. Patenaude, Quebec's lieutenant-governor, and Montreal mayor Adhemar Raynault.

The game itself was difficult for most of the All–Stars, few of whom were familiar with each other's style of play. Eddie Shore was in mid-season form for the All–Stars, and Marty Barry, Charlie Conacher, and Cecil Dillon also acquitted themselves well. Teammates Babe Siebert and Johnny Gagnon sparkled for the Montreal side, but the highlight of play was the second period, when both goalies made several spectacular stops. And it came to a close on a high note. The All–Stars had built a comfortable lead of 6–2 with only

five minutes left when the Montreal team rallied furiously to score three times in as many minutes and then almost tied the score in the final moments.

Pall-bearers take Howie Morenz into the Montreal Forum one last time.

Although he only played one year with the Canadiens,
Nels Crutchfield was given a special Benefit Night
by the team after his career-ending car accident in 1936.

All–Stars 6   Montreal All–Stars 5

Montreal All–Stars
Cecil Hart, coach (Canadiens)

All–Stars
Jack Adams, coach (Detroit)

1	G	Wilf Cude (Canadiens)
3	D	King Clancy (Maroons)
4	LW	Aurel Joliat (Canadiens)
5	D	Cy Wentworth (Maroons)
6	D	Walt Buswell (Canadiens)
8	C	Pit Lepine (Canadiens)
9	RW	Jimmy Ward (Maroons)
10	RW	Earl Robinson (Maroons)
11	C	Paul Haynes (Canadiens)
12	C	Russ Blinco (Maroons)
14	LW	Toe Blake (Canadiens)
15	D	Babe Siebert (Canadiens)
16	RW	Johnny Gagnon (Canadiens)
17	LW	Baldy Northcott (Maroons)
19	LW	Georges Mantha (Canadiens)
20	LW	Dave Trottier (Maroons)
2	G	Bill Beveridge (Maroons) did not play

2	G	Tiny Thompson (Boston)
3	D	Ebbie Goodfellow (Detroit)
4	D	Eddie Shore (Boston)
5	D	Red Horner (Toronto)
6	D	Dit Clapper (Boston)
7	LW	Sweeney Schriner (N.Y. Americans)
8	RW	Charlie Conacher (Toronto)
9	LW	Harvey Jackson (Toronto)
10	C	Art Chapman (N.Y. Americans)
11	RW	Cecil Dillon (N.Y. Rangers)
12	LW	Johnny Gottselig (Chicago)
14	RW	Mush March (Chicago)
15	LW	Hap Day (N.Y. Americans)
16	C	Frank Boucher (N.Y. Rangers)
17	C	Marty Barry (Detroit)
1	G	Normie Smith (Detroit) did not play

First Period
1. Montreal: Gagnon (Blinco) 2:12
2. All–Stars: Clapper (Conacher) 13:06
3. All–Stars: Gottselig (Chapman) 15:44
Penalties: Horner (AS)

Second Period
4. All–Stars: Dillon (Gottselig, Barry) 4:30
Penalties: None

Third Period
5. Montreal: Lepine (Ward, Blake) 0:51
6. All–Stars: Conacher (unassisted) 2:08
7. All–Stars: Schriner (unassisted) 2:51
8. All–Stars: Barry (Dillon, Shore) 15:00
9. Montreal: Siebert (Gagnon) 16:13
10. Montreal: Gagnon (Siebert, Mantha) 17:03
11. Montreal: Haynes (unassisted) 19:15
Penalties: None

In Goal
Montreal—Cude
All–Stars—Thompson

Referees Eusebe Daignault and Mickey Ion

Attendance 8,683

Babe Siebert
Memorial Game

Montreal Forum, Sunday, October 29, 1939

Babe Siebert won a Stanley Cup in his rookie season (1925–26) and achieved lasting fame as a member of the Montreal Maroons' famous S Line with Nels Stewart and Hooley Smith. Though this line stayed together for only three seasons, it left an indelible mark for production and tough play. Sometimes called the Ironback Babe or Iron Stick, Siebert was as good a defender as scorer, and no less a critic than rough, tough Eddie Shore once called him the greatest player in the game.

Acquired by Montreal general manager Cecil Hart the same summer he re-acquired Howie Morenz (1936), Siebert played for the Canadiens for three years and retired at 35 after 14 years in the league. Almost immediately, he was appointed coach of the Habs for the upcoming 1939–40 season. But then tragedy struck in late August 1939 at the resort town of St. Joseph, Ontario. Just before 4 p.m. on the 25th, Babe was swimming with his two daughters, Judie (11) and Joan (10), and a friend, Clayton Hoffman. The girls had been playing in the water with an inflated tire, but when it was time to come in, somehow they lost control of it. They pleaded with dad to go get it and he started to swim. Then something went wrong for the normally strong, able swimmer and he screamed out for help. By the time Hoffman tried to reach him, Siebert had gone under. His family and friends could only think he got tired swimming after the tube, which was steadily being blown farther away from him. His body was found three days later.

Siebert was not only a fine hockey player, he was also devoted to his wife, Bernice, who had been paralysed from the waist down since their second child had been born. Babe was well-known in Montreal for carrying his wife to her rinkside seat in his arms before each game and to the car after. As league president Frank Calder duly noted: "He was not only a fine man from a point of view of hockey, but he was a model father and a fine husband to his sick wife. He was a

LA PRESSE, MONTRÉAL, SAMEDI 5 JANVIER 1929

BABE SIEBERT

L'un des piliers de la défense du Montréal, et l'un des plus rapides joueurs de la ligue professionnelle. Siebert est un artiste du hockey. Il est l'un des hommes les plus brillants et les plus effectifs sur le club de M. James Strachan.

model of self-sacrifice." Former teammate Wilf Cude agreed. "It's really a double tragedy," he said, "because he meant so much to his wife." It was she who would benefit from the Siebert Memorial Game played that fall both to honour her husband and provide some financial support. As with the Morenz game before it, however, the Montreal attendance was weak as just 6,000 watched the game at the Forum. Still, with program and advertising sales factored in, the game raised more than $15,000 for the Siebert family.

Syl Apps was the standout player of the evening, scoring once and setting up three other all–star goals. Though the game was not terribly lively, Eddie Shore stole the show just before the third period started. As the orchestra played, he skated out and danced a "shag" to the music. A dour and venomous opponent at the best of times, Shore brought down the house, which hooted and hollered for an encore. He obliged them and won—at least temporarily—the hearts of the Montreal crowd.

Team-mates and friends attend Babe Siebert's funeral in Montreal.

A. C. "Babe" Siebert Memorial Fund

ALL PROCEEDS
FOR FAMILY
OF LATE
BELOVED CANADIEN
HOCKEY
STAR

★

TOUTES LES RECETTES
IRONT
A LA FAMILLE
DU
REGRETTE JOUEUR
ETOILE DU
CLUB DE HOCKEY
CANADIEN

N. H. L. ALL-STARS vs. CANADIENS
FORUM - MONTREAL - SUN., OCT. 29th, 1939
SOUVENIR PROGRAMME
TWENTY-FIVE CENTS

All–Stars 5   Montreal Canadiens 2

		Montreal Canadiens Pit Lepine, coach				All–Stars Art Ross, coach (Boston)
1	G	Wilf Cude		1	G	Frank Brimsek (Boston)
2	D	Cy Wentworth		2	D	Art Coulter (N.Y. Rangers)
3	D	Walt Buswell		2	D	Eddie Shore (Boston)
4	C	Polly Drouin		5	D	Dit Clapper (Boston)
5	RW	Rod Lorrain		5	D	Ebbie Goodfellow (Detroit)
6	LW	Toe Blake		6	C	Neil Colville (N.Y. Rangers)
8	LW	Louis Trudel		7	LW	Johnny Gottselig (Chicago)
10	C	Paul Haynes		8	RW	Syd Howe (Detroit)
11	C	Ray Getliffe		8	LW	Tom Anderson (N.Y. Americans)
12	LW	Georges Mantha		10	C	Syl Apps (Toronto)
14	RW	Johnny Gagnon		11	LW	Harvey Jackson (N.Y. Americans)
15	RW	Earl Robinson		12	RW	Gord Drillon (Toronto)
16	D	Red Goupille		17	RW	Bobby Bauer (Boston)
17	LW	Armand Mondou		17	D	Earl Seibert (Chicago)
20	D	Doug Young				

First Period
1. All–Stars: Bauer (Apps, Gottselig) 8:30
2. All–Stars: Shore (Apps, Gottselig) 10:07
Penalties: None

Second Period
3. All–Stars: Apps (Bauer). 2:05
4. Montreal: Robinson (Mantha, Getliffe). 5:49
5. All–Stars: Gottselig (Apps, Coulter) 7:49
6. All–Stars: Seibert (unassisted) 11:21
7. Montreal: Trudel (Drouin, Lorrain) 19:15
Penalties: Goupille (Mtl), Goodfellow (AS), Wentworth (Mtl)

Third Period
No Scoring
Penalties: Jackson (AS)

In Goal
Montreal—Cude
All–Stars—Brimsek

Referees King Clancy and Bill Stewart

Attendance 6,000

The NHL Establishes a Players' Pension Fund

Maple Leaf Gardens, Monday, October 13, 1947

When the NHL agreed at its 1947 spring meeting to stage an All–Star Game of some sort in the fall, there was no immediate consensus that the receipts would go toward establishing a pension fund. These notes from the board of governors' meetings indicate that the issue had hardly been settled:

Players Pensions and Savings Plan

A proposal for the establishment of a Players Pensions and Savings Plan was received from the Players Committee and the President reported upon his conference with that Committee held on May 23rd. After considerable discussion it was the general opinion that the proposal's feature to provide pensions in respect to "past service" would impose an unreasonably onerous burden and probably could not be undertaken. There was a great deal of doubt in the minds of the Governors as to whether the plan without its "past service" feature would arouse sufficient interest and support on the part of the players to warrant further examination of the plan.

It was agreed that the President should communicate this opinion to the Players Committee and if there was a further desire on their part to pursue the matter, the President and a committee to be nominated by him should meet the Players Committee and explore the possibilities of the other feature of the proposal.

It was also agreed that the Management of each club would contact its players and their representatives to discuss certain features of the proposals from the club standpoint.

All–Star Charity Game

The applications of Chicago and Toronto to stage the All–Star Charity Game and the alternative suggestion to stage two such games in the Season 1947–48 were considered and it was the opinion of the Meeting that only one such game should be staged. The President reported that he had drafted the schedule so as to make the staging of the game in Chicago possible on December 10, 1947. The Toronto application called for the game to be played before the opening of the season on October 13, 1947, and would involve no expenses with the rink, the staff or promotional costs.

It was finally agreed upon the motion of Mr. Ross, seconded by Senator Raymond that in view of the special circumstances arising from this year's All–Star selections that the game between the NHL All–Stars and the Stanley Cup Winners be staged at Toronto on October 13, 1947, and that the All–Star game in the season 1948–49 be allocated definitely to Chicago.

The following points were also agreed upon:

(a) The Team should be composed of the First and Second NHL All–Star teams plus an additional player from Detroit and Chicago and three players from New York Rangers, and all Clubs agreed to make the designated players available.

(b) The Coach of the team will be Dick Irvin.

(c) Each Club will be responsible for the expenses of all its personnel taking part in any capacity.

(d) The All–Star uniforms and the officiating will be the responsibility of the League.

(e) There are to be no deductions from the

Gross Gate receipts for rink rental, staff, promotion, advertising or other expenses, and appropriate action should be taken to secure exemption from Federal Amusement Tax.

(f) The proceeds are to be divided as follows:

One-third of the proceeds to local charities to be designated by the Toronto Club.

Two-thirds of the proceeds to the Players Emergency (Benevolent and Disability) Fund.

The financial groundswell for the All–Star Game was formalized at the board of governors' meeting in New York on September 5, 1947. Representing the players were Syl Apps of Toronto, Sid Abel of Detroit and Glen Harmon of Montreal. Everyone agreed a pension for players was essential to their welfare, and to that end the players agreed to put $900 of their salary into a pension fund every season (a hefty sum, given that most were only making about $5,000 per season). In return, the owners would contribute to the fund in two ways: 25 cents from the sale of every playoff ticket and two-thirds of the proceeds from the All–Star Game would go into the fund. As a result, when he reached 45, a player could start collecting a pension that would pay out $8 per year of service per month. For example, a player with 10 years of play in the league would receive $80 a month for the rest of his life. And if he could defer the start date for the pension, the amount would increase. Proceeds from this particular game went to both the players' pension fund and the Community Chest of Greater Toronto welfare project. In the end, the 1947 game raised $25,865 for the pension fund.

The team that was fielded for this game was much more a lineup of star combinations than individual players. Both defensive pairings were regular-season partners (Reardon and Bouchard with the Canadiens, Stewart and Quackenbush with Detroit) and the forwards were also set lines from league play. The Bruins' Kraut Line of Schmidt, Dumart, and Bauer was of signal importance because Bobby Bauer had retired at the end of the previous season and was playing by special invitation from the NHL in his last career game. Chicago provided the top Pony Line of Bill Mosienko and the Bentley brothers (Max and Doug), while the Rangers sent their famous threesome of Laprade, Leswick, and Warwick. Maurice Richard and Ted Lindsay were also on hand for the action as forwards.

But the very formation of an all–star team was attended by divergent opinions. Art Ross of Boston claimed that this would be "the greatest team ever assembled," while a more cautious Frank Boucher included the caveat that:

"If an all–star team played several games together, I have not the slightest doubt they could beat all comers easily. But since this is not so, I shouldn't be surprised if Toronto defeated the all–star aggregation."

The Leafs came to the game with an extra motivation. They were Stanley Cup champions, but the other coaches in the league hadn't voted a single Leaf on to either the First or Second All–Star Team for the previous year. (Coaches couldn't vote for players on their own team, so Hap Day had in no way been culpable here.) According to the rules at the time, the All–Stars coach had to have at least three players from each team on his roster so Irvin added Laprade, Warwick, and Leswick of the Rangers, Mosienko of Chicago, and Lindsay of Detroit to reach the numbers he needed.

To host this inaugural game, the Gardens had been the first rink in the league to replace its wire fencing with new Herculite glass. The reviews for the glass on this opening night were not glowing, however. Two players (Jack Stewart and Bob Goldham) were cut after smashing their faces against the glass standards, and a good many fans complained they missed some of the sounds and thus what was perhaps most exciting in the play of the game.

Pre-Game Events

A full itinerary was cramped into one afternoon on the day of the game. Hockey's luminaries were guests of the Leafs at the annual Thanksgiving Day football game between the CFL's Argos and the Hamilton Tiger Cats at Varsity Stadium. Then there was a dinner at 5:30 p.m. at the Royal York Hotel. Organized by Leafs management, it included 185 special guests, most notably Ontario Premier George Drew, Toronto mayor Robert Saunders, and NHL president Clarence Campbell (all of whom would take part in the opening faceoff just three hours later). Campbell also took the opportunity to formally announce that Chicago would host the next All–Star clash.

Pre-Game Ceremonies

In what would become a tradition, the pre-game presentations represented a bundle of very mixed loot. Each member of the First All–Star Team from the 1946–47 season received a miniature engraved gold puck. (During the second intermission, an additional 11 gold pucks were given to each of the Leafs who had been selected to the First Team since All–Star Teams had first been selected in 1931: Sweeney Schriner, Charlie Conacher, Lorne Carr, Gord Drillon, Syl Apps, Wally Stanowski, King Clancy, Gaye Stewart, Harvey Jackson, Turk Broda, and Babe Pratt.) In addition, Howie Meeker was presented with his Calder Trophy for the previous year by a member of the board of directors for the Leafs, W.A.H. (Bill) MacBrien. The government of Ontario pitched in with a set of gold cufflinks for each player from the 1947 Stanley Cup champion Leafs team and, not to be outdone, Leafs owner Conn Smythe presented each champion player with a lifetime pass to the Gardens. Sponsors chipped in with more stuff than a Boxing Day sale could provide: All the Leafs garnered sweater coats from Eaton's, hats from Simpsons, table lighters from Birks, golf balls from CCM, ties from Sammy Taft (better known for his hats), cigarette boxes from

Sweeney Schriner of the All–Stars and captain Syl Apps of Toronto take the ceremonial faceoff.

the Gardens, pocket knives from Dick Dowling, team photos from Alexandra Studios, silver tea trays from the NHL, engraved gold wrist watches from the city of Toronto, and silver watch chains from Conn Smythe (again) and Dick Irvin.

Prior to the player introductions, the house lights were dimmed and two regal trumpeters stepped out onto the ice to acknowledge each player from the First All-Star Team with a couple of eye- and ear-opening blasts. Ken Reardon would later recall it as "one of the most moving moments of my career." And, as a member of the traditionally archrival Canadiens, he was surely reflecting the mood of excitement in Maple Leaf Gardens that night.

The Game

In an attempt to introduce some variety, the referee and linesmen were decked out in midnight blue sweaters and slacks for the first of what was now

When all was at last said and done, the game was a success on the ice as well as at the box office. Overall, Kenny Reardon perhaps said it best when he later recalled of the historic night:

"We were so determined to win that game you could almost hear the fellows grinding their teeth as they walked to the ice. I never saw a group so fired up in all my hockey career."

Bill Durnan started with a game effort in the All-Stars net despite a knee injury that could have used a rest. Although he had required surgery a few weeks before for torn cartilage, he deemed himself fit for the glamour game. Perhaps not surprisingly, he lost his half of the tilt 3–1 and was the one All-Star who "failed to twinkle," as legendary hockey writer Red Burnett described. When Frank Brimsek replaced Durnan, the All-Stars mounted a game-winning

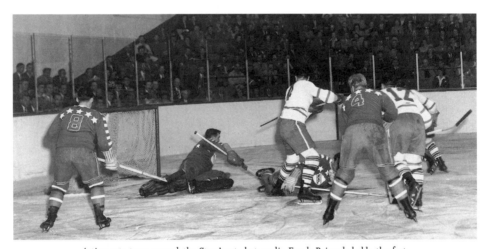

Action gets tense around the Stars' net, but goalie Frank Brimsek holds the fort.

being proposed as an annual game. The fans loved it, but league president Clarence Campbell ordered the on-ice officials back into traditional white for the regular season. For their part, the All-Stars wore bright scarlet sweaters with white stripes on the arms and rows of white stars across the chest, above the NHL shield.

comeback. The outcome was marred when Bill Mosienko fractured his ankle early in the second period after an innocuous-looking check by Jim Thomson. While Mosienko was having his leg put in a cast at the Wellesley Hospital later that night, his wife was back in Winnipeg giving birth. Furthermore, as a result of this serious injury, Mosienko

William Hewitt makes a presentation to a Leaf at the All–Star dinner preceding the game itself.

missed the first 20 games of the regular season.

After the first period, All–Star coach Dick Irvin played Schmidt–Richard–Doug Bentley as the first line and Max Bentley–Bauer–Dumart as the second. Rocket Richard led the attack early in the third, first with a goal, then with a nice three-way play with Doug Bentley and Schmidt. Reardon was a physical presence all night. He received a major penalty for cutting Bob Goldham on the head after taking a dirty cross-check, and at the final bell he exchanged stick swings with both Ezinicki and Mortson. Vic Lynn was counting

four stitches to the corner of his left eye from another high stick from Warwick, who nicked him just as he had a great chance on goal. Brimsek was sensational in the crease, especially in the final minute when coach Day pulled Broda for an extra attacker and the Leafs scrambled to tie.

Perhaps the most notable aspect of the All–Stars was the singular fact that the bitterest of enemies during the season were now, for one game, on a team. Of course, it could not make a silk purse of every pig's ear. The immersion course in sportsmanly camaraderie didn't transform Maurice Richard one iota, and he all but ignored temporary teammate and perpetual nemesis Ted Lindsay.

"I didn't talk to him," the Rocket spat after the game. "We didn't even say hello. He tried talking to me, but I just ignored him. I don't like him, not even for an All–Star Game."

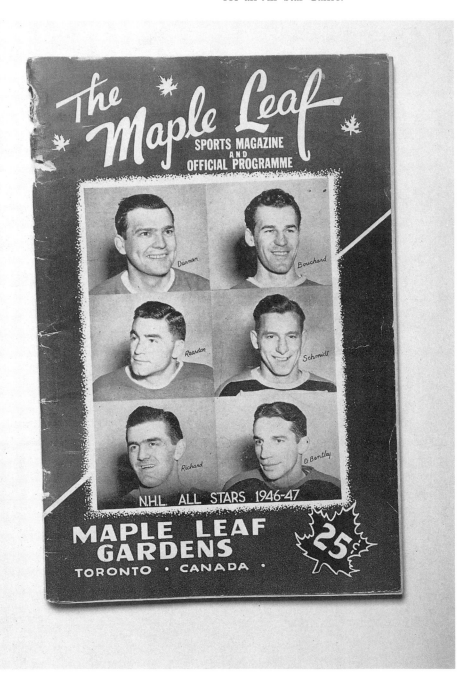

All–Stars 4   Toronto Maple Leafs 3

			Toronto Maple Leafs Hap Day, coach
1	G		Turk Broda
2	D		Bob Goldham
3	D		Wally Stanowski
4	L		Harry Watson
5	RW		Don Metz
7	C		Bud Poile
9	C		Ted Kennedy
10	C		Syl Apps "C"
12	RW		Bill Ezinicki
14	D		Vic Lynn
15	RW		Howie Meeker
16	LW		Gaye Stewart
17	LW		Joe Klukay
19	D		Gus Mortson
20	D		Jim Thomson
21	D		Bill Barilko
22	C		Fleming Mackell

			All–Stars Dick Irvin, coach (Montreal)
1b	G		Frank Brimsek (Boston)
1a	G		Bill Durnan (Montreal)
2b	D		Jack Stewart (Detroit)
3a	D		Butch Bouchard (Montreal)
4b	D		Bill Quackenbush (Detroit)
5b	C		Max Bentley (Chicago)
6	RW		Bill Mosienko (Chicago)
7a	LW		Doug Bentley (Chicago)
8	RW		Grant Warwick (New York)
9a	RW		Maurice Richard (Montreal)
10	C		Edgar Laprade (New York)
11	LW		Ted Lindsay (Detroit)
14b	LW		Woody Dumart (Boston)
15a	C		Milt Schmidt (Boston)
17b	LW		Bobby Bauer (Boston)
17a	D		Ken Reardon (Montreal)
18	LW		Tony Leswick (New York)

a=selected to First All–Star Team for 1946–47

b=selected to Second All–Star Team for 1946–47

First Period

1. Toronto: Watson (Ezinicki) 12:29

Penalties: Mortson (Tor), Leswick (AS), Ezinicki (Tor), Ezinicki (Tor), Bauer (AS)

Second Period

2. Toronto: Ezinicki (Apps, Watson) 1:03
3. All–Stars: M. Bentley (Reardon) 4:39
4. Toronto: Apps (Watson) 5:01
5. All–Stars: Warwick (Laprade, Reardon) 17:35

Penalties: Lynn (Tor—minor, major) and Reardon (AS—minor, major)

Third Period

6. All–Stars: Richard (unassisted) 0:28
7. All–Stars: D. Bentley (Schmidt, Richard) 1:26

Penalties: Mortson (Tor), Mortson (Tor), Bouchard (AS), Ezinicki (Tor), Schmidt (AS)

In Goal

Toronto—Broda

All–Stars—Durnan/Brimsek [Brimsek (no goals) replaced Durnan (3 goals) at 11:00 of 2nd period]

Referee King Clancy

Linesmen Jim Primeau and Ed Mepham

Attendance 14,169

The Mosienko Effect

Chicago Stadium, Wednesday, November 3, 1948

Blackhawks president Bill Tobin had been instrumental in establishing the inaugural game. In its second year, it was to be held in Chicago (even though the Leafs had won the Cup), as promised in the previous season's negotiations. So it was that in 1948 Tobin helped raise $23,018 for the players' pension fund at the Stadium.

The day of the game, John P. Carmichael, sports editor of the *Chicago Daily News*, the event's official sponsor, hosted a lunch at the LaSalle Hotel. A portion of the profits was earmarked for the *News'* veterans' fund. (The LaSalle was the veritable pulse of the Windy City the day of the game, not only because of the NHL presence but because Thomas Dewey's Republican Party headquarters were set up there and the U.S. election—in which he was heavily favoured by the locals—was just a few days away. Alas, Dewey went down to defeat at the hands of Harry S. Truman.) Speaking at the noontime feed were league president Clarence Campbell; Conn Smythe; James Norris; Syl Apps, president of the NHL pension fund; and Lou Boudreau, player–manager of baseball's world champion Cleveland Indians and a season ticket holder for Hawks games. After Boudreau spoke, Conn Smythe and Art Ross exchanged heated—and this time mock—insults for the better part of 45 minutes, much to the delight of a crowd that had witnessed this sort of exchange in earnest countless times over the years.

Leaf goalie Turk Broda withstands a Stars' attack during the 1948 game.

Additionally, profits from Foster Hewitt's broadcast of the game were to go to the Red Feather campaign in Toronto.

There were some peculiarities to the scheduling of this particular game. Rather than bringing an end to the training camp season, as it had in the previous year and would for about the next 20, this All–Star Game was played three weeks *after* the start of the season. Thus, the players were coming together already well into play and had practically no time to spare. In fact, the All–Stars met in Chicago only one day before and didn't have a single practise together.

The core of the All–Star Team was automatically formed by the players selected to the First and Second All–Star Teams at the end of the previous season. Only two did not play, Turk Broda, who instead minded goal for Toronto's Cup champion team, and Buddy O'Connor of Montreal, who had been hurt in a car crash a few weeks before in Quebec on his way to his team's training camp in Lake Placid. This time, the All–Stars were selected by the six NHL coaches (though a coach still couldn't vote for a player who was on his own team). Each coach made three selections for each position. The first place was accorded five points, the second three, the third one. Only one player, Ted Lindsay, received the maximum 25 points.

The rest of the team was assembled by diminutive coach Tommy Ivan, whose Red Wings had made it to the Stanley Cup finals in the previous season. He began by replacing Broda with Bill Durnan (also considered the finest softball pitcher in Canada at the time) and O'Connor with Milt Schmidt. Ivan's only restriction in filling out the roster was that each team had to be represented by at least three players. To this end, he also added Woody Dumart of Boston, Butch Bouchard of Montreal, Edgar Laprade and Tony Leswick of the Rangers, Doug Bentley of Chicago, and Detroit's Gordie Howe.

The Leafs' lineup excluded Syl Apps, captain emeritus, who had retired after 10 NHL years with Toronto, and Nick Metz, who had also hung up his blades despite pleas to return from Conn Smythe. Metz had recurring health problems, the result of a chest injury suffered two years before in the playoffs against Montreal. And Syl Apps was a serious loss. The previous spring, Apps scored a hat trick, goals 199, 200, and 201 of his career, in his final regular-season game. In the playoffs, he led the Leafs to the Cup even more impressively than he had in the previous year. The Leafs eliminated Boston in five games in the semifinals and swept the Wings in four straight in the finals, outscoring Detroit 18–7. Ted "Teeder" Kennedy led the league with eight goals in the playoffs and was duly rewarded when he was appointed to succeed Apps as Leafs captain. Howie Meeker's playing time was limited because of a broken toe he'd incurred in the season's first game and Joe Klukay took his place most of the night. Leafs coach Day used the All–Star Game to experiment with two five-man playing units, keeping the same defencemen with the same forward lines all night long while he spotted the third blue line tandem of Bill Juzda and Frank Mathers.

In light of Bill Mosienko's serious ankle injury in the first All–Star Game, players tended to avoid any hard contact for fear of another accident. But it didn't dampen the spirits of Gordie Howe and Gus Mortson, who dropped their gloves and went at it with full vim and vigour in the course of a second period that also generated the bulk of excitement and the total sum of the scoring. In a startling departure from the routine of a regular game, the combatants were not forced to share the penalty box to serve out their major penalties. Instead, each was held under police guard at his respective bench! Only one other hostile encounter, between perpetual foes Jim Thomson and Rocket Richard in the third period, threatened the placid proceedings, however, and for the second year in a row the Cup-winning Leafs lost to the All–Stars.

THINGS YOU NEVER SEE IN HOCKEY

OF all the spectator sports, hockey is the toughest to follow in detail. The action moves so swiftly and players enter and leave the game so frequently the average hockey fan has all he can do to keep his eyes on the man with the puck.

Fights start, players spill on the ice, goals are scored and most of the crowd never knows why or how it happened.

On these pages, the Magic Eye camera shows you some of the things you usually miss at a hockey game. The action pix were taken at the second annual National Hockey League All-Star classic at Chicago just before the start of the '48-'49 season.

Magic Eye action pictures exclusively for SPORT by Hugh Broderick of International

THE BRAWL . . .

Brawls and fisticuffs are dime a dozen in hockey, yet the average fan leaps to his feet without knowing what started the argument.

The Rocket slips in a short left to the jaw and Thomson immediately loses all interest in the puck at his feet.

Cal Gardner is the only witness who seems anxious to separate the battlers. Linesman just watches the fight.

Ted Lindsay (7) of the All-Stars and Toronto's Cal Gardner skate in for a ringside view of the bout as the action gets hotter.

Richard is on the defense as the referee arrives to stop the bout. Toronto's Gus Morison (3) is the one other pacifist in the group.

2

3

Here's the kind of action fights are made of. Combatants are All-Star Rocket Richard, vet NHL scrapper, and Jim Thomson.

Richard bangs Thomson into the boards as the Maple Leaf defenseman tries to move the puck toward All-Star goal.

6

7

As Richard ducks away from a Thomson left and succeeds in sticking a mitt in Jim's face, a linesman and Bill Ezinicki watch.

Despite the ref's efforts, Thomson manages to get in a final punch as Maple Leafs and another linesman pull Richard away.

Fights like this make headlines in baseball, but hockey players and officials are used to such belligerent demonstrations.

Most scraps on the ice end with the pugilists seated side by side in jug. Richard and Thomson both drew penalties.

10

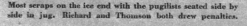

11

All–Stars 3   Toronto Maple Leafs 1

<table>
<tr><td colspan="3">Toronto Maple Leafs
Hap Day, coach</td><td colspan="3">All–Stars
Tommy Ivan, coach (Detroit)</td></tr>
<tr><td>1a</td><td>G</td><td>Turk Broda</td><td>0b</td><td>G</td><td>Frank Brimsek (Boston)</td></tr>
<tr><td>2</td><td>D</td><td>Jim Thomson</td><td>1</td><td>G</td><td>Bill Durnan (Montreal)</td></tr>
<tr><td>3</td><td>D</td><td>Gus Mortson</td><td>2a</td><td>D</td><td>Jack Stewart (Detroit)</td></tr>
<tr><td>4</td><td>LW</td><td>Harry Watson</td><td>3a</td><td>D</td><td>Bill Quackenbush (Detroit)</td></tr>
<tr><td>5</td><td>D</td><td>Garth Boesch</td><td>4</td><td>D</td><td>Butch Bouchard (Montreal)</td></tr>
<tr><td>7</td><td>C</td><td>Max Bentley</td><td>6b</td><td>C</td><td>Neil Colville (New York)</td></tr>
<tr><td>8</td><td>LW</td><td>Joe Klukay</td><td>7a</td><td>LW</td><td>Ted Lindsay (Detroit)</td></tr>
<tr><td>9</td><td>C</td><td>Ted Kennedy "C"</td><td>8</td><td>LW</td><td>Doug Bentley (Chicago)</td></tr>
<tr><td>11</td><td>RW</td><td>Howie Meeker</td><td>9a</td><td>RW</td><td>Maurice Richard (Montreal)</td></tr>
<tr><td>12</td><td>RW</td><td>Bill Ezinicki</td><td>10</td><td>C</td><td>Edgar Laprade (New York)</td></tr>
<tr><td>14</td><td>D</td><td>Vic Lynn</td><td>11</td><td>RW</td><td>Gordie Howe (Detroit)</td></tr>
<tr><td>15</td><td>LW</td><td>Les Costello</td><td>12b</td><td>LW</td><td>Gaye Stewart (Chicago)</td></tr>
<tr><td>16</td><td>C</td><td>Fleming Mackell</td><td>14</td><td>LW</td><td>Woody Dumart (Boston)</td></tr>
<tr><td>17</td><td>C</td><td>Cal Gardner</td><td>15</td><td>C</td><td>Milt Schmidt (Boston)</td></tr>
<tr><td>18</td><td>D</td><td>Bill Juzda</td><td>16a</td><td>C</td><td>Elmer Lach (Montreal)</td></tr>
<tr><td>19</td><td>D</td><td>Bill Barilko</td><td>17b</td><td>D</td><td>Ken Reardon (Montreal)</td></tr>
<tr><td>20</td><td>D</td><td>Frank Mathers</td><td>18</td><td>LW</td><td>Tony Leswick (New York)</td></tr>
<tr><td></td><td></td><td></td><td>19b</td><td>C</td><td>Bud Poile (Chicago)</td></tr>
</table>

a=selected to First All–Star Team for 1947–48

b=selected to Second All–Star Team for 1947–48

First Period
No Scoring
Penalties: Ezinicki (Tor), Reardon (AS)

Second Period
1. All–Stars: Lindsay (Richard, Lach). 1:35
2. All–Stars: Dumart (unassisted). 3:06
3. Toronto: M. Bentley (Costello) 5:13
4. All–Stars: G. Stewart (D. Bentley). . . . . 19:32(pp)
Penalties: Mortson (Tor—major) and Howe (AS—major),
J. Stewart (AS), Bouchard (AS), Juzda (Tor)

Third Period
No Scoring
Penalties: Bouchard (AS)

In Goal
Toronto—Broda
All–Stars—Brimsek/Durnan [Durnan (no goals) replaced Brimsek (one goal) at 10:00 of 2nd period]

Referee Bill Chadwick

Linesmen Sammy Babcock and Mush March

Attendance 12,794

The Leafs Dynasty Plays Its Third in a Row

Maple Leaf Gardens, Monday, October 10, 1949

The Leafs won their third Stanley Cup in a row in an identical manner to the 1948 sweep, defeating Detroit in four games after beating Boston in five in the semi-finals. So overcome were the Wings by the Leafs that in the fourth and last game of the finals, the Detroit team resorted to using oxygen tanks at the bench in an effort to help players recover more quickly. Needless to say, their efforts were wasted and the Leafs won three consecutive Cups for the first time in league history.

Again scheduled for Thanksgiving Monday in Toronto, the third All–Star Game hoped to repeat both the ceremony and quality of the inaugural event at Maple Leaf Gardens. This time the game was officially held in the Stanley Cup winners' city, and

this would become the tradition for the next 20 years. The game was also played the day after the Yankees beat the Brooklyn Dodgers to win the World Series, an unfortunate overlap that was a constant worry to the NHL as it strove to gain greater recognition for hockey in the United States.

The unseasonably warm, sunny day began with an All–Star luncheon at the Royal York Hotel, where Montreal manager Frank Selke took advantage of the confabulation to acquire right winger Knobby Warwick from Boston for cash. Courtesy of the NHL, Leafs alumnus Syl Apps presented his former teammates (and current champions) with silver table lighters. Then the bright lights and dignitaries headed over to Varsity Stadium to watch the Toronto

Rocket Richard moves in on goal, only to face the tough Leaf defence and goaler Turk Broda guarding the cage with characteristic poise.

Argonauts play the Hamilton Tiger Cats in the annual Canadian Football League classic.

The All–Stars selection was again made by Tommy Ivan, coach of the Cup finalists for the third year straight. He filled his lineup sheet with the 12 men on the First and Second Team and then added Bill Mosienko and Bob Goldham of Chicago, Paul Ronty of the Bruins and four Rangers—Pat Egan, Buddy O'Connor, Tony Leswick, and Edgar Laprade. (As usual in the years of the Original Six, the Rangers had the most additions to the team because they rarely had anyone named to the All–Star Teams by the writers.) Ivan kept two of the best lines in the game intact by playing the Detroit Production Line of Howe, Lindsay, and Abel and Chicago's top post-Pony line of Doug Bentley, Roy Conacher, and Bill Mosienko and their familiarity with each other's play clearly gave the glitter-blades an advantage.

As in 1947, not one member of the Leafs' Cup-winning team had been named to either the First or Second All–Star Team. The Leafs were without three regulars due to injury, Gus Mortson, Frank Mathers and, most notably, Wild Bill Ezinicki, who had torn ligaments in his ankle the previous week in an exhibition game in St. Catharines. Up front, coach Day used the first line of Cal Gardner and Harry Watson with Howie Meeker filling in for Ezinicki, the second line was made up of Max Bentley, Ray Timgren, and Joe Klukay; and the third line had the great Ted Kennedy centring Sid Smith and Flem Mackell.

Two-thirds of the $25,892 profits from the night went to the players' pension fund and the other third went to local charities. The Red Feather campaign received $4,000; the Hospital for Sick Children $2,000; Queen Elizabeth Hospital $1,000; and the remainder was dispersed between the Canadian Paraplegic Association and the Ontario Society for Crippled Children, an organization with which Conn Smythe was to become increasingly involved over the post-war years.

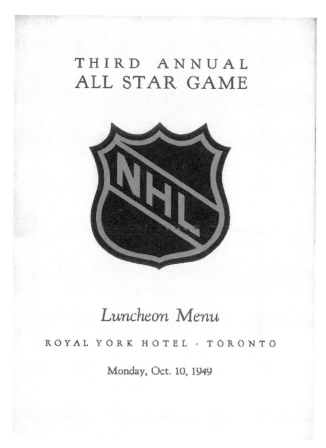

THIRD ANNUAL
ALL STAR GAME

Luncheon Menu

ROYAL YORK HOTEL · TORONTO

Monday, Oct. 10, 1949

Pre-Game Ceremonies

During the pre-game ceremonies, league president Campbell presented each member of the previous year's First All–Star Team with gold pucks about the size of a pocket watch. The two coaches were also granted the perk. In fact, Hap Day was receiving his first special puck even though he was the first coach to have ever guided a team to three consecutive Stanley Cup victories. The gold pucks had been previously reserved for the All–Stars coach, but Clarence Campbell amended this tradition when he saw its inequity. As Day walked out to receive his gold disc, the band played "Happy Days Are Here Again." This spirit was somewhat betrayed by a few of the locals, however. While a round of applause greeted most of the players for the centre ice presentation, discriminating Toronto fans joined in a lusty chorus of boos for Maurice Richard and Ken Reardon, both of the much-hated and reviled Canadiens.

The Game

Syl Apps faced the first puck off between Ted Kennedy and Sid Abel and then the game got under way. Bob Goldham was the outstanding player, scoring the first goal, setting up the second, and negating rush after rush by his former mates on the Leafs. Perhaps he had pretty strong motives after having been traded from the Leafs to Chicago in the huge five-for-two deal that saw Toronto acquire Max Bentley. All in all, the game was as thrilling as the inaugural match and a good deal more exciting than the previous one in Chicago. For the third year running, the Leafs lost to the best of the league, but, as both Day and Ivan echoed after the game, it was far better to lose the All–Star Game as the host after taking the Stanley Cup home in the spring.

The game was defensively minded and to that end a bit on the rough side. Ted Lindsay was cut for eight stitches around his right eye after knocking heads with archrival Jim Thomson. Pat Egan took seven to the side of his head when he lifted Watson's stick with an excess of vigour and it came up on him. For the Leafs, Garth Boesch had six laced into the back of his head courtesy of a Roy Conacher high stick near game's end and Ray Timgren took a deuce over his left eye after being guided into the end glass by Ken Reardon.

Max Bentley's commemorative lighter is a gift from another era,
one which allowed the players a relaxing cigarette, cigar, or pipe for brief social diversion.

All–Stars 3   Toronto Maple Leafs 1

		Toronto Maple Leafs Hap Day, coach				All–Stars Tommy Ivan, coach (Detroit)
1	G	Turk Broda		1a	G	Bill Durnan (Montreal)
2	D	Jim Thomson		1b	G	Charlie Rayner (New York)
4	LW	Harry Watson		2a	D	Jack Stewart (Detroit)
5	D	Garth Boesch		3	D	Bob Goldham (Chicago)
7	C	Max Bentley		4	D	Pat Egan (New York)
8	LW	Joe Klukay		5	C	Buddy O'Connor (New York)
9	C	Ted Kennedy "C"		6a	LW	Roy Conacher (Chicago)
11	RW	Howie Meeker		7b	LW	Doug Bentley (Chicago)
14	D	Vic Lynn		8	RW	Bill Mosienko (Chicago)
16	C	Fleming Mackell		9a	RW	Maurice Richard (Montreal)
17	C	Cal Gardner		10	C	Edgar Laprade (New York)
18	D	Bill Juzda		11a	D	Bill Quackenbush (Boston)
19	D	Bill Barilko		12a	C	Sid Abel (Detroit)
22	LW	Ray Timgren		14b	RW	Gordie Howe (Detroit)
23	D	Bobby Dawes		15b	D	Glen Harmon (Montreal)
24	LW	Sid Smith		16b	LW	Ted Lindsay (Detroit)
				17b	D	Ken Reardon (Montreal)
				18	LW	Tony Leswick (New York)
				20	C	Paul Ronty (Boston)

a=selected to First All–Star Team for 1948–49
b=selected to Second All–Star Team for 1948–49

First Period

1. Toronto: Barilko (Watson, Gardner) 15:22
2. All–Stars: Goldham (Laprade) . . . . 18:03(sh)

Penalties: Richard (AS), Meeker (Tor), Thomson (Tor), Howe (AS)

Second Period

3. All–Stars: Ronty (Goldham) . . . . 14:42(pp)

Penalties: Harmon (AS), Thomson (Tor), Boesch (Tor), Egan (AS), Smith (Tor)

Third Period

4. All–Stars: D. Bentley (Quackenbush) 2:38

Penalties: None

In Goal

Toronto—Broda
All–Stars—Durnan/Rayner [Rayner (no goals) replaced Durnan (one goal) at 9:30 of 2nd period]

Referee Bill Chadwick

Linesmen Ed Mepham and Jim Primeau

Attendance 13,541

4th All–Star Game

The Stars
Get Hammered

Detroit Olympia, Sunday, October 8, 1950

The NHL pension fund had been started just three years before with two-thirds of All–Star Game gross receipts and, among other small sources, a special 25-cent assessment on all playoffs tickets (which in the spring of 1950 alone added more than $50,000 to the balance). The fund was now up to $460,564.85 in deposits and swelled further with this year's contribution of $17,513. NHL president Clarence Campbell hoped the amount would reach $1.5 million by the time payouts would begin on October 1, 1957, to players who were 45 years or older. By that time, a player with 10 years of service would be eligible to collect $80 a month for life. And if he waited until he turned 60, that figure would double.

To ensure an honest system for maintaining the fund, Campbell demanded that every team have three representatives who would be apprised of how the money was handled, one a retired player who would keep his team's alumni informed and two current players to keep his team up to date. For this year, those members included: Syl Apps, alumnus, and Ted Kennedy and Gus Mortson, current Maple Leafs; Toe Blake, alumnus, and Glen Harmon and Maurice Richard, current Canadiens; Johnny Crawford, alumnus, and Milt Schmidt and Paul Ronty, current Bruins; Red Hamill, alumnus, and Harry Lumley and Gus Bodnar, current Blackhawks; Neil Colville, alumnus, and Frank Eddolls and Buddy O'Connor, current Rangers players.

The powerful Wings had won the 1950 Cup in dramatic fashion, with an overtime goal from Leo Reise in game seven that eliminated the Leafs in the semi-finals. In the finals, this time against the Rangers, they went to double overtime in game

seven. Pete Babando finally scored midway through the fifth period of play to take the Silver Mug to the Motor City. Ironically, two of New York's home games had been played at Maple Leaf Gardens in Toronto because Madison Square Garden had been booked for a circus.

The Red Wings' 7–1 win in the 1950 All–Star Game was the most lopsided yet, but Red Kelly remarked how little coach Tommy Ivan had to say to motivate the players:

"He didn't have to tell us much," Kelly said. "We thought to ourselves, we were playing against the best, the All–Stars, and we wanted to put on a good show." And they did.

The game's result generated impassioned debate about every detail of the game. The coaches had not begun selecting the First and Second All–Star Teams until 1946–47, and the feeling was that they sometimes selected inferior players from other teams to ensure a spot for one of their own. There was talk of returning to the old system whereby sportswriters had chosen the teams. Also, because the Red Wings had five players on the First or Second Team, the quality of the All–Star Team left something to be desired because those players suited up for the Red Wings and not for the All–Stars. They included the entire Production Line of Gordie Howe–Sid Abel–Ted Lindsay as well as defencemen Red Kelly and Leo Reise.

Furthermore, Art Ross suggested that the game should be played around American Thanksgiving (in late November) so that it wouldn't compete with baseball and football in the U.S. and so that players would be in better physical condition for the contest and therefore able to put on a much better show. Stan

Saplin, who was in charge of public relations for the Rangers, proposed an East–West game with the East represented by New York, Boston, and Montreal. Ross countered that such a format would lose the interest of the home team fans and suggested a better change might be to have Canada (represented by Toronto and Montreal) play the United States. Another possibility was to choose the All–Star Team after the Stanley Cup was decided, thus preventing the possibility of Cup champs being named to the All–Stars. This was immediately rejected by the players, who traditionally received a $1,000 bonus for All–Star Team honours. A final suggestion had the All–Star Game being scrapped and the Cup finals becoming a best-of-nine with receipts for the final two extra games going to the pension fund. This too was ultimately rejected.

Pre-Game Events

The night before the 1950 All–Star Game in Detroit, a banquet was held in honour of the champion Wings. Each of the local players received silver trays and flower bowls, and all the All–Stars were given travelling clocks as well. Clarence Campbell chaired the evening, while Glen Harmon spoke for the players' pension fund interests and General John Kilpatrick represented the owners in this respect. The meal itself was delectable: fresh shrimp cocktail, cream of mushroom soup, sliced tenderloin of beef in a fresh mushroom sauce, Anna potatoes, asparagus hollandaise, chef's salad, frozen strawberry ice cream pie, and coffee.

Pre-Game Ceremonies

In a pre-game ceremony, Campbell presented the annual gold pucks to the six First Team All–Stars. Referee George Gravel and Leaf participants Ted Kennedy and Gus Mortson were vociferously booed during introductions to the Olympia fans (though they numbered only 9,166, by far the smallest All–Star Game crowd before or since). In turn, Gravel took a deep bow in mock appreciation of his derisive reception.

*Doug Bentley at the game-day practice
prior to the 1950 contest in Detroit.*

The Game

The game featured the incomparable Production Line of Abel–Howe–Lindsay of Detroit, with the result that Lindsay scored the first hat trick in All–Star history and Howe scored a superb goal in the second on a give-and-go with Terrible Ted. It would be 33 years before another three-goal game was recorded (by a guy named Gretzky). Lindsay scored on Detroit's first rush of the game, 19 seconds in, and the Red Wings never looked back. The All–Stars featured just two players from the previous year's First Team (Rocket Richard and Gus Mortson), thus seriously compromising their claim to be called an all–star team. Abel and Lindsay were with the Red Wings and both Bill Durnan and Ken Reardon of the Canadiens had retired.

The game's best moments were provided by Detroit rookie goalie Terry Sawchuk, who had

(l-r) *Howe, Abel, and Lindsay, the most feared line of its era.*

inherited the number one job in Motown after Harry Lumley was traded to Chicago in the summer. Sawchuk's rookie game shutout was spoiled in the dying minutes of the game, but time and again he foiled Richard from in close and established himself instantly as one of the netminding superstars of the NHL. At the other end of the ice, Leaf Turk Broda had a bad night in the All–Stars' net and his team's poor defensive play was exacerbated by his perambulations from the crease to stop the attack. "Looks like Broda has turned into a rover," quipped Boston scout and former Leaf Baldy Cotton at one point during the night.

Once the game was clearly out of reach, play became noticeably rougher. Lindsay hit his head on the ice early in the third after being upended, and Leo Reise barely escaped serious injury after being dazed by a Jack Stewart slash.

Detroit Red Wings 7   All–Stars 1

		Detroit Red Wings Tommy Ivan, coach				All–Stars Lynn Patrick, coach (Boston)
1	G	Terry Sawchuk		1	G	Turk Broda (Toronto)
2	D	Bob Goldham		1b	G	Charlie Rayner (New York)
4b	D	Red Kelly		2	D	Jack Stewart (Chicago)
5b	D	Leo Reise		3a	D	Gus Mortson (Toronto)
7a	LW	Ted Lindsay		4	D	Jim Thomson (Toronto)
8	C	George Gee		5	D	Glen Harmon (Montreal)
9b	RW	Gordie Howe		6	D	Butch Bouchard (Montreal)
10	RW	Jim Peters		7	LW	Doug Bentley (Chicago)
11	LW	Gaye Stewart		8	RW	Bill Mosienko (Chicago)
12a	C	Sid Abel "C"		9	RW	Maurice Richard (Montreal)
14	C	Metro Prystai		10	C	Edgar Laprade (New York)
15	LW	Marty Pavelich		11	D	Bill Quackenbush (Boston)
16	C	Jim McFadden		12b	C	Ted Kennedy (Toronto)
17	RW	Joe Carveth		18b	LW	Tony Leswick (New York)
18	C	Gerry Couture		20	C	Paul Ronty (Boston)
19	LW	Steve Black		23	RW	Johnny Peirson (Boston)
21	D	Lee Fogolin		24	LW	Sid Smith (Toronto)
22	D	Marcel Pronovost				

a=selected to First All Star Team for 1949–50
b=selected to Second All–Star Team for 1949–50

First Period
1. Detroit: Lindsay (Howe) 0:19
2. Detroit: Lindsay (Abel) . . . . 17:12(pp)
Penalties: Richard (AS) 7:57, Leswick (AS) 9:09, Abel (Det) 9:15, Pronovost (Det) 11:45, Bentley (AS) 15:13, Leswick (AS) 16:54

Second Period
3. Detroit: Howe (Lindsay, Kelly) 11:12
4. Detroit: Peters (Kelly, Prystai) 18:36
5. Detroit: Pavelich (Prystai, Peters) 19:44
Penalties: Couture (Det) 4:30

Third Period
6. Detroit, Prystai (Pavelich) 7:36
7. Detroit: Lindsay (unassisted) . . . . 14:28(sh)
8. All–Stars: Smith (Peirson) 18:27
Penalties: Detroit: too many men (served by Peters) 5:03, G. Stewart (Det) 13:10

In Goal
Detroit—Sawchuk
All–Stars—Rayner/Broda [Broda (4 goals) replaced Rayner (3 goals) at 11:12 of 2nd period]

Referee George Gravel

Linesmen George Hayes and Doug Young

Attendance 9,166

A New Format

Maple Leaf Gardens, Tuesday, October 9, 1951

Officially, the 1951 game pitted the First All–Star Team against the Second, but it was almost a Canadian team–American team format similar to what had been proposed the previous year. The only two exceptions were that Toronto coach Joe Primeau was in charge of an all-American First Team and three American-based players—Charlie Rayner (New York), Leo Reise and Sid Abel (both with Detroit)—were with a Toronto–Montreal Second Team. The change in format was made after the previous year's game, when five Red Wings had been selected to the First or Second All–Star Team but played for the Wings against a much-depleted best of the rest because the Wings won the Cup. The result was a 7–1 thrashing of the All–Stars and a speedy move to alter the format (though the game was still hosted by the current Cup champs).

This year, a pall hung over the Leafs' dramatic Stanley Cup win. That August, Bill Barilko, the fine young Toronto defenceman who had scored the Stanley Cup–winning goal, had been lost in a plane accident in Ontario's remote north and hadn't been found. His goal had come in game five against Montreal, and to this day that finals is the only series ever played in which every game went into overtime.

Second Team coach Dick Irvin noted the tragedy with all due respect by announcing how sad he was that Bashin' Bill wouldn't be on his team.

Irvin did elicit shocked reactions from the hockey world when he chose the tiny Gerry McNeil (not Al Rollins) as his second goalie. McNeil had been in goal when Barilko scored to win the Cup, while the Leafs' Rollins had just won a Stanley Cup, and Vezina Trophy and been runner-up in Calder Trophy voting. Still Irvin casually declared:

"We'll see how McNeil does with a good team in front of him. I know he is much better than Rollins, and besides, I want the best players on my team. I don't consider Mr. Rollins a very good goaler."

Thus it was that, for the first time, the Vezina winner didn't play as an All–Star.

Because the game was scheduled at the start of the year, rule changes implemented over the summer were always first witnessed at the glitter game. This year, for instance, fans in Toronto were the first to see an enlarged goal crease, meant to provide added protection for the twine-tending brethren. The crease grew larger by one foot out from the goal line and six inches beyond each post, making the total crease area four by eight feet. Also, this marked the first year a defending player other than the goalie had to touch the puck on icing calls. Previously, only the goalie could touch the puck for an icing call, and this alteration was intended to make players hustle back to get to the puck and also to incorporate the possibility of an offensive player racing to it first and negating the icing.

Pre-Game Events

The game-day lunch at the Royal York Hotel was attended by almost the entire National Hockey League. Everyone involved in the game itself received a specially engraved tie clip and cufflinks presented to them by Syl Apps, and the writers and broadcasters throughout the league received pocket knives. As a member of the Stanley Cup championship team, each Leaf was given a silver plate, cufflinks and a cigarette lighter. The tradition of giving a gold puck to each member of the First All–Star Team was also upheld this year.

The Game

The opening ceremonies culminated with Syl Apps facing off the first puck. The game was recorded by a movie camera and the league made a 20-minute film using All–Star Game footage to help promote the NHL. While the game was entertaining and Howe, Richard et al. shone bright, critics again made some frustrated noise after the final bell. Whereas the pre-

vious year they had lamented the one-sided score, this year they clamoured with equal relish over the lack of a winner and suggested a 10-minute overtime be implemented in the future. Referee-in-chief Carl Voss also took the time to announce that this year his referees were going to clamp down on all the hooking, holding, and interference that was slowing the game down and reducing the level of skill that fans had for so long expected. *Plus ça change…!*

There were only two brief moments of contact in the game, one when Ted Kennedy gave Lindsay an elbow and Terrible Ted retaliated in kind, and the

Game action from the 1951 game in Toronto,
one of only two that pitted stars against stars before the expansion era.

second when Richard wrestled Howe to the ice to no great effect.

Hot Stove Leaguer Elmer Ferguson selected as his three stars Charlie Rayner, Gerry McNeil (to coach Irvin's delight), and Tod Sloan. The First Team wore red sweaters, the Second Team the same style of sweater in white. All told, the evening raised $25,307 for the players' pension fund.

First All–Stars 2   Second All–Stars 2

		First All–Stars				Second All–Stars
		Joe Primeau, coach (Toronto)				Dick Irvin, coach (Montreal)
1a	G	Terry Sawchuk (Detroit)	1	G	Gerry McNeil (Montreal)
1	G	Harry Lumley (Chicago)	1b	G	Charlie Rayner (New York)
2	D	Frank Eddolls (New York)	2b	D	Jim Thomson (Toronto)
4a	D	Red Kelly (Detroit)	3	D	Gus Mortson (Toronto)
5	C	Don Raleigh (New York)	4	LW	Harry Watson (Toronto)
6	LW	Ed Sandford (Boston)	5b	D	Leo Reise (Detroit)
7a	LW	Ted Lindsay (Detroit)	6	RW	Floyd Curry (Montreal)
8	D	Al Dewsbury (Chicago)	7	C	Max Bentley (Toronto)
9a	RW	Gordie Howe (Detroit)	8bc	C	Ted Kennedy (Toronto)
11a	D	Bill Quackenbush (Boston)	9b	RW	Maurice Richard (Montreal)
12	LW	Doug Bentley (Chicago)	10	D	Doug Harvey (Montreal)
15a	C	Milt Schmidt (Boston)	11	D	Butch Bouchard (Montreal)
16	LW	Gaye Stewart (New York)	12bc	C	Sid Abel (Detroit)
17	C	Gus Bodnar (Chicago)	15	C	Tod Sloan (Toronto)
20	D	Lee Fogolin (Chicago)	18	C	Ken Mosdell (Montreal)
21	RW	Reg Sinclair (New York)	20	LW	Paul Meger (Montreal)
23	RW	Johnny Peirson (Boston)	24b	LW	Sid Smith (Toronto)

a=selected to First All-Star Team for 1950–51
b=selected to Second All-Star Team for 1950–51
c=tied in voting

First Period
1. First Team: Howe (Lindsay, Schmidt) . . . . 7:59(pp)

Penalties: Curry (2nd) 6:38, Eddolls (1st) 10:41, Sloan (2nd) 15:58

Second Period
2. Second Team: Sloan (Watson, M. Bentley) . . . . . 2:26(pp)
3. First Team: Peirson (Stewart, Raleigh) 16:49

Penalties: Raleigh (1st) 1:46, Lindsay (1st) 13:26

Third Period
4. Second Team: Mosdell (Sloan, Mortson) 9:25

Penalties: Lindsay (1st) 1:25, Howe (1st) 5:53

In Goal
First Team—Sawchuk/Lumley [Lumley (one goal) replaced Sawchuk (one goal) at 9:28 of 2nd period]
Second Team—Rayner/McNeil [McNeil (one goal) replaced Rayner (one goal) at 9:28 of 2nd period]

Referee Bill Chadwick

Linesmen Sammy Babcock and Scotty Morrison

Attendance 11,469

Another Tie

Detroit Olympia, Sunday, October 5, 1952

The 1952 game was truly dull in the extreme for all but the last five minutes and prompted a unanimous decision by the NHL governors that the previous format—Cup champions versus the best of the rest, in the Cup-winning city—would prevail the next year. Terry Sawchuk was forced to play the whole game for the First All–Stars after his partner Charlie Rayner was injured in a Rangers exhibition game in Guelph a few days before and Ukey's play was, as usual, spectacular. Otherwise, the Detroit fans were only interested in the action when Red Wings had the puck. There was no heavy hitting and little intensity or excitement, and the players seemed uncharacteristically content to skate to a 1–1 tie.

The dinner the night before succeeded where the game itself was uneventful. The head table consisted of NHL president and pension fund chairman Clarence Campbell and dignitaries from each team: General Kilpatrick of New York, James Norris and Jack Adams of Detroit, Frank Selke of Montreal, Walter Brown of Boston, Bill Tobin and Bruce Norris of Chicago, and Colonel Bill MacBrien of Toronto (Conn Smythe and Art Ross missed both the dinner and the game). Other members of the head table included player representative Leo Reise and both All–Star coaches, Tommy Ivan and Dick Irvin. The evening's music was provided by Eddie John and his quartet, a group from Sault Ste. Marie, Michigan, that was the Red Wings' official orchestra. The dinner itself was elegant and featured roast Michigan turkey with cranberry sauce, Anna potatoes and string beans, a chef's salad and *statler bombe* ice cream.

The day of the game, Gordie Howe and NHL director of publicity Ken McKenzie appeared on the television show "So You Know Sports" and that night the usual festival of pre-game events took place. Press and radio men all received leather key holders and players were given pocket-sized binoculars, courtesy of the NHL. Each member of the Cup-winning Wings received a silver tray and bowl, and the game added $17,470 to the players' pension fund.

The starting six players for the First and Second

Referee Bill Chadwick watches the puck slide by the Second All–Stars goal during the 1952 Game.

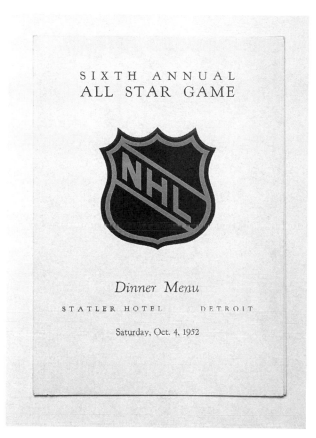

SIXTH ANNUAL
ALL STAR GAME

NHL

Dinner Menu

STATLER HOTEL   DETROIT

Saturday, Oct. 4, 1952

Teams were selected by 18 hockey writers and broadcasters, three from each NHL city. The First Team roster was then augmented by players from the four U.S. teams and the Second Team from the two Canadian teams, Toronto and Montreal. Coaches were responsible for selecting those additional players, and this process produced controversy in at least one instance.

Max Bentley of the Second Team was forced to withdraw from the game because of a groin injury, and coach Dick Irvin named Ted Kennedy his replacement. Leafs owner Conn Smythe intervened and declared Kennedy unavailable for the game after feeling slighted that Billy Reay of Montreal had been named to the team instead of Teeder in the first place.

"They can't keep the captain of our club waiting around to substitute at the last minute," fumed the Hollerin' Major. "They asked if Kennedy would be available now that Maxie is out, and I told them Kennedy was unavailable." Irvin retorted in kind: "I chose Reay because I am looking for checkers on the club. And Kennedy can't check. Anyway, if I remember rightly, Reay played in the Stanley Cup finals last season." The next day, Irvin eventually chose his own Floyd Curry as Max's replacement, though not without adding one final thrust: "With Smythe's kind permission, I will put Tod Sloan at centre because he has also played that position and I'll take along Canadiens right winger Floyd Curry for the wing job."

Defensive coverage is the order of the day, every white-shirted Second Team player covering his man.

Criticism of the game and format focused on a number of salient issues. Many thought it seemed counterproductive to have players from the same team competing against one another. Too, holding the game at the start of the year meant that players were not in top shape and thus were not able to provide a suitable display of their skills. Red Burnett of the *Toronto Star* suggested that the game be played at mid-season and that fans vote on which players should participate, both of which proved to be prophetic suggestions. Bob Hesketh joined the glitter bashing and opined that there should be a winner-take-all cash award for the game and that the venue should change each year so the game wasn't always in Toronto, Montreal, or Detroit.

First All–Stars 1   Second All–Stars 1

First All–Stars
Tommy Ivan, coach (Detroit)

1a	G	Terry Sawchuk (Detroit)
2a	D	Doug Harvey (Montreal)
3	D	Gus Mortson (Toronto)
4a	D	Red Kelly (Detroit)
5	C	Dave Creighton (Boston)
6	LW	Ed Sandford (Boston)
7a	LW	Ted Lindsay (Detroit)
8	D	Leo Reise (New York)
9a	RW	Gordie Howe (Detroit)
10	LW	Marty Pavelich (Detroit)
11	D	Bill Quackenbush (Boston)
12	RW	Bill Mosienko (Chicago)
14	D	Bob Goldham (Detroit)
15	LW	Tony Leswick (Detroit)
16a	C	Elmer Lach (Montreal)
21	RW	Reg Sinclair (Detroit)
1	G	Charlie Rayner (New York) did not play

Second All–Stars
Dick Irvin, coach (Montreal)

1b	G	Sugar Jim Henry (Boston)
1	G	Gerry McNeil (Montreal)
2b	D	Jim Thomson (Toronto)
3b	D	Hy Buller (New York)
4	LW	Harry Watson (Toronto)
5	RW	Bernie Geoffrion (Montreal)
6	RW	Floyd Curry (Montreal)
9b	RW	Maurice Richard (Montreal)
10	D	Tom Johnson (Montreal)
11	D	Butch Bouchard (Montreal)
12	D	Fern Flaman (Toronto)
14	C	Ken Mosdell (Montreal)
15b	C	Milt Schmidt (Boston)
16	C	Tod Sloan (Toronto)
17	C	Billy Reay (Montreal)
20	LW	Paul Meger (Montreal)
24b	LW	Sid Smith (Toronto)

a=selected to First All–Star Team for 1951–52
b=selected to Second All–Star Team for 1951–52

First Period
No Scoring
Penalties: Buller (2nd) 0:23, Thomson (2nd) 12:46, Richard (2nd) 18:03

Second Period
1. First Team: Pavelich (Mosienko, Creighton) 9:57
Penalties: Sandford (1st) 3:51, Bouchard (2nd) 4:53, Thomson (2nd) 7.50, Thomson (2nd) 16:39

Third Period
2. Second Team: Richard (Buller). 1:36
Penalties: Howe (1st) 6:34, Lach (1st) 15:09

In Goal
First Team—Sawchuk
Second Team—Henry/McNeil [McNeil (no goals) replaced Henry (one goal) at 9:57 of 2nd period]

Referee Bill Chadwick

Linesmen George Hayes and Doug Young

Attendance 10,680

Le Gros Bill
Joins the NHL

Montreal Forum, Saturday, October 3, 1953

The big news of the day came in the afternoon when the Habs announced they had signed sensational rookie Jean Béliveau to a five-year contract (meaning he could play in the All–Star Game that night). According to Montreal general manager Frank Selke, the price paid was the highest in league history. Certainly the 22-year-old Béliveau was easily the most celebrated rookie to begin his career at the All–Star Game.

Béliveau had played the previous two years with the Quebec Aces in Quebec senior hockey despite pleas from Montreal to join the NHL Habs. He'd been paid well enough with the Aces ($20,000 a year) and had been in no hurry to move. In some respects, his was the longest holdout of Original Six history.

And that October night in 1953, Béliveau did not disappoint his fans in the Forum or look out of place even though this was his first NHL game. He centred Richard and Eddie Mazur, and he kept pace with the Rocket from start to finish. Le Gros Bill, as he was fondly dubbed in the French media (after a popular song of the same name), became such a hit that the fans booed coach Irvin when he replaced Béliveau's line during a power-play.

The format for this All–Star Game reverted to the previous setup of Cup champion against the best of the rest although, for the first time, league president Clarence Campbell admitted difficulty with the timing.

"It might be nicer to stage the game later in the season, when hockey interest is at a peak, but that would mean one entire week of the schedule would be wiped out so that clubs could let their players free. This is a much more convenient setup as long as either Montreal or Toronto or Detroit is the host city. However, if any other city in the league should be host, competition with football and baseball would force us to play the game later in the season."

Of course, that was no problem this year; Montreal had beat Boston in five games to win the '53 Cup.

This was to be the last year for the current system of voting for the All–Star Teams. To this point, three hockey writers from each NHL city had made the selections, and since many cities had more than three writers, each chose its voting members on a rotating basis. The voting had to be completed by the end of the regular season, and announcements for the First and Second Teams were made right after the Stanley Cup was decided. Starting the next year, the same people would vote (no coaches would be involved), but they would cast ballots twice, by January 1st and again at the end of the regular season. Each half was weighted equally in the final analysis, and this method was deemed to provide better balance if some players had a particularly strong first or second half of the season (and were thus either ignored or given more favourable judgement in the previous system). First Team All–Stars received $1,000 and Second Team All–Stars $500, an important addition to any player's salary.

The most notable rule change to go into effect this year was a change in icing calls further to the amendment of two years before. A linesman no longer had discretionary power to waive off an icing if he thought the errant puck was an attempted pass. If the pass or shot originated before the centre line and the defence could not get to the puck, an icing call had to be made. Also, this was the first year the Norris Trophy was awarded, named in honour of Detroit owner James Norris, who had died the previous winter.

The NHL players' pension plan was the main impetus to participate in the annual game. To become a member, a player had to have played two full 70-game seasons in the NHL (or 140 games over any number of years). The players' own annual and obligatory $900 fee was tax-deductible, but the fund wouldn't have gotten to where it was now without the receipts from the Game. And the one in 1953 broke records for both attendance (14,153) and receipts ($26,795), bringing the fund to a whopping $1,003,783.93.

Two players who were supposed to participate in this All–Star Game but didn't were goaler Sugar Jim Henry, who was injured, and Fleming Mackell, a First Team All–Star and holdout who was judged not to be in good enough shape to join the twinkle team after signing with Boston just a few days before.

Pre-Game Events

The head table at the banquet the night before the game included Clarence Campbell, Bill Northey, Lynn Patrick, Colonel Bill MacBrien, Leo Reise, General Kilpatrick, Walter Brown, Frank Selke, Dick Irvin, and Jack Adams. Numerous oldtime Montreal stars attended the tribute dinner: Joe Malone, Newsy Lalonde, Sylvio Mantha, Georges Mantha, Armand Mondou, Ray Getliffe, Buddy O'Connor, Glen Harmon, and Gerry Heffernan. Reise, who had been acting as a player rep, officially became vice-president of the pension fund at the dinner after incumbent Syl Apps retired, while Ted Kennedy replaced Reise as director.

Pre-Game Ceremonies

During the pre-game festivities, players were given leather shaving kits and representatives of the press

Jean Béliveau was an icon in Quebec City and was in no hurry to leave the Aces to join the Habs in the NHL.

and radio received pens. The Cup-winning Habs got gold stick pins from their manager, Frank Selke, and the NHL gave the same players silver rose bowls. Montreal captain Butch Bouchard then returned the favour, giving Selke an oil painting depicting his former farm at Maple, Ontario, on behalf of the team. Players were also given shoes, lighters, blazers, stickpins, sweater coats, hats, and fishing rods.

The Game

The game was called the most successful ever, with the crowd creating an intense atmosphere and the players skating up to the fans' expectations despite extreme heat in the Forum. Both All–Star goals came on the same first-period power-play (two-minute penalties were served to the full until 1956), and the game's outcome was in doubt until an empty-net goal by Alex Delvecchio in the final minute. Terry Sawchuk was again brilliant in the Stars' net and fended off the champion Canadiens, who held a wide edge in territory and play.

And this time Forum fans witnessed the rarest of all All–Star Game occurrences: a fight. Mild-mannered Red Kelly and Bert Olmstead threw punches because, according to Kelly, he had absorbed three successive elbows to the head from Bert and would brook no more. Linesman Sammy Babcock stepped into the fray early, and although major penalties were assessed, this was hardly a true dustup in the Howe–Olmstead All–Star tradition. Earlier, Jim Thomson and Dickie Moore had wrestled for a good length of time but without incurring a penalty.

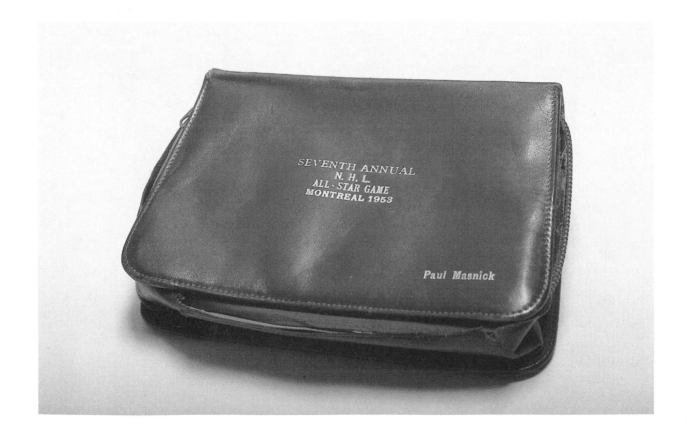

All–Stars 3   Montreal Canadiens 1

Montreal Canadiens
Dick Irvin, coach

1b	G	Gerry McNeil
2a	D	Doug Harvey
3	D	Butch Bouchard "C"
4	C	Jean Béliveau
5	RW	Bernie Geoffrion
6	RW	Floyd Curry
8	LW	Dick Gamble
9b	RW	Maurice Richard
10	D	Tom Johnson
12	RW	Dickie Moore
14	LW	Calum MacKay
15b	LW	Bert Olmstead
16	C	Elmer Lach
17	C	John McCormack
18	C	Ken Mosdell
19	D	Dollard St. Laurent
20	LW	Paul Meger
21	D	Bud MacPherson
22	RW	Lorne Davis
24	LW	Eddie Mazur

All–Stars
Lynn Patrick, coach (Boston)

1a	G	Terry Sawchuk (Detroit)
2	D	Jim Thomson (Toronto)
3b	D	Bill Quackenbush (Boston)
4a	D	Red Kelly (Detroit)
6	LW	Ed Sandford (Boston)
7a	LW	Ted Lindsay (Detroit)
8	LW	Sid Smith (Toronto)
9a	RW	Gordie Howe (Detroit)
10	C	Metro Prystai (Detroit)
11	RW	Wally Hergesheimer (New York)
12	RW	Bill Mosienko (Chicago)
14b	D	Bill Gadsby (Chicago)
15b	C	Alex Delvecchio (Detroit)
16	D	Gus Mortson (Chicago)
17	D	Leo Reise (New York)
18	C	Paul Ronty (New York)
24	LW	Harry Watson (Toronto)

a=selected to First All–Star Team for 1952–53
b=selected to Second All–Star Team for 1952–53

First Period
1. All–Stars: Hergesheimer (Ronty, Kelly) . . . . 4:06(pp)
2. All–Stars: Hergesheimer (Kelly) . . . . 5:25(pp)
Penalties: Meger (Mtl) 4:00, MacPherson (Mtl) 4:37, Lindsay (AS) 8:55

Second Period
No Scoring
Penalties: Mortson (AS) 5:03, St. Laurent (Mtl) 11:28, Howe (AS) 12:52, Richard (Mtl) 15:18, Mosdell (Mtl) 19:58

Third Period
3. Montreal: Richard (Harvey, Béliveau) . . . . 4:30(pp)
4. All–Stars: Delvecchio (unassisted) . . . . 19:27(en)
Penalties: Kelly (AS—fighting major) and Olmstead (Mtl—fighting major) 2:34, Smith (AS) 3:30

Shots on Goal

Montreal	12	8	11	**31**
All–Stars	7	4	9	**20**

In Goal
Montreal—McNeil
All–Stars—Sawchuk

Referee Red Storey

Linesmen Sammy Babcock and Doug Davies

Attendance 14,153

Pride of the Goalies

Detroit Olympia, Saturday, October 2, 1954

Eliminated in 1953 by Boston in the semi-finals, the Red Wings played with a vengeance in the spring of 1954. They easily eliminated the Leafs in five and then played one of the most memorable final series of all time, taking Montreal to seven games and finally clinching the Cup at 4:29 of overtime on a goal by Tony Leswick. It was the Wings' third championship in five years and the climax of an era for general manager Jack Adams and a great team that featured Gordie Howe, Ted Lindsay, and Terry Sawchuk at its core.

Pre-Game Events

Pension fund members held their annual meeting in the afternoon before the game. It was attended by NHL president Clarence Campbell and representatives from four teams: Bob Goldham and Marty Pavelich of the Wings; Ted Kennedy of Toronto; Bill Quackenbush, Fleming Mackell, and Ed Sandford of the Bruins; and Gus Mortson of Chicago. Meanwhile, the NHL provided a bus and a packed lunch for those who wanted to attend a football game in Ann Arbor.

Guests at the banquet honouring the Wings the

Bill Quackenbush played in his eighth and final All–Star Game in 1954.

night before the game featured members of the International Hockey Hall of Fame: Newsy Lalonde, Joe Malone, Frank Nighbor, Dickie Boon, and Nels Stewart. At the head table were John Digby Chick, president of the AHL, Tommy Ivan, Colonel Bill MacBrien, Bruce and Marguerite Norris, Frank Selke, Walter Brown, Jack Adams, and Leo Reise, who toasted Clarence Campbell for the wonderful work he had done in establishing the pension fund back in 1947 (this year's edition raised $18,355). Adams began the evening with a bang:

"I claim," he orated, "that we have the greatest game in the world—regardless of what's going on in Cleveland [where the World Series was being contested by the Cleveland Indians and the New York Giants]—and we have the world's greatest competitors, too."

Players from both the Leafs and the Habs who were playing in the game begged off attending the dinner, however. The Leafs had played an exhibition game the previous night in Niagara Falls and the Montrealers were grounded in Moncton after winding up a tour of the Maritimes.

Pre-Game Ceremonies

As an experiment, the ice at the Olympia was not painted white but a soft green that helped eliminate glare. Players were happy with the results, but white was considered too traditional to tamper with and was back for the regular season. Before the game, Clarence Campbell gave miniature gold pucks to all members of the First All-Star Team and to coaches King Clancy and Jimmy Skinner.

The Game

All three goalies in the game were somewhat less than ready to play. Al Rollins was dressed despite having fractured his cheekbone and sustaining a bad cut a few nights before in an exhibition game in Buffalo. Terry Sawchuk featured a black eye and stitches in his cheek from fielding one too many pucks in practice. And Harry Lumley was suffering bouts of dizziness from a collision in an exhibition tilt in Port Perry a couple of days before. Even so, Lumley stole the show in the first half of the game and kept the All-Stars in contention as they familiarized themselves with the ice and each other. Rollins, too, was heroic. Said Al with both pride and conviction: "This is the first time I've been invited to an All-Star Game, and it may be the last."

The quality of the all-stars roster was greatly diminished because three of its number—Red Kelly, Gordie Howe, and Ted Lindsay—played for the Red Wings (Delvecchio, Lindsay, and Howe played as an all-Detroit line). And not only was Ted Lindsay playing in his eighth All-Star Game but, incredibly, he had never been on the losing side. Warren Godfrey was scheduled to play but broke his foot and was replaced by teammate Bill Quackenbush.

When Gus Mortson scored, it was only the third time a defenceman had accomplished the feat (the others were Bill Barilko and Bob Goldham, both in 1949). And both Tim Horton and Fleming Mackell wore contact lenses. It was Mackell's first time, but Horton had been using them for two years and couldn't see his hand without them.

Detroit Red Wings 2   All–Stars 2

		Detroit Red Wings Jimmy Skinner, coach				All–Stars King Clancy, coach (Toronto)
1b	G	Terry Sawchuk		1a	G	Harry Lumley (Toronto)
2	D	Bob Goldham		1	G	Al Rollins (Chicago)
3	D	Marcel Pronovost		2a	D	Doug Harvey (Montreal)
4a	D	Red Kelly		3	D	Gus Mortson (Chicago)
5	D	Benny Woit		4b	D	Bill Gadsby (Chicago)
7a	LW	Ted Lindsay "C"		5	RW	Bernie Geoffrion (Montreal)
8	LW	Tony Leswick		6	C	Fleming Mackell (Boston)
9a	RW	Gordie Howe		8	LW	Sid Smith (Toronto)
10	C	Metro Prystai		9b	RW	Maurice Richard (Montreal)
11	LW	Marty Pavelich		10	D	Harry Howell (New York)
12	C	Glen Skov		11	D	Bill Quackenbush (Boston)
14	C	Earl Reibel		12b	C	Ted Kennedy (Toronto)
15	C	Alex Delvecchio		14	C	Jean Béliveau (Montreal)
16	LW	Johnny Wilson		15b	LW	Ed Sandford (Boston)
17	RW	Bill Dineen		16	C	Don Raleigh (New York)
18	D	Keith Allen		17a	C	Ken Mosdell (Montreal)
19	C	Don Poile		18b	D	Tim Horton (Toronto)
20	LW	Marcel Bonin		20	C	Paul Ronty (New York)
				23	D	Doug Mohns (Boston)

a=selected to First All–Star Team for 1953–54

b=selected to Second All–Star Team for 1953–54

First Period

1. Detroit: Delvecchio (Lindsay, Reibel) . . . . 9:50(pp)
2. Detroit: Howe (Reibel, Kelly) . . . . 19:55(pp)

Penalties: Mortson (AS) 1:37, Bonin (Det) 5:48, Mackell (AS) 8:30, Bonin (Det) 13:18, Howell (AS) 18:03, Horton (AS) 18:26

Second Period

3. All–Stars: Mortson (Gadsby, Kennedy) . . . . 4:19(pp)
4. All–Stars: Mohns (Béliveau) 13:10

Penalties: Dineen (Det) 4:01, Bonin (Det) and Howell (AS) 7:53, Sandford (AS) 13:27, Mohns (AS) 19:51

Third Period

No Scoring

Penalties: Lindsay (Det) 1:09, Mortson (AS) 3:57, Woit (Det) 9:09

Shots on Goal

All–Stars	6	11	7	**24**
Detroit	16	7	8	**31**

In Goal

Detroit—Sawchuk

All–Stars—Lumley/Rollins [Rollins (no goals) replaced Lumley (2 goals) at 10:59 of 2nd period]

Referee Bill Chadwick

Linesmen George Hayes and Doug Young

Attendance 10,689

The Production Line

Detroit Olympia, Sunday, October 2, 1955

Stanley Cup winners for the fourth time in six years, the Wings played the Habs in another brilliant seven-game final series with Detroit taking the last game 3–1 at the Olympia. Ironically, it was to be their last Cup for the next 40 years while Montreal's consecutive near misses would soon become years of unparalleled success, beginning in 1956.

At the annual banquet, NHL publicity director Ken McKenzie was handing out souvenir wallets to one and all. So caught up in his efforts did he become that he gave away his own—$200 and all. The recipient turned out to be Detroit timekeeper Fred Pike, who held on to the valuable keepsake long enough to worry poor Ken and enjoy a hearty laugh before returning it not too much later. At the head table were General Kilpatrick, Leo Reise, and Ted Lindsay, Marguerite Norris, Jack Adams, Walter Brown, Colonel Bill MacBrien, Clarence Campbell, Frank Selke, Tommy Ivan and Al Leader, president of the WHL. Reise retired as vice-president of the pension society and was replaced by Lindsay, who saw this year's game add $20,310 to the players' fund.

Because of trades, there were only nine Red Wings in the 1955 All–Star Game who had been with the Cup-winning team in the spring. In the most important of these moves, Terry Sawchuk had gone to Boston in the summer, so in this game he actually played against his own Stanley Cup team. The nine newcomers to Detroit included Real Chevrefils, Gord Hollingworth, Ed Sandford, Norm Corcoran, Larry Hillman, Warren Godfrey, and rookies Norm Ullman and John Bucyk, whose ability to step into the NHL confirmed Detroit's tremendous depth.

The Red Wings were dominant in this game, their

The incomparable Terry Sawchuk prepares to face the Stars in his fifth All–Star Game.

25th straight home game without a loss, dating back to December of the previous year. The only club ever to beat the collection of stars before this (in 1950), Detroit won for the second time. The new version of the Production Line, Howe–Lindsay–Earl

N.H.L. NINTH ANNUAL

ALL-STAR GAME

Sunday, October 2, 1955

OLYMPIA STADIUM

DETROIT

25c

DETROIT RED WINGS

1954-55 STANLEY CUP CHAMPIONS

versus

N.H.L. ALL-STARS

Riebel, created mayhem around Lumley and Sawchuk in goal all night long. A second line consisted of Delvecchio–Dineen–Chevrefils, while a third was made up of Ullman, Bucyk, and Jerry Toppazzini. Ullman and Bucyk had played together on the number one line for the Wings' farm team, the Edmonton Flyers, while "Topper" was an off-season acquisition from the Chicago Blackhawks.

The All–Stars' most impressive line was made up of the threesome of Jean Béliveau–Maurice Richard–Sid Smith. The other line put together by coach Dick Irvin featured the all-Chicago trio of Red Sullivan–Ed Litzenberger–Harry Watson. Danny Lewicki and Leo Boivin were slated to play for the glamour team but injuries prevented either from suiting up.

This was the first league game for Maurice Richard since he had attacked an official in a game in Boston toward the end of the 1954–55 season. As a result, Clarence Campbell had suspended him for the final three games of the regular season and all of the play-offs. The attack very likely cost Richard what would have been his only scoring title, as teammate Boom Boom Geoffrion finished one point ahead (76–75) after scoring three points on the second last day of the season. The suspension also cost the Habs first place in the standings (on the final night, to Detroit) and contributed to an early exit from the playoffs. And it led to the infamous "Richard Riot" at the Forum just days after the suspension was handed down. Richard wasn't popular everywhere, though, and his introduction in Detroit earned him a rousing chorus of boos commemorating his reputation in the Motor City. Immediately after the game, Habs general manager Frank Selke announced that the club had signed Richard's younger brother, Henri, more informally known as the "Pocket Rocket."

In the dying moments of the game, All–Stars coach Dick Irvin pulled Terry Sawchuk for an extra attacker, but the plan backfired and Riebel scored an empty-net freebie after Hall had made a fine save at the other end. Harry Lumley was a standout in the All–Stars net, especially in the first period when his team was short-handed five times and outshot 16–4. He made particularly spectacular saves on Geoffrion and Litzenberger and the fans rose to their feet in appreciation during one stoppage in play. Lumley's efforts were eclipsed, however, by the mid-game appearance of Sawchuk, now twine-minding for Boston after six years and three Stanley Cups in the Red Wings cage. He was greeted by a deafening ovation in honour and memory of his many previous efforts in the Olympia as he skated out to his crease. At the other end, his rookie replacement, Glenn Hall, stood on his head to shut down a team that had collectively scored more than 300 goals in the previous season.

Detroit Red Wings 3   All–Stars 1

		Detroit Red Wings Jimmy Skinner, coach				All–Stars Dick Irvin, coach (Chicago)
1	G	Glenn Hall		2a	D	Doug Harvey (Montreal)
2b	D	Bob Goldham		3b	D	Fern Flaman (Boston)
3	D	Marcel Pronovost		4a	C	Jean Béliveau (Montreal)
4a	D	Red Kelly		5b	RW	Bernie Geoffrion (Montreal)
5	D	Warren Godfrey		6	RW	Leo Labine (Boston)
7	LW	Ted Lindsay "C"		7	RW	Ed Litzenberger (Chicago)
8	C	Earl Reibel		8b	LW	Danny Lewicki (New York)
9	RW	Gordie Howe		9a	G	Harry Lumley (Toronto)
10	C	Alex Delvecchio		10	D	Jim Morrison (Toronto)
11	LW	Marty Pavelich		11b	C	Ken Mosdell (Montreal)
12	LW	Ed Sandford		12a	RW	Maurice Richard (Montreal)
14	LW	Real Chevrefils		13a	LW	Sid Smith (Toronto)
15	D	Larry Hillman		14	D	Allan Stanley (Chicago)
16	C	Norm Ullman		15b	G	Terry Sawchuk (Boston)
17	RW	Bill Dineen		16	C	Red Sullivan (Chicago)
18	D	Gord Hollingworth		17	RW	Ron Stewart (Toronto)
19	RW	Jerry Toppazzini		18	LW	Harry Watson (Chicago)
20	LW	Johnny Bucyk		20	D	Frank Martin (Chicago)
21	C	Norm Corcoran				

a=selected to First All–Star Team for 1954–55
b=selected to Second All–Star Team for 1954–55

First Period

No Scoring

Penalties: Flaman (AS) 1:28, Corcoran (Det) 8:46, Geoffrion (AS) 9:04, Stewart (AS) 10:32, Bucyk (Det) 15:16, Stanley (AS) 16:14, Morrison (AS) 19:14

Second Period

1. Detroit: Howe (Reibel, Delvecchio) . . . . 0:57(pp)
2. Detroit: Reibel (Howe, Lindsay). 5:43
Penalties: Corcoran (Det) 6:40, Hollingworth (Det) 16:01

Third Period

3. All–Stars: Harvey (Béliveau, Smith) 16:38
4. Detroit: Reibel (Goldham, Lindsay) . . . . 19:33(en)
Penalties: Hollingworth (Det) 10:54, Harvey (AS) 12:28

Shots on Goal

All–Stars	4	16	10	**30**
Detroit	16	8	18	**42**

In Goal

Detroit—Hall
All–Stars—Lumley/Sawchuk [Sawchuk (one goal) replaced Lumley (2 goals) at 12:10 of 2nd period]

Referee Frank Udvari

Linesmen George Hayes and Scotty Morrison

Attendance 10,111

Ted Lindsay's Unbeaten Streak Continues

Montreal Forum, Tuesday, October 9, 1956

The early 1950s saw Montreal come tantalisingly close to winning the Cup every year, but 1956 saw the start of something remarkable. That spring, the Habs faced the same Detroit team that had beaten them in game seven in the two previous finals. But this year it was the *Club de hockey* that won, in five hard-fought games.

Rocket Richard was just beginning his first year as team captain, replacing the outgoing Butch Bouchard, who was finally calling it quits. At the pre-game lunch, Richard received numerous gifts on behalf of the NHL. For the game itself, the All–Stars wore white and the home Habs red sweaters in what was to be the fourth tie in 10 years of the game.

Toronto's George Armstrong played on a line with fellow Leaf wingmen Dick Duff and Tod Sloan and Gadsby and Mortson on the defence. Another line created by bench boss Jimmy Skinner had Alex Delvecchio at centre with Ted Lindsay and Leo Labine at his sides. A third trio was formed by Dave Creighton, Johnny Wilson, and Wally Hergesheimer. In total, the All–Stars had combined to score 316 goals in the previous season, 100 more than the Habs.

The two Montreal lines were made up of the Richard brothers with Dickie Moore and a second unit of Béliveau–Geoffrion–Olmstead. A makeshift third line included Claude Provost and Floyd Curry on the wings with alternating centres Jackie LeClair and Don Marshall. The only members of the Cup Canadiens not playing were Butch Bouchard and Ken Mosdell, now with Chicago. Gordie Howe had been selected a Second Team All–Star but missed the game with a sore ankle after being hit by a shot in practise a few days before, and his spot was taken by Leo Labine. There was plenty of heavy hitting in the game for a change, though only Henri Richard came out of it injured, slightly (a sore knee).

Detroit's Glenn Hall made the difference in goal with four sensational, sure-goal saves off Richard, Geoffrion, Moore and, finally, Floyd Curry on a breakaway. In the second period, he robbed the Rocket twice more before giving way to Terry Sawchuk. The only two men who had played in all of the All–Star Games to date were the ones who scored goals, the 35-year-old Lindsay incredibly not having been on the losing side yet. Maurice Richard's goal was scored with Red Sullivan in the penalty box, and with that goal Sullivan skated back onto the ice, the first time a new rule was implemented whereby a power-play goal terminated the manpower advantage. It was certainly appropriate that the Habs scored the goal, since it had been their explosive playing in the previous year that had forced the rule change when they routinely scored two or more goals during the one-man advantage, and it was a rule that foreshadowed the so-called "Edmonton Rule" in the early 1980s (when the Oilers excelled to an even greater degree), when offsetting minors meant teams played five men a side rather than four-on-four.

Gordie Drillon was at the game, as was malapropistic "honourary trainer" Tim Daly, who had been serving the Leafs since the days the team had been called the Arenas (1918) during his self-proclaimed "remarketable" career.

This game raised $24,897 for the pension fund, which now exceeded $1.5 million, according to Ian Johnston, the pension society director. Because players could start claiming pension fund money at 45,

Montreal coach Toe Blake would be the first eligible player if he wished to collect. In other words, as he jokingly pointed out, when the fund was started, he was the oldest eligible player in the league.

It was after this game that Lindsay secretly called together a select group of players to discuss forming a union. Over the next few months, he got every player in the league (except Ted Kennedy of Toronto) to put up $100 for membership dues. Once the initiative was public, the owners stepped in and drove a wedge into the union plans, destroying the group before it could be formalized or gain popular momentum.

The three stars of the game were Richard, Hall, and Lindsay.

Terrible Ted Lindsay played in eleven All–Star Games, never on the losing side.

All–Stars 1   Montreal Canadiens 1

Montreal Canadiens
Toe Blake, coach

1a	G	Jacques Plante
2a	D	Doug Harvey
4a	C	Jean Béliveau
5	RW	Bernie Geoffrion
6	RW	Floyd Curry
8	C	Jackie LeClair
9a	RW	Maurice Richard "C"
10b	D	Tom Johnson
11	D	Bob Turner
12	RW	Dickie Moore
14	RW	Claude Provost
15b	LW	Bert Olmstead
16	C	Henri Richard
17	D	Jean-Guy Talbot
19	D	Dollard St. Laurent
22	LW	Don Marshall

All–Stars
Jimmy Skinner, coach (Detroit)

1b	G	Glenn Hall (Detroit)
2	D	Gus Mortson (Chicago)
3	D	Jim Morrison (Toronto)
4b	D	Red Kelly (Detroit)
5	D	Hugh Bolton (Toronto)
6	LW	Dick Duff (Toronto)
7a	LW	Ted Lindsay (Detroit)
8	C	Alex Delvecchio (Detroit)
9	RW	Leo Labine (Boston)
10	RW	George Armstrong (Toronto)
11	LW	Nick Mickoski (Chicago)
12b	C	Tod Sloan (Toronto)
14	D	Fern Flaman (Boston)
15	LW	Johnny Wilson (Chicago)
16a	D	Bill Gadsby (New York)
18	RW	Wally Hergesheimer (Chicago)
19	C	Dave Creighton (New York)
20	C	Red Sullivan (Chicago)
24	G	Terry Sawchuk (Boston)

a=selected to First All–Star Team for 1955–56
b=selected to Second All–Star Team for 1955–56

First Period
No Scoring
Penalties: Flaman (AS) 1:42, Béliveau (Mtl) 7:44, Béliveau (Mtl) 18:29

Second Period
1. Montreal: M. Richard (Olmstead, Harvey) . . . . 14:58(pp)
2. All–Stars: Lindsay (Mortson) 18:48
Penalties: Mortson (AS) 8:14, Sullivan (AS) 14:25

Third Period
No Scoring
Penalties: Labine (AS) 2:17, Mortson (AS) 9:42

Shots on Goal

All–Stars	12	11	7	**30**
Montreal	13	14	8	**35**

In Goal
Montreal—Plante
All–Stars—Hall/Sawchuk [Sawchuk (no goals) replaced Hall (one goal) at 9:30 of 2nd period]

Referee Red Storey

Linesmen Doug Davies and Bill Roberts

Attendance 13,095

Howe and Lindsay Reunited

Montreal Forum, Saturday, October 5, 1957

After what has been called the most exciting All–Star Game ever played, four stars were named at the game's conclusion: Dean Prentice, Maurice Richard, Bill Gadsby, and Tom Johnson. Sentimental coach Milt Schmidt happily put Gordie Howe and Ted Lindsay on the same line, and the two of course played well together while Detroit owner James Norris Jr. no doubt cringed in his seat. Lindsay had been traded to Chicago in the summer after infuriating general manager Jack Adams by trying to form a players' union, so after the glitter game Howe and Lindsay became opponents for the first time in their careers. Still a fan favourite, Lindsay was given a rousing round of applause prior to the second period when the players were introduced on ice for the benefit of television viewers.

(l-r) Maurice Richard, his brother, Henri, and Lorne Davis.

Coach Milt Schmidt did his part to promote the game and motivate his players by saying, "It'll be one really good game, and while all of us know how strong the Canadiens are, we feel we have an excellent chance to come out on top." He was right on both counts. Montreal was hosting its second straight game after winning the Cup almost without competition in the previous spring, when the Habs beat the Rangers in five, outscoring the Blueshirts 22–12, and then Boston in five, allowing only six goals while scoring 15 of their own in the series.

Boom Boom Geoffrion was out of the Montreal lineup with a serious case of the flu, the only Habs no-show after the bug had swept through the team's training camp. Floyd Curry replaced him on the line with Jean Béliveau and Bert Olmstead. The only new players from Montreal's previous Cup-winning year were Stan Smrke and Marcel Bonin, both promoted from the Quebec league. Junior Langlois, impressive in the Habs workouts, was a last-minute cut who was sent to Rochester for development.

Since four of the First and Second Team All–Stars played for the Canadiens and were not available to his team, Schmidt added 10 players of his choice to the All–Star Team to fill out the roster: Jim Morrison, Allan Stanley, Marcel Pronovost, Alex Delvecchio, Rudy Migay, Don McKenney, Andy Bathgate, George Armstrong, Dick Duff, and Dean Prentice. Only one member of the hapless Blackhawks (Ed Litzenberger) was on the All–Star Team, but the Hawks could console themselves in Glenn Hall's performance. Acquired along with Lindsay in July, Hall played remarkably in the third period to preserve the Stars' win.

But it was Dean Prentice who stole the show with his determined play. He was in on three of the All–Stars' goals, setting up the one that led to a tie and scoring the insurance marker on a blistering shot to the top corner. The goal came as a relief to Glenn Hall, who had been called upon to make many spectacular saves off the Habs' best shooters—Béliveau, Moore, and Richard—in quick succession as Montreal tried to tie a 4–3 game.

Prentice's winning shot came on the power-play. Ted Lindsay had been speared by Bert Olmstead and he dropped his gloves, fully prepared to pummel poor Bert. The linesmen quickly stepped in, however, and Olmstead was the only one given a penalty. Fern Flaman also expressed himself forcefully, hammering the Richard brothers every chance he got.

A record $29,347 was raised for the pension fund this year.

All–Stars 5   Montreal Canadiens 3

Montreal				All–Stars			
Toe Blake, coach				Milt Schmidt, coach (Boston)			

		Montreal				All–Stars
1b	G	Jacques Plante		1a	G	Glenn Hall (Detroit)
2a	D	Doug Harvey		3	D	Jim Morrison (Toronto)
4a	C	Jean Béliveau		4a	D	Red Kelly (Detroit)
6	RW	Floyd Curry		5	RW	Andy Bathgate (New York)
8	LW	Stan Smrke		6	D	Marcel Pronovost (Detroit)
9b	RW	Maurice Richard "C"		7a	LW	Ted Lindsay (Detroit)
10	D	Tom Johnson		8	LW	Dick Duff (Toronto)
11	D	Bob Turner		9a	RW	Gordie Howe (Detroit)
12	RW	Dickie Moore		10	C	Alex Delvecchio (Detroit)
14	RW	Claude Provost		11b	LW	Ed Litzenberger (Chicago)
15	LW	Bert Olmstead		12b	LW	Real Chevrefils (Boston)
16	C	Henri Richard		14b	D	Fern Flaman (Boston)
17	D	Jean-Guy Talbot		15	LW	Dean Prentice (New York)
18	LW	Marcel Bonin		16	C	Rudy Migay (Toronto)
19	D	Dollard St. Laurent		17	RW	George Armstrong (Toronto)
20	C	Phil Goyette		18	C	Don KcKenney (Boston)
22	LW	Don Marshall		19	D	Allan Stanley (Boston)
23	LW	André Pronovost		24b	D	Bill Gadsby (New York)

a=selected to First All–Star Team for 1956–57
b=selected to Second All–Star Team for 1956–57

First Period
1. All–Stars: Kelly (unassisted) 1:06
2. Montreal: M. Richard (H. Richard, Moore) 10:53
3. All–Stars: Stanley (Prentice, Migay) . . . . 19:55(sh)
Penalties: Migay (AS) 5:36, Talbot (Mtl) 14:25, Howe (AS) 15:55, Harvey (Mtl) 16:05, Howe (AS) 19:14

Second Period
4. Canadiens: Olmstead (Johnson) . . . . 0:33(pp)
5. Canadiens: Smrke (Bonin) 9:13
6. All–Stars: Bathgate (Litzenberger, Prentice) 18:14
Penalties: Talbot (Mtl) 5:54, Chevrefils (AS) 12:36, Johnson (Mtl) 18:59

Third Period
7. All–Stars: Howe (Chevrefils, Morrison) . . . . 8:11(pp)
8. All–Stars: Prentice (Bathgate, Litzenberger) 16:50
Penalties: Flaman (AS) 5:48, Olmstead (Mtl) 6:24, Flaman (AS) 9:46

Shots on Goal
Montreal	10	13	9	**32**
All–Stars	14	12	12	**38**

In Goal
Montreal—Plante
All–Stars—Hall

Referee Red Storey

Linesmen Doug Davies and Scotty Morrison

Attendance 13,095

Canadiens Sont Là!

Montreal Forum, Saturday, October 4, 1958

Montreal won the Cup again in 1958 by sweeping Detroit 4–0 in the semis and beating Boston for the second year in a row in a six-game final. Maurice Richard's 11 playoff goals led the Habs, and the core of the team was so strong it seemed no contender could usurp this most powerful of dynasties (which

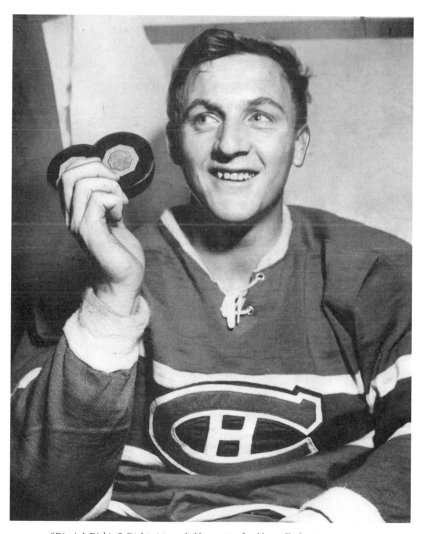

"Diggin' Dickie," Dickie Moore holds a pair of rubber pills for photographers.

was only the second team to win three in a row after Toronto pulled the Cup hat trick from 1947 to 1949).

At the pre-game banquet, All–Star players were given mementos and league winners their trophies. Dickie Moore was awarded the Art Ross, Gordie Howe the Hart, Camille Henry the Lady Byng, Jacques Plante his third straight Vezina, Frank Mahovlich the Calder, and Doug Harvey his fourth consecutive Norris. Conn Smythe gave four of the league's senior trainers gold pucks: Tim Daly of the Leafs, Win Green of Boston, Carl Mattson of the Red Wings, and Ernie Cook of the Canadiens. Ever quick with a quip, Daly made a brief but hilarious acceptance speech:

"Your son Stafford asked me tonight if I would retire. I told him as long as I'm getting the soft money I'm getting from you, I'll never retire."

The Leafs also took advantage of the general managers' gathering to send defenceman Jim Morrison to Boston for Allan Stanley.

Ted Lindsay was in Montreal not as an all–star player but as a team representative. He had been instrumental in trying to organize a players' union for two years before this. When he failed, he'd been traded to cellar-dweller Chicago in a stiff rebuke by Detroit's Norris family. On the morning of the All–Star Game, the NHL Players' Association (which was not recognized by the NHL owners) huddled for a couple of hours of discussion. In the afternoon, the team owners and players held their formal discussions, but not surprisingly nothing in the way of formalising a union was accomplished.

During the All–Star meetings, Doug Harvey, vice-president and director of the players' pension fund, asked Sun Life to conduct an audit of the NHL to determine just how the pension money was being handled. Sun Life duly reported that it was one of the finest pension plans it had ever perused. Along with player-president Lindsay, Harvey publicly thanked Clarence Campbell on behalf of all the players for his fine work and dedication in ensuring the health of the fund (which was now over two million dollars, thanks to this year's take of $31,510). Said Harvey:

"We had an independent survey of our pension plan, and I am satisfied with the result. Now I feel if a little television money comes in, it will look after our families a little better."

In an unusual twist, the coaches introduced their players over the public address system for the benefit of fans at the game and those watching on television. The recently traded Dollard St. Laurent was greeted with enthusiastic and prolonged applause. Like Hall and Lindsay the year before, he'd been sent to Chicago during the summer and so represented the All–Stars rather than his former Cup-winning team.

Coach Milt Schmidt's stellar defence was formed by keeping his Bruins tandem of Mohns and Flaman together and pairing Pronovost and Gadsby as a second set and Kelly and St. Laurent as a third. Up front, he formed lines of Litzenberger–Henry–Bathgate, Delvecchio–Duff–Howe, Sullivan–McKenney–Toppazzini and Harris and Pulford at centre and left with the three rotating right wingers. The only Montreal regular not in the lineup for the game was Al Langlois, who was out for six weeks after separating his shoulder in an exhibition game against the Rochester Americans in Sudbury on September 30. Ian Cushenan, bought from Chicago the previous day, filled in for him.

The only casualty of the evening was Boom Boom Geoffrion, who reached for a puck near his blue line midway through the second and boom! was hammered cleanly by Red Kelly. Geoffrion lay on the ice for 10 minutes and missed the rest of the game. Fortunately, he'd only pulled some neck muscles and didn't miss any action with the Habs. "I remember hitting Geoffrion," Kelly said some time later. "He didn't see me; his vision was blocked."

Montreal Canadiens 6   All–Stars 3

Montreal Canadiens
Toe Blake, coach

1b	G	Jacques Plante
2a	D	Doug Harvey
4b	C	Jean Béliveau
5	RW	Bernie Geoffrion
6	C	Ralph Backstrom
9	RW	Maurice Richard
10	D	Tom Johnson
11	D	Bob Turner
12a	RW	Dickie Moore
14	RW	Claude Provost
15	LW	Ab McDonald
16a	C	Henri Richard
17	D	Jean-Guy Talbot
18	LW	Marcel Bonin
20	C	Phil Goyette
21	D	Ian Cushenan
22	LW	Don Marshall
23	LW	André Pronovost

All–Stars
Milt Schmidt, coach (Boston)

1a	G	Glenn Hall (Chicago)
3b	D	Marcel Pronovost (Detroit)
4a	D	Bill Gadsby (New York)
5	D	Red Kelly (Detroit)
7	C	Red Sullivan (New York)
8b	RW	Andy Bathgate (New York)
9a	RW	Gordie Howe (Detroit)
10	C	Alex Delvecchio (Detroit)
11	RW	Jerry Toppazzini (Boston)
12b	C	Camille Henry (New York)
14b	D	Fern Flaman (Boston)
15	C	Billy Harris (Toronto)
16	LW	Dick Duff (Toronto)
17	RW	Ed Litzenberger (Chicago)
18	C	Don McKenney (Boston)
19	D	Doug Mohns (Boston)
20	LW	Bob Pulford (Toronto)
24	D	Dollard St. Laurent (Chicago)

a=selected to First All–Star Team for 1957–58
b=selected to Second All–Star Team for 1957–58

First Period

1. Montreal: M. Richard (Harvey, Moore) . . . . 9:19(pp)
2. Montreal: Geoffrion (H. Richard) 16:20
Penalties: Henry (AS) 7:29, Harvey (Mtl) 11:41

Second Period

3. Montreal: Marshall (Provost) . . . . 2:33(sh)
4. Montreal: H. Richard (Talbot, Moore) 5:08
5. All–Stars: Pulford (Toppazzini, Harris) 11.39
Penalties: Turner (Mtl) 2:24

Third Period

6. All–Stars: Bathgate (Litzenberger, Henry) 3:55
7. Montreal: McDonald (Provost, Marshall) . . . . . . 7:43(pp)
8. All–Stars: Bathgate (Pulford, Sullivan) . . . . 13:54(pp)
9. Montreal: M. Richard (Moore, H. Richard) 16:04
Penalties: Mohns (AS) 4:25, Duff (AS) 7:36, Provost (Mtl) 12:52

Shots on Goal

Montreal	17	11	11	**39**
All–Stars	7	8	12	**27**

In Goal

Montreal—Plante
All–Stars—Hall

Referee Eddie Powers

Linesmen George Hayes and Scotty Morrison

Attendance 13,989

A Year of No-Shows

Montreal Forum, Saturday, October 3, 1959

The Habs won their fourth Cup in a row, but the Stanley Cup story of the spring of 1959 occurred at Maple Leaf Gardens. After a bad start to the year, Punch Imlach took over as coach and vowed to take the Leafs to the playoffs. As the regular season wound down, they were still in fifth place. With five games to play, Toronto was still seven points behind the fourth-place Rangers but Imlach still promised a place in the playoffs. On the last day of the season, the Leafs were only one point back. Then they beat Detroit 6–4, Montreal took the Rangers 4–2 and the Leafs were in. They went on to beat Boston in a seven-game semi-final while Montreal defeated the Blackhawks in six to set up

all-Canadian finals for the first time since 1951. But at that point the Leafs' fortunes ran into Montreal's dynasty. Five games later, Montreal was again the unequivocal champion.

For the first time in All–Star Game history, the NHL proviso that players had to be under contract to play finally caught up with all parties concerned. Designed to intimidate players into signing by a particular date on terms they might otherwise not have accepted, the ploy backfired this year as it presented a tainted "All–Star" game featuring a number of players who wouldn't normally have made the grade.

Dickie Moore was close to missing the game but autographed a contract for coach Toe Blake the day

Tom Johnson (left) and Doug Harvey (right) engage in a warm conversation with referee Frank Udvari.

before the contest. Two Leafs (Frank Mahovlich and George Armstrong) signed contracts on the day of the game and thus became eligible to play. All–Star coach Punch Imlach was not able to use three of his Leafs (Tim Horton, Dick Duff, and Bob Pulford) or three top-notch Blackhawks (Bobby Hull, Tod Sloan, and Pierre Pilote) and was forced to fill in these meaningful gaps with inferior last-minute additions. Add to that the fact that six Habs who were selected to the First and Second All–Star Teams also played for their club in this game and Imlach didn't stand much of a chance with his All–Stars, though, as usual, he put up a brave front. "We're going to win," he shouted to anyone who would listen on the morning of the game. "I've got the best players going for me, and I didn't come down here on a social trip."

Pre-Game Events

As a result of not signing (or playing), the six top players named above also missed out on the souvenir table lighters handed out at the annual pre-game banquet. Bert Olmstead found out the hard way. He had replaced the unsigned Bob Pulford, but when he went to get a second lighter for Pully, he was rebuffed. Similarly, Carl Brewer (another late invitee) received a gift with Pierre Pilote's name on it because Pilote too was a last-minute no-show.

Toe Blake was given a thank-you puck with seven diamonds in it, representing each of his Stanley Cups, four as a coach and three as a player. Jean Béliveau received a puck with four studs, Bill Gadsby got three, and Jacques Plante and Dickie Moore two. Bathgate, Johnson, and Punch Imlach were given their first All–Star pucks. Cooper Smeaton, long-time referee and custodian of the Stanley Cup, was given a mini-

replica of the hallowed hardware as thanks for his 20-odd years of devotion to the league.

The game raised $35,186 for the pension fund, and preliminary talks were initiated to get the referees and linesmen into the fund. Again, both coaches introduced their players on ice during the first intermission for the added excitement of fans in the stands and watching on TV. Maurice Richard played in his 13th consecutive game, the only man to appear in all of the games to date, and received a standing ovation from his hometown fans during the introductions, as did Gordie Howe and Bert Olmstead. The tough Fern Flaman of Boston received the coldest chorus of whistles and boos.

The Game

Béliveau led Montreal with his first two goals in this, his seventh All–Star Game, and Sawchuk had a rare off night, allowing all six Montreal goals. The All–Stars' best line consisted of Howe–Delvecchio–Mahovlich. Alex Delvecchio scored a disputed goal in the second, but referee Udvari ruled that he had already blown the play dead. The Habs had two rookies in the lineup, Bill Hicke and J.C. Tremblay, who combined to replace Jean-Guy Talbot, who had separated his shoulder in practise the previous week and was convalescing.

Although Jacques Plante had announced before the start of the season he would wear a mask for every game (as he'd been doing for practices), he was bare-faced for his superb performance against the Stars. Generally speaking, the game was fast and friendly, but players were cautious along the boards. One of the loudest cheers of the night came midway through the third when referee Udvari whistled his first penalty of the game.

Montreal Canadiens 6   All–Stars 1

		Montreal Canadiens Toe Blake, coach				All–Stars Punch Imlach, coach (Toronto)
1a	G	Jacques Plante		1b	G	Terry Sawchuk (Detroit)
2b	D	Doug Harvey		3b	D	Marcel Pronovost (Detroit)
4a	C	Jean Béliveau		4a	D	Bill Gadsby (New York)
5	RW	Bernie Geoffrion		5	D	Carl Brewer (Toronto)
6	C	Ralph Backstrom		7	C	Red Sullivan (New York)
8	RW	Bill Hicke		8a	RW	Andy Bathgate (New York)
9	RW	Maurice Richard "C"		9b	RW	Gordie Howe (Detroit)
10a	D	Tom Johnson		10b	C	Alex Delvecchio (Detroit)
11	D	Bob Turner		11	RW	Jerry Toppazzini (Boston)
12a	RW	Dickie Moore		14	D	Fern Flaman (Boston)
14	RW	Claude Provost		15	LW	Frank Mahovlich (Toronto)
15	LW	Ab McDonald		16	LW	Bert Olmstead (Toronto)
16b	C	Henri Richard		17	LW	Ed Litzenberger (Chicago)
18	LW	Marcel Bonin		18	C	Don McKenney (Boston)
19	D	Al Langlois		19	D	Doug Mohns (Boston)
20	C	Phil Goyette		24	RW	George Armstrong (Toronto)
21	D	J.C. Tremblay				
22	LW	Don Marshall				
23	LW	André Pronovost				

a=selected to First All–Star Team for 1958–59

b=selected to Second All–Star Team for 1958–59

First Period

No Scoring

Penalties: None

Second Period

1. Montreal: Béliveau (Hicke, Harvey) 4:25
2. Montreal: McDonald (Backstrom, Geoffrion) 13:43
3. All–Stars: McKenney (Litzenberger) 18:30

Penalties: None

Third Period

4. Montreal: Moore (H. Richard, Johnson) 7:44
5. Montreal: H. Richard (Moore, Harvey) 9:31
6. Montreal: Béliveau (Hicke, Bonin) 11:54
7. Montreal: A. Pronovost (Harvey) 15:51

Penalties: Tremblay (Mtl) 8:43, Bathgate (AS) 9:21, Turner (Mtl) 12:45

Shots on Goal

Montreal	9	14	10	**33**
All–Stars	14	16	5	**35**

In Goal

Montreal—Plante

All–Stars—Sawchuk

Referee Frank Udvari

Linesmen George Hayes and Bob Frampton

Attendance 13,818

The Rocket Is Honoured

Montreal Forum, Saturday, October 1, 1960

For the first time since the game's inception in 1947, the now retired Maurice "Rocket" Richard would not be playing in the All–Star Game. Bill Hicke took his spot on the line with Dickie Moore and the other Richard, younger brother Henri, while the Habs' new captain was 35-year-old defenceman Doug Harvey. Coach Toe Blake mourned Rocket's loss when he noted, "On the ice, there's nobody around to get that important goal for us...nobody." Ab McDonald, a key member of the team that won the 1959–60 Stanley Cup in a minimum eight games, had been sold to Chicago during the summer, and an injured Phil Goyette was the only other Cup player to miss the game. Otherwise, the Habs lineup was man for man the same for this All–Star Game as the one that had claimed the Cup in the spring for an unprecedented fifth time in succession. Blake wanted to use some of the four rookies that he had in camp (Cliff Pennington, Bobby Rousseau, Wayne Connelly, and J.C. Tremblay), but his team had encountered so little real challenge during exhibition games that he needed to use his veterans in a difficult situation as a tuneup for the regular season. This year marked the continuation of another streak, though, since Harvey was playing in his ninth consecutive tinsel tilt.

The All–Stars sweater underwent a design change for this year, deviating from the traditional red, blue, and white to a combination of orange and black (the NHL's official colours) coordinated with pants supplied by the Boston Bruins.

Pre-Game Events

The All–Star dinner the night before the game was a briskly paced evening of fun and entertainment at the Sheraton Mount-Royal, masterfully arranged by league president Clarence Campbell. Rocket Richard left the festivities laden with gifts celebrating both his last Stanley Cup and his recent retirement. The donations included an alarm clock and a mini replica of the Cup with an engraving of each Montreal player mounted on the wood base. On the way back to his table, Richard's new alarm sounded and sounded, unchecked. "I couldn't stop the damn thing," he grinned as he sat down. All the NHL trophies were also awarded. Bobby Hull won his first Art Ross Trophy; Gordie Howe won the Hart; Don McKenney of Boston won the Lady Byng; Jacques Plante won his record fifth successive Vezina; Bill Hay won the Calder; and Doug Harvey won the Norris. And of course the All–Stars received their gold pucks and then went out and raised $33,048 for their collective pension benefits to swell their bank account to almost $2.5 million.

Player introductions were made between the first and second periods again, with Gordie Howe was accorded the loudest applause. Unfortunately, he sprained his knee in the first period when he took a check from Bob Turner and watched the rest of the game from the press box. What was more, he wound up missing Detroit's home opener, his first opening-night absence in 15 seasons.

Between the second and third periods, Sylvio Mantha and Maurice Richard, the most recent introductions to civilian life and the Hockey Hall of Fame, were given ovations when they were introduced to the Forum crowd. The only absentee from either of the two All–Star Teams was Dean Prentice (Second Team), who was still recovering from surgery for

Jacques Plante does what he made famous—comes out of the net to play the puck.

torn cartilege. Red Sullivan ably stepped in and set up the game-winning goal.

The Game

Generally thought to be one of the best ever played, the game garnered particularly strong accolades for Stars goalie Glenn Hall, who repelled all Montreal comers in an active third period in which he made a number of spectacular saves. After playing defence in the first period, Red Kelly moved up to forward on a line with Frank Mahovlich and Norm Ullman and formed the most effective trio on the ice for the last 20 minutes. Almost equally spectacular was the second threesome of Bobby Hull, Red Hay, and Andy Bathgate. Coach Punch Imlach's third glory line featured Bronco Horvath, Bob Pulford, and Vic Stasiuk.

All the scoring was done in the second period, but with 11 seconds left in the game, Habs coach Toe Blake pulled goalie Jacques Plante with a faceoff in the All–Stars end to try to tie the score. It was all for naught. The puck skidded away harmlessly and Hall didn't have to make a stop. The win was particularly sweet for coach Imlach, whose Leafs had lost to the Habs for the past two years in the finals, winning only one game of nine. His All–Star Team had also been clobbered 6–1 the previous year. Playing for the fifth year in a row, the Habs were winning with such consistency that plans to move the game to mid-season for the benefit of U.S. teams were put on hold. In Montreal, conflict with the World Series was not uppermost in anyone's mind at the time.

All–Stars 2   Montreal Canadiens 1

Montreal Canadiens Toe Blake, coach				All–Stars Punch Imlach, coach (Toronto)		
1 b	G	Jacques Plante		1 a	G	Glenn Hall (Chicago)
2 a	D	Doug Harvey "C"		2	D	Bob Armstrong (Boston)
4 a	C	Jean Béliveau		3 a	D	Marcel Pronovost (Detroit)
5 b	RW	Bernie Geoffrion		4	D	Red Kelly (Toronto)
6	C	Ralph Backstrom		5 b	D	Pierre Pilote (Chicago)
8	RW	Bill Hicke		6 b	D	Bronco Horvath (Boston)
10	D	Tom Johnson		7	LW	Vic Stasiuk (Boston)
11	D	Bob Turner		8	C	Norm Ullman (Detroit)
12	RW	Dickie Moore		9 a	RW	Gordie Howe (Detroit)
16	C	Henri Richard		10	RW	Andy Bathgate (New York)
17	D	Jean-Guy Talbot		11	C	Bill Hay (Chicago)
18	LW	Marcel Bonin		12	RW	Andy Hebenton (New York)
19	D	Al Langlois		14	D	Bill Gadsby (New York)
22	LW	Don Marshall		15	C	Red Sullivan (New York)
23	LW	André Pronovost		16 a	LW	Bobby Hull (Chicago)
24	RW	Claude Provost		17	C	Don McKenney (Boston)
				18 b	D	Allan Stanley (Toronto)
				19	LW	Frank Mahovlich (Toronto)
				20	LW	Bob Pulford (Toronto)

a=selected to First All–Star Team for 1959–60

b=selected to Second All–Star Team for 1959–60

First Period

No Scoring

Penalties: Talbot (Mtl) 7:22

Second Period

1. All–Stars: Mahovlich (Pilote, Kelly)............... 0:40
2. Montreal: Provost (Backstrom, A. Pronovost) 11:40
3. All–Stars: Hebenton (Sullivan) .... 15:15(sh)

Penalties: Sullivan (AS) 12:17, Hull (AS) 14:47, Johnson (Mtl) 17:03

Third Period

No Scoring

Penalties: Hicke (Mtl) 2:58, Gadsby (AS) 5:44, Pilote (AS) 6:54, Harvey (Mtl) 10:20

Shots on Goal

Montreal	9	8	9	**26**
All–Stars	7	10	10	**27**

In Goal

Montreal—Plante

All–Stars—Hall

Referee Eddie Powers

Linesmen George Hayes and Neil Armstrong

Attendance 13,949

Celebration in the Windy City

Chicago Stadium, Saturday, October 7, 1961

The second time Chicago hosted the glitter game was also the first time it did so as Stanley Cup champions. And only one player in 1961's game was in the 1948 game as well—Gordie Howe. Moreover, the Hawks had accomplished their stunning Cup victory the previous spring even though none of their players had been named to the First All–Star Team. They climaxed their historic season by eliminating Montreal in six games in the semi-finals (thus ending the Canadiens' unprecedented five-year Stanley Cup run) and then beat Detroit in six in the finals to win their first Cup since 1937–38, largely thanks to spectacular goaltending from the legendary Glenn Hall.

To help celebrate the team's first Stanley Cup in 23 years, the Hawks used the All–Star Game to dedicate their new Blackhawks Hall of Fame. The team inducted the first 16 members and displayed memorabilia related to those stars in the corridors of Chicago Stadium. Those honoured included Dick Irvin, Paul Thompson, and Johnny Gottselig (as coaches); all the members of the two most potent lines in Hawks history, the Pony Line of Doug Bentley–Max Bentley–Bill Mosienko and a line from the 1930s consisting of Paul Thompson, Doc Romnes, and Mush March; Earl Seibert, Johnny Mariucci, and Chuck Gardiner; and oldtimers already enshrined in the Hockey Hall of Fame, Mickey MacKay, Herb Gardner, George Hay, Duke Keats, and Hugh Lehman.

The Stars' goalie Johnny Bower watches play as the Blackhawks move the puck around during the 15th All–Star Game.

75

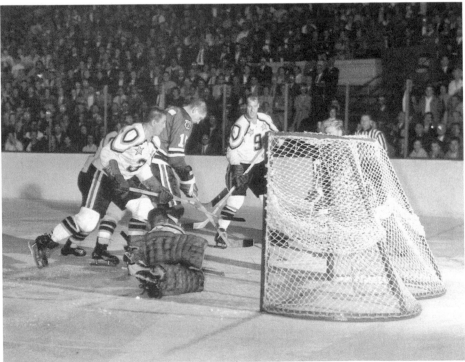

Action from the Chicago Stadium around goalie Gump Worlsey (top) as Eric Nesterenko scores on the power-play. The Gumper has better luck (bottom) as Gordie Howe watches him make a fine save.

As coach of the finalists, Detroit bench boss Sid Abel selected the remaining spots on the All–Star Team after First and Second stars had been slotted in, but he was given more than a little grief for naming Phil Goyette to the roster ahead of Red Kelly. Abel explained that because he had already selected Carl Brewer for defence, he needed a Montreal player for balance. Interestingly, Doug Harvey, a First Team selection, had now become player–coach with the Rangers and thus became the first and only coach to play in an All–Star Game (although he had yet to play his first game as a coach).

Abel had no control over the participation of other All–Stars, however. Allan Stanley (a Second Team selection) didn't play because of salary problems that prevented him from signing his contract. And both Jean Béliveau (First Team) and Dickie Moore (Second Team) were sidelined with injuries, with Goyette filling in for Le Gros Bill.

For Chicago, coach Rudy Pilous went down to the wire before setting his lineup. A day before the game, five players from his Cup team had not yet signed contracts and were doubtful starters. But Reggie Fleming, Ron Murphy, and Dollard St. Laurent all inked deals prior to the faceoff, leaving only Stan Mikita and Earl Balfour unsigned and absent.

Pre-Game Events

At the All–Star Game dinner at the Bismark Hotel, Clarence Campbell performed his chores as president and host briskly, doling out All–Star pucks, gifts, and NHL awards in a record 20 minutes. Hawks owners Arthur Wirtz and Jim Norris led the gift-giving by allotting each of their Cup-winning players diamond-studded rings.

Players were again introduced between the first and second periods, with goaler Glenn Hall extended an ovation everyone agreed was the finest ever granted a player, greater even than Gordie Howe's in Detroit or Maurice Richard's in Montreal. The standing ovation lasted three minutes, during which Hall stood at centre ice alone and near tears.

"I was afraid I was going to burst out crying," he said later. "It was marvellous considering that there were so many truly great players on the ice tonight. If that kind of a greeting doesn't make me play better, I doubt if anything ever will."

The Game

One of the highlights came when Donnie Marshall was speeding down the wing on a breakaway. Bobby Hull, sitting on the bench, leaned over and poked the puck away from the skater, a move that earned him a deuce in the penalty box for interference. On another occasion in the second, Frank Mahovlich and Eric Nesterenko had a set-to with their sticks that ended with a Big M fist to a Nester jaw. Referee Udvari insulted the combatants by deeming the scuffle so tame as not to deserve major penalties and issued double minors instead.

"He stuck his stick in my face and scratched like a woman instead of fighting," claimed big Frank.

"That Mahovlich thinks he can't be touched. He's a real prima donna," retorted Nester.

Gordie Howe and Reg Fleming also came close to blows in the second, though no real damage was done and no penalties needed.

The game raised a record $43,652 for the pension fund and a record crowd of 14,534 witnessed the action, despite stiff competition from the World Series.

All–Stars 3   Chicago Blackhawks 1

Chicago Blackhawks
Rudy Pilous, coach

1b	G	Glenn Hall
2	D –	Bob Turner
3b	D –	Pierre Pilote "C"
4	D –	Elmer Vasko
5	D –	Jack Evans
6	LW –	Reggie Fleming
7	C –	Murray Hall
9	C –	Bronco Horvath
10	LW –	Ron Murphy
11	C –	Bill Hay
12	C –	Gerry Melnyk
14	LW –	Ab McDonald
15	RW –	Eric Nesterenko
16	LW –	Bobby Hull
17	RW –	Ken Wharram
18	RW –	Chico Maki
19	D –	Dollard St. Laurent

All–Stars
Sid Abel, coach (Detroit)

1a	G	Johnny Bower (Toronto)
1	G	Gump Worsley (New York)
2a	D –	Doug Harvey (New York)
3a	D –	Marcel Pronovost (Detroit)
4	C –	Phil Goyette (Montreal)
5a	RW –	Bernie Geoffrion (Montreal)
6	RW –	Andy Bathgate (New York)
7	C –	Norm Ullman (Detroit)
8a	LW –	Frank Mahovlich (Toronto)
9b	RW –	Gordie Howe (Detroit)
10	C –	Alex Delvecchio (Detroit)
12	LW –	Don Marshall (Montreal)
14	RW –	Claude Provost (Montreal)
15	LW –	Dean Prentice (New York)
16b	C –	Henri Richard (Montreal)
17	C –	Don McKenney (Boston)
18	D –	Tim Horton (Toronto)
19	D –	Doug Mohns (Boston)
20	D –	Leo Boivin (Boston)

a=selected to First All–Star Team for 1960–61
b=selected to Second All–Star Team for 1960–61

First Period
1. All–Stars: Delvecchio (Howe, Ullman) 11:37
Penalties: Mahovlich (AS) 8:26, Hay (Chi) 15:02, Vasko (Chi) 19:15

Second Period
2. All–Stars: McKenney (Bathgate, Pronovost) 2:37
3. Chicago: Nesterenko (Hull, Pilote) . . . . 6:26(pp)
4. All–Stars: Howe (Delvecchio, Ullman) 12:38
Penalties: Goyette (AS) 4:46, Nesterenko (Chi—double minor) and Mahovlich (AS—double minor) 7:36, Nesterenko (Chi) 16:21, McKenney (AS) 19:47

Third Period
No Scoring
Penalties: Pilote (Chi) 1:38, Richard (AS) 11:49, Hull (Chi) 19:24

Shots on Goal

Chicago	6	9	8	**23**
All–Stars	11	13	11	**35**

In Goal
Chicago—Hall
All–Stars—Bower/Worsley [Worsley (no goals) replaced Bower (one goal) at 10:00 of 2nd period]

Referee Frank Udvari

Linesmen Neil Armstrong and George Hayes

Attendance 14,534

A Million-Dollar Offer for The Big M

Maple Leaf Gardens, Saturday, October 6, 1962

Punch Imlach, twice a Stanley Cup finalist, proved his worth as a champion coach when he led the Leafs to their first Cup since 1951 and their first of four rounds of champagne in the 1960s. The finals, a four-game sweep of the Habs, couldn't have provided a more satisfying a triumph, and the Leafs, led by Bower, Armstrong et al., were on their way to Blue and White glory. But the win became legendary in part because of Bill Barilko, who had scored the Cup-winning overtime goal in 1951 and then died in a plane crash in northern Ontario that summer. Eerily enough, his body wasn't found until the Leafs won the Cup again in 1962. It was as if with his body not found and his death not confirmed, the restless soul of the Leafs couldn't hope to win glory.

The days leading up to the game featuring the Cup-winning Leafs and the NHL All–Stars were curious and unsettling, to say the least. As always, the league's rules prescribed that players had to be under contract by game time in order to play. However, 10 days before the game, only two Leafs (George Armstrong and Kent Douglas) had signed for the coming season while the rest were hoping to increase their salaries based on their outstanding performance the previous spring. Punch Imlach was not inclined to negotiate money matters in the off-season, however, because he felt a signed contract made players slack and too comfortable in training camp. By the time this All–Star Game rolled around, all the Leafs had signed, but on Imlach's terms, not theirs. Stan Mikita (First Team) was the only one of the dozen All–Star Team selections not to play in the game, but this was due to a badly sprained ankle incurred in an exhibition game with Chicago in Ottawa.

Pre-Game Events

The banquet the day before the game attracted 200 people, including a retired Bert Olmstead, who drew the loudest applause, and the game raised $36,519—plus an additional $15,000 for the TV and radio rights—for the pension fund.

But the game in 1962 is perhaps best remembered not for the contest itself but for a stunning midnight offer Chicago owner Jim Norris publicly made to the Leafs the night before—a cheque for a cool $1 million for left winger Frank Mahovlich. While some called it a publicity stunt to toss the World Series off the front pages of newspapers (in which case it worked), Norris displayed the cheque as concrete proof of his offer. And it made an enormous impression on everyone except Leafs executive Stafford Smythe, who firmly rejected the deal the next day.

Here's what happened. After the All–Star dinner, a number of owners and executives moved to suite 11-268 of the Royal York Hotel, where conversation eventually turned to the problems Toronto was having signing the Big M (who seemed destined to miss the game as a result). Norris asked Harold Ballard, a member of the team's Silver Seven managing committee, what it would take to pry Mahovlich away from the Leafs, and Ballard growled, "A million dollars!" Norris pulled out 10 $100-bills as a down payment and the men shook on the deal. Ballard then wrote a note of confirmation: "We except [sic] on behalf of Maple Leaf Gardens," and Jack Amell, another of the Silver Seven, also signed the agreement. Next, Norris conferred with his publicity director, former player Johnny Gottselig, who relayed the stunning news to reporters for Associated Press and United Press

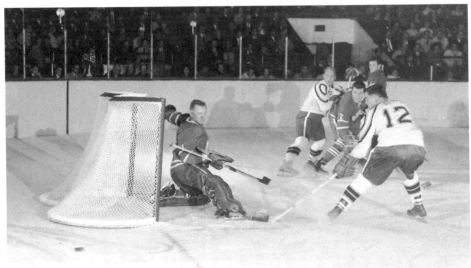

Johnny Bower faces All–Star heat around his cage in 1962. After a dozen years in the minors, he won his first Stanley Cup with the Leafs in the spring of '62, his first of four with Toronto in the '60s.

International. Stafford Smythe was at the other end of the room and didn't find out about the "deal" until then, at which point he proceeded to comment on the World Series and then said there was no deal until a formal meeting at a suitable—and sober—time could be arranged. The next day, the principals met at the Gardens, and Norris walked in with a $1-million cheque and walked right back out with the same. Meanwhile, Frank Mahovlich was in another office with Punch Imlach, signing his new Leafs contract, a four-year deal for an unheard of $110,000.

Pre-Game Ceremonies

Before the game got under way, the Stanley Cup was presented to Leafs captain George Armstrong by John Buchanan, great-grandson of Lord Stanley of Preston, who was seeing the great trophy for the first time. League president Clarence Campbell once more presented gold pucks to the First Team All–Stars and the two coaches. All the members of the 1947 All–Star Team were also on hand and were introduced to the crowd, with Maurice Richard getting the loudest applause from the fans in the Gardens now that he was in street clothes. (The original Stars would all also appear on the Hot Stove League during the second intermission while Foster Hewitt was introducing the current All–Stars to the crowd as each player skated into an on-ice spotlight.)

The Game

When he named three goalies to the All–Star Team, coach Rudy Pilous began a new trend of handling twine-tenders that gave fans of the game a chance to see three of the best play in one night. It would be 1992 before the goalie-a-period was adopted as the usual practice, however.

For the first time, the league awarded an MVP for the game and the inaugural winner was Eddie Shack. And his prize? "Just like everybody else—a jewellery case with no jewellery," he quipped later. Appropriately, he was one of only two men to win MVP honours and receive a penalty in the same game (the other would be the milder-tempered Henri Richard in 1967).

George Armstrong (left) and Gordie Howe (right) shake prior to the 1963 glitter game in Toronto.

Toronto Maple Leafs 4   All–Stars 1

Toronto Maple Leafs		All–Stars	
Punch Imlach, coach		Rudy Pilous, coach (Chicago)	

		Toronto Maple Leafs				All–Stars
1	G	Johnny Bower	1b	G	Glenn Hall (Chicago)
2b	D	Carl Brewer	1a	G	Jacques Plante (Montreal)
4	C	Red Kelly	1	G	Gump Worsley (New York)
7	D	Tim Horton	2a	D	Doug Harvey (New York)
9	LW	Dick Duff	3b	D	Pierre Pilote (Chicago)
10	RW	George Armstrong "C"	4a	D	Jean-Guy Talbot (Montreal)
11	RW	Bob Nevin	5	RW	Bernie Geoffrion (Montreal)
12	RW	Ron Stewart	6a	RW	Andy Bathgate (New York)
14b	C	Dave Keon	7	C	Norm Ullman (Detroit)
15	C	Billy Harris	9b	RW	Gordie Howe (Detroit)
19	D	Kent Douglas	10	C	Alex Delvecchio (Detroit)
20	LW	Bob Pulford	11a	LW	Bobby Hull (Chicago)
21	D	Bobby Baun	12	C	Ralph Backstrom (Montreal)
22	D	Larry Hillman	14	RW	Claude Provost (Montreal)
23	RW	Eddie Shack	17	C	Don McKenney (Boston)
24	RW	John MacMillan	18	D	Jack Evans (Chicago)
25	RW	Ed Litzenberger	19	D	Doug Mohns (Boston)
26	D	Allan Stanley	20	D	Leo Boivin (Boston)
27b	LW	Frank Mahovlich			

a=selected to First All–Star Team for 1961–62

b=selected to Second All–Star Team for 1961–62

First Period
1. Toronto: Duff (Douglas, Armstrong) . . . . 5:22(pp)
2. All-Stars: Howe (Delvecchio, Pilote) . . . . 7:26(pp)
3. Toronto: Pulford (Stewart) 10:45
4. Toronto: Mahovlich (Stanley) 13:03
5. Toronto: Shack (Keon) 19:32
Penalties: Mohns (AS) 4:32, Nevin (Tor) 6:16, McKenney (AS) and Brewer (Tor) 12:41, Howe (AS) and Shack (Tor) 15:39

Second Period
No Scoring
Penalties: Kelly (Tor) 1:56, Howe (AS) 16:33, Brewer (Tor) 18:30

Third Period
No Scoring
Penalties: Baun (Tor) 13:03, Boivin (AS) 17:35, Shack (Tor) 19:21

Shots on Goal

Toronto	16	10	10	**36**
All-Stars	10	12	11	**33**

In Goal
Toronto—Bower
All-Stars—Plante (1st period, 4 goals), Hall (2nd period, no goals), Worsley (3rd period, no goals)

Referee Eddie Powers

Linesmen Matt Pavelich and Ron Wicks

Attendance 14,236

MVP Eddie Shack (Toronto)

The Big M's Game

Maple Leaf Gardens, Saturday, October 5, 1963

Johnny Bower comes out to make the stop while a Leaf defenceman takes Bobby Hull out of the play.

Like the Leafs in the 1940s, the Red Wings in the early 1950s and the Habs in the late 1950s, the Leafs of the 1960s got stronger and stronger with each passing season, with the result that the 1963 playoffs provided little drama or test of their mettle as they beat both Montreal and Detroit in five games to win their second Cup in a row.

Worried over unsigned players and a lacklustre performance by his defence in pre-season play, Leafs coach Punch Imlach recalled Kent Douglas and Al Arbour from the Rochester Americans for the All–Star Game, though he only played Douglas because Arbour was having trouble with the cartilage in his knee. Imlach also had another interesting issue to consider when it came time to fill out his roster.

He had brought two Swedish players (Carl Oeberg and Kjell "Ollie the Goalie" Svensson) to his Maple Leafs camp. Although he considered them unlikely starters for the All–Star Game, he did offer them contracts with Rochester. Instead, they passed up the chance to pursue their NHL dream and went home to prepare for the Olympics in their yellow and blue Tre Kronor colours.

All–Stars coach Sid Abel added 11 players to his team, eight by necessity after the 12 starting players were named and another three because Mahovlich, Horton, and Bower would of course skate for the Leafs. Carl Brewer had been named to the First All–Star Team but missed the game because he'd broken an arm in the playoffs the previous spring (ironically, he was in town for the game undergoing intense physiotherapy). Another First Team All–Star, Stan Mikita, missed the game for the second time because of a contract dispute, looking to practically double his previous salary of $14,000 by 10 grand. His spot was filled by Murray Oliver.

Abel added Marcel Pronovost, Norm Ullman, and Alex Delvecchio from his own Red Wings; Harry Howell and Camille Henry from the Rangers; Jean Béliveau, Bernie Geoffrion, and Claude Provost from the Canadiens; and Dean Prentice and Johnny Bucyk from the Bruins. Leo Boivin had also been added but had to be replaced by another Bruin, Tom Johnson,

because of an injury. Johnson's inclusion proved to be something of a miraculously happy ending for the defenceman. After 15 seasons with Montreal, he had suffered a terrible eye injury near the end of the previous season when he was cut by a teammate's skate. The injury left him with double vision and, in the opinion of the Montreal management, ended his career. Boston claimed Johnson at the draft on a bit of a flier, but over the summer his condition improved and he regained his visual health. Abel used him as fifth defenceman on the blue line to go with Chicago partners Pilote and Vasko as the first pair and Pronovost and Howell as their subs. Unfortunately,

*Goaler Terry Sawchuk feels the heat from Toronto's Bob Pulford,
but manages to make the save.*

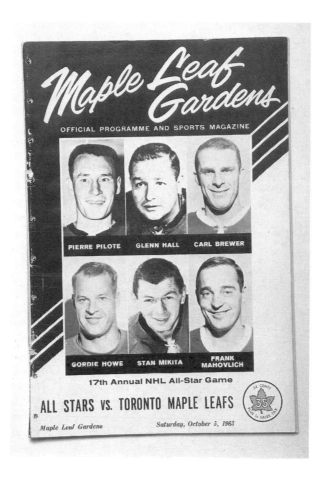

Abel had to leave right after the game to go to Melville, Saskatchewan, to his mother's funeral.

Gordie Howe was performing double duty in Toronto. Apart from representing the All–Stars in the game, he was also the showpiece of a press conference sponsored by Campbell Soup Company in support of his new book, written with Bob Hesketh, called *Hockey—Here's Howe!* Heading into this 1963–64 season, Mr. Hockey needed only five goals to break Maurice Richard's all-time NHL record of 544. The prescient book cover featured Howe on the ice at the Olympia with his two young sons, Marty and Mark, the latter wearing number 9. Although he was already in his 16th season in Detroit, he would play with those two sons in the NHL some 16 years later!

The night-before dinner at the Royal York Hotel attracted a record 222 people, including former Leaf great Gord Drillon, who had come all the way from New Brunswick for the occasion. Drillon got to talking about the current state of the game as opposed to when he had been playing and concluded the league was getting thinner on talent. "There are six or seven NHLers on each team," he said, "and eight or nine minor leaguers." He also arrived with a new version of his name and asked that it be spelled "Drillen."

Dit Clapper, the only man to have played 20 years for one NHL team, was also an honoured guest at the dinner and concurred with Drillon/Drillen. Recollecting the passing skills common in his generation of players, he claimed: "We had more combinations.

Today, they shoot the puck in and chase it."

One player at the banquet suggested the league put a limit on the number of exhibition games a team could play before the start of the season. When the number exceeds 10, he maintained, the players should start getting paid. The suggestion was made for two reasons: (1) players didn't get paid until the start of the regular season; and (2) Leafs coach Punch Imlach inflicted an egregious 17-game pre-season schedule on his team—all played, of course, free of charge. Needless to say, the league vetoed the player's suggestion.

The Game

The first and third periods of the game were fast-skating affairs, but the second was plodding. The only excitement in the 20 minutes in the middle came when Bobby Hull tried to duplicate his great solo rush of the first period. Horton tied him up and the two had a brief swordfight before being given minor penalties. Leafs captain George Armstrong said of the scuffle:

"Tim is probably the strongest man in the league, but he can't fight. Hull is strong and he can punch. Hull hit me on the top of the head with his fist one time—I had a headache for a month."

The star of the night was Frank Mahovlich, who played on a line with Red Kelly and Ed Litzenberger, scored two goals and was voted the MVP. He seemed to fly up and down the port side all night until a Harry Howell chop to the ankle in the third forced him to the bench. Afterward, Armstrong made a bold prediction for the Big M. "There is no doubt that Frank can score 75 goals during the season if he gets determined enough," he opined. Imlach's second line featured Dave Keon with Armstrong and Dick Duff, and the last trio was a pair of Bobs—Pulford and Nevin—with the Entertainer himself, Eddie Shack.

The three stars were Mahovlich, Hull, and Litzenberger, and the game raised $42,534 for the players' pension fund.

Toronto Maple Leafs 3   All–Stars 3

Toronto Maple Leafs
Punch Imlach, coach

I	G	Johnny Bower
4	C	Red Kelly
7b	D	Tim Horton
8	RW	John MacMillan
9	LW	Dick Duff
10	RW	George Armstrong "C"
11	RW	Bob Nevin
12	RW	Ron Stewart
14	C	Dave Keon
15	C	Billy Harris
19	D	Kent Douglas
20	RW	Bob Pulford
21	D	Bobby Baun
22	D	Larry Hillman
23	RW	Eddie Shack
24	G	Don Simmons
25	RW	Ed Litzenberger
26	D	Allan Stanley
27a	LW	Frank Mahovlich

All–Stars
Sid Abel, coach (Detroit)

I a	G	Glenn Hall (Chicago)
2	D	Marcel Pronovost (Detroit)
3a	D	Pierre Pilote (Chicago)
4b	D	Elmer Vasko (Chicago)
5	RW	Bernie Geoffrion (Montreal)
6	C	Norm Ullman (Chicago)
7b	LW	Bobby Hull (Chicago)
8b	RW	Andy Bathgate (New York)
9a	RW	Gordie Howe (Detroit)
10	C	Alex Delvecchio (Detroit)
11	D	Harry Howell (New York)
12	C	Camille Henry (New York)
14	RW	Claude Provost (Montreal)
15	C	Murray Oliver (Boston)
16b	C	Henri Richard (Montreal)
17	LW	Johnny Bucyk (Boston)
18	LW	Dean Prentice (Boston)
19	C	Jean Béliveau (Montreal)
20	D	Tom Johnson (Boston)
24b	G	Terry Sawchuk (Detroit)

a=selected to First All–Star Team for 1962–63
b=selected to Second All–Star Team for 1962–63

First Period
1. Toronto: Mahovlich (Armstrong, Baun) 2:22
2. All–Stars: Richard (Henry, Howe) . . . . 4.08(pp)
3. Toronto: Mahovlich (Keon, Litzenberger) 12:11
4. All–Stars: Hull (Geoffrion) . . . . 19:27(pp)
Penalties: Stanley (Tor) 2:42, Howell (AS) 15:18, Duff (Tor) 18:15

Second Period
No Scoring
Penalties: Pronovost (AS) 11:47, Horton (Tor) 16:32, Baun (Tor) 18:55, Hull (AS) and Horton (Tor) 19:27

Third Period
5. Toronto: Litzenberger (Mahovlich, Kelly) 2:56
6. All–Stars: Pronovost (Bucyk, Oliver) 3:23
Penalties: Stanley (Tor) 17:04

Shots on Goal

Toronto	12	10	14	**36**
All–Stars	14	12	12	**38**

In Goal
Toronto—Bower/Simmons [Simmons (one goal) replaced Bower (2 goals) to start 3rd period]
All–Stars—Hall/Sawchuk [Sawchuk (one goal) replaced Hall (2 goals) at 11:03 of 2nd period]

Referee Frank Udvari

Linesmen Neil Armstrong and Matt Pavelich

Attendance 14,034

MVP Frank Mahovlich (Toronto)

The NHL Introduces Two New Trophies

Maple Leaf Gardens, Saturday, October 10, 1964

In the 1964 playoffs, the Leafs did what had been done only once before when they won both series in seven games en route to the championship (Detroit had accomplished the feat in 1950). The highlight of the playoffs came in game six of the finals in Detroit when Bobby Baun scored the overtime game-winner on a cracked ankle. Then the teams went back to Maple Leaf Gardens, where the home side shut out the Wings 4–0. For the third year running, the Leafs had won the Cup and, with it, the right to host the All–Star Game.

The Leafs entered the All–Star fray exhausted after a two-week, nine-game exhibition tour of western Canada, a trademark Punch Imlach series designed to get everything out of the players at no cost to the club. It was a strategy that had contributed to the Leafs having played a total of 101 games the previous year. The players grumbled, but it was tough to argue with the winning results.

For the All–Star Game, the most notable absentee from the Leafs Cup-winning roster was Red Kelly, who was now a member of Parliament and had been sent to the Olympic Games in Tokyo as a representative of the Canadian government. Newcomers since the Cup win in the spring were Terry Sawchuk (claimed from Detroit in the June draft) and rookie Ron Ellis. Goaler Don Simmons was now playing in Tulsa, and Allan Stanley was a late scratch after pulling a knee ligament in the team's final exhibition game in Portland a few nights before. Dickie Moore had also been drafted from Montreal in the spring and the Leafs were trying to talk him out of retirement, but he remained the other no-show on the Leafs roster (Moore was listed in the program as number 16 but

Bower juggles and saves, while the legend himself, Gordie Howe, fights for position in case of a rebound.

Goalie Charlie Hodge extends himself while Stars mark their Leaf men
and referee John Ashley adjudicates play from the safety of the corner.

he watched the game from the seats). Bob Pulford, a late holdout, signed his contract shortly before game time and was thus qualified to play.

Detroit's Sid Abel was the All Star coach once again (the third time he had earned the honour as the Stanley Cup finalist), and his selection of 10 extra players included Harry Howell, Rod Gilbert, and Camille Henry of the Rangers; Murray Oliver, Leo Boivin, and Johnny Bucyk of Boston; Bill Gadsby, Norm Ullman, and Alex Delvecchio from his own Wings; and Henri Richard of the Canadiens. These selections were over and above the automatic players from the First and Second All–Star Teams. One player Abel didn't choose was the legendary Jacques Plante, most recently of the Rangers, who had been sent to the AHL's Baltimore Clippers by the Broadway Blueshirts for reconditioning after injuring his right knee during the summer.

Although they'd been selected, Henri Richard, Bill Gadsby, and Camille Henry were unable to play because of injuries. First Team All–Star Ken Wharram also had to bow out after sustaining a frightening skull fracture in an exhibition game between Chicago and the Leafs in Peterborough on September 22.

Pre-Game Events

At the pre-game banquet, emceed by comedian Johnny Wayne, league president Campbell announced that the pension fund was now in excess of $3.5 million. He explained that a player who was in the NHL for 20 years would receive a monthly pension of $1,640 at age 65. Alternatively, if he decided to claim benefits earlier, the same player would get $500 a month at 45, $657 at 50, $875 at 55, or $1,187 at 60. Death benefits would amount to $182,098 at age 65 down to $27,313 for a player with three years' experience in the league.

Campbell also announced the introduction of a new trophy to honour the late Lester Patrick that would go to men who had made an outstanding contribution to hockey in the United States. The trophy would be voted on by a committee that would include Campbell himself as well as one NHL

governor, a U.S. national news service writer, a U.S. sports columnist, a member of the Hockey Hall of Fame and the sports director of a U.S. national radio or TV network. An informal poll instantly offered Walter Brown as the first recipient of the Patrick Trophy. A second new trophy was also introduced, this one to honour Conn Smythe, that would be voted on by the six governors. Each would make three selections for the outstanding performer in the Stanley Cup playoffs, and the winner would also receive a cheque for $1,000.

Campbell then handed out special gold tie clips for players who had scored more than 250 career goals: Gordie Howe, Jean Béliveau, Andy Bathgate, Alex Delvecchio, and Dickie Moore. Then it was decided that in future such honours would be accorded 300-goal scorers but only after the player retired (and the

clip would also include his final scoring records set in diamonds). Howe then went out and extended two All–Star records, one for games played (16) and the other for points (12), while Sawchuk set a new one for the number of games played in goal (10).

The annual presentation of NHL awards followed the dinner, and a glittering gathering was on hand. Frank Boucher presented the Lady Byng Trophy to Ken Wharram; Syl Apps presented the Calder Trophy (which he himself had won in his heyday) to Jacques Laperrière; Jim Norris gave his namesake award to Pierre Pilote; and Bill Durnan, six-time winner of the Vezina, now gave it over to Charlie Hodge. Blackhawks teammates Bobby Hull and Stan Mikita shook hands when the former handed the latter the Art Ross, and Gordie Howe gave the Hart Trophy up to Jean Béliveau. Cooper Smeaton and Red Dutton, trustees of the Stanley Cup, presented the silver mug to Toronto and the Prince of Wales Trophy to first-place finishers Montreal.

In pre-game festivities, NHL president Clarence Campbell presented each of the league's All–Stars and both coaches with the traditional gold puck. Cooper Smeaton made the official presentation of the Stanley Cup to Leafs captain George Armstrong, and the crowd in the Gardens produced a deafening roar of approval. Fellow trustee Red Dutton then faced off the ceremonial first puck between the two captains, George Armstrong and Jean Béliveau.

The Game

When coach Abel abandoned the tradition of putting a club's players on the same line, the result was one of the greatest lines ever (Gordie Howe, Jean Béliveau, and Bobby Hull). Imlach played four lines for the Leafs all night, and one of the few notes of interest came when referee John Ashley penalised goalie Charlie Hodge for intentionally holding the puck, the first penalty given out to a goalie in All–Star Game history (for the record, the minor was served by Rod Gilbert). Murray Oliver scored the game-winning goal, but as he moved to retrieve the souvenir puck from the net, Leafs defenceman Carl Brewer flipped in into the stands. Years later, Béliveau recalled the game:

"I remember in the room having the opportunity to speak to players that I had always looked at as opponents. When you played together, you recognized their great ability. Even if you didn't talk to them much during the course of the year, they were great guys."

All–Stars 3   Toronto Maple Leafs 2

		Toronto Maple Leafs Punch Imlach, coach				All–Stars Sid Abel, coach (Detroit)
1	G	Johnny Bower		1a	G	Glenn Hall (Chicago)
2	D	Carl Brewer		2b	D	Jacques Laperrière (Montreal)
7a	D	Tim Horton		3	D	Harry Howell (New York)
8	RW	Gerry Ehman		4b	C	Jean Béliveau "C" (Montreal)
9	RW	Andy Bathgate		5b	D	Elmer Vasko (Chicago)
10	RW	George Armstrong "C"		7a	LW	Bobby Hull (Chicago)
11	RW	Ron Ellis		8	C	Norm Ullman (Detroit)
12	RW	Ron Stewart		9b	RW	Gordie Howe (Detroit)
14	C	Dave Keon		10	C	Alex Delvecchio (Detroit)
15	C	Billy Harris		11a	D	Pierre Pilote (Chicago)
17	C	Don McKenney		12	RW	Rod Gilbert (New York)
18	RW	Jim Pappin		15	C	Murray Oliver (Boston)
19	D	Kent Douglas		16	RW	Claude Provost (Montreal)
20	LW	Bob Pulford		20	C	Camille Henry (New York)
21	D	Bobby Baun		21a	C	Stan Mikita (Chicago)
22	D	Larry Hillman		22	LW	Johnny Bucyk (Boston)
23	RW	Eddie Shack		23	D	Leo Boivin (Boston)
24	G	Terry Sawchuk		25b	G	Charlie Hodge (Montreal)
27b	LW	Frank Mahovlich				

a=selected to First All–Star Team for 1963–64
b=selected to Second All–Star Team for 1963–64

First Period
No Scoring
Penalties: Bathgate (Tor) 1:05, Howell (AS) 7:25, Baun (Tor) 15:38, Douglas (Tor) and Oliver (AS) 17:42

Second Period
1. All–Stars: Boivin (Laperrière, Oliver) 10:47
2. Toronto: Douglas (Bathgate, Mahovlich) . . . . . . 11:45(pp)
3. All–Stars: Béliveau (Hull, Howe) 13:52
Penalties: Laperrière (AS) 2:27, Mikita (AS) and Baun (Tor) 9:43, Howell (AS) 11:03, Hodge (AS) 15:31

Third Period
4. All–Stars: Oliver (Bucyk, Howell) 6:11
5. Toronto: Pappin (Ehman) 13:35
Penalties: Stewart (Tor) 5:32, Pilote (AS) 5:43, Douglas (Tor) 8:35, Provost (AS) 10:51

Shots on Goal

Toronto	8	8	12	**28**
All–Stars	9	14	9	**32**

In Goal
Toronto—Bower/Sawchuk [Sawchuk (3 goals) replaced Bower (no goals) at 9:43 of 2nd period]
All–Stars—Hall/Hodge [Hodge (2 goals) replaced Hall (no goals) at 9:43 of 2nd period]

Referee John Ashley

Linesmen Neil Armstrong and Matt Pavelich

Attendance 14,232

MVP Jean Béliveau (Montreal)

The Governors Capitulate

Montreal Forum, Wednesday, October 20, 1965

Attending the All–Star dinner in 1965 was the legendary Frank Fredrickson, who had played on the 1920 Canadian Olympic team and then in the NHL and was not without an opinion when he was asked what he thought of Bobby Hull's salary demands during the Golden Jet's acrimonious negotiations with the Hawks.

"I read some place," he began, "where Bobby was quoted as saying that he'd be glad to reveal the terms of his contract to any other player in the NHL who asked him. That's hard to believe. I think it's been the experience of most professional athletes that salaries are private matters, just as they are in the business world. You don't go around telling your associates how much you're making."

Incredibly, Stan Mikita missed the game for the fourth time, although this year it was because of a groin strain and not a contract dispute. Not that his— and other players'—contract talks were proceeding smoothly. Hull was asking for a salary of $50,000 a year, a figure that would make him the highest-paid player in the history of the game. The problems with Hull's negotiations prompted the board of governors to vote for the first time that players could skate in the All–Star Game even if they hadn't yet signed with their team. Ironically, just before the opening faceoff, Hull settled for $40,000 a season in a multi-year deal.

The decision was made out of desperation, not charity. In addition to Hull and Mikita, Roger Crozier, Rod Gilbert, Bobby Baun, and Carl Brewer—that is, six players who were scheduled to play—were still not signed as game day approached. The cumulative effect of so many possible no-shows would have created an embarrassment for the NHL because the game was to be broadcast nationwide by CTV. In the end, Gilbert, Crozier, and Hull all signed at the last minute, but Dave Keon, who was asked to fill in for the injured Mikita, refused to play because he was embroiled in a contract dispute with Leafs coach Punch Imlach. And after all that, a bad case of the flu felled First Team goalie Roger Crozier in the pre-game skate and he ended up on the sidelines for the game.

Bobby Baun was perhaps the most recalcitrant of the six holdouts, despite an appeal by coach Billy Reay at the dinner.

"Baun owes it to other NHL players [to play]," Reay said. "This game means a lot to the players' pension fund. I was playing when the fund was started, and believe me, we accomplished something.... It's his duty to play."

Baun, however, was Carl Brewer's roommate and best friend, and Carl had advised Baun to hold out. He managed to sign before the game and played anyway, but Brewer's advice was not without malice. Elected to the Second All–Star Team, Brewer stunned the Leafs by retiring two days before the game, the result of one in a series of particularly bitter feuds with Imlach. After consulting his friend and lawyer Alan Eagleson, Brewer announced he'd still play with the All–Stars under two conditions to which Leafs owner Stafford Smythe had to agree. First, should he suffer a serious injury, he'd be paid a year's salary plus $2,000 by the Leafs; and, second, Smythe had to announce during the TV broadcast that Brewer's participation did not mean he'd return to the Leafs. The Leafs refused to meet these outlandish conditions and Brewer didn't play in the game. He was determined to return to the University of Toronto to finish his

*Mr. Goalie, Glenn Hall, has played in more All-Star Games (13),
for more minutes (540) and more victories (4)
than any other masked, or unmasked, net guardian.*

B.A., as he had threatened to do many times before. But this time he was serious, and he stayed retired for four years.

Earlier in the day, at the governors' semi-annual meetings, Vancouver and San Francisco–Oakland were named as two cities of six that would pay $2 million to join the NHL in 1966–67, when the league would double in size. Los Angeles and St. Louis had already been chosen, and that left two cities to fill the expansion list that would increase the schedule to 74 games and change the geography of the game forever. Still in the running were Baltimore, Minnesota, Philadelphia, and Pittsburgh. A Vancouver bid (which wouldn't succeed until 1970) was spearheaded by two groups, one led by Cy McLean of the WHL Canucks and another by Frank McMahon of West Coast Transmission.

Pre-Game Events

The night before the pre-game dinner, there was a special tribute to Frank Selke, who had retired as general manager of the Canadiens at the end of the 1963–64 season after one of the most successful careers ever in hockey. He had been right-hand man to Conn Smythe in Toronto from the formation of the Leafs in 1927 until 1946, a period which saw Toronto win three Stanley Cups, and he'd won another seven in Montreal. He was presented with a farewell cheque for $6,000 but promptly returned it with words of pride:

"The game doesn't owe me a cent. I feel that I have been one of the luckiest men in the world to have been associated with hockey and all the great players and wonderful people connected with it."

The four presidents of North America's pro hockey leagues were in Montreal for the game: Clarence Campbell, National Hockey League; Al Leader, Western Hockey League; Jack Riley, American Hockey League; and Jack Adams, Central Professional Hockey League. The All–Star dinner was held in downtown Montreal at the Queen Elizabeth Hotel. Danny Gallivan and René Lecavalier, Canadiens broadcasters in English and French on the CBC, were co-emcees of the evening, and players received their individual trophies for the previous year. Jacques Laperrière presented Roger Crozier with the Calder Trophy; Bobby Hull acquired two mantle pieces, the Hart from Jean Béliveau and the Lady Byng from Kenny Wharram; Wings owner Bruce Norris handed the Norris Trophy to Pierre Pilote; Mr. Hockey, Gordie Howe, gave the Art Ross to Stan Mikita; and Charlie Hodge put the Vezina in the hands of Frank Mahovlich, who was representing Leafs teammates Johnny Bower and Terry Sawchuk. In keeping with the trophies' family theme, Stafford Smythe presented his father's namesake Conn Smythe Trophy to Béliveau. Last, league president Campbell gave Maurice Richard a diamond tie clip with the number 544 embossed on it to commemorate his total career goals. Yet another of the evening's highlights was a film of the 1965 Stanley Cup finals that featured highlights from all the games in the playoffs and was shown and produced by Molson's brewery.

The Game

This Montreal game marked the seventh time the Habs faced the best of the rest, a new record surpassing the six times Toronto had played the All–Stars. Montreal's Stanley Cup victory had come at the expense of the Blackhawks in seven games, the last a 4–0 shutout. Both teams came out for the pre-game skate adorned in new sweaters. Although it had been suggested that the teams should warm up on the ice at different times, this idea was dismissed at the last minute and both took part in the traditional loosening up at either end at the same time.

The Howe–Ullman–Hull line stole the show in a game played without incident. Howe was starting his 20th NHL season (he and Bill Gadsby were on the verge of tying Dit Clapper's record as the only 20-year men in league history) and he played a particularly star-like game, scoring two goals and helping on two others and giving a strong two-way performance that left the MVP decision no decision at all. The Béliveau–Rousseau–Duff unit was the only threesome that impressed coach Billy Reay for the Habs. Although this Montreal threesome scored the first goal of the game, they went on be repeatedly thwarted by Glenn Hall (Eddie Johnston of Boston was his backup but did not play). Yvan Cournoyer had a groin injury and was the only regular Hab not to play.

All–Stars 5   Montreal Canadiens 2

		Montreal Canadiens Toe Blake, coach
1b	G	Charlie Hodge
2a	D	Jacques Laperrière
3	D	J.C. Tremblay
4	C	Jean Béliveau "C"
6	C	Ralph Backstrom
8	LW	Dick Duff
10	D	Ted Harris
11	RW	Claude Larose
14a	RW	Claude Provost
15	RW	Bobby Rousseau
16	C	Henri Richard
17	D	Jean-Guy Talbot
19	D	Terry Harper
20	LW	Dave Balon
21	LW	Gilles Tremblay
22	LW	John Ferguson
24	C	Red Berenson
26	RW	Jim Roberts
30	G	Gump Worsley

		All–Stars Billy Reay, coach (Chicago)
2	D	Bobby Baun (Toronto)
3	D	Harry Howell (New York)
4b	D	Bill Gadsby (Detroit)
5	D	Marcel Pronovost (Detroit)
6	D	Ted Green (Boston)
7a	LW	Bobby Hull (Chicago)
8a	C	Norm Ullman (Detroit)
9b	RW	Gordie Howe (Detroit)
10	C	Alex Delvecchio (Detroit)
11	RW	Ron Ellis (Toronto)
12	LW	Vic Hadfield (New York)
14	D	Doug Mohns (Chicago)
15	RW	Rod Gilbert (New York)
16	C	Murray Oliver (Boston)
18a	D	Pierre Pilote (Chicago)
21	LW	Johnny Bucyk (Boston)
22b	LW	Frank Mahovlich (Toronto)
23	RW	Eric Nesterenko (Chicago)
24	G	Glenn Hall (Chicago)

a=selected to First All–Star Team for 1964–65
b=selected to Second All–Star Team for 1964–65

First Period

No Scoring
Penalties: Gadsby (AS) 0:48, Béliveau (Mtl) 7:13, Harris (Mtl) 9:48, Larose (Mtl) 13:27, Pronovost (AS) 16:08, Harris (Mtl) 16:33

Second Period

1. Montreal: Béliveau (Duff, Rousseau) 6:48
2. Montreal: Laperrière (Backstrom, Larose) 11:00
3. All–Stars: Ullman (Hull, Howe) 12:40
4. All–Stars: Hull (Howe, Oliver) . . . . 16:35(pp)
5. All–Stars: Howe (Ullman, Baun) 19:19
Penalties: Balon (Mtl) 16:31

Third Period

6. All–Stars: Bucyk (Gadsby, Oliver) 10:52
7. All–Stars: Howe (unassisted) . . . . 18:39(sh)
Penalties: Ellis (AS) 6:20, Ferguson (Mtl) 11:57, Howell (AS) 14:31, Howell (AS) 18:31

Shots on Goal

Montreal	13	14	14	**41**
All–Stars	8	12	5	**25**

In Goal

Montreal—Worsley (one goal) Hodge (4 goals): Hodge replaced Worsley at 5:00 of 1st; Worsley replaced Hodge at 9:48 of 1st; Hodge replaced Worsley at 14:25 of 1st period. Worsley started 2nd; Hodge replaced Worsley at 5:14 of 2nd; Worsley replaced Hodge at 11:00 of 2nd; Hodge replaced Worsley at 16:31 of 2nd period. Worsley started 3rd; Hodge replaced Worsley at 5:45 of 3rd; Worsley replaced Hodge at 11:05 of 3rd; Hodge replaced Worsley at 15:44 of 3rd period. All–Stars—Hall

Referee Art Skov

Linesmen Neil Armstrong and Matt Pavelich

Attendance 14,284

MVP Gordie Howe (Detroit)

The Game Goes Mid-Season

Montreal Forum, Wednesday, January 18, 1967

For the first time, the 1967 All–Star Game was played at mid-season, a format for scheduling that has endured to this day and accounts for the fact that there wasn't a game in the 1966 calendar year. And it was televised in "living colour" to the United States by MSG-RKO with the Detroit Red Wings' own voice, Bruce Martyn, doing the play-by-play. The league's board of governors had announced the details of an expansion that would include six new American clubs (each of which had paid $2 million to join the league). Since play would begin in the fall, the league needed as much southern exposure as possible and this broadcast had enormous symbolic importance. National TV provided the perfect forum for early promotion of the NHL in its newest cities: Los Angeles, Oakland, Minnesota, St. Louis, Pittsburgh, and Philadelphia.

CBS also signed a new contract with the NHL for the upcoming 12-team season that was worth an unprecedented $3.6 million over three years and made a commitment to an unspecified number of regular-season games plus the All–Star Game and the playoffs. Business was quickly replacing sports, entertainment, or athletic endeavour as the focus of hockey.

In addition to all this expansion and TV talk, the idea of a players' union was gathering momentum on two fronts. The NHLers were impressed by how Alan Eagleson had been able to negotiate the richest contract ever for Bobby Orr before Orr had played a single game in the NHL (two years at $70,000 per). Eagleson was also the centre of attention in resolving the Springfield Indians players' strike against their much-hated owner, Eddie Shore. In addition, Eagleson had been integral in having Carl Brewer

Goalie Gary Bauman played just 20 minutes of All–Star hockey in his brief career, here on Forum ice with the Cup-champion Habs.

Bobby Hull (9) and Stan Mikita (21) won more scoring championships in the 1960s than any other.
Hull appeared in every All–Star Game of the decade, but Mikita missed three because of contract disputes.

reinstated as an amateur after Clarence Campbell had at first refused outright to grant the request. The Eagle was quickly showing players that they had more power than they knew and that they were an essential part of the past, present, and future success of the league. By the summer of 1967, a players' union was not just fantasy, talk, or hope, as it had been a decade earlier in Ted Lindsay's day; it was reality.

At the same time, hockey writers were forming the NHL Writers' Association, with Tom Fitzgerald of the *Boston Globe* as its first president and Jacques Beauchamp of *Montréal-Matin* as vice-president. The secretary-treasurer was Jack Dulmage of the *Windsor Star* and founding members included George Gross of the *Toronto Telegram*, Red Fisher of the *Montreal Star*, Ted Damata of the *Chicago American*, and Barney Kremenko of the *New York World Journal-Tribune*.

Even though the game was played at mid-season, the automatic starters for the All–Stars were still those selected to the First and Second Teams from 1965–66, almost a full year before. Bobby Orr's exclusion from the game highlighted what had by now become an outdated method of player selection. The All–Star Teams were put together by means of two ballots, one for the first half of the season and one for the second. Many players felt the mid-season game should feature players who made the First and Second Teams from the current season's first-half balloting so extraordinary rookies such as Orr could participate. As it was, coach Abel had little leeway and didn't add Orr of his own accord because his additions were supposed to be based on the 1965–66 season (when Orr was not in the league). Furthermore, there was general consensus that it no longer made sense to pit the Cup winners against the All–Stars because by mid-season the Cup champion team might be vastly different from the one that had won the big bowl some eight or nine months earlier.

Montreal was hosting for the second year running thanks to a 3–2 overtime victory in game six of the 1966 finals against the Red Wings and in spite of Roger Crozier's heroics in the Detroit net. Montreal captain Jean Béliveau, a Second Team All–Star selection, missed the game with an eye injury, while Gump Worsley had already been out for six weeks after knee surgery and didn't play. Jim Roberts had a bruised foot and Leon Rochefort a bad leg and were the other Montreal regulars who were unable to play. Noel Price was recalled from Quebec to patrol the blue line, and Gary Bauman, who had played his first NHL game just four nights before, took the Gumper's spot in the nets. For the All–Stars, Johnny Bucyk had not yet fully recovered from a charley horse and would miss this year's game.

Coach Sid Abel augmented the All–Stars with his own selections and managed to produce a rare controversy over what might be called reverse discrimination. It was common for the All–Star coach to select players from his own team whenever possible. This year, however, Abel chose Ed Giacomin in goal over his own Crozier despite the fact that Crozier finished third in All–Star Team voting and won the Conn Smythe Trophy for his performance in the previous Stanley Cup finals against the Habs. Selecting him could not possibly have been questioned as biased. Still, Abel put together three competent lines, the first consisting of Stan Mikita, Gordie Howe, and Bobby Hull; the second of Dave Keon, Frank Mahovlich, and Rod Gilbert; and the third of Norm Ullman, Alex Delvecchio, and Bob Nevin.

Pre-Game Events

Danny Gallivan was again an entertaining emcee at the All–Star dinner that featured the usual presentations of trophies to the honoured players at the Queen Elizabeth Hotel. Additionally, three men were saluted for their life's work in the league: trainers Tommy Naylor of the Leafs and Hammy Moore of Boston, and physiotherapist Bill Head of the Canadiens. One special guest at the dinner was Leroy Goldsworthy, an NHLer in the 1930s who had a particular connection with Montreal coach Toe Blake.

"I broke into the Canadiens lineup in a combination with Paul Haynes and Goldie," Blake recalled of the successful forward line. "I replaced Georges Mantha, who was hurt, at left wing. I scored my first NHL goal off a pass from Goldie at the Forum when we beat the Americans 1–0."

Now a golf pro in Vancouver, Goldie was the toast of the crowd at the Queen Elizabeth.

The Game

The game itself was a dull and timorous affair that produced light humour among the members of newly formed writers' association. "As lively as the expansion draft meeting," "Hardly as exciting as an Irish wake," and "As rough as the second day of a Polish wedding" were a few of the deprecating remarks penned by journalists who no doubt hoped to provoke change. The fact that only three minors were whistled by the referee also accurately reflected the lack of physical contact throughout the night's light scrimmage. In fact, John Ferguson not only got two goals but also scored the only punch of the evening when he knocked Norm Ullman to the ice and earned a penalty for the jab.

"He slashed me behind the goal," Fergie recounted, "and broke my stick. Then I hit him with a good shoulder check, and he cross-checked me under the chin. So I just zinged him one, right on the nose."

It was the first and is still the only shutout in All–Star Game history.

Montreal Canadiens 3   All–Stars 0

		Montreal Canadiens Toe Blake, coach				All–Stars Sid Abel, coach (Detroit)
I	G	Charlie Hodge		Ia	G	Glenn Hall (Chicago)
2a	D	Jacques Laperrière		2b	D	Allan Stanley (Toronto)
3	D	J.C. Tremblay		3	D	Harry Howell (New York)
6	C	Ralph Backstrom		4	D	Jim Neilson (New York)
8	LW	Dick Duff		7	C	Norm Ullman (Detroit)
10	D	Ted Harris		8	RW	Bob Nevin (New York)
11	RW	Claude Larose		9a	RW	Gordie Howe (Detroit)
12	RW	Yvan Cournoyer		10	C	Alex Delvecchio (Detroit)
14	RW	Claude Provost		11a	LW	Bobby Hull (Chicago)
15b	RW	Bobby Rousseau		12b	D	Pat Stapleton (Chicago)
16	C	Henri Richard		14	C	Dave Keon (Toronto)
17	D	Jean-Guy Talbot		15	RW	Rod Gilbert (New York)
18	LW	André Boudrias		16	C	Murray Oliver (Boston)
19	D	Terry Harper		18a	D	Pierre Pilote (Chicago)
20	LW	Dave Balon		21a	C	Stan Mikita (Chicago)
21	LW	Gilles Tremblay		22b	LW	Frank Mahovlich (Toronto)
22	LW	John Ferguson		24	G	Ed Giacomin (New York)
23	D	Noel Price				
30	G	Gary Bauman				

a=selected to First All–Star Team for 1965–66

b=selected to Second All–Star Team for 1965–66

First Period
1. Montreal: Richard (Rousseau, Harper) 14:03
2. Montreal: Ferguson (Larose) 15:59
Penalties: None

Second Period
No Scoring
Penalties: Howell (AS) 6:58, Richard (Mtl) 7:19, Ferguson (Mtl) 10:00

Third Period
3. Montreal: Ferguson (Richard, Rousseau) 19:52
Penalties: None

Shots on Goal

Canadiens	14	7	9	**30**
All–Stars	10	10	15	**35**

In Goal
Canadiens—Hodge/Bauman [Bauman (no goals) played 2nd period only]

All–Stars—Hall/Giacomin [Giacomin (one goal) replaced Hall (2 goals) at 10:00 of 2nd period]

Referee Vern Buffey

Linesmen Neil Armstrong and Matt Pavelich

Attendance 14,284

MVP Henri Richard (Montreal)

In Memory of Bill Masterton

Maple Leaf Gardens, Tuesday, January 16, 1968

While the purpose of the All–Star Game had always been to showcase the league's best players and the game's speed and skill, the game was heavy with sorrow in 1968. On January 14, just two days before it was played, a player had died from injuries suffered during a game, for the first time in league history. Checked by two Oakland Seals, Bill Masterton lost his balance, fell, hit his head on the ice, and was carried off on a stretcher. The next day, he was dead. The NHL immediately donated $60,000 to Masterton's widow from the pension fund, and the All–Star Game proceeded in a spirit that was suitably sombre.

As a result of the tragic circumstance in which it was held, the All–Star tilt became less a celebration than a heated debate about helmets: whether their use should be mandatory, whether they affect a player's skill, whether safety should come first even if performance and ability might be somewhat diminished. Bobby Hull said he would consider wearing one; Stafford Smythe said that everyone should. Gordie Howe was not swayed. "No, I won't wear a helmet," he said when he got to Toronto for the game, "but I'd recommend youngsters wear them." Frank Mahovlich perhaps captured the essence of the dilemma when he said that he'd wear a helmet tomorrow—if he were ordered to do so. But league president Campbell made clear that such a directive wasn't about to be legislated:

> "I don't believe regimentation is necessary...I think they [the players] should be encouraged to wear them, but I don't believe it can be made mandatory. I believe most players in the next generation will have learned to play with helmets."

Leafs Al Smith and Dave Keon watch Gordie Howe play in his 18th All–Star Game.

After Masterton's death, Brian Conacher of the Leafs showed up wearing a helmet for the first time in All–Star Game history. Still, the only other player to make use of the protective headgear was Montreal defenceman J.C. Tremblay, who had worn one all year. In the following days, many others adopted the practice when they realised they were not immune to serious injury and even tragedy.

"Number Five, Bobby Orr." It doesn't sound right, but this was his first All–Star Game and as yet he didn't have the clout to take Jean Béliveau's number four.

On game day, the NHL Writers' Association hosted a brunch. Guests included Jack Bownass (manager of Canada's national team, Eastern section), current player Bob Berry, and two former NHLers, Cy Wentworth and Jack Church. The writers' association decreed during their annual All–Star meetings that an honourary trophy be struck for the league in Masterton's name. Later in the season, they made a formal suggestion to this effect to the league and it carried.

This year marked perhaps the worst weather for a city hosting the game even though it was only the second truly winter game. Getting into Toronto was difficult for many (Norm Ullman missed the dinner because of a bad storm), and leaving was equally treacherous.

Johnny Bower, whose injured left elbow was causing him grief, had to bow out of the game for the Leafs. Coach Punch Imlach replaced him with Al Smith, goaler at the time with their farm team in Tulsa. Smith was in goal against the All–Stars, but he didn't play at all in the 1967–68 season and thus became the only man ever to take part in the All–Star Game who didn't play in the NHL in the same season. As usual, the All–Stars were made up of First and Second Team selections, and rules ensured that each team from the expansion clubs also had one player named to the team.

Also at the game were a number of members of the original Ace Bailey Benefit contest in 1934. Red Dutton was an honoured guest; Baldy Cotton, who scored the first goal in that game, was on hand as a scout for Minnesota; and King Clancy and Joe Primeau were Torontonians through and through and wouldn't have missed the game for the world.

Pre-Game Events

The pre-game dinner took place at the Royal York Hotel with Johnny Wayne as the outstanding host for the evening. In an effort not to put too great a damper on the game, president Campbell paid only brief respects to Bill Masterton (he noted that playing in the NHL had been a dream come true). The previous year's All–Stars received their gold pucks and individual NHL trophies were handed out. Wayne quipped to Stan Mikita as he won the Lady Byng that $1,000 "and a beaded purse" came with the trophy. William "Bingo" Christie was given a special gold plaque by the league in recognition of his many years of service (from 1929 to 1964) as the Leafs' penalty timekeeper.

At every dinner setting was a brochure promoting Vancouver as a beautiful city...and where the league should move next. This none-too-subtle promotional attempt had been authorized by Campbell himself and was meant to prove that the city had serious intentions when the NHL next considered expanding (which it did two years later). Vancouver was also the front-running option if the Oakland Seals moved, which at the time seemed more likely than getting the franchise for a new team. It was still their first year, but the Seals were in difficulty and their leaving the city seemed imminent.

The Game

One of the more exciting All–Star Games was played before the largest crowd in game history—15,753. It was also the last year the Cup champions faced the best of the rest of the league. As time would tell, it was also the last time the Leafs won the Cup and the last game played at the greatest hockey rink of them all, Maple Leaf Gardens.

From his seat at the game, Clarence Campbell hinted that next year's game was likely to be a bona fide East versus West All–Star battle. In explaining the

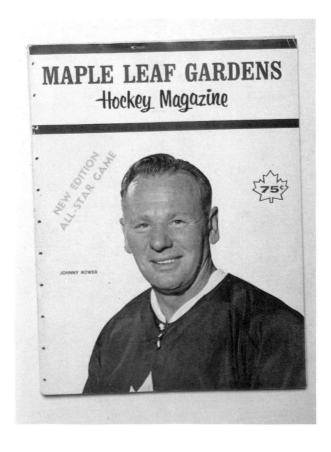

"new look," Campbell said that: "Once we make the change, there'll be no excuse to hold the game in any one city because there'll be no home team. We'll be able to move the game anywhere." The intention was to alternate each year between an East Division city and a city in the West Division. (Even though this was adopted, it was put on hold for a year.) The announcement also had significant implications for choosing the teams. Rather than basing them on All–Star Teams selected the season before (now almost a year previous since the game was played mid-year), the idea of assembling the preeminent players at the time of the game was gathering stronger and stronger support.

At the age of 20, Bobby Orr had been the youngest participant in All–Star history to that point. Some time later, he reflected on this, his second All–Star Game:

"At first, I was nervous about playing. Just rubbing shoulders with all those guys, the Howes and Richards and Hulls and Mikitas and Halls and Plantes. I wondered, 'how should you act?'

"I think the most thrilling thing is simply sitting with them in the dressing room, looking around the room and seeing the greatest collection of players in the game.

"I was always nervous about keeping up with them and about putting on a game the fans would like.... I remember just trying to get to Toronto in a blinding snowstorm. There was no way I wanted to miss it."

A clean Pete Stemkowski check broke Orr's collarbone late in the game. Even so, Orr outshone everyone else on the ice except Bruce Gamble in the Leafs net. Orr's rushing was brilliant, his shot devastating, and his competitive spirit reflected the true nature of what an All–Star Game had to offer. Unfortunately, it all came at a cost when he wound up missing 10 games with the Bruins because of the injury.

The only fight of the evening was aborted before things got too heated. Mike Walton and Gordie Howe—now in his millionth game—jousted before dropping their gloves and grappling, but the linesmen stepped in (much to Walton's relief) and kept their sentences to a two-minute rest. Howe played with teammate Norm Ullman and Don Marshall of the Rangers. A second All–Star trio was made up of Jean Béliveau, Johnny Bucyk, and Leon Rochefort, and the third trio put Stan Mikita, Dave Balon, and Ken Schinkel together.

With 61 seconds left in the game, coach Blake pulled Glenn Hall for an extra attacker to try to tie the score. In the Leafs goal, Al Smith faced these six players: Howe, Hull, Mikita, Orr, Wharram, and Ullman. At 39, Hall was on a daily retirement plan. "Every game I have to play these days," he said, "is an hour or so of hell." All–Star co goalie Ed Giacomin saw things differently. "That guy is unbelievable. It's his hands. It's his reactions. He's the best." His coach, young Scotty Bowman, agreed. "I've yet to see anybody better than Glenn Hall."

Gamble, Mikita, and Orr were selected the three stars of the evening by radio lord Foster Hewitt while Punch Imlach and his wife, Dodo, celebrated not only the Leafs' victory but also their silver wedding anniversary.

Toronto Maple Leafs 4   All–Stars 3

		Toronto Maple Leafs Punch Imlach, coach

1	G	Al Smith
2	D	Larry Hillman
3	D	Marcel Pronovost
4	D	Duane Rupp
7b	D	Tim Horton
8	RW	Ron Ellis
10	RW	George Armstrong "C"
11	C	Murray Oliver
12	C	Pete Stemkowski
14	C	Dave Keon
16	C	Mike Walton
18	RW	Jim Pappin
20	LW	Bob Pulford
22	LW	Brian Conacher
25	LW	Wayne Carleton
26	D	Allan Stanley
27	LW	Frank Mahovlich
30	G	Bruce Gamble

		All–Stars Toe Blake, coach (Montreal)

1a	G	Ed Giacomin (New York)
2a	D	Pierre Pilote (Chicago)
3a	D	Harry Howell (New York)
4	C	Jean Béliveau (Montreal)
5b	D	Bobby Orr (Boston)
6	D	Jacques Laperrière (Montreal)
7b	C	Norm Ullman (Detroit)
8	D	Bobby Baun (Oakland)
9b	RW	Gordie Howe (Detroit)
10a	LW	Bobby Hull (Chicago)
11	LW	Johnny Bucyk (Boston)
12	RW	Ken Schinkel (Pittsburgh)
14	D	J.C. Tremblay (Montreal)
15	RW	Leon Rochefort (Philadelphia)
17a	RW	Ken Wharram (Chicago)
18	LW	Dave Balon (Minnesota)
21a	C	Stan Mikita (Chicago)
22b	LW	Don Marshall (New York)
24	G	Terry Sawchuk (Los Angeles)
25b	G	Glenn Hall (St. Louis)

a=selected to First All–Star Team for 1966–67
b=selected to Second All–Star Team for 1966–67

First Period

1. Toronto: Oliver (Mahovlich, Hillman) 5:56
2. All–Stars: Mikita (B. Hull, Tremblay) . . . . 19:53(sh)

Penalties: Stemkowski (Tor) 14:10, Howell (AS) 17:54

Second Period

3. All–Stars: Wharram (Mikita). 0:35
4. Toronto: Stanley (Stemkowski, Carleton) 7:56
5. Toronto: Stemkowski (Carleton, Rupp) 16:36

Penalties: Howe (AS) 3:53

Third Period

6. Toronto: Ellis (Mahovlich, Hillman) 3:31
7. All–Stars: Ullman (Howe, Orr) 8:23

Penalties: Howe (AS) and Walton (Tor) 14:42

Shots on Goal

Toronto	9	18	14	**41**
All–Stars	19	11	10	**40**

In Goal

Toronto—Gamble/Smith [Smith (one goal) replaced Gamble (2 goals) to start 3rd period]

All–Stars—Giacomin (1st period, one goal); Sawchuk (2nd period, 2 goals); Hall (3rd period, one goal)

Referee Bill Friday

Linesmen Brent Casselman and Pat Shetler

Attendance 15,753

MVP Bruce Gamble (Toronto)

An Expansion Surprise

Montreal Forum, Tuesday, January 21, 1969

For the last time the All–Star Game would be played in the Cup-champion's city, members of the NHL Writers' Association selected the first 12 players for the East and West teams. Only three players were awarded the unanimous 90 points from the writers—Gordie Howe, Bobby Hull, and Bobby Orr. Howe was in his 20th game, Hull his ninth, and Orr only his third (but then he'd started young—the youngest in game history, in fact). The writers' selections were augmented by the All–Star coaches, who filled in the final seven positions for their teams. East Division coach Toe Blake came out of retirement to coach his side (rather than current Habs coach Claude Ruel) because of his place in the Stanley Cup the previous spring, before he had hung up his hat. "This was my last game," he said afterward to squelch any rumours of a comeback. He added Ted Harris and Bobby Rousseau from his Montreal team; Stan Mikita and Dennis Hull from Chicago; Ted Green (Boston), Norm Ullman (Toronto), and Rod Gilbert (New York). St. Louis coach Scotty Bowman was even more biased, using four of his seven spots to swell the Blues' contingent to eight. Doug Harvey, Noel Picard, Jim Roberts, and Ab McDonald were bluenotes who joined non-Blues players Danny O'Shea (Minnesota), Ken Schinkel (Pittsburgh), and Bernie Parent (Philadelphia).

The All–Stars uniforms were supplied by Gerry Cosby of New York. The West wore red and blue sweaters with their names on them (for the first time) and the East simple white. In a further innovation, for the first time players would be paid for their participation: winning-team members were to get $500 and losers $250. In fact, the game went to a tie, so all the players on both teams got $375. This was reduced in the West's dressing-room when Red Berenson went around collecting $15 from everyone to give to the injured Fred Barrett, who'd been unable to play. "He's an All–Star, too," the loyal Berenson reasoned, and everyone happily parted with their share.

The result of the game—a tie—was a morale booster for the expansion West, which by rights should have been slaughtered by the superior talent from the established East. Coach Bowman kept with the tried and true All–Star method of keeping players from the same club teams together. He played Berenson on a St. Louis line with Ab McDonald and Jim Roberts and an all-Minnesota line of O'Shea, Claude Larose, and Danny Grant. An Oakland line of Ted Hampson, Bill Hicke, and Carol Vadnais was formed, but only after Vadnais (a First Team selection to the West) replaced Gary Jarrett, who had to withdraw from the game because of a serious eye injury. Another St. Louis defenceman, Al Arbour, called Radar for his terrible eyesight (which caused him to wear glasses even on the ice), was playing in his first game at age 36, the oldest first-timer in All–Star Game history to that point.

Toe Blake had much more to work with. He put the incomparable threesome of Gordie Howe, Bobby Hull, and Phil Esposito together to start. However, he was asked by Chicago coach Billy Reay to use Hull sparingly. The Golden Jet had lost 17 pounds in the past few weeks after breaking his jaw and was in no condition to go all out for 30 minutes of game time. Blake remained faithful to the writers' selection for the Second Team by making a line of Jean Béliveau, Frank Mahovlich, and Bob Nevin. Rod Gilbert was another doubtful starter because of an eye injury, but

The Big M, Frank Mahovlich, won All–Star MVP honours
as both a Maple Leaf (1963) and a Red Wing (1968).

he was in uniform nonetheless come the opening faceoff at the Forum.

The league's governors held their semi-annual meetings as part of the All–Star festivities, but the talks revolved mostly around the corpse that was the Oakland Seals and two prospective vultures—in Buffalo and Vancouver—who wanted to take the ailing California team to their respectively fairer hockey climes. Stafford Smythe succinctly summed up the meetings when he commented that, "Buffalo may not be dead, but Oakland is one hell of a mess." In the end, league president Clarence Campbell gave the Seals a month to come up with proper financing and improve management to the point where they could guarantee continued operation of a franchise that had seemed doomed almost from the start. In the end, the reprieve eked out a few more years for the Seals.

At their annual meetings, the NHL Writers' Association named Red Fisher its president for the year and Ryerson Press rented a suite at the Sheraton– Mount Royal Hotel to showcase its newest hardback publications on hockey.

The day before the NHL game, another All–Star affair was played at the Forum. The Western All–Stars beat the Quebec Oldtimers 5–3 in a game that featured the great players of previous years. Hall of Fame skaters included the Bentley brothers (Max and Doug), Gerry Heffernan, Buddy O'Connor, Edgar Laprade, Elmer Lach, and Connie Broden, all playing for charity in a game that anticipated the Heroes of Hockey game that became a part of the larger All–Star weekend in the early 1990s.

In the All–Star Game itself, the West stunned the East throughout, twice taking the lead and then in the third period rallying from 3–2 down to tie the score late in the game. It was an improbable showing for a division that was less than two years old playing against one that had 52 years of stories to tell.

East 3   West 3

East Division All–Stars
Toe Blake, coach (Montreal)

1a	G	Ed Giacomin (New York)
2a	D	Bobby Orr (Boston)
3b	D	J.C. Tremblay (Montreal)
4b	C	Jean Béliveau (Montreal)
5	D	Ted Harris (Montreal)
6	D	Ted Green (Boston)
7a	D	Tim Horton (Toronto)
8b	RW	Bob Nevin (New York)
9a	RW	Gordie Howe (Detroit)
10	LW	Dennis Hull (Chicago)
11a	C	Phil Esposito (Boston)
12b	D	Pat Stapleton (Chicago)
14	C	Norm Ullman (Toronto)
15	RW	Bobby Rousseau (Montreal)
16a	LW	Bobby Hull (Chicago)
17	RW	Rod Gilbert (New York)
21	C	Stan Mikita (Chicago)
27b	LW	Frank Mahovlich (Detroit)
30b	G	Gerry Cheevers (Boston)

West Division All–Stars
Scotty Bowman, coach (St. Louis)

1b	G	Glenn Hall (St. Louis)
2b	D	Ed Van Impe (Philadelphia)
3a	D	Al Arbour (St. Louis)
4b	D	Elmer Vasko (Minnesota)
5	D	Doug Harvey (St. Louis)
6	D	Noel Picard (St. Louis)
7a	C	Red Berenson (St. Louis)
8	C	Danny O'Shea (Minnesota)
9b	RW	Bill Hicke (Oakland)
10b	C	Ted Hampson (Oakland)
11	RW	Ken Schinkel (Pittsburgh)
14	RW	Jim Roberts (St. Louis)
15	D	Carol Vadnais (Oakland)
16a	RW	Claude Larose (Minnesota)
20	LW	Ab McDonald (St. Louis)
21a	D	Bill White (Los Angeles)
22b	LW	Danny Grant (Minnesota)
29	G	Bernie Parent (Philadelphia)
30a	G	Jacques Plante (St. Louis)

a=selected to First All–Star Team for first half of season by NHL Writers' Association

b=selected to Second All–Star Team for first half of season by NHL Writers' Association

First Period
1. West: Berenson (Harvey, Picard) 4.43
2. East: Mahovlich (Rousseau, Stapleton) 17:32
Penalties: Vadnais (West) 12:55

Second Period
3. West: Roberts (Berenson, Picard) 1:53
Penalties: Horton (East) 11:41, White (West) 17:50

Third Period
4. East: Mahovlich (Harris, Gilbert) 3:11
5. East: Nevin (Ullman) 7:20
6. West: Larose (Grant, O'Shea) 17:07
Penalties: White (West) 10:18, Harvey (West) 11:55, Horton (East) 18:46

Shots on Goal

East	12	10	15	**37**
West	10	10	7	**27**

In Goal
East—Giacomin/Cheevers [Cheevers (one goal) played 2nd period only]

West—Hall (1st period, one goal); Parent (2nd period, no goals); Plante (3rd period, 2 goals)

Referee John Ashley

Linesmen Neil Armstrong and Matt Pavelich

Attendance 16,260

MVP Frank Mahovlich (Detroit)

The Game Starts Rotating

St. Louis Arena, Tuesday, January 20, 1970

To kick off the 1970s, the NHL held the All–Star classic outside the Cup champion's home rink for the first time since 1948. The governors selected St. Louis as the first road show city because of that team's impressive record in its three years in the league since expansion (though it appeared that they chose the wrong date. When they discovered the NBA's All–Star Game was scheduled for the same night, the NHL was forced to push the start time back to 9 p.m. for American television). Furthermore, the league announced that in future the game would continue to rotate from city to city, giving the fans of every NHL team the chance to see the glittering game played at home. At the league's pre-game meetings,

A young Bernie Parent, playing in his second straight All–Star Game,
blocks Gordie Howe's wrap-around attempt during the 23rd Game in St. Louis.

the game was awarded to Boston for 1971, Minnesota for 1972, and Madison Square Garden in New York the year after.

The players and the owners also held meetings. Representing the players were NHL Players' Association president Red Berenson (who was replacing the outgoing Norm Ullman), vice-president Lou Angotti, and Alan Eagleson, executive director of the NHLPA. For the league, Bill Wirtz of Chicago was on hand with colleagues Charles Mulcahy of Boston and Bill Putnam of Philadelphia. Tops on the agenda was player involvement in the next round of expansion, which was expected within three or four years. League president Campbell had suggested this expansion might include international play as well as European involvement in the NHL playoffs. The NHLPA responded that it wanted equal voice in all decisions or it simply wouldn't endorse any of them.

A motion to make the wearing of helmets mandatory was rejected by the league. Instead, the governors voted to allocate $5,000 toward research to design and produce more effective headgear. Further business discussions resulted in the players giving Eagleson full support to follow Curt Flood's case and assess its relevance to hockey. As his game's first free agent, Flood was challenging baseball's reserve clause in court and the hockey players rightly felt any outcome in that case would have enormous repercus-

sions for the NHL, even though at the All–Star dinner, the comedian, a fellow called Buck, made light of it all when he joked, "I heard today that Curt Flood is learning how to skate."

For the first time, the dinner the night before the game was open to the public, some 900 of whom paid $25 each to dine with the stars and see all of hockey's trophies on display at the Chase-Park Plaza Hotel. Proceeds from the dinner went to the upkeep of the aquatic display for children at the world-famous St. Louis Zoo. The evening was co-hosted by Buck and Dan Kelly and encompassed the bizarre and hilarious. For starters, a chimp, a llama, and a snake were brought in by the zoo as honoured dinner guests. And Punch Imlach was on hand—after he had been ignominiously fired by Toronto's Stafford Smythe immediately after the 1969 playoffs and rehired as general manager of the new Buffalo team for the coming fall. When Smythe came over with a hand extended in hearty regard, Imlach chuckled and took a step back, as if to say, "The game is on, and we're on opposite sides now." Another special guest was Carl Voss, former NHL referee-in-chief, who had played for the old St. Louis Eagles in 1933–34. "This was a great hockey town even then," he enthused. The ritual trophy presentation was a huge success in St. Louis, where most fans had never seen the league's famous silverware. But the loudest reception was reserved for Charles Schulz, the creator of Snoopy and future winner of the Lester Patrick Trophy for his contributions to the game in the U.S.

Controversy raged at the news that St. Louis Blues organist Norm Kramer would play at the game. It had been rumoured that East coach Claude Ruel objected to Kramer's playing for fear his tunes would whip the West into a frenzy and create an imbalance in the contest. Fully entering the fray, Bill Wirtz had his own Chicago (East Division) organist, Al Melgard, flown down and demanded his man get a chance to play during the game. In the end, both organists got equal playing time.

Again, the two coaches were each allowed seven players above the dozen selected to the team by the NHL Writers' Association. East coach Claude Ruel added Carl Brewer, Jean Ratelle, Dave Keon, Rod Gilbert, Ron Ellis, Bobby Hull, and Frank Mahovlich. From behind the West bench, Scotty Bowman added Bill White, Harry Howell, Dean Prentice, J.P. Parise, Jim Roberts, Claude Larose, and Danny O'Shea. And because of his popularity in St. Louis and career-long contribution to the game, Glenn Hall was a special addition to Bowman's squad (though he didn't play because of a groin pull).

Bobby Clarke was one of only two rookies to play in this game (the other was Tony Esposito), and his inclusion came only after Phil Goyette's late withdrawal as a result of a knee injury. Goyette had been named to the First Team and led the league in shooting percentage with 17 goals on just 74 shots. The Serge Savard story was even more serendipitous. In town only to attend the All–Star dinner, Savard found himself subbing for Jim Neilson, another First Team selection whose bruised ankle was healing too slowly to allow him to skate. The only other roster change was made when Gary Sabourin replaced Al Arbour, who was out with a knee injury (Jim Roberts moved back to defence while Sabourin skated at right wing).

Jacques Plante almost single-handedly kept the West in the game and was the lone reason for the

hometown Blues fans to cheer play that was otherwise thoroughly dominated by the East. Bernie Parent started for the West and gave up all of the four goals scored by the East before Jake the Snake came in and stopped the league's best in all of the 26 shots he faced in the final half-hour. Bobby Hull played on a line with two stellar Leafs, Keon and Ellis, and this trio was the best for the East. And the other top line of Frank Mahovlich, Gordie Howe, and Phil Esposito was perhaps one of the finest threesomes ever to skate together at an All–Star Game.

Opening ceremonies included renditions of both anthems with the U.S. Marines National Colour Guard overseeing the occasion. The three stars were Bobby Hull, Jacques Plante, and Bobby Orr.

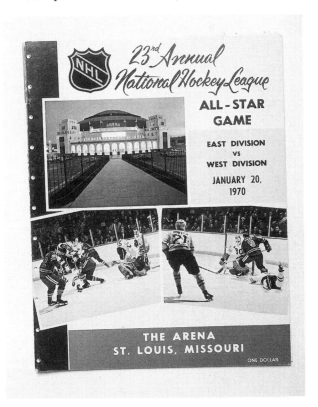

East 4   West 1

East Division All–Stars
Claude Ruel, coach (Montreal)

1a	G	Ed Giacomin (New York)
2b	D	Jacques Laperrière (Montreal)
3b	D	Brad Park (New York)
4a	D	Bobby Orr (Boston)
5	D	Carl Brewer (Detroit)
7a	C	Phil Esposito (Boston)
8a	LW	Johnny Bucyk (Boston)
9a	RW	Gordie Howe (Detroit)
10	C	Jean Ratelle (New York)
11b	C	Walt Tkaczuk (New York)
12	RW	Ron Ellis (Toronto)
14	C	Dave Keon (Toronto)
15b	LW	Jacques Lemaire (Montreal)
16	LW	Bobby Hull (Chicago)
17	RW	Rod Gilbert (New York)
18	D	Serge Savard (Montreal)
21b	RW	John McKenzie (Boston)
27	LW	Frank Mahovlich (Detroit)
30b	G	Tony Esposito (Chicago)

West Division All–Stars
Scotty Bowman, coach (St. Louis)

2	D	Bill White (Los Angeles)
4b	D	Carol Vadnais (Oakland)
5b	D	Bob Woytowich (Pittsburgh)
6	D	Harry Howell (Oakland)
7b	C	Red Berenson "C" (St. Louis)
8a	D	Barclay Plager (St. Louis)
9b	RW	Frank St. Marseille (St. Louis)
10	C	Bobby Clarke (Philadelphia)
11	LW	J.P. Parise (Minnesota)
12	LW	Dean Prentice (Pittsburgh)
14	RW	Jim Roberts (St. Louis)
15	C	Danny O'Shea (Minnesota)
16	RW	Claude Larose (Minnesota)
17	RW	Gary Sabourin (St. Louis)
20a	LW	Ab McDonald (St. Louis)
21a	RW	Bill Goldsworthy (Minnesota)
22b	LW	Danny Grant (Minnesota)
29b	G	Bernie Parent (Philadelphia)
30a	G	Jacques Plante (St. Louis)

a=selected to First All–Star Team for first half of season by NHL Writers' Association

b=selected to Second All–Star Team for first half of season by NHL Writers' Association

First Period

1. East: Laperrière (unassisted) 0:20
2. West: Prentice (Berenson, Woytowich) 0:37
3. East: Howe (B. Hull, Lemaire) . . . . 7:20(pp)

Penalties: Park (East) 1:52, St. Marseille (West) 6:00

Second Period

4. East: B. Hull (Brewer) 1:53
5. East: Tkaczuk (McKenzie, Bucyk) 9:37

Penalties: Woytowich (West) 15:47

Third Period

No Scoring

Penalties: Woytowich (West) 2:12

Shots on Goal

East	10	14	20	**44**
West	6	5	6	**17**

In Goal

East—Giacomin/Esposito [Esposito (no goals) replaced Giacomin (one goal) at 9:37 of 2nd period]

West—Parent/Plante [Plante (no goals) replaced Parent (4 goals) at 9:37 of 2nd period]

Referee Art Skov

Linesmen Claude Bechard and Matt Pavelich

Attendance 16,587

MVP Bobby Hull (Chicago)

Coaches, Not Coaches

Boston Garden, Tuesday, January 19, 1971

(l-r) *Phil Esposito, Bobby Hull, and Gordie Howe, the greatest scorers of their generation, enjoy a light moment at the All–Star Game dinner leading up to the 24th edition of the affair in Boston.*

For the first time in 17 years, Gordie Howe was not an automatic choice to play the right wing position in 1971. The 42-year-old had missed much of the first half of the season with a rib injury. When he was nevertheless extended a courtesy invitation by coach Harry Sinden, he at first declined, saying: "I don't deserve it...I don't want to fool anybody. If I went, I'd just sit anyway." The very next day,

however, he changed his tune. "When I read it in the paper, it sounded so bad I decided to play even if I had to walk." Ken Schinkel had also been voted onto the First Team, but, unlike Gordie, he had to be replaced (by Gary Sabourin) when he broke his shoulder in Montreal the month before the All–Stars were to meet.

This was the first time Boston had hosted the game,

and the timing couldn't have been more appropriate. Although the league had agreed in 1969 to rotate the event rather than have it played in the Cup champion's city, Boston had in fact been victorious the previous spring.

The selection of players was again carried out by a vote among members of the NHL Writers' Association, with three men from each NHL city being eligible to decide on the starting 12 players. As it happened, the Hawks had just transferred from the Original Six East Division to the expansion (and weaker) West Division and ended up with nine representatives at the game.

Harry Sinden had coached the Bruins to a Cup the previous spring and then retired. Now he announced that he would return to boss the East Division bench for one more special night—much as Billy Reay had done in 1967—at the invitation of Bruins chairman Weston Adams Sr. When he'd first been hired for the 1966–67 season, Sinden, then 32, was the youngest-ever NHL coach. He was accorded the strongest ovation in the pre-game introductions, but after losing the game he was subject to a Gordie Howe verbal elbow: "If you can't win with a lineup like this, Harry, you better stay retired." Sinden duly spent the balance of the season in Rochester, New York, as part

of the marketing division of Sterling Houses, a company that produced factory-built homes.

Similarly, Scotty Bowman had moved from coach of the Blues to general manager and took his post behind the bench for this night only. "My fires were running out as a coach," he explained. "I never wanted to go back." He would later recant what turned out to be a premature retirement as coach. Today, in the year 2000, the fires are raging as strongly as ever.

Sinden's line combinations read like a veritable who's who of the Hockey Hall of Fame. Frank Mahovlich, Dave Keon, and Gordie Howe were the first line; Phil Esposito, Ken Hodge, and Johnny Bucyk formed an all-Boston troika; Jean Ratelle, Dave Balon, and Yvan Cournoyer were the third line; and the "checking line" featured Gil Perreault with Pete Mahovlich and Eddie Westfall. The power-play consisted of Espo, the Big M, Orr, Howe, and J.C. Tremblay.

Three rookies took part in this year's game, Gil Perreault, Dale Tallon, and Greg Polis. Aside from Schinkel, John McKenzie was the only other player of the 24 starters elected to the rosters by the NHL Writers' Association who didn't play after he separated his shoulder the day before in a game against the Leafs

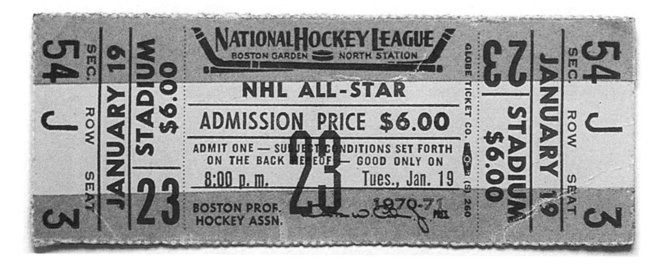

and was replaced by Boston teammate Ed Westfall.

Johnny Wayne emceed the All–Star banquet again. Receipts from the dinner went to the Jimmy Fund of Boston, while the game itself produced a record take of $79,009 for the players' pension fund.

The "tinsel tilt" was lacklustre after the first few minutes, when all the goals were scored, and both teams settled in to playing defensive, hitless hockey that failed to strike sparks outside a few special performances. The brilliant Perreault shone with many a rush, and Bobby Hull played impassioned hockey with and without the puck, as both scorer and checker. Everyone in the building was rooting for Gordie Howe to play well, of course, and while all the Stars played something that could be called hockey, Bobby Orr played something completely superior. Scotty Bowman mixed lines, and once threw a five-man Boston combination out, but to little effect. Tony Esposito stymied the East in goal all night long, and fans left a bit disappointed when the East failed to tie the score late and was humbled by going down to defeat at the hands of the purportedly weaker West Division.

After the game, winning coach Bowman handed out cigars to all his players. The three stars of the night were Hull, Orr, and Perreault.

West 2   East 1

West Division All–Stars
Scotty Bowman, coach (St. Louis)

2b	D	Bill White (Chicago)
3a	D	Keith Magnuson (Chicago)
4	D	Ted Harris (Minnesota)
5	D	Doug Roberts (California)
6b	C	Pit Martin (Chicago)
7	C	Red Berenson (St. Louis)
8b	D	Barclay Plager (St. Louis)
9a	LW	Bobby Hull (Chicago)
10b	LW	Dennis Hull (Chicago)
11	RW	Gary Sabourin (St. Louis)
12a	D	Pat Stapleton (Chicago)
14b	LW	Tim Ecclestone (St. Louis)
15	C	Bobby Clarke (Philadelphia)
16	RW	Chico Maki (Chicago)
17	RW	Bill Flett (Los Angeles)
20	LW	Danny Grant (Minnesota)
21a	C	Stan Mikita (Chicago)
22	LW	Greg Polis (Pittsburgh)
30b	G	Ernie Wakely (St. Louis)
35a	G	Tony Esposito (Chicago)

East Division All–Stars
Harry Sinden, coach (Boston)

1a	G	Ed Giacomin (New York)
2a	D	Brad Park (New York)
3b	D	J.C. Tremblay (Montreal)
4a	D	Bobby Orr (Boston)
5	D	Dale Tallon (Vancouver)
6a	LW	Johnny Bucyk (Boston)
7a	C	Phil Esposito (Boston)
8a	RW	Ken Hodge (Boston)
9	RW	Gordie Howe (Detroit)
10	RW	Ed Westfall (Boston)
11	LW	Gilbert Perreault (Buffalo)
12	RW	Yvan Cournoyer (Montreal)
14	C	Dave Keon (Toronto)
15b	D	Jim Neilson (New York)
17b	LW	Dave Balon (New York)
18b	C	Jean Ratelle (New York)
20	D	Dallas Smith (Boston)
21	C	Pete Mahovlich (Montreal)
27	LW	Frank Mahovlich (Montreal)
30b	G	Gilles Villemure (New York)

a=selected to First All–Star Team for first half of season by NHL Writers' Association

b=selected to Second All–Star Team for first half of season by NHL Writers' Association

First Period
1. West: Maki (unassisted) 0:36
2. West: B. Hull (Flett). . . . . 4:38(pp)
3. East: Cournoyer (D. Smith, Balon). 6:19
Penalties: Harris (West) 2:17, F. Mahovlich (East) 3:09, B. Hull (West) 11:14

Second Period
No Scoring
Penalties: Bucyk (East) 1:22

Third Period
No Scoring
Penalties: Stapleton (West) 2:48, Magnuson (West) 8:34

Shots on Goal

West	13	8	7	**28**
East	13	12	2	**27**

In Goal
West—T. Esposito/Wakely [Wakely (no goals) replaced T. Esposito (one goal) at 10:41 of 2nd period]
East—Giacomin/Villemure [Villemure (no goals) replaced Giacomin (2 goals) at 10:41 of 2nd period]

Referee Bill Friday

Linesmen Neil Armstrong and John D'Amico

Attendance 14,790

MVP Bobby Hull (Chicago)

A Suicide Mars the Celebrations

Met Sports Center, St. Paul, Minnesota, Tuesday, January 25, 1972

The Radisson South Hotel in St. Paul, Minnesota, was the place to be for the two-day festivities surrounding the All–Star Game of 1972. The NHL's board of governors held meetings there on January 24 and 25, and the banquet the night before the game was once again open to the public for $25 per person. Emceed by Al Shaver, the dinner drew more than 1,500 people and all the profits went to the local Variety Club Heart Hospital. In addition to the dinner and special guests, the night featured a special ceremony presenting all the major trophies to the previous spring's winners: Bobby Orr the Norris and Hart; Johnny Bucyk the Lady Byng; Phil Esposito the Art Ross; Gil Perreault the Calder; and the tandem of Ed Giacomin and Gilles Villemure the Vezina.

But on the afternoon of the game, the players were surrounded by police for most of the day—and it had nothing to do with NHL security. As part of the All–Star meetings, a number of officials from the Western Hockey League had come to St. Paul to discuss merging with the Central League. During one of their meetings, the owner of the Salt Lake City Golden Eagles, Daniel Myers, excused himself to make a phone call from his room. Next door, Pit Martin and Paul Henderson were getting set for a pre-game nap when they heard loud crashes from Myers's room. Martin looked out his window to see Myers climb onto the ledge, hoist himself over a beam and let go.

The West Division All–Stars, 1972.

"I called Paul and told him there's a guy going to jump.... He had a very determined look on his face. Then he climbed over the beam like a kid climbing over a fence. I saw him hang there by his hands for a couple of moments, then let go."

Myers crashed into the cabana complex below, and everyone in the hotel lobby thought a bomb had gone off. Bobby Hull, who was staying directly below Myers, came up to the room and found the key in the door.

"I went in and found traces of blood on the door handle inside the room, as well as blood in the bathroom and along some casing," Hull said. "There was a chair overturned near the window and a lamp on the floor."

"You can't open those windows," Martin surmised of the scene. "I guess he must have thrown the chair through it a couple of times."

Investigators questioned everyone who had been at the hotel. Some of the players were even interviewed at the game that night. Hull and Mikita were so shaken they almost didn't play. "It's probably the worst thing I've ever experienced," Hull said.

Quite apart from this extra, unwanted attention, NHL president Clarence Campbell took advantage of the world stage for the All–Star Game to make a huge announcement: For the fourth time since 1967, the league was expanding, this time to Atlanta and Long Island. Additionally, two more teams would be added for the 1974–75 season, bringing the league to 18 teams and tripling its size in just seven years. Campbell also suggested that the NHL would have to grow to 24 teams during the 1970s, with such cities as Kansas City, Cleveland, Washington, Miami, San Diego, and Indianapolis among future candidates. In coordinating the merger of the Western and Central Hockey Leagues, he promised those teams first dibs on expansion.

Behind closed doors, the NHL meetings focused on how these new teams would affect the major realignment of divisions now needed to accommodate all future teams. The upshot of the discussions proved historic. The governors decided to go with two eight-team divisions for now, envisioning expansion to 24 teams by 1980. There had been strong impetus to create four divisions, but the governors felt this would create too many disparities within each. Furthermore, it became clear during the meetings that while a four-division format seemed inevitable, getting all the governors to agree on which teams would be in which divisions was at that point virtually impossible.

The great Bobby Orr, fresh from scoring the Cup-winning goal, won MVP honours at this year's All–Star Game in the friendly confines of the Boston Garden.

Bill White (standing) and Carol Vadnais (falling) manage to knock Phil Esposito off the puck.

A small game within the All–Star Game was continued from the previous year as players tried to smuggle their sweaters out of the building (at $30 each, the league wanted to collect them to use the next year). Quite a few were as successful as they had been year before, when only eight of 22 were accounted for. Certainly the players could justify feeling entitled to this little perk. Despite Alan Eagleson's clout as NHL Players' Association executive director—and the increase in salaries that resulted from his negotiations with the league—the winning team still received a meagre $500 and the losers $250, though the game brought in a record purse of $85,101 for the pension fund.

As in the previous year, when Harry Sinden unretired for a night to coach the East, Al MacNeil played NHL coach even though he was currently coaching the Habs' farm team (the Nova Scotia Voyageurs of the AHL) far away from the NHL spotlight. MacNeil had led Montreal to the 1971 Stanley Cup in his first season, but he ultimately preferred the less pressured and slower pace of life in the minors.

Before and after the game, both MacNeil and Billy Reay were put under the gun for their putatively biased selections to their respective teams. Reay had included two of his own Hawks (Pit Martin and Keith Magnuson) among his seven additions and incurred the wrath of host city coach Jack Gordon, who felt his North Stars (notably Murray Oliver and Tom Reid) had been hard done by. Ned Harkness was equally miffed that Detroit scoring sensation Mickey Redmond was given the pass by MacNeil, who made it clear that since the Habs had traded Redmond the previous year, it would reflect badly on them to select him as an All–Star this year. Gordon then demanded that in future the coach be left out of the decision-making, which would be left to a panel of NHL managers or governors. While both coaches vigorously defended their selections, both seemed equally amenable to this alternative.

This game marked the first time in 23 years Gordie Howe, now retired, didn't play (with one exception in 1956 when he was injured), while Jean Béliveau, another future Hall of Famer, was also recently retired and unavailable for the first time since 1952. But another oldtimer, veteran Minnesota goalkeeper Gump

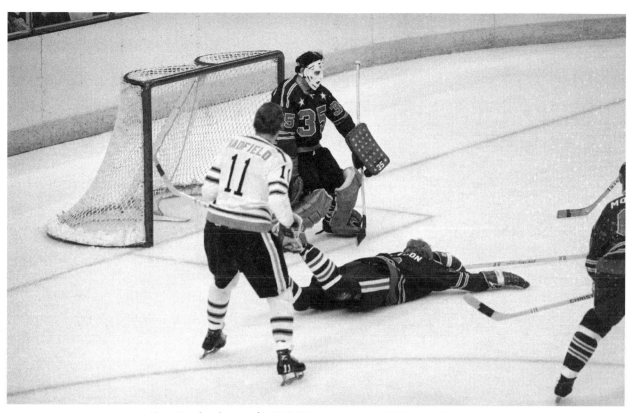

Tony O makes the save after Keith Magnuson just misses blocking an East shot.

Worsley, fondly remembers playing in the game:

"I was 42 and playing for the North Stars. I got the biggest ovation of anyone. It wouldn't stop, really, and I didn't know what to do. I was enjoying it and it also was a little embarrassing. I was anxious to get started.

"I was standing next to Bobby Orr, and I said, 'What do I do now?' He said, 'Just stay there—you have no place to go—and soak it up.' He said I deserved it all....

"The style of play changes a little from a regular game. We'd go all out but we didn't want it to get too rough. Guys would take more chances skating-wise because someone wasn't going to hang him. A guy could go along the boards and, instead of getting run, they would just get cut off or get a lane down the wing....

"The fans are there to see their favourites do their things, so it was up to each guy to put out his best.... What's really great is that there are a lot of guys you play against for years and never get to talk to. At All–Star Games, you finally get that chance. You have the start of many friendships."

The spirit of the All–Star Game was never more clearly epitomized than it was by Bobby Orr in the dying minutes of this contest. With his team up 3–2 and hanging on for dear life, Orr charged across the ice to confront Bobby Hull, who was moving in over the blue line ready to let loose one of his patented slappers. Orr got in front of the shot in time, but the puck hit him somewhere between the knees and the shoulders. He cleared the puck out and then headed off to the bench, barely able to stay on his skates. He walked around in the hallway for half a minute, returned to the ice to help ensure victory, and then skated off with the rest of the team. Later, in a talk with Dick Irvin, Orr clarified what had happened on the Hull shot. "It wasn't the knee," he said. "The puck hit me right in the crown jewels!" Orr was named the game's first star, Hull the second, and goaler Gilles Villemure the third.

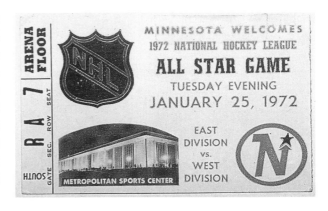

East 3   West 2

East Division All–Stars
Al MacNeil, coach (Montreal)

1a	G	Ken Dryden (Montreal)
2a	D	Brad Park (New York)
3b	D	J.C. Tremblay (Montreal)
4a	D	Bobby Orr (Boston)
5	C	Red Berenson (Detroit)
6	LW	Rick Martin (Buffalo)
7a	C	Phil Esposito (Boston)
8a	RW	Rod Gilbert (New York)
9	D	Dale Tallon (Vancouver)
10	C	Gilbert Perreault (Buffalo)
11a	LW	Vic Hadfield (New York)
12b	RW	Yvan Cournoyer (Montreal)
16	D	Rod Seiling (New York)
17	LW	Paul Henderson (Toronto)
18	RW	John McKenzie (Boston)
19b	C	Jean Ratelle (New York)
20b	D	Dallas Smith (Boston)
27b	LW	Frank Mahovlich (Montreal)
30b	G	Gilles Villemure (New York)

West Division All–Stars
Billy Reay, coach (Chicago)

1b	G	Gump Worsley (Minnesota)
2a	D	Bill White (Chicago)
3	D	Keith Magnuson (Chicago)
4b	D	Ted Harris (Minnesota)
5	D	Carol Vadnais (California)
6b	D	Doug Mohns (Minnesota)
7b	C	Garry Unger (St. Louis)
8a	RW	Bill Goldsworthy (Minnesota)
9a	LW	Bobby Hull (Chicago)
10b	LW	Dennis Hull (Chicago)
11	LW	Ross Lonsberry (Los Angeles)
12a	D	Pat Stapleton (Chicago)
14	C	Pit Martin (Chicago)
15	C	Bobby Clarke (Philadelphia)
16b	RW	Chico Maki (Chicago)
17	RW	Simon Nôlet (Philadelphia)
21a	C	Stan Mikita (Chicago)
22	LW	Greg Polis (Pittsburgh)
35a	G	Tony Esposito (Chicago)

a=selected to First All–Star Team for first half of season by NHL Writers' Association

b=selected to Second All–Star Team for first half of season by NHL Writers' Association

First Period

1. West: B. Hull (P. Martin, Maki) 17:01
Penalties: Hadfield (East) 6:22

Second Period

2. West: Nôlet (D. Hull). 1:11
3. East: Ratelle (Tremblay, Gilbert) 3:48
4. East: McKenzie (Park, Seiling). 18:45
Penalties: White (West) 5:26

Third Period

5. East: Esposito (Smith, Orr). 1:09
Penalties: White (West) 2:28, Esposito (East) 5:34, Tremblay (East) 8:42, Mohns (West) 19:05

Shots on Goal

East	9	8	13	**30**
West	10	11	6	**27**

In Goal

East—Dryden/Villemure [Villemure (no goals) replaced Dryden (2 goals) at 10:24 of 2nd period]
West—T. Esposito/Worsley [Worsley (2 goals) replaced T. Esposito (one goal) at 10:24 of 2nd period]

Referee Bruce Hood

Linesmen Claude Bechard and Matt Pavelich

Attendance 15,423

MVP Bobby Orr (Boston)

Greg Polis Shines Brightest

Madison Square Garden, New York, Tuesday, January 30, 1973

At the 1973 pre-game dinner at the Waldorf Astoria, the NHL honoured two disparate figures. Walter Bush, president of the North Stars, was given the Lester Patrick Memorial Trophy for outstanding service to hockey in the United States and Bob Hope was given a special award for founding the Eisenhower Medical Center in California, which had been built on a large parcel of land Hope donated. For the first time, the dinner was a black tie affair. Ticket prices escalated from $25 the previous year to $100 this time around and the enhanced proceeds all went to the Center. Tim Ryan of NBC was the emcee, and of course Hope kept up the quips through the night of festivities. Of the new Center itself, he said: "Zsa Zsa Gabor had a checkup a few days ago for $1,000. The doctors were glad to pay for it." Earl Ingarfield was a late arrival. He'd been pleasantly minding his own business on Long Island until Islanders coach Phil Goyette was fired two days before the All–Star Game and he was named the new coach. Ingarfield got a tux and hustled off in a cab to Manhattan as the Islanders' team representative.

Vintage Bobby Orr, in his prime. He rarely used more than a strand or two of tape on his stick.

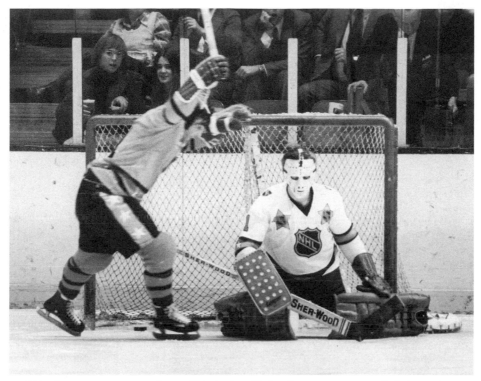

Eddie Giacomin, appearing in what would be his last All–Star Game, gives one up to the bad guys here.

One significant piece of news came out of the governors' meetings. Conditional expansion franchises were awarded to Kansas City and Washington for the 1974–75 season, which would bring the total number of teams to 18 and triple the size of the league from what it had been just seven years before.

As the league continued rotating the All–Star Game from city to city, the list of those that were hosting it for the first time expanded to include Madison Square Garden in New York in 1973. The team selection process remained the same, though, and three members of the NHL Writers' Association from each NHL city voted for the first 12 players to the team in their division. Bobby Hull was the only member of the previous year's All–Star Teams not at the game (he had signed with the World Hockey Association in the summer of 1972 and was persona non grata with the NHL), while Ken Dryden was selected to the First

Team by the writers' association but didn't play because of a severe back strain that had kept him out of the Montreal lineup for three weeks (he was replaced by Ed Giacomin). Even though he was flat on his back in Montreal when the puck was dropped in New York, he was not without some responsibility, though. At the annual players' meetings, Red Berenson had resigned as NHL Players' Association president and Dryden was elected to replace him. The other significant cancellation came when a battered Johnny Bucyk gave up all hope of playing and Tom Johnson replaced him with Leafs winger and Summit Series hero extraordinaire, Paul Henderson.

Many fans and executives were incensed that Gil Perreault had not been selected to the East Team. Coach Johnson brushed aside suggestions that he didn't select Perreault at the behest of his general manager in Boston, Harry Sinden. The inference was

Wearing an unfamiliar number 1, Tony Esposito clears the puck from Bobby Orr.

that this was payback for Perreault's abandoning the Sinden-coached Team Canada in Moscow midway through the Summit Series in September 1972. Simply, Johnson said of the player he selected instead, "Ratelle isn't bad." Opposing coach Reay came to Johnson's defence and explained that, "By picking Ratelle, he [Johnson] has the crowd with him." In any event, Sinden had extracted his measure of revenge on Perreault some time earlier. Summit Series players had finally received their pay at Christmastime. Each "full share" amounted to $4,487, but Perreault—and the three other members who left early, Vic Hadfield, Rick Martin and Jocelyn Guevremement—received only a quarter share each. And not one complained.

Johnson got into another ruckus with Phil Esposito the morning of the game. The East players were slated to have a team picture taken at 11:30 a.m. before a one-hour practice. Espo and teammate Ken Hodge arrived 20 minutes late, but everyone waited for

them. Hodge put a sweater on over his jacket and tie, and then Johnson hollered at Esposito to "get out here," to which Espo replied, "I don't have to take this crap," and left the building. Thus it was that, along with the injured Eddie Westfall, Phil was absent from the 1973 East All–Stars Team picture.

When coach Billy Reay added Syl Apps Jr. to the roster, it marked the first time an All–Star Game player's son would participate (Apps' father, of course, was the great Leafs captain of the 1940s). Unfortunately, Apps Jr. hurt his elbow two days before the big game and was replaced by Penguins teammate Lowell MacDonald and the history books had to wait.

Reay's forward lines consisted of Mikita–Parise–Dornhoefer, Clarke–Pappin–Hull, Unger–Johnston–Berry, and Martin–Polis–MacDonald. Ironically, Reay was initially criticised for selecting Apps and Polis over MacDonald, but even though he added MacDonald when Apps withdrew, it was Polis who

Tony Esposito makes two stops during action from the 26th game, in Madison Square Garden, as his brother Phil looks on (top) and a fallen Orr (bottom) is unable to get to the puck.

The Iron Man, Garry Unger.

shone brightest and took home a car as game MVP. (The Dodge Charger awarded to Polis was the first of what was to become a traditional automotive bonbon for the All–Star player of the game, but the post-game presentation was not broadcast by the CBC because the car was considered a conflict of interest with Hockey Night in Canada's prime sponsor, Ford.)

It was a busy, happy few days for Polis, who missed the pre-game dinner to be with his pregnant wife. He arrived in New York only hours before the game but in his state of elation scored two goals for the West. For teammate Stan Mikita, it was an expensive trip. "I gave her [his wife] $500 to take to Bergdorf's," he recalled, "and then she asked for a dollar for a taxi." He recouped half of his money (the winning players got $500 and the losers $250), but not the buck. "You should feel that every game is important because you're in it," Mikita said. "A game like this, the money is the least of it."

The highlight of the evening, and its funniest moment, came when Bobby Orr tripped ignominiously as he was introduced to the fans, much as teammate Phil Esposito had fallen in the Summit Series. Orr's teammates had a good laugh at the gaffe while fans hooted and hollered. No more preposterous image could be imagined than that of the fastest, most fluid skater of all time slipping on a banana peel—while standing still.

The unsung Greg Polis bested all comers and was awarded the car as game MVP in MSG.

East 5   West 4

East Division All–Stars
Tom Johnson, coach (Boston)

1	G	Ed Giacomin (N.Y. Rangers)
2b	D	Brad Park (N.Y. Rangers)
3	D	Gary Bergman (Detroit)
4a	D	Bobby Orr (Boston)
5a	D	Guy Lapointe (Montreal)
6a	LW	Rick Martin (Buffalo)
7a	C	Phil Esposito (Boston)
8	RW	Ken Hodge (Boston)
9	RW	Bobby Schmautz (Vancouver)
12a	RW	Yvan Cournoyer (Montreal)
14	C	Dave Keon (Toronto)
15b	RW	René Robert (Buffalo)
17	RW	Ed Westfall (N.Y. Islanders)
18b	D	Serge Savard (Montreal)
19	C	Jean Ratelle (N.Y. Rangers)
20	D	Dallas Smith (Boston)
21	LW	Paul Henderson (Toronto)
25b	C	Jacques Lemaire (Montreal)
27b	LW	Frank Mahovlich (Montreal)
30b	G	Gilles Villemure (N.Y. Rangers)

West Division All–Stars
Billy Reay, coach (Chicago)

1a	G	Tony Esposito (Chicago)
2a	D	Bill White (Chicago)
3b	D	Terry Harper (Los Angeles)
4b	D	Gilles Marotte (Los Angeles)
5a	D	Barry Gibbs (Minnesota)
6	D	Barclay Plager (St. Louis)
7	C	Pit Martin (Chicago)
8a	RW	Jim Pappin (Chicago)
9	C	Garry Unger (St. Louis)
10a	LW	Dennis Hull (Chicago)
11b	LW	J.P. Parise (Minnesota)
12b	RW	Gary Dornhoefer (Philadelphia)
14	D	Randy Manery (Atlanta)
16b	C	Bobby Clarke (Philadelphia)
18	LW	Bob Berry (Los Angeles)
21a	C	Stan Mikita (Chicago)
22	LW	Greg Polis (Pittsburgh)
23	LW	Joey Johnston (California)
26	RW	Lowell MacDonald (Pittsburgh)
30b	G	Rogie Vachon (Los Angeles)

a=selected to First All–Star Team for first half of season by NHL Writers' Association

b=selected to Second All–Star Team for first half of season by NHL Writers' Association

First Period
No Scoring
Penalties: Orr (East) 11:11, Bergman (East) 14:52

Second Period
1. West: Polis (Clarke, MacDonald) 0:55
2. East: Robert (Park) 3:56
3. East: Mahovlich (unassisted) 16:27
4. East: Henderson (Esposito, Hodge) 19:12
5. West: P. Martin (Hull, Pappin) 19:29
Penalties: Hodge (East) 6:26

Third Period
6. East: Lemaire (Mahovlich, Lapointe) 3:19
7. West: Polis (Harper) 4:27
8. West: Harper (Mikita) 9:27
9. East: Schmautz (Savard) 13:59
Penalties: White (West) 10:03

Shots on Goal

East	16	9	9	**34**
West	8	10	12	**30**

In Goal
East—Villemure/Giacomin [Giacomin (3 goals) replaced Villemure (one goal) at 9:16 of 2nd period]
West—T. Esposito/Vachon [Vachon (4 goals) replaced T. Esposito (one goal) at 9:16 of 2nd period]

Referee Lloyd Gilmour

Linesmen Neil Armstrong and John D'Amico

Attendance 16,986

MVP Greg Polis (Pittsburgh)

The Players' Association Gains Strength

Chicago Stadium, Tuesday, January 29, 1974

(l-r) *Stan Mikita, Bill White, and Bobby Clarke in fancy dress, enjoy a relaxing yuck or two at the pre-game dinner.*

The All–Star dinner remained upscale and black tie in 1974. The $100-a-plate affair was hosted by the Palmer House Hotel in Chicago with the proceeds going to a local settlement house, Hull House (no connection to Bobby or Dennis). Local broadcasters Jim West and Jack Brickhouse were emcees while Joan Rivers was the guest entertainer. The ever-popular and always hilarious Dennis Hull took a turn as speaker-comedian as well.

High on the list of priorities for the league's governors that year was a meeting to consider the most recent attempt by the WHA to settle its lawsuit with the NHL over the Reserve Clause. The new one-year clause was just starting to appear in players' contracts because the WHA had claimed that a player signing a contract with a team was not bound to that team for his entire career (as the NHL argued) but only for the length of the contract (as the WHA argued). In essence, the WHA was taking the NHL to court over a form of free agency, claiming the established league had no rights to a player after a contract expired. More simply, an NHL player whose contract was up could legally sign with a WHA team.

While the two leagues were trying to cohabit

amicably under the same hockey roof, they were forgetting the players, or, more specifically, the players' association. The day of the game, the battling leagues announced they had settled their differences and as a show of peaceful co-existence agreed to a 15-game exhibition series against one another during training camp to prepare for the coming season. Alan Eagleson promptly stepped in and said no such games would be played because at no time during the NHL–WHA resolution were the players either consulted or in the end even notified of the terms of the agreement. "We won't play against the WHA," he said tersely. "It's one of our rights under the standard player's contract."

The league also had to deal with the impending demise of the California Golden Seals, who were suffering from the lack of a fan base and poor on-ice performance, problems that had plagued the team since day one in 1967. Their last home game had attracted just 2,833 fans. To make matters worse, dissent was rampant within the team. Of coach Fred Glover, winger Reg Leach said simply: "It doesn't

matter what Glover thinks. He's crazy. Nobody listens to him." Meanwhile, league president Clarence Campbell had a plan in place to buy the team from owner Charlie Finley and keep it up and running for the rest of the season.

For the first time in All–Star Game history, controversy dominated conversation as a result of no fewer than five East players withdrawing at the last minute. First Team selection Bobby Orr hurt his knee just two days before the game after being tripped viciously by Bill Barber in a game versus the Flyers; Serge Savard (Second Team) was told by team doctors to rest; Guy Lapointe (Second Team) separated his shoulder; Jacques Lemaire was slowed by a lingering knee injury; and Gil Perreault also had leg problems and was replaced by Henri Richard.

East coach Scotty Bowman began looking around for replacements, keeping in mind that each team had to have at least one player in the game, but offers were few and far between. Boston's general manager Harry Sinden refused to allow Carol Vadnais to play because of injuries to teammates Bobby Orr and Darryl

Edestrand. Bowman wanted Darryl Sittler, Borje Salming, and Jim McKenny from Toronto, but Sittler's wife was having a baby and Leafs coach Red Kelly didn't want both of the other defencemen to go because Mike Pelyk was also injured. Buffalo's ageless Tim Horton declined an invitation, citing his father's death the previous week. In New York, Emile Francis refused to allow any of his players to go (namely, Rod Gilbert, Walt Tkaczuk, or Jean Ratelle) because the inferior cross-town rival Islanders already had two players on the team to his one. In the end, Bowman added Jocelyn Guevremont from Vancouver, Red Berenson from Detroit, and Larry Robinson from Montreal.

McKenny, a.k.a. "Howie," was already in Chicago to attend the NHL meetings as the Leafs' rep, so he was allowed to play. His sense of humour was legendary and he experienced a lighter, less flattering side of the game:

"Scotty Bowman asked me if I could suit up. They were a little strapped for bodies on defence. Man, I didn't belong there. I was by no means an All–Star. I was paired with Larry Robinson, but even that didn't help. I went minus-four for the game. Afterwards, in the dressing-room, Clarence Campbell went around shaking all the players' hands. When he got to me, he became silent, causing all the guys to burst into laughter. I just said, 'Don't worry, Mr. Campbell, I don't know what I'm doing here either!'"

On the other hand, Frank Mahovlich more than belonged. Playing for the East, he came into the game with 12 All–Star points in his career—one more than the entire West roster.

*Tony Esposito fields a few practice shots during warm up
for the All–Star Game in his NHL home of Chicago.*

For the first time, the league instituted a no limit, sudden-death overtime policy for the All–Star Game, meaning a winner would be decided even if it took all night. It turned out a fourth period wasn't required, but it was still one of the more exciting games in recent times, as the line of Garry Unger, Stan Mikita, and Bob Berry gelled as though they had played together all season. Arguably the best three-some of the night, though, was the Ullman–Cournoyer–Mahovlich line that scored twice in the first period and created scoring chances on literally every shift. The goaltending was also outstanding, particularly by Parent and Esposito, and again winning players took home $500 and losers half that. The three stars were Unger, Mikita, and Cournoyer, while Unger, an employee of Dodge-Chrysler in Detroit during the off-season, was relieved the car that accompanied selection as the MVP was a Chrysler. "It's my fourth [car], would you believe, all Dodge," he revealed. "It's a good thing this was a Chrysler product because it means I can drive it."

Although Dennis Hull (left) is the funny man of the NHL,
he can't hold a candle to the master of the one-liner, Mr. Bob Hope.

West 6   East 4

West Division All–Stars
Billy Reay, coach (Chicago)

1a	G	Bernie Parent (Philadelphia)
2a	D	Bill White (Chicago)
3b	D	Ed Van Impe (Philadelphia)
4b	D	Dave Burrows (Pittsburgh)
5	D	Barclay Plager (St. Louis)
6	C	Garry Unger (St. Louis)
7	C	Pit Martin (Chicago)
8a	RW	Bill Goldsworthy (Minnesota)
9b	RW	Al McDonough (Atlanta)
10a	LW	Dennis Hull (Chicago)
11	RW	Jim Pappin (Chicago)
12	LW	Bob Berry (Los Angeles)
14	D	Joe Watson (Philadelphia)
16a	C	Bobby Clarke (Philadelphia)
17	LW	Joey Johnston (California)
18b	LW	Lowell MacDonald (Pittsburgh)
21	C	Stan Mikita (Chicago)
22b	C	Dennis Hextall (Minnesota)
26a	D	Don Awrey (St. Louis)
35b	G	Tony Esposito (Chicago)

East Division All–Stars
Scotty Bowman, coach (Montreal)

1a	G	Gilles Gilbert (Boston)
2a	D	Brad Park (N.Y. Rangers)
3	D	Denis Potvin (N.Y. Islanders)
5	D	Jocelyn Guevremont (Vancouver)
6a	LW	Rick Martin (Buffalo)
7a	C	Phil Esposito (Boston)
8a	RW	Ken Hodge (Boston)
9b	C	Norm Ullman (Toronto)
10	RW	Bobby Schmautz (Vancouver)
11	C	Red Berenson (Detroit)
12b	RW	Yvan Cournoyer (Montreal)
14b	LW	Wayne Cashman (Boston)
15	D	Larry Robinson (Montreal)
16	C	Henri Richard (Montreal)
18	D	Jim McKenny (Toronto)
19	RW	Ed Westfall (N.Y. Islanders)
20	D	Dallas Smith (Boston)
21	RW	Mickey Redmond (Detroit)
27	LW	Frank Mahovlich (Montreal)
30b	G	Dave Dryden (Buffalo)

a=selected to First All–Star Team for first half of season by NHL Writers' Association

b=selected to Second All–Star Team for first half of season by NHL Writers' Association

---

First Period
1. East: Mahovlich (Cournoyer, Ullman) 3:33
2. East: Cournoyer (Ullman). 16:20
Penalties: P. Martin (West) 11:17

Second Period
3. West: Berry (Mikita). 5:59
4. West: McDonough (Clarke, MacDonald) 13:55
5. West: MacDonald (Plager, Awrey) . . . . 19:07(pp)
Penalties: Hextall (West) 7:42, Berenson (East) 18:35

Third Period
6. West: Mikita (Unger, White) 2:25
7. West: Unger (White, Mikita) . . . . 7:54(sh)
8. East: Potvin (unassisted) 9:55
9. East: Redmond (Berenson) 14:55
10. West: P. Martin (Pappin) 19:13
Penalties: Plager (West) 6:27

Shots on Goal

West	8	8	12	**28**
East	15	10	10	**35**

In Goal
West—Parent/T. Esposito [T. Esposito (2 goals) replaced Parent (2 goals) at 9:59 of 2nd period]
East—Gilbert/Dryden [Dryden (5 goals) replaced Gilbert (one goal) at 9:59 of 2nd period]

Referee Art Skov

Linesmen Matt Pavelich and Will Norris

Attendance 16,426

MVP Garry Unger (St. Louis)

A Controversial Suspension

Montreal Forum, Tuesday, January 21, 1975

Although the tradition of Cup champs facing the best of the rest had long been abandoned, the coaches for the 1975 game were decided on the basis of having won their division in the previous season. Fred Shero was named West coach for leading the Flyers to the West Division title and the Stanley Cup. Finding that he'd be without Bill White (a Second Team selection) and Bill Goldsworthy (a First Team selection) because of injury, he added a total of nine players to his roster: Doug Jarrett and Stan Mikita of Chicago; Tom Lysiak and Curt Bennett of Atlanta; Tracy Pratt of Vancouver; Ed Van Impe of his own Flyers; Simon Nôlet of Kansas City; Ed Westfall of the

Islanders; and Dennis Hextall of Minnesota. Shero also made All-Star Game history in the same way he had previously made NHL history, by bringing his assistant coach Mike Nykoluk to the bench.

"People are still under the impression that Mike is like other assistant coaches," he explained. "He's not. We're co-coaches. If he wants to take a player aside and give him hell, he'll do it."

Prince of Wales coach Bep Guidolin was there because he had led the Bruins to first place in the East Division in the previous year. When he learned Gil Perreault, a Second Team starter, would miss the game after straining his knee in a game against

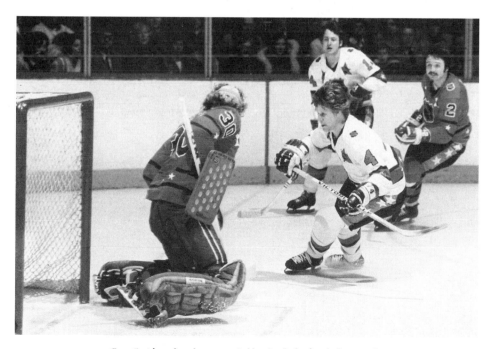

Gary Smith makes the save as Bobby Orr looks for the loose puck.
A moustachioed Brad Park and René Robert look on in the background.

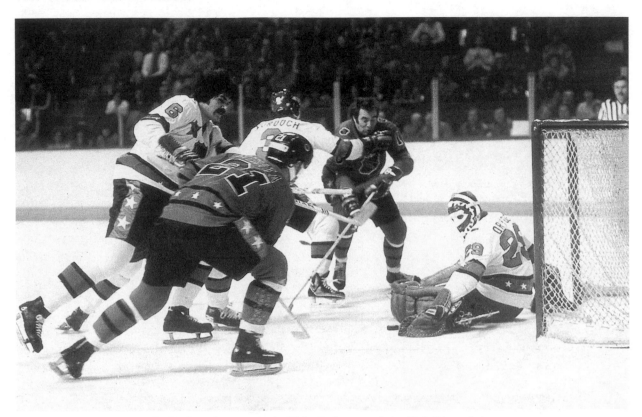

Ken Dryden makes a save in the Wales Conference net during his half-hour of play
made unusual because he started the second and stayed in until midway through the third.

Vancouver just three days before, Guidolin added nine players to his team rather than eight: Syl Apps and Jean Pronovost of Pittsburgh; Jerry Korab and Don Luce of Buffalo; Bob Murdoch of Los Angeles; Marcel Dionne of Detroit; Darryl Sittler of Toronto; Joey Johnston of California; and Denis Dupere of Washington. At the last minute, Guidolin also had to replace Second Team starter Johnny Bucyk, who injured his foot in the Bruins' last game before the All-Star tilt. Despite his desire to replace Bucyk with Dave Forbes, Guidolin had to use Terry O'Reilly at Clarence Campbell's insistence because Forbes was under suspension. Guidolin was furious, though, because O'Reilly was another right winger while Bucyk played on the left side.

"As I understand it," Guidolin said, "it's the right of the sports writers to pick the team, and then it's the right of the coaches to pick the rest of the players. They [the league] should at least phone me and ask me what I need."

Furthermore, Bep was almost forced to add four more players to his side when the four Boston Bruins threatened to boycott the game because of what they considered an unduly harsh 10-game suspension teammate Forbes had received from Campbell. The league president was punishing Forbes for a vicious attack on Henry Boucha that had left Boucha nearly blind in one eye and eventually forced him to retire. Still, the Bruins were infuriated by what was the third-longest suspension ever meted out and it took

Twenty-Eighth Annual
National Hockey League
All Star Dinner

Menu

Vancouver Shrimp Cocktail
Relish Tray
Consommé Imperial

Roast Prime Rib of Beef
Parisian Potatoes
Green Beans Amandine
Mixed Green Salad, Radishes, Celery

Ice Cream Bombe Aida
Strawberry Sauce
Petits Fours

Coffee or Tea

Rolls and Butter

(Gratuities have been provided by your host)

Hotel Bonaventure
Montreal
January 20, 1975

Vins: Château Timberlay (Bordeaux)

by the Soviets because they wanted a big cut of the TV revenues from such games.

At the NHL board of governors' meetings, Campbell had more immediate problems to contend with. Initially granted expansion franchises for 1976, Denver and Seattle were ready to join the league a year early, in the upcoming season, but as transferred clubs rather than new entries. The league had been operating the California team for a year and was tired of this financially unstable setup, and Campbell admitted that a second team (which remained nameless) was in such a poor state that it would be leaving its home at the end of the season. (This was almost certainly the Pittsburgh Penguins, a team for which owner Tad Potter had been quietly trying to find a buyer for months.) Campbell's ambitious plans to expand the NHL by one city a year until the league was 24 teams by 1980 was being scaled back until Denver and Seattle had had a chance to set up properly with their transferred franchises.

More than 1,000 people attended the $100-a-plate banquet at the Hotel Bonaventure the night before the game and the proceeds went to the Montreal Children's Hospital and Hopital Sainte-Justine. Every player and both coaches received commemorative watches for their participation in the game.

The game that year was fast but cautious and, ironically, it was the competitive spirit of late replacement

Evidently, the entertainment during the dinner was not the high-end, glitzy sort the All–Star Game would provide in future years.

Forbes himself to persuade his Bruins teammates to play in the All–Star showcase.

At their annual get-together, the NHL Players' Association discussed the fallout of the Forbes incident. The members agreed that players assessed a penalty for a deliberate attempt to injure should be suspended until the incident was reviewed. They also wanted to get working on a new eight-game Summit Series with the Soviets for 1976, but with one emendation: The first four games would be played in the USSR and the last four in Canada. Additionally, there was talk of a Soviet team playing NHL teams during the season, in the same format that had previously been agreed to and then reneged on at the last minute

Terry O'Reilly that put some life into the contest.

"The other guys were pulling up on checks," he said afterward, "but I wanted to play a really good game and one of my best assets is bodychecking so I just kept working."

Tracy Pratt, also known as a checker, snuck in a couple of hits, as did Ed Van Impe. Guy Lafleur, playing in his home building on a line with Darryl Sittler and Phil Esposito, had three assists in his first All–Star appearance. Goalie Ken Dryden, who had been criticised in the media for recent poor outings, came in midway through the second period and played his way back into the hearts of Montreal fans with some excellent close-in stops. Otherwise, nothing much happened during the night.

The highlight of the night went to Syl Apps Jr. His father had dropped the puck for the first All–Star Game in 1947 and was on hand to watch his son score twice and win MVP honours in 1975, when they became the first father and son to have played in the All–Star Game. The historic event had been a year in the making, as a last-minute injury had forced the younger Apps to withdraw after he'd been selected the previous year.

After it was over, most aficionados agreed that the All–Star Game had become tedious and unemotional. It was suggested that the game revert to the old system of pitting the Cup champion team against the best of the rest. Other suggestions (from Guidolin) included the NHL All–Stars versus the WHA All–Stars or a team of NHL Stars against a Soviet All–Star Team. He also proposed that each team be required to have an all-rookie line to help showcase young talent. The very fact that all the teams had to be represented was further cause for complaint. Bona fide stars such as Borje Salming, Yvan Cournoyer, and Walt Tkaczuk were staying at home while lesser lights such as Denis Dupere, Dennis Hextall, and Tracy Pratt were playing to fill the team requirements.

Perhaps the liveliest moments of the night came in the Prince of Wales dressing room before the game when two female reporters—Michelle St. Cyr from a Montreal radio station and Robin Herman of the *New York Times*—entered the room unannounced, much to the birthday-suit embarrassment of Bobby Orr, Phil Esposito, et al. The policy of admitting women reporters had been accepted before the game by both coaches. "Without women, there wouldn't be any men. A woman can come into my room any time," Guidolin quipped in a tone appropriate to the game's usual banter. Ms Herman had been covering the Islanders for the past year and had been slowly making her way through the dressing rooms of other league teams. But it would take years for women to gain access on a regular basis and for players to be comfortable in "mixed media" situations such as this.

Wales 7   Campbell 1

		Wales Conference All–Stars Bep Guidolin, coach (Kansas City)			Campbell Conference All–Stars Fred Shero, coach (Philadelphia)
1a	G	Rogie Vachon (Los Angeles)	1a	G	Bernie Parent (Philadelphia)
2b	D	Terry Harper (Los Angeles)	2a	D	Brad Park (N.Y. Rangers)
3	D	Bob Murdoch (Los Angeles)	3	D	Ed Van Impe (Philadelphia)
4a	D	Bobby Orr (Boston)	4	D	Doug Jarrett (Chicago)
5a	D	Guy Lapointe (Montreal)	5a	D	Denis Potvin (N.Y. Islanders)
6	D	Jerry Korab (Buffalo)	6a	LW	Bill Barber (Philadelphia)
7a	C	Phil Esposito (Boston)	7b	C	Garry Unger (St. Louis)
8a	LW	Rick Martin (Buffalo)	8b	RW	Jim Pappin (Chicago)
10b	D	Carol Vadnais (Boston)	9b	LW	Steve Vickers (N.Y. Rangers)
12	C	Marcel Dionne (Detroit)	10	RW	Rod Gilbert (N.Y. Rangers)
14b	RW	René Robert (Buffalo)	11	C	Curt Bennett (Atlanta)
15	LW	Denis Dupere (Washington)	12	C	Tom Lysiak (Atlanta)
16a	RW	Guy Lafleur (Montreal)	16a	C	Bobby Clarke (Philadelphia)
19	RW	Jean Pronovost (Pittsburgh)	17	RW	Simon Nôlet (Kansas City)
20	C	Don Luce (Buffalo)	18	RW	Ed Westfall (N.Y. Islanders)
22	LW	Joey Johnston (California)	19	D	Tracy Pratt (Vancouver)
24	RW	Terry O'Reilly (Boston)	20b	D	Jim Watson (Philadelphia)
26	C	Syl Apps Jr. (Pittsburgh)	21	C	Stan Mikita (Chicago)
27	C	Darryl Sittler (Toronto)	22	C	Dennis Hextall (Minnesota)
29b	G	Ken Dryden (Montreal)	30b	G	Gary Smith (Vancouver)

a=selected to First All–Star Team for first half of season by NHL Writers' Association

b=selected to Second All–Star Team for first half of season by NHL Writers' Association

First Period

1. Wales: Apps (Johnston, Vadnais) 9:38
2. Wales: Luce (O'Reilly, Dupere) 12:02
3. Wales: Sittler (Lafleur) 14:22
4. Campbell: Potvin (Unger) 19:41

Penalties: None

Second Period

5. Wales: Esposito (Lafleur, Murdoch) 19:16

Penalties: Vickers (CC) 0:16, Luce (WC) 4:51, Harper (WC) 12:11, Korab (WC) 19:37

Third Period

6. Wales: Apps (Robert, Martin) 3:25
7. Wales: O'Reilly (unassisted) 5:43
8. Wales: Orr (Lafleur, Sittler) . . . . 7:19(pp)

Penalties: Watson (CC) 6:42, Clarke (CC) 13:32

Shots on Goal

Wales	14	9	14	**37**
Campbell	10	9	10	**29**

In Goal

Wales—Vachon/Dryden [Dryden (no goals) replaced Vachon (one goal) from start 2nd to 10:39 of 3rd period]

Campbell—Parent/Smith [Smith (4 goals) replaced Parent (3 goals) at 9:17 of 2nd period]

Referee Wally Harris

Linesmen Leon Stickle and Claude Bechard

Attendance 16,080

MVP Syl Apps Jr. (Pittsburgh)

Broad Street Rules

The Spectrum, Philadelphia, Tuesday, January 20, 1976

In 1976, the NHL's All–Star Game kick-started the year-long bicentennial celebration of America's birth in Philadelphia, which had also provided a home for the Stanley Cup for the past two years. Once again, the $100 black tie pre-game dinner, this time at the Mariott Hotel, was a hugely successful extravaganza that greatly benefited that year's charity of choice, the Police Athletic League, or PAL.

The City of Brotherly Love had anticipated the glitter game with perhaps the worst moment in league history when the brawling Flyers forced the touring Soviet Union's Red Army Team off the ice in the first period of their exhibition game just nine days before. It took threats and persuasions from league president Clarence Campbell to get the CCCPs back on the ice, but the 4–1 Flyers' win was a moot point. As a team, the Flyers seemed almost incapable—and certainly unwilling—to play clean hockey or represent the league with a pride based on skill, speed, and sportsmanship. Instead, the Broad Street Bullies continued to damage the game's reputation during their reign of violence, intimidation, and terror. That they were Stanley Cup champions in 1974 and 1975 spoke volumes about the state of the game in the 1970s, and hockey purists longed for a team that could supplant the bench-clearing menace that was the Flyers.

Off ice, there was more exciting news than the game itself could provide. As a bargaining tactic, the Salomon

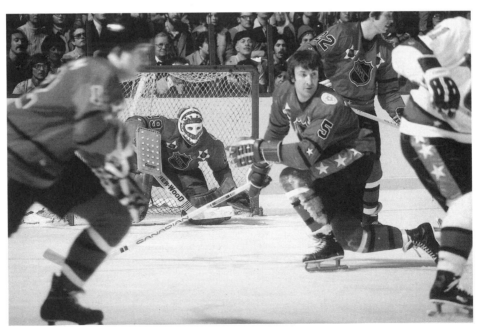

Ken Dryden goes low, in the crease, to follow the puck during the 29th All–Star Game.

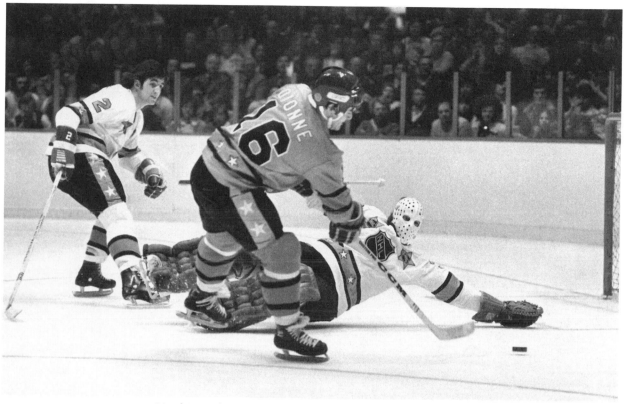

*Marcel Dionne beats Wayne Stephenson midway through the second period,
while defenceman Carol Vadnais watches helplessly.*

family, which owned the St. Louis Blues, had demanded a better tax break in the upcoming year when the city refused to allow the team to install air-conditioning or build a bridge over a highway that would connect the arena to new parking facilities. Now the Blues were given official permission to move the franchise if city officials didn't oblige. Also, the NHL and the NHL Players' Association had signed an historic five-year deal to ensure financial success for the teams and also guaranteed there would be no negotiations between the NHLPA and the rival WHA.

Furthermore, Clarence Campbell had indicated his intention to retire in the near future. After 29 years, he was hinting that it would soon be time to leave running the league in the hands of a successor. However, the governors refused to acquiesce to his suggestion

that they should create the position of chairman for him so that he might tutor his replacement for a year and instead formed a five-man committee to find the right man. Four club presidents—Bruce Norris (Detroit), Bill Jennings (N.Y. Rangers), Jacques Courtois (Montreal), and Roy Boe (N.Y. Islanders)—and Campbell himself would seek the ideal replacement. "If he doesn't have a legal background," Campbell said of the imminent newcomer, "he'll most certainly have to have a full-time attorney available."

Meanwhile, the Pittsburgh situation, which had become an all but yearly (if not daily) concern for the league, peaked in 1976 when it was learned that the Penguins were certain to move to Miami for the next year if attendance didn't increase to 13,000 a game. When the Pens filed for bankruptcy in the previous season, Al Savill (chairman of the board) and Wren Blair (president and chief operating officer) had put $3.8 million into the team's empty bank account to keep it going in the short term, but transfer to Florida seemed a necessity for the franchise to endure.

And to add to the fray, Campbell Conference coach Fred Shero got a few heads turning and ears bristling when he suggested that the coaches form a united front:

"The players have an association, so do the trainers and managers, so why can't we have a coaches' association? To me, an association would mean we could hold seminars to help ourselves and the game. The NHL has never brought coaches together by suggesting a week where we can talk hockey. We're asked to attend league meetings where we do nothing. In all the years I've coached at the pro level, I've never heard of the possibility of seminars."

In addition to the players selected to the starting team by the NHL Writers' Association, the coaches added eight players each. Floyd Smith chose Jerry Korab, Dave Burrows, Bill Clement, Al MacAdam, Dan Maloney, Greg Sheppard, Pierre Larouche, and Craig Ramsay. When Smith had to find a replacement for Second Team selection Serge Savard (who had bruised his knee), the sub turned out to be Larry Robinson. Smith had named Gil Perreault to his roster, but Gil's pride was bruised because he hadn't been chosen to one of the two starting positions by the writers and he declined to play. Coach Smith's lines included Ramsay–Clement–Sheppard; Larouche–Maloney–MacAdam; Mahovlich–Lafleur–Martin; and Shutt–Dionne–Pronovost.

Shero added Carol Vadnais, André Dupont, Bryan Trottier, Tom Lysiak, Bill Goldsworthy, Wilf Paiement, Dennis Ververgaert, and Curt Bennett. In the pre-game warmup, Bobby Clarke realised his bruised heel was causing him too much pain to play and he was replaced at the last minute by teammate Rick MacLeish. Second Team selection Dick Redmond also had to withdraw after tearing lateral cartilage in his right knee.

Rather than attend the team's morning practice, scoring sensation Phil Esposito filled his agenda in other ways. "I've been over to San Francisco, where I taped a show for Larry Solway at the Fairmount," he chortled later that day.

Eventually, Roger Doucet of Montreal Forum fame sang "O, Canada" with his usual flourish and *joie de chanson* and the party began. The game was non-physical, as usual, but Guy Lapointe injured his knee and ligament damage was feared. Fortunately, he missed only three games for the Habs and returned in good health. Peter Mahovlich won the traditional car as game MVP but sold the new wheels right away and split the profits with his All-Star teammates from Montreal. But perhaps the hero of the game—if not the main event of the whole weekend—was Garry Unger, who was closing in on the all-time NHL Iron Man record of 914 games (which he was to break a couple of months later). Two games before the All-Star tilt, he tore rib cartilage. Afraid he might be replaced in the All-Star Game, he continued to play even though it might jeopardize (if not end) his consecutive-game streak. And it didn't. He rejoined the Blues and kept playing and playing.

Wales 7   Campbell 5

Wales Conference All–Stars
Floyd Smith, coach (Buffalo)

1b	G	Wayne Thomas (Toronto)
2	D	Larry Robinson (Montreal)
3	D	Dave Burrows (Pittsburgh)
4	D	Jerry Korab (Buffalo)
5a	D	Guy Lapointe (Montreal)
6	C	Bill Clement (Washington)
7a	LW	Rick Martin (Buffalo)
8	LW	Dan Maloney (Detroit)
9	C	Pierre Larouche (Pittsburgh)
10a	RW	Guy Lafleur (Montreal)
11	LW	Craig Ramsay (Buffalo)
12	RW	Al MacAdam (California)
14	C	Gregg Sheppard (Boston)
16b	C	Marcel Dionne (Los Angeles)
17b	LW	Steve Shutt (Montreal)
19b	RW	Jean Pronovost (Pittsburgh)
20a	C	Pete Mahovlich (Montreal)
21b	D	Borje Salming (Toronto)
22a	D	Brad Park (Boston)
29a	G	Ken Dryden (Montreal)

Campbell Conference All–Stars
Fred Shero, coach (Philadelphia)

1a	G	Glenn Resch (N.Y. Islanders)
2	D	Carol Vadnais (N.Y. Rangers)
4b	D	Phil Russell (Chicago)
5a	D	Denis Potvin (N.Y. Islanders)
6	D	André Dupont (Philadelphia)
7b	C	Garry Unger (St. Louis)
8b	LW	Steve Vickers (N.Y. Rangers)
9	RW	Wilf Paiement (Kansas City)
10	RW	Dennis Ververgaert (Vancouver)
11a	LW	Bill Barber (Philadelphia)
12	RW	Bill Goldsworthy (Minnesota)
14	D	John Marks (Chicago)
15b	RW	Billy Harris (N.Y. Islanders)
17	LW	Curt Bennett (Atlanta)
18	C	Tom Lysiak (Atlanta)
19	C	Bryan Trottier (N.Y. Islanders)
20a	D	Jim Watson (Philadelphia)
21	C	Rick MacLeish (Philadelphia)
27a	RW	Reggie Leach (Philadelphia)
35b	G	Wayne Stephenson (Philadelphia)

a=selected to First All–Star Team for first half of season by NHL
Writers' Association

b=selected to Second All–Star Team for first half of season by NHL
Writers' Association

First Period

1. Wales: Martin (Mahovlich, Lafleur) 6:01
2. Campbell: Bennett (Dupont) 16:59
3. Wales: Mahovlich (Lapointe, Lafleur) 18:31
4. Wales: Park (Mahovlich, Martin) 19:00

Penalties: None

Second Period

5. Wales: MacAdam (Maloney) 9:34
6. Wales: Lafleur (Mahovlich, Martin) 11:54
7. Wales: Dionne (unassisted) 13:51
8. Wales: Maloney (Larouche, MacAdam) 16:59

Penalties: Barber (CC) 17:29

Third Period

9. Campbell: Ververgaert (Trottier, Harris) 4:33
10. Campbell: Ververgaert (Trottier, Harris) 4:43
11. Campbell: Potvin (unassisted) 14:17
12. Campbell: Vickers (Unger, Potvin) 14:46

Penalties: Marks (CC) 15:26

Shots on Goal

Wales	13	17	12	**42**
Campbell	9	6	9	**24**

In Goal

Wales—K. Dryden/Thomas [Thomas (4 goals) replaced Dryden (one goal) at 9:34 of 2nd period]
Campbell—Resch/Stephenson [Stephenson (4 goals) replaced Resch (3 goals) at 9:18 of 2nd period]

Referee Lloyd Gilmour

Linesmen Neil Armstrong and John D'Amico

Attendance 16,436

MVP Pete Mahovlich (Montreal)

The NHL Goes International

Pacific Coliseum, Vancouver, Tuesday, January 25, 1977

For the first time, the NHL's governors stayed in Vancouver a day after the All–Star Game in 1977 to finish discussions on many fronts. Included on the agenda were changing the playoffs structure, divisional realignment, the NHL–junior hockey relationship, and financially troubled franchises. After meetings at the Bayshore Inn, Alan Eagleson said, "I think there is a good chance Cleveland [Barons] will not finish the season."

The Barons had only moved from California to Ohio at the start of the year and were already looking for about $600,000 just to meet the next payroll. In the end, they got about half the money, along with assurances from owner George Gund that the team would continue through to the end of the regular season at least. On the juniors front, the NHL and NHL Players' Association agreed that any player selected in the amateur draft but not signed in the following 12 months could be re-drafted the following year. And on realignment, league president Clarence Campbell felt that a perfectly balanced schedule was imperative to the future success of the league (though certain teams didn't want to give up prestige dates; i.e. a game against Toronto for a game against Cleveland). The balanced-schedule idea all but eliminated rivalries. With an 18-team, 80-game season, each team would play every other one only three times a year.

After the great success of the 1976 Canada Cup, the league meetings also marked an historic return to international hockey when the International Ice Hockey Federation relented and allowed professionals to compete at the world championships, thus ensuring Canada would play on a global stage for the first time since it withdrew from international competition in 1970 to protest the disparity in interpretation of the terms "amateur" and "pro." To this end, the NHL said it would allow any player on a team that didn't make the playoffs to play at the world championships, to be held that year in Vienna. The participation of European countries in future Canada Cups was contingent on Canada sending a top-flight team to the world championships each year. And the arrangement immediately assumed monumental significance when players including Phil Esposito and Marcel Dionne took part in what became a violent and controversial championship round during the Vienna tournament that sullied Canada's already debatable international reputation.

For the Campbell Conference, coach Fred Shero included on his roster Tom Bladon, Harold Snepsts, Gary Unger, Phil Esposito, Wilf Paiement, Gary Dornhoefer, Tom Lysiak, and Tim Young, though in truth he hadn't made the selections. "I left that up to Mike and Barry," Shero said, referring to assistant coaches Mike Nykoluk and Barry Ashbee. "I'm too busy watching my own team to know who to pick for an All–Star Game." In the end, it hardly mattered. Shero lost his third straight All–Star Game and, with the talented Montreal Canadiens on a Stanley Cup roll, the coach's goon squad in Philadelphia was on its way out.

Selected to play with the Stars, Darryl Sittler suffered torn rib cartilage in a game against Los Angeles just days before the big show and was unable to attend. As per the rules, his spot was filled by another Leaf, Ian Turnbull. Clark Gillies, a Second Team selection, took himself off the roster because of sickness and was replaced by Islander teammate Bob Nystrom.

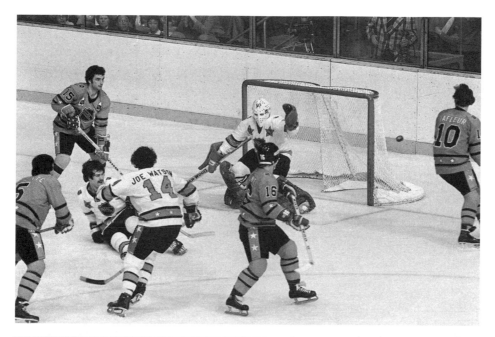

Action at both ends of the ice as one shot flies by the glove of Bernie Parent (top), while Phil Esposito beats Gerry Desjardins (bottom) at the other end.

And Steve Shutt, a First Team selection, elected to stay by the side of his pregnant wife and was replaced by Bob Gainey.

Once again, the league approved the overtime clause, which meant that a game that was tied after 60 minutes would be played to the death in overtime for however long it took.

The All–Star dinner at the Bayshore Inn the night before was attended by popular Vancouverites Babe Pratt, Frank Griffiths, Bill Hughes, Greg Douglas and local residents, and Hall of Fame members Frank Fredrickson and Cyclone Taylor were honoured. A total of 572 seats at $125 each were sold for the evening's festivities.

On game night, Wales Conference coach Scotty Bowman stole the show with his line combinations. He used his own Montreal defenceman Larry Robinson on left wing (facilitated by the late addition of defenceman Turnbull for a forward, Sittler), and from the port side "Big Bird" set up two of his team's goals. In another All–Star Game rarity, Bowman double-shifted Gil Perreault, while the line of Dionne–Martin–Lafleur excelled most of the night. Bowman also caused a bit of controversy when he benched Turnbull and MacAdam in the third period, but his response was terse and confident: "You play to win."

Rick Martin, winner of the MVP car, came up with what had become the annual auto witticism when he quipped, "If I'd known I was going to win the car, I wouldn't have bought my wife one for Christmas."

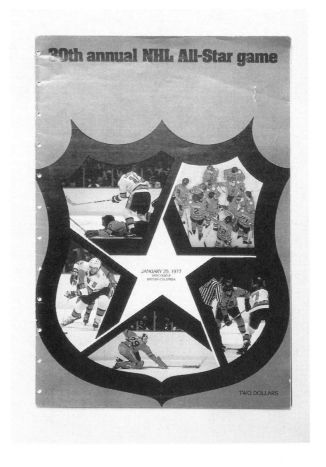

<h1 style="text-align:center">Wales 4   Campbell 3</h1>

Wales Conference All–Stars
Scotty Bowman, coach (Montreal)

2	D	Ian Turnbull (Toronto)
5b	D	Guy Lapointe (Montreal)
6	D	Jim Schoenfeld (Buffalo)
7b	LW	Rick Martin (Buffalo)
8	C	Peter McNab (Boston)
9b	RW	Lanny McDonald (Toronto)
10a	RW	Guy Lafleur (Montreal)
12b	C	Gilbert Perreault (Buffalo)
14	LW	Nick Libbett (Detroit)
15	C	Guy Charron (Washington)
16	C	Marcel Dionne (Los Angeles)
18	D	Serge Savard (Montreal)
19a	D	Larry Robinson (Montreal)
20	RW	Jean Pronovost (Pittsburgh)
21a	D	Borje Salming (Toronto)
22b	D	Brad Park (Boston)
23	LW	Bob Gainey (Montreal)
25	RW	Al MacAdam (Cleveland)
29a	G	Ken Dryden (Montreal)
30b	G	Gerry Desjardins (Buffalo)

Campbell Conference All–Stars
Fred Shero, coach (Philadelphia)

1b	G	Bernie Parent (Philadelphia)
2	D	Harold Snepsts (Vancouver)
3	D	Tom Bladon (Philadelphia)
4b	D	Phil Russell (Chicago)
5a	D	Denis Potvin (N.Y. Islanders)
7a	RW	Rod Gilbert (N.Y. Rangers)
8	C	Garry Unger (St. Louis)
10	RW	Wilf Paiement (Colorado)
11	C	Tom Lysiak (Atlanta)
12	RW	Gary Dornhoefer (Philadelphia)
14b	D	Joe Watson (Philadelphia)
15b	RW	Don Murdoch (N.Y. Rangers)
16a	C	Bobby Clarke (Philadelphia)
17	C	Tim Young (Minnesota)
19b	C	Rick MacLeish (Philadelphia)
20a	D	Jim Watson (Philadelphia)
23	RW	Bob Nystrom (N.Y. Islanders)
27a	LW	Eric Vail (Atlanta)
30	G	Glenn Resch (N.Y. Islanders)
77	C	Phil Esposito (N.Y. Rangers)

a=selected to First All–Star Team for first half of season by NHL Writers' Association

b=selected to Second All–Star team for first half of season by NHL Writers' Association

---

First Period
1. Campbell: Vail (Potvin) 2:54
2. Wales: McDonald (Gainey, McNab) 6:22
Penalties: Campbell (too many men) 15:32, Dornhoefer (CC) and Lapointe (WC) 16:24

Second Period
3. Campbell: MacLeish (Nystrom, Potvin) 11:56
4. Wales: McDonald (Perreault, Robinson) 19:27
Penalties: Potvin (CC) 4:11, Lapointe (WC) 5:08, Paiement (CC) 8:34, Joe Watson (CC) 14:02

Third Period
5. Wales: Martin (Dionne, Robinson) . . . . 4:00(pp)
6. Campbell: Esposito (Gilbert, Dornhoefer) 12:23
7. Wales: Martin (Dionne, Lafleur) 18:04
Penalties: Russell (CC) 3:17, Salming (WC) 15:48

Shots on Goal

Wales	14	10	12	**36**
Campbell	10	8	7	**25**

In Goal
Wales—K. Dryden/Desjardins [Desjardins (2 goals) replaced Dryden (one goal) at 11:27 of 2nd period]
Campbell—Parent/Resch [Resch (3 goals) replaced Parent (one goal) at 11:27 of 2nd period]

Referee Bruce Hood

Linesmen Matt Pavelich and Ron Finn

Attendance 15,607

MVP Rick Martin (Buffalo)

The Last of Its Kind

Buffalo Memorial Auditorium, Tuesday, January 24, 1978

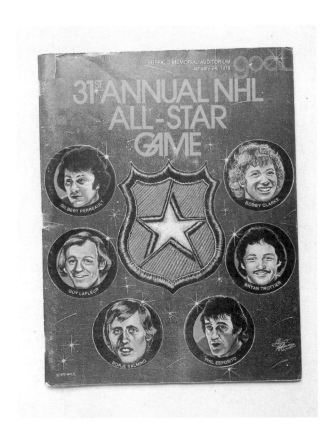

The 1978 All–Star Game was former NHL chairman of the board John Ziegler's first since taking over from Clarence Campbell as league president at the beginning of the regular season, and as if to mark the magnitude of the change in his status, Ziegler tripped on the red carpet on his walk out to centre ice for the pre-game ceremonies but regained his balance and got the show on the road in good style.

The pre-game dinner was hosted by Ted Darling, the voice of the Buffalo Sabres, and featured songstress Anne Murray and comedian Norm Crosby entertaining more than 800 guests. Danny Gare formally opened the dinner, Rick Jeanneret introduced all the players to the dinner crowd and singer Joe Byron offered renditions of both "O, Canada" and "The Star-Spangled Banner." The $100-a-head profits went to the Buffalo Children's Hospital and the stick-boy and stickgirl for the game were patients who had both had successful heart surgery at Children's.

But many executives in the league were saying this

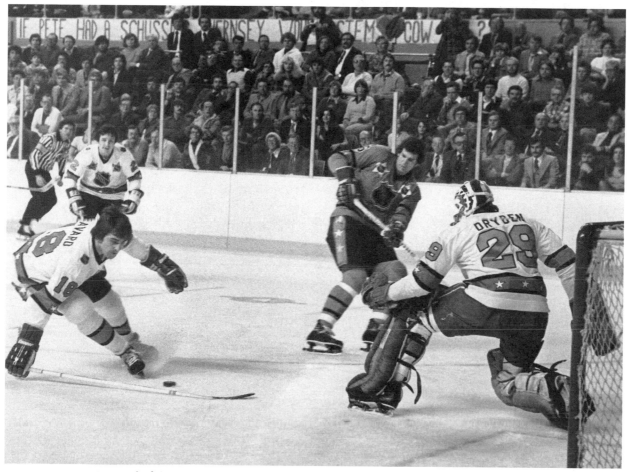

Barry Beck of the Campbells slides the puck across the front of the goal only to see Serge Savard block it, while Montreal goalie Ken Dryden follows the play from his crease.

would be the last game of its kind. "I think this game is a joke," Alan Eagleson stated just hours before the 1978 All–Star skate.

The league's international profile, and the popularity of the international game, had been steadily increasing through the 1970s, from the 1972 Summit Series to the 1976 Super Series tours of Soviet and Czech teams culminating with that year's Canada Cup to the return of Canada to international hockey with professional players at the 1977 world championships. To capture (and capitalize on) this momentum, the NHL had announced that for 1979 a Super Series featuring the league's stars and the best from

the Soviet Union would play a three-game mini-series to replace the classic All–Star Game, which everyone admitted had run its course in terms of quality and fan interest. Such an All–Star series for 1979 seemed to be the best way for the NHL to maintain an international presence but at the same time replace the tired routine of touring Soviet teams. Furthermore, such a series was deemed to be more interesting to American television networks and thus a superior means of generating greater amounts for the players' pension fund. Initially scheduled to be a three- or four-game series, the event was presumed to be a permanent replacement for the All–Star Game and would be strategically scheduled two weeks after the Super Bowl to accommodate television.

"Call it All–Star week or NHL week," Ziegler said, "but we would expect that not only North America but the whole world will be watching and will be very excited about it."

As a related concern, there were also heated discussions between players and owners regarding continued participation at the world championships. Incensed by their treatment the year before in Vienna, the players made it clear that they had no desire to go to Prague this time unless conditions improved. Otherwise, they said, they'd be happy to see WHA skaters represent Canada at the championships.

The difficulty lay in the nature of the reciprocity agreement between the International Ice Hockey Federation and the NHL, which made other countries' participation in future Canada Cup tournaments contingent on Canada sending a top-notch pro team to the world championships every year. The Canadian team had been hooted and jeered at and treated like barbarians in Vienna in 1977. In retrospect, it can all be seen as part of the growing pains of international participation, but at the time the controversy was real and indeed it threatened future hockey peace.

To the Wales Conference roster, Scotty Bowman added Tom Bladon, Carol Vadnais, Bill Clement, Phil Esposito, Dennis Ververgaert, Roland Eriksson, Garry Unger, and Ivan Boldirev. Coach Fred Shero of the Campbells added Dave Burrows, Reed Larson, Dennis Maruk, Bob Sirois, Marcel Dionne, Bob Gainey, Jacques Lemaire, and Terry O'Reilly. Guy Lapointe was selected to the starting team by the NHL Writers' Association but couldn't play because of a serious eye injury and was replaced by teammate Serge Savard; Dave Burrows had to bow out of the game because of a knee injury and was replaced by Jean Pronovost; and Jacques Lemaire's similar injury forced him to watch the game on TV and allowed teammate Yvan Cournoyer to go in the lineup.

The Campbells played an all-Islanders line of Trottier–Gillies–Bossy and their others consisted of Clarke–Barber–Paiement, Esposito–Unger–Ververgaert, and Boldirev–Eriksson–Clement, but the number one Wales line of Lafleur–Perreault–Shutt dominated the game and the Campbells were lucky their two goals held up long enough to get them into overtime. For the most part, the Wales were the overwhelming favourites and in fact they won their third game in a row and gave Campbells coach Fred Shero an unprecedented fourth consecutive loss (he never returned to the NHL's showcase game) while the Campbells set a record in underachievement by taking only 12 shots at the enemy net in the whole game. Fans booed bitterly when goaler Billy Smith and not their own overtime hero Perreault won MVP honours.

Wales 3   Campbell 2 (OT)

Wales Conference All–Stars
Scotty Bowman, coach (Montreal)

1b	G	Rogie Vachon (Los Angeles)
6	RW	Jean Pronovost (Pittsburgh)
7a	LW	Rick Martin (Buffalo)
8b	LW	Steve Shutt (Montreal)
9b	RW	Lanny McDonald (Toronto)
10a	RW	Guy Lafleur (Montreal)
11a	C	Gilbert Perreault (Buffalo)
12	RW	Bob Sirois (Washington)
14	RW	Yvan Cournoyer (Montreal)
16	C	Marcel Dionne (Los Angeles)
18	D	Serge Savard (Montreal)
19b	D	Larry Robinson (Montreal)
20	C	Dennis Maruk (Cleveland)
21a	D	Borje Salming (Toronto)
22a	D	Brad Park (Boston)
23	LW	Bob Gainey (Montreal)
24	RW	Terry O'Reilly (Boston)
27b	C	Darryl Sittler (Toronto)
28	D	Reed Larson (Detroit)
29a	G	Ken Dryden (Montreal)

Campbell Conference All–Stars
Fred Shero, coach (Philadelphia)

2a	D	Bob Dailey (Philadelphia)
3	D	Tom Bladon (Philadelphia)
4	D	Carol Vadnais (N.Y. Rangers)
5a	D	Denis Potvin (N.Y. Islanders)
6b	D	Barry Beck (Colorado)
7b	LW	Bill Barber (Philadelphia)
8b	RW	Wilf Paiement (Colorado)
9a	LW	Clark Gillies (N.Y. Islanders)
10	C	Bill Clement (Atlanta)
11	RW	Dennis Ververgaert (Vancouver)
12	C	Ivan Boldirev (Chicago)
16b	C	Bobby Clarke (Philadelphia)
17	C	Garry Unger (St. Louis)
19a	C	Bryan Trottier (N.Y. Islanders)
20b	D	Jim Watson (Philadelphia)
21	C	Rollie Eriksson (Minnesota)
22a	RW	Mike Bossy (N.Y. Islanders)
31a	G	Billy Smith (N.Y. Islanders)
35b	G	Wayne Stephenson (Philadelphia)
77	C	Phil Esposito (N.Y. Rangers)

a=selected to First All–Star Team for first half of season by NHL Writers' Association

b=selected to Second All–Star Team for first half of season by NHL Writers' Association

---

First Period
1. Campbell: Barber (unassisted) 1:25
2. Campbell: Potvin (Clarke) 12:12
Penalties: Salming (WC) 7:42, Gillies (CC) 18:30

Second Period
3. Wales: Sittler (Robinson, Park) . . . . 19:32(pp)
Penalties: Dailey (CC) 2:25, Smith (CC) and McDonald (WC) 3:36, Vadnais (CC) 18:12

Third Period
4. Wales: Martin (Dionne, O'Reilly) 18:21
Penalties: None

Overtime
5. Wales: Perreault (Shutt, Salming) 3:55
Penalties: None

Shots on Goal

Wales	7	16	15	2	**40**
Campbell	7	2	3	0	**12**

In Goal
Wales—K. Dryden/Vachon [Vachon (no goals) replaced Dryden (2 goals) at 9:26 of 2nd period]
Campbell—Smith/Stephenson [Stephenson (3 goals) replaced Smith (no goals) at 9:26 of 2nd period]

Referee Bruce Hood

Linesmen John D'Amico and Leon Stickle

Attendance 16,433

MVP Billy Smith (N.Y. Islanders)

1979 Challenge Cup

The 1979 Challenge Cup (which took its name from the original Stanley Cup) completed nearly a decade of unparalleled growth and interest in international hockey that began with Team Canada's victory in the Summit Series in 1972.

In 1970, Canada had decided to boycott the world championships because it was not allowed to send even semi-professional players to the then amateur tournament. Every year, young Canadian teams were soundly beaten by the best the Soviet Union had to offer (although the Soviets vehemently claimed not to have any pros in their country), and slowly but surely this huge discrepancy in talent led to negotiating a series that would decide all future bragging rights. Thus it was that in 1972, the best players in Canada, regardless of league, affiliation, or professional status, played the best from the USSR.

The result of the eight-game series was both dramatic and favourable and produced further interest in the international game. The NHL became directly involved when it hosted a series of exhibition games during the ensuing seasons against the two top teams from the Soviet Union, the Wings and Central Army. This was followed by the inaugural Canada Cup in

Guy Lafleur gives a little hook and tug to Victor Zhluktov of the Soviet Union during game one of the Challenge Cup.

the fall of 1976 and another round of exhibition tours by both Soviet and Czech teams. Finally, in the face of continued and unflagging fan support, the NHL decided it was time to replace the All–Star Game (which had featured the best in the league) with a mini-Summit in which the best in the NHL, regardless of nationality, would form one team to play the best from the Soviet Union.

Given the importance of the series—the Challenge Cup was being touted as a world championship, a mini–Canada Cup of sorts for all bragging rights—the selection process for the NHL team was particularly casual. For the first time, fan balloting determined the starting lineup for Team NHL. Each city's team was given 200,000 ballots to distribute to fans during home games, and across the continent millions of ballots were available in stores.

Controversy erupted early on when teams claimed that the Rangers were stuffing ballots, a charge that was easily supported by the fact that four of five starting positions were led by Blueshirts throughout the

voting (which ended on January 14). It got to the point where during stoppages in play in Montreal, the public address announcer would declare that Guy Lafleur was trailing Pat Hickey of the Rangers by some 5,000 votes. Elsewhere in the league, fans seemed apathetic about voting players to the team until near the end, when justice prevailed and none of the Rangers made the first team. Fans also voted one goalie to the team, but the NHL coach, Scotty Bowman, had the final decision about who to start for the three games.

The final Team NHL roster was announced at a press conference at the Nassau Coliseum prior to the Islanders–Rangers game of January 27, 1979. All additional player decisions were made by general manager Bill Torrey of the Islanders and assistants Harry Sinden (Boston) and Cliff Fletcher (Atlanta). Ultimately, only 20 players could dress for each game, so the 32-man roster was pared to 25 for the first practise in New York on February 5, while the roster's seven-man cushion was used to accommodate

Four NHLers are back—(l-r) Barry Beck, Denis Potvin, Lanny McDonald,
and Gerry Cheevers protecting the goal during game three of the series.

*A victorious Boris Mikhailov holds the Challenge Cup trophy high
for all to see what his mighty CCCP team
had accomplished at Madison Square Garden.*

slightly injured players (notably Darryl Sittler, Steve Shutt, and Denis Potvin) who might not be healthy enough for the series.

Over in Moscow, coach Viktor Tikhonov shrunk the dimensions of his team's practice rink to acclimatise his players to the smaller NHL rink. He also had to deal with two significant lineup changes, with forward Aleksandr Maltsev out with a broken wrist and rising star Boris Alexandrov suspended from the team for drinking violations. By the time Tikhonov made out

his final roster, he still had plenty of talent, however. His first line was Zhluktov, Kapustin, and Balderis; the second was Petrov, Mikhailov, and Kharlamov; and the third was Golikov, Kovin, and Priordin. But the lines never told the whole story with Tikhonov, who preferred to use five-man units and set plays based on a specific set of defencemen playing every shift with the same forwards.

In addition, the Challenge Cup battle was a culturally based clash of styles with the democratic versus communist political differences serving as a metaphor for on-ice variations. On offence, the Soviets passed the puck and skated like the wind. They looked for the perfect pass, the perfect play on each rush. As a result, they were susceptible to hitting and over-passing. On defence, they were not used to clearing a man (such as Phil Esposito) from the slot and their blueliners were unaccustomed to fast, heavy forechecking.

An All–Star dinner the night of February 9 at the Waldorf Astoria was attended by former league president Clarence Campbell. (Unfortunately, Campbell collapsed the next night during the game and was rushed to hospital, where he had successful abdominal surgery.) The recently retired Bobby Orr was also

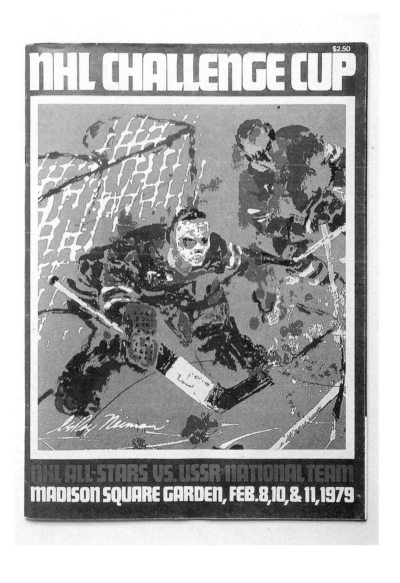

honoured at the Challenge Cup dinner with the Lester Patrick Award for contributions to hockey in the United States.

While the NHL had just three practices to prepare, the Soviets had been training for months with only this tournament in mind. After splitting the first two games, the lopsided score of game three did not necessarily prove Soviet superiority so much as the NHL's arrogance in thinking it needed so little time to put a winning team together.

One suggestion that came out of the debacle that was this lost Challenge Cup was an expressed desire on the part of the Soviets to play the Stanley Cup champions in a three-game showdown in Moscow—a real Challenge Cup for the only real trophy. This never materialized because the concept of the Cup winners being open to challenge had been abandoned in 1914.

But after watching game three, most people involved in the NHL would have been leery about further competition anyway. The game was exciting in the first period and still close after the second, with the score still only 2–0 for the bad guys. Then, midway through the third, the Soviets exploded for four more goals on Gerry Cheevers and the rout proved an embarrassing anticlimax to what had looked like a favourable alternative to the All–Star Game.

After the final game, referee John McCauley (who was in New York for the series but not officiating any of the games) went to a Manhattan bar with two linesmen for drinks. McCauley was openly critical of the Canadian method of playing and suggested North Americans could learn something from the Soviet style. Out of nowhere, a fan sucker-punched him in the eye. A few days later, his vision was so bad he had to leave a Toronto–Philadelphia game at Maple Leaf Gardens. It took five operations just to restore his vision and McCauley's career as an official was over.

The Soviets earned $200,000 for participating while every Team NHL player received a mere $3,000 whether he played or not.

1979 CHALLENGE CUP

Madison Square Garden, New York

Game 1 February 8	Game 2 February 10	Game 3 February 11
NHL All–Stars 4 USSR 2	**USSR 5 NHL All–Stars 4**	**USSR 6 NHL All–Stars 0**

NHL All–Stars
Scotty Bowman, coach (Montreal)

			G	A	P	Pim
3 d	D	Guy Lapointe (Montreal)	0	0	0	0
4	D	Barry Beck (Colorado)	0	1	1	2
5 ad	D	Denis Potvin (N.Y. Islanders)	0	0	0	0
7	LW	Bill Barber (Philadelphia)	0	1	1	0
8	RW	Lanny McDonald (Toronto)	0	0	0	2
9	LW	Clark Gillies (N.Y. Islanders)	1	2	3	2
10 a	RW	Guy Lafleur (Montreal)	1	2	3	0
11	C	Gilbert Perreault (Buffalo)	1	1	2	2
12 c	C	Ulf Nilsson (N.Y. Rangers)	0	0	0	0
15 c	RW	Anders Hedberg (N.Y. Rangers)	0	0	0	0
16 a	C	Bobby Clarke (Philadelphia)	0	1	1	0
17 b	C	Marcel Dionne (Los Angeles)	0	1	1	0
18	D	Serge Savard (Montreal)	0	0	0	0
19 a	D	Larry Robinson (Montreal)	1	0	1	0
20	C	Bryan Trottier (N.Y. Islanders)	1	1	2	2
21 e	LW	Don Marcotte (Boston)	0	0	0	2
22 ab	LW	Steve Shutt (Montreal)	0	1	1	0
23	LW	Bob Gainey (Montreal)	1	0	1	0
25	RW	Mike Bossy (N.Y. Islanders)	2	2	4	0
26	D	Borje Salming (Toronto)	0	0	0	2
27	C	Darryl Sittler (Toronto)	0	1	1	0
29 b	G	Ken Dryden (Montreal)	0	0	0	0
30 e	G	Gerry Cheevers (Boston)	0	0	0	0

D	Ron Greschner (N.Y. Rangers) did not play	
D	Robert Picard (Washington) did not play	
Ga	Tony Esposito (Chicago) did not play	

USSR
Victor Tikhonov, coach

			G	A	P	Pim
1 d	G	Vladimir Myshkin	0	0	0	2
2	D	Yuri Federov	0	0	0	0
4 b	D	Sergei Babinov	0	0	0	0
5	D	Vasili Pervukhin	0	0	0	0
6	D	Valeri Vasiliev	0	3	3	2
7 c	D	Gennady Tsygankov	0	0	0	2
8	F	Sergei Kapustin	2	1	3	0
9	C	Vladimir Kovin	1	0	1	2
10	F	Mikhail Varnakov	1	1	2	0
11	F	Alexander Skvortsov	0	2	2	0
12	D	Sergei Starikov	0	1	1	0
13	F	Boris Mikhailov	3	0	3	2
14	D	Zinetula Bilyaletdinov	0	0	0	0
16	F	Vladimir Petrov	0	1	1	2
17 c	F	Valeri Kharlamov	0	1	1	0
18 d	F	Irek Gimayev	0	1	1	0
19	F	Helmut Balderis	1	1	2	0
20 a	G	Vladislav Tretiak	0	0	0	0
21 b	F	Victor Tyumenev	0	0	0	0
22	F	Victor Zhluktov	1	1	2	4
23 a	F	Alexander Golikov	1	2	3	0
24	F	Sergei Makarov	1	2	3	0
25	F	Vladimir Golikov	2	0	2	0

D   Alexei Kasatonov, did not play

	GP	Mins	W-L-T	GA	SO	Avg
Ken Dryden	2	120	1-1-0	7	0	3.50
Gerry Cheevers	1	60	0-1-0	6	0	6.00

	GP	Mins	W-L-T	GA	SO	Avg
Vladislav Tretiak	2	120	1-1-0	8	0	4.00
Vladimir Myshkin	1	60	1-0-0	0	1	0.00

a	voted to roster by fan ballot
b	played February 8 and 10
c	played February 8 and 11
d	played only February 10
e	played only February 11

a	played February 8 and 10
b	played February 10 and 11
c	played only February 8
d	played only February 11

Game One
NHL All–Stars 4   USSR 2

First Period
1. NHL: Lafleur (Shutt, Clarke) 0:16
2. NHL: Bossy (Perreault, Lafleur) . . . . 6:22(pp)
3. USSR: Mikhailov (Vasiliev, Kharlamov) . . . . 11:25(pp)
4. NHL: Gainey (Barber, Beck) 15:48
Penalties: Zhluktov (USSR) 0:59, Petrov (USSR) 5:13, McDonald (NHL) 8:31, Gillies (NHL) 10:59, Zhluktov (USSR) 12:21

Second Period
5. NHL: Gillies (Bossy) 8:14
Penalties: Tsygankov (USSR) 10:48

Third Period
6. USSR: V. Golikov (A. Golikov, Makarov) 3:02
Penalties: None

Shots on Goal

NHL	10	9	5	**24**
USSR	6	5	9	**20**

In Goal
NHL—Dryden
USSR—Tretiak

Referee Bob Myers

Linesmen John D'Amico and Ray Scapinello

Attendance 17,210

Game Two
USSR 5   NHL All–Stars 4

First Period
1. USSR: Kapustin (Starikov) 8:10
2. NHL: Bossy (Trottier, Gillies) . . . . 13:35(pp)
3. NHL: Trottier (Bossy, Gillies) 18:21
Penalties: Kovin (USSR) 12:32, Perreault (NHL) 15:13

Second Period
4. NHL: Perreault (Sittler) 0:27
5. USSR: Varnakov (Skvortsov) 2:05
6. NHL: Robinson (Lafleur, Dionne) 5:06
7. USSR: Mikhailov (Petrov, Vasiliev) . . . . 17:02(pp)
8. USSR: Kapustin (Zhluktov) 17:47
Penalties: Salming (NHL) 8:04, Beck (NHL) 15:07

Third Period
9. USSR: V. Golikov (Makarov) 1:31
Penalties: None

Shots on Goal

USSR	7	14	10	**31**
NHL	5	5	6	**16**

In Goal
USSR—Tretiak
NHL—Dryden

Referee Victor Dombrovski

Linesmen   Matt Pavelich and Ron Finn

Attendance 17,239

Game Three
USSR 6   NHL All–Stars 0

First Period
No Scoring
Penalties: None

Second Period
1. USSR: Mikhailov (A. Golikov). 5:47
2. USSR: Zhluktov (Balderis, Vasiliev) . . . . 7:44(pp)
Penalties: Marcotte (NHL) 6:27, Vasiliev (USSR) 10:48, Myshkin (USSR) and Trottier (NHL) 12:27

Third Period
3. USSR: Balderis (Gimayev). 8:44
4. USSR: Kovin (Skvortsov, Varnakov). 10:21
5. USSR: Makarov (Kapustin) 12:44
6. USSR: A. Golikov (unassisted) . . . . 14:46(sh)
Penalties: Mikhailov (USSR) 14:22

Shots on Goal
USSR	6	6	7	**19**
NHL	7	7	10	**24**

In Goal
USSR—Myshkin
NHL—Cheevers

Referee Andy van Hellemond

Linesmen Claude Bechard and Leon Stickle

Attendance 17,329

32nd All–Star Game
Gordie Says Goodbye
Joe Louis Arena, Detroit, Tuesday, February 5, 1980

In 1980, Scotty Bowman did the only thing a man could do in his capacity as head coach: He named 51-year-old Gordie Howe to his Wales Conference roster to play just one more time.

Howe had first played as an All–Star in 1948.

"I remember that first All–Star Game," Howe later said in Detroit. "It was in Toronto and they gave us our game sweater as a souvenir. I didn't keep mine. I gave it to my buddy on a fishing trip. I wish I hadn't now. It would have been a good keepsake."

At his 23rd appearance, Howe received the most resounding ovation in All–Star history and managed an assist while he took a regular shift. "It was unbelievable how much love poured from those people," Howe said of his longtime Detroit fans. "It's one of the memories I'll carry with me forever." It was also an All–Star reunion of sorts for Wayne Gretzky, who had played with his idol at the 1979 WHA All–Star Game against the Soviets and was now playing in his first as an NHLer.

Similarly, Campbell Conference coach Al Arbour added Phil Esposito to the lineup to fill in for the injured Anders Hedberg, a sentimental move meant to acknowledge Espo's great contribution to the game in what was to be his final full season in the NHL (he retired midway through 1980–81).

Still, the All–Star weekend was marred by controversy over continuing and emerging problems within the league. Boston's attempt to oust Alan Eagleson from the NHL Players' Association failed miserably; criticism of league president John Ziegler for losing control of the players in new acts of on-ice violence was rampant; and general consensus had it that the NHL was losing ground and fading in popularity instead of progressing onward and upward. It was conceded that only 11 of the 21 teams in the league were making money; ironically, only the clubs based in Canada seemed certain of long-term prosperity.

The campaign to oust Eagleson was championed first and foremost by Boston's Mike Milbury. He had polled players throughout the league to determine whether they would prefer another full-time executive director, rather than Eagleson, who wore many hats as player agent, NHLPA executive, Canada Cup director, and chief negotiator between the players and the NHL in the collective bargaining agreement. Milbury refused to reveal the results of the poll in light of the fact that Eagleson was returned as unanimous choice as executive director until 1982, when he planned to step down anyway. In the interim, the players created a committee consisting of Milbury, Darryl Sittler, Tony and Phil Esposito (Phil was the newly-elected NHLPA president) and two players to be named later whose job was to look for a candidate to apprentice under Eagleson until he retired and then to replace him.

But the perennial topic of free agency became the top priority for both the league and the players at meetings that year. As a starting point, the owners wanted a lifetime option for all players under contract and the players wanted total freedom at the expiration of a contract. To say a schism existed would be generous in the extreme. The current system called for a team to be compensated for like talent when a free agent was signed by another team, which was more like a forced trade than actual free agency. The owners offered a compromise: equal compensation for players earning more than $100,000 a year; a first-

Marcel Dionne and Gordie Howe, ranked one-two in scoring until Wayne Gretzky came along,
pose for the cameras prior to Howe's last All–Star Game in 1980. His first came back in 1948.

round draft choice for players earning $80,000 to $100,000; and no compensation for a player making less than $80,000. The players countered not with an offer but by forming a committee of eight to study this proposal and initiate a counter-proposal.

Typically, both sides defended their demands.

"Our studies show that players who are subject to equalization, whether they stayed with their existing club or moved, did so with an average increase of 30 per cent of salary," Ziegler said.

Eagleson countered with his own figures: Of the past year's 139 free agents, only 22 changed clubs. Thus, he hypothesized, bidding on the open market seemed to be minimal and the current system of compensation prevented players from realizing their true worth because solicitation from competing clubs was not being encouraged.

Held at the brand-spanking-new Joe Louis Arena in Detroit, the 1980 All–Star Game returned to what it had been before the failure that was the 1979 Challenge Cup. The two conferences played each other, and the first 12 players to each team were selected by the Professional Hockey Writers' Association.

On the injury front, Borje Salming, a First Team selection, could not play because he was recovering from an operation to his vocal cords. He was replaced by another Leaf defenceman, Dave Burrows. When Ranger Barry Beck was injured, Arbour added another Blueshirt, Ron Greschner. Gary Sargent, a Second Team selection to the Wales, had to be replaced by rookie teammate Craig Hartsburg. Dave Taylor (First Team) and Charlie Simmer (Second Team), two-thirds of L.A.'s famed Triple Crown Line, also couldn't play and were replaced by the Kings' Mike Murphy and Butch Goring. Four other great defencemen were also unavailable (Brad Park, Denis Potvin, Serge Savard and Guy Lapointe), leaving the blue line

far from all–star in quality fans hoped to see.

The banquet at the Detroit Plaza Hotel the night before the game featured entertainer Mac Davis and comedian Norm Crosbie, and the highlight of the night came when Detroit's famed Production Line of Lindsay–Howe–Abel was honoured in front of a record 1,500 guests. Proceeds from the $150-a-ticket banquet went to the United States Special Olympics.

To celebrate the 1980 Olympic Winter Games, the All–Star Game was preceded by a special 20-minute period of hockey between the Canadian and American Olympic teams. The mini-game was won by Canada 1–0 on a goal by Cary Farelli, and the night as a whole set a record for attendance at an All–Star Game (ironically, it had also been in Detroit that the smallest crowd, 9,166, had watched an All–Star Game at the old Olympia in 1950).

In one anomaly, goalie Tony Esposito played the fewest minutes of any All–Star goalie in history when he left just 15 minutes into the first period. He had injured his hand a few nights before and was stung by a rising Howe slapper. Pete Peeters came in for the final 45 minutes, thus playing longer than any goalie since 1965, when Glenn Hall had played the whole game for the All–Stars.

Wayne Gretzky played against the Wales' top line of Perreault–Cloutier–Lafleur and was not really a factor in the game. Afterwards, his father came up to him and put the game puck in his hand.

"Go ahead," Walter Gretzky said, "touch it."

"What for?" Wayne asked, surprised.

"You didn't get a chance to touch it all game, so maybe you'd like to touch it now," the elder Gretzky replied with a smile.

But even though that year's was one of the best All–Star Games ever played (and without doubt one of the most successful events off the ice), the game's future itself was up in the air. Most felt a change had to be made—a new format, another Challenge Cup, something—but no conclusive results emerged from the board of governors' meetings. However, the tradition of naming the next year's host city at the game was suspended and everyone left the Joe Louis Arena not knowing where the 1981 game would be played, let alone under what circumstances.

Wales 6   Campbell 3

Wales Conference All–Stars
Scotty Bowman, coach (Buffalo)

1a	G	Don Edwards (Buffalo)
3	D	Ron Stackhouse (Pittsburgh)
4	D	Craig Hartsburg (Minnesota)
6b	D	Jim Schoenfeld (Buffalo)
7	C	Jean Ratelle (Boston)
8	RW	Real Cloutier (Quebec)
9	RW	Gordie Howe (Hartford)
10a	RW	Guy Lafleur (Montreal)
11b	C	Gilbert Perreault (Buffalo)
12	RW	Mike Murphy (Los Angeles)
15	C	Butch Goring (Los Angeles)
16a	C	Marcel Dionne (Los Angeles)
17	RW	Danny Gare (Buffalo)
19a	D	Larry Robinson (Montreal)
23	LW	Bob Gainey (Montreal)
24	D	Dave Burrows (Toronto)
26b	LW	Steve Payne (Minnesota)
27	C	Darryl Sittler (Toronto)
28	D	Reed Larson (Detroit)
30b	G	Gilles Meloche (Minnesota)

Campbell Conference All–Stars
Al Arbour, coach (N.Y. Islanders)

2	D	Lars Lindgren (Vancouver)
4a	D	Mike McEwen (Colorado)
5	D	Robert Picard (Washington)
6	D	Ron Greschner (N.Y. Rangers)
7a	LW	Bill Barber (Philadelphia)
12	LW	Morris Lukowich (Winnipeg)
14b	LW	Blair MacDonald (Edmonton)
16	C	Kent Nilsson (Atlanta)
18	C	Rick MacLeish (Philadelphia)
19a	C	Bryan Trottier (N.Y. Islanders)
20b	D	Jim Watson (Philadelphia)
22	RW	Mike Bossy (N.Y. Islanders)
24	C	Bernie Federko (St. Louis)
25b	D	Norm Barnes (Philadelphia)
26b	LW	Brian Propp (Philadelphia)
27a	RW	Reggie Leach (Philadelphia)
33b	G	Pete Peeters (Philadelphia)
35a	G	Tony Esposito (Chicago)
77	C	Phil Esposito (N.Y. Rangers)
99b	C	Wayne Gretzky (Edmonton)

a=selected to First All–Star Team for first half of season by Professional Hockey Writers' Association

b=selected to Second All–Star Team for first half of season by Professional Hockey Writers' Association

---

First Period
1. Wales: Robinson (unassisted) 3:58
2. Wales: Payne (Murphy, Goring) 4:19
3. Campbell: Leach (McEwen) 7:15
Penalties: Hartsburg (WC) 12:23

Second Period
4. Campbell: Nilsson (Federko, MacLeish) 6:03
Penalties: None

Third Period
5. Campbell: Propp (Esposito, Leach) 4:14
6. Wales: Stackhouse (Sittler, Lafleur) 11:40
7. Wales: Hartsburg (Cloutier, Ratelle) 12:40
8. Wales: Larson (Payne, Perreault) 13:12
9. Wales: Cloutier (Howe) 16:06
Penalties: None

Shots on Goal

Wales	10	5	17	**32**
Campbell	15	4	11	**31**

In Goal
Wales—Edwards/Meloche [Meloche (one goal) replaced Edwards (2 goals) at 9:27 of 2nd period]
Campbell—T. Esposito/Peeters [Peeters (4 goals) replaced Esposito (2 goals) at 15:10 of 1st period]

Referee Dave Newell

Linesmen John D'Amico and Ray Scapinello

Attendance 21,002

MVP Reggie Leach (Philadelphia)

Ennui Sets In

The Forum, Los Angeles, Tuesday, February 10, 1981

Despite trying to end a five-year jinx in which the Campbells hadn't won a game, Philadelphia coach Pat Quinn added a number of his own Flyers to his All–Star team (with the knowledge that each city had to be represented) who fell under the rubrik of "iffy." He chose forwards Paul Holmgren and Eddie Johnstone, and in so doing bypassed Lanny McDonald, Dennis Maruk, Wayne Babych, and Anders Hedberg. Quinn later commented that he saw nothing wrong with picking players from his own team over others: "I feel an obligation to pick my own players," he admitted. "If it hadn't been for my players, I wouldn't be here to pick them." All of which began pledges anew, led by Emile Francis, to have a committee of general managers select the additional players to fill out the roster.

This was the first West Coast game ever played by the All-Stars, and needless to say the glitzy L.A. dinner was, if nothing else, spectacular. Guest entertainers at the Century Plaza Hotel included George Burns, Harvey Korman, Tim Conway, and Gordon Lightfoot. But all these names together couldn't outperform the recently-retired Phil Esposito who danced with a dozen long-legged showgirls to a stylish recording of "The Hockey Sock Rock." The proceeds from the evening went to the Juvenile Diabetes Foundation, and Charles Schulz, the creator of the Peanuts comic strip, was given the Lester Patrick Trophy. In 1975, he had established the Senior World Hockey Tournament for 40–60-year olds, held at the Redwood Empire Ice Arena in Santa Rosa, California that he built himself (first prize for the winning teams was a Golden Snoopy Trophy). It was, to him, a tournament founded on love for the game for those who

never could have made it to the NHL. Pre-game and intermission entertainment came in the form of skaters from the Topanga Plaza Ice Capade Chalet in the San Fernando Valley, choreographed by Gail Pitts.

In an ever-increasing state of controversy, the free agency debate between owners and players once again got all het up at meetings surrounding the All–Star game. "We're at zero, they're at ten," Alan Eagleson said in describing the gap between the two sides. Although he threatened a players' strike, he vowed to pursue a compromise solution that would see salaries rise and teams fairly compensated for loss of players.

The league, meanwhile, approved the sale of the Colorado Rockies to Peter Gilbert who hoped to keep the team in Denver, thereby scuttling earlier rumours the team was on its way to the Meadowlands in New Jersey (rumours that were ultimately prescient).

This was, officially, Scotty Bowman's last game as a head coach. He announced he would never return behind the bench, so immensely content was he as the Sabres' general manager, a position he assumed at the start of the year. History has seen that statement turned on its head as it had after the 1970 game when he promised to remain general manager in St. Louis rather than coach.

Again, the format of All–Star play was challenged, and legendary scribe Frank Orr made a couple of novel suggestions for the game's alteration and improvement. One was to have the Canadian-born players play the best from the rest of the world. Two, to have the Canadian-team players play the American-team players. Part of the greater worry over the game lay not just in the format, but in what was being seen as ennui among players, many

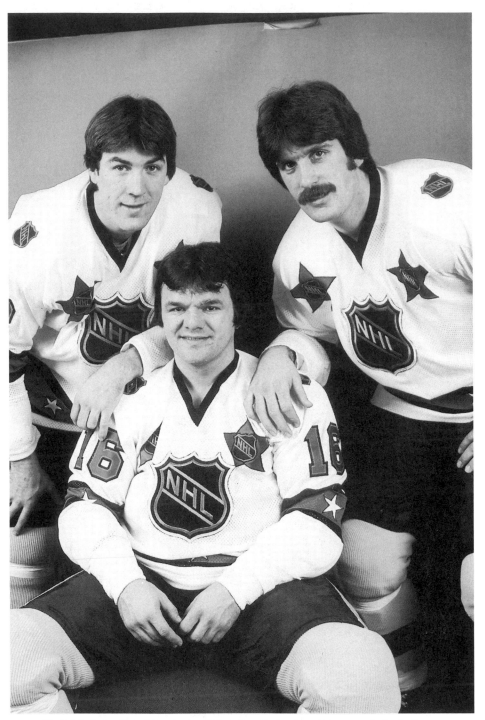

The Triple Crown Line of Los Angeles of (l-r) Dave Taylor, Marcel Dionne, and Charlie Simmer was one of the highest-scoring threesomes of the modern era.

of whom felt little or no obligation any longer to play and preferred a restful long weekend in an ever-demanding hockey season. Bryan Trottier (knee), Larry Robinson (flu), Borje Salming (sinuses), Bill Hajt (ankle), and Guy Lafleur (numerous small wounds) all bowed out of the game, yet all played in their respective team's first game after the All–Star tilt. In short, they could have played in L.A.—they just didn't feel much like it. No incentive. Mark Howe was the most legitimate cancellation after suffering a life-threatening injury. He was named to the team but had to be replaced by Wales boss Bowman because of a serious cut he suffered when he was stabbed in the buttock by the lower plate at the base of the net in a recent game.

Marcel Dionne was particularly critical of Lafleur's withdrawal from the game because of a groin injury, among other things. "I think he should have been with us," the Little Beaver said of the Flower. "When things were going well for him, he showed up. I don't think he should be embarrassed about what he's done in this game in the last nine years." Bowman used Rick Middleton to replace Lafleur, and Robert Picard took Salming's place. The game, in Los Angeles, was also particularly relevant for the Kings' Triple Crown line of Taylor-Dionne-Simmer, all of whom were chosen to last year's team, but only Dionne of which played because of injuries to his linemates. This year was their first All–Star appearance, then, as a line, and they were introduced as one at the end and received a deafening ovation from the hometown fans.

Rod Langway was initially selected by Bowman to replace Robinson but had been bed-ridden with the flu and didn't feel strong enough to play. So, Bowman added Reed Larson instead. But then on the weekend Bill Hajt re-aggravated a sore ankle and Langway was given a second chance. "It's an opportunity I couldn't miss," he said shortly after arriving the day before the game, weak and convalescing.

The game was particularly costly for Bill Barber.

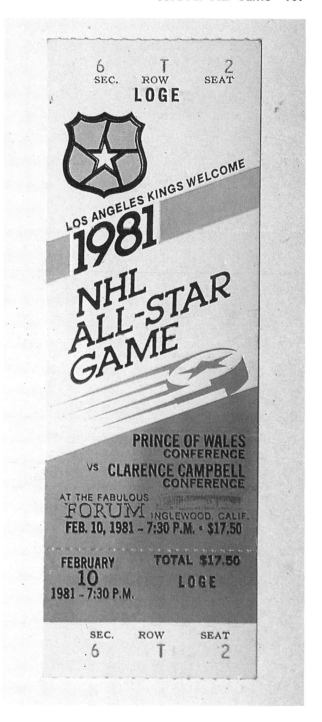

During the game, maintenance workers cleaned the dressing rooms, including all stray paper cups, one of which contained Barber's dentures! But the prize money increased for this year's game: winners got $1,000, losers $750, so Barber still made a little coin after replacement costs for his ivories.

Campbell 4   Wales 1

		Campbell Conference All–Stars Pat Quinn, coach (Philadelphia)				Wales Conference All–Stars Scotty Bowman, coach (Buffalo)
1a	G	Mike Liut (St. Louis)		1b	G	Mario Lessard (Los Angeles)
2	D	Bob Dailey (Philadelphia)		2	D	Rod Langway (Montreal)
3b	D	Behn Wilson (Philadelphia)		4	D	Robert Picard (Toronto)
4a	D	Rob Ramage (Colorado)		5a	D	Mark Howe (Hartford)
5a	D	Denis Potvin (N.Y. Islanders)		7	D	Ray Bourque (Boston)
6	D	Bob Murray (Chicago)		11a	LW	Charlie Simmer (Los Angeles)
7a	LW	Bill Barber (Philadelphia)		12	RW	Rick Middleton (Boston)
10	RW	Wayne Babych (St. Louis)		14	RW	Rick Kehoe (Pittsburgh)
11b	C	Mike Gartner (Washington)		15	C	Bobby Smith (Minnesota)
12	LW	Morris Lukowich (Winnipeg)		16a	C	Marcel Dionne (Los Angeles)
14	C	Bob Bourne (N.Y. Islanders)		17b	C	Mike Rogers (Hartford)
15	C	Kent Nilsson (Calgary)		18a	RW	Dave Taylor (Los Angeles)
17	RW	Paul Holmgren (Philadelphia)		20b	RW	Danny Gare (Buffalo)
18	RW	Eddie Johnstone (Rangers)		22b	LW	Steve Shutt (Montreal)
22b	LW	Dave Williams (Vancouver)		23	LW	Bob Gainey (Montreal)
23a	RW	Mike Bossy (N.Y. Islanders)		25b	D	Randy Carlyle (Pittsburgh)
24	C	Bernie Federko (St. Louis)		26	C	Peter Stastny (Quebec)
25b	D	Kevin McCarthy (Vancouver)		27	RW	John Ogrodnick (Detroit)
33b	G	Pete Peeters (Philadelphia)		28	D	Reed Larson (Detroit)
99b	C	Wayne Gretzky (Edmonton)		33a	G	Don Beaupre (Minnesota)

a=selected to First All–Star team for first half of season by Professional Hockey Writers' Association

b=selected to Second All–Star team for first half of season by Professional Hockey Writers' Association

---

First Period
1. Campbell: Nilsson (Barber, Holmgren) 0:45
2. Campbell: Barber (Johnstone) .... 8:02(sh)
Penalties: Bourne (CC) 7:47, Williams (CC) 10:37

Second Period
3. Campbell: Babych (Johnstone, Federko) 16:12
Penalties: None

Third Period
4. Wales: Ogrodnick (Howe, Kehoe) 6:13
5. Campbell: Wilson (Bossy, Gretzky) 10:18
Penalties: None

Shots on Goal

Campbell	18	13	12	43
Wales	9	8	8	25

In Goal
Campbell—Liut/Peeters [Peeters (one goal) replaced Liut (no goals) at 11:43 of 2nd]
Wales—Beaupre/Lessard [Lessard (2 goals) replaced Beaupre (2 goals) at 11:43 of 2nd]

Referee Bryan Lewis

Linesmen Jim Christison and Gerard Gauthier

Attendance 15,761

MVP Mike Liut (St. Louis)

Gretzky Champions
the Elimination of Fighting

The Capital Center, Landover, Maryland, Tuesday, February 9, 1982

As part of the All–Star festivities in 1982, the players, governors, and league officials were received at the White House at a luncheon hosted by President Ronald Reagan. The menu included crab bisque and cheese straws, roast tenderloin of beef with potatoes mascotte, mushrooms, and tomatoes St. Germain. The head table included Reagan, Wayne Gretzky, Gordie Howe, league president John Ziegler, Bob Hope, Canadian Ambassador Allan Gotlieb, and Ken Taylor, hero, the former Canadian ambassador to Iran who had helped save the lives of six American hostages. In 1939, "Dutch" Reagan had worn a New York Americans sweater in the movie *Hell's Kitchen*, starring the Dead End Kids. Now Ziegler presented the president with an All–Star sweater with the number 1 and his name on it.

As player president of the NHL Players' Association, Tony Esposito was a last-minute invitee. When he showed up at the White House, there was no invitation for him and he wasn't admitted to the luncheon. At the NHLPA meeting, he took just as tough a stance on behalf of the negotiating players as the White House had on his sudden appearance.

"It's all money," he said. "Teams are replacing veterans with kids to decrease their payrolls. They're moving the veterans out because they don't want to pay them the sizeable contracts they've earned. The owners like it the way it is, but it's not going to stay like this and they know it. We're not going to accept all their terms, even if it means a strike."

Undeterred, the NHL board of governors' meeting

consisted mostly of discussions about salvaging the Colorado Rockies franchise. Owner Peter Gilbert had been losing millions since acquiring the team just a year before and he wanted to move the team to New Jersey. John Ziegler hoped a new owner could be found in Denver, so he put off any decision to move the team until all local avenues had been exhausted.

Given the financial climate in his team's city, Colorado's Don Lever, for one, found himself in the lineup with mixed emotions.

"I played the right side with Secord and Savard, and it's a tremendous experience for any player to be in an All–Star Game," he recalled some time later. "But I was a little preoccupied that night. The league was having meetings on our franchise [the Rockies] and I didn't know if I was going to be representing a team or a former team. I know it would have been a much more enjoyable experience without that kind of thing hanging over our team."

The only other matters the owners discussed included an agreement to have general managers vote on the winner of the Vezina Trophy at the end of the regular season. Ziegler also named 15 people to a committee to review the procedure by which disciplinary matters were handled, which had become relevant in the aftermath of Flyers goon Paul Holmgren incurring what many felt was not a stiff enough sentence for assaulting referee Andy van Hellemond.

As usual, not everybody was happy with the players the two coaches added to their rosters. Some wondered why Dino Ciccarelli was named to play but Guy Lafleur, Marcel Dionne, and Bob Gainey were not. Bob Manno of the Leafs replaced Borje Salming, who was again injured when it came time for the game. John Van Boxmeer, a First Team starter for the Wales, broke a finger on his left hand just days before the game and also had to withdraw.

In a remarkable twist to the 1982 game, the Prince of Wales had only one player (Ray Bourque) who was under 25 years of age while the Campbells had but one (Dave Taylor) who was over that age. Youth

Perennial All–Star Mike Bossy tries to break free from traffic in Washington during the 34th All–Star Game.

versus Experience was the theme of the game, and it was the latter that won it that year.

The official pre-game banquet was held the night of February 8 in the International Ballroom at the Washington Hilton Hotel and was attended by 1,600 people, with proceeds going to the Juvenile Diabetes Foundation. Entertainment was provided by Bob Hope, Gloria Loring, Rich Little, Larry King, and the Sammy Shreiber Orchestra.

Pre-game ceremonies at centre ice featured Gordie Howe and Phil Esposito with Ken Taylor between them to face off the opening puck.

By now, Wayne Gretzky was the darling of the NHL. At game time, he had already scored an unheard of 69 goals, and the reception given him by the Capital Center fans was testament to his league-wide popularity. He dazzled under the spotlight, and the crowd was treated to an exciting game that featured speed and a little hitting and renewed calls for the league to eliminate fighting. Wayne Gretzky was first to champion the cause and Phil Esposito seconded the motion:

"Both teams played well, and the amount of hitting was somewhat surprising. But, you know, the big thing this proved to me is that fighting should be out of the game. Hockey doesn't need it, and tonight proved it."

A rare All–Star Game injury that kept Rod Langway on the shelf for three weeks occurred when he hurt his knee in a three-way collision with Ray Bourque and Doug Wilson. On the humourous side, Paul Coffey, playing in his first game, recalled hitting Bill Barber "kind of from behind. He [Barber] turned to me and said: 'Relax, kid. It's the All–Star Game.' I told him, 'Oops, sorry.'"

For the sixth straight year, an unlimited sudden-death overtime rule was in effect in case of a tie after 60 minutes, but it wasn't required. Playing as an all-Islanders line, Bossy, Tonelli, and Trottier dominated play and Bossy won the traditional car as the MVP. "I had a little extra incentive," Bossy revealed afterward. "My wife doesn't drive, but she said she was going to learn to drive if I won the car."

Two of the greats meet on ice, goalie Grant Fuhr of the dynastic Edmonton Oilers and Quebec's Peter Stastny, the highest-scoring player of the '80s with but one exception-Wayne Gretzky.

Wales 4   Campbell 2

Wales Conference All–Stars
Al Arbour, coach (N.Y. Islanders)

1b	G	Don Edwards (Buffalo)
3	D	Barry Beck (N.Y. Rangers)
5	D	Mike Ramsey (Buffalo)
6a	D	Ray Bourque (Boston)
7a	LW	Bill Barber "C" (Philadelphia)
8b	LW	Marc Tardif (Quebec)
9b	C	Bryan Trottier (N.Y. Islanders)
10	C	Ron Duguay (N.Y. Rangers)
12	C	Keith Acton (Montreal)
16b	RW	Rick Middleton (Boston)
17	D	Rod Langway (Montreal)
19b	D	Larry Robinson (Montreal)
20	C	Dennis Maruk (Washington)
21	LW	Blaine Stoughton (Hartford)
22a	RW	Mike Bossy (N.Y. Islanders)
25b	D	Randy Carlyle (Pittsburgh)
26a	C	Peter Stastny (Quebec)
27	LW	John Tonelli (N.Y. Islanders)
28	LW	Brian Propp (Philadelphia)
29	G	Michel Dion (Pittsburgh)

Campbell Conference All–Stars
Glen Sonmor, coach (Minnesota)

1a	G	Grant Fuhr (Edmonton)
2	D	Bob Manno (Toronto)
3	D	Pekka Rautakallio (Calgary)
4b	D	Craig Hartsburg (Minnesota)
7a	D	Paul Coffey (Edmonton)
9	C	Don Lever (Colorado)
10	C	Dale Hawerchuk (Winnipeg)
11a	LW	Mark Messier (Edmonton)
12	LW	Brian Sutter (St. Louis)
15	C	Bobby Smith (Minnesota)
17b	C	Denis Savard (Chicago)
18a	RW	Dave Taylor "C" (Los Angeles)
19b	RW	Dino Ciccarelli (Minnesota)
20b	LW	Al Secord (Chicago)
22	RW	Rick Vaive (Toronto)
24a	D	Doug Wilson (Chicago)
26	RW	John Ogrodnick (Detroit)
27b	G	Gilles Meloche (Minnesota)
28	D	Harold Snepsts (Vancouver)
99a	C	Wayne Gretzky (Edmonton)

a=selected to First All–Star Team for first half of season by Professional Hockey Writers' Association   b=selected to Second All–Star Team for first half of season by Professional Hockey Writers' Association

---

First Period
1. Campbell: Vaive (Sutter) 2:32
2. Wales: Bourque (Maruk, Carlyle) . . . . 12:03(pp)
3. Wales: Tardif (Middleton, P. Stastny) 13:27
Penalties: Tardif (WC) 5:40, Hartsburg (CC) 10:36

Second Period
4. Campbell: Gretzky (Coffey, Ciccarelli) 0:26
5. Wales: Bossy (Beck, Tonelli) 17:10
Penalties: Hawerchuk (CC) 3:52, Tardif (WC) 13:13

Third Period
6. Wales: Bossy (Robinson) 1:19
Penalties: Stoughton (WC) 2:37

Shots on Goal

Wales	8	16	7	31
Campbell	17	5	6	28

In Goal
Wales—Dion/Edwards [Edwards (no goals) replaced Dion (2 goals) at 10:23 of 2nd period]
Campbell—Fuhr/Meloche [Meloche (2 goals) replaced Fuhr (2 goals) at 10:23 of 2nd period]

Referee Wally Harris

Linesmen Ron Finn and Swede Knox

Attendance 18,130

MVP Mike Bossy (N.Y. Islanders)

Gretzky Versus Marini

Nassau County Coliseum, Long Island, Tuesday, February 8, 1983

What had by now become the annual criticise-the-format fest featured Alan Eagleson's proposal to return to the tried and true with the Stanley Cup winners—or, more originally, the host city's team—playing the All–Stars. And Oilers coach Glen Sather lambasted the writers for their selections, notably because his own Mark Messier was left off the First Team.

"How is a guy who is second in league scoring left off the First All–Star Team?" he began before

The Great One and the Great One Sr., Walter Gretzky.

broadening his palette of complaints. "I don't think the system is right.... Only travelling media should vote. Plus, there should be some sort of collaboration between media and coaches."

For the first time, the All–Star dinner was held on ice, at the Nassau Coliseum, where some 2,000 seats were sold at $200 for the dinner while another 6,000 fans paid a more modest $15 to listen in from the stands to entertainment that included Anne Murray and Billy Crystal. Islanders general manager Bill Torrey was given the Lester Patrick Award and popular local comedian and radio DJ Don Imus was emcee for the night. Imus riled the nearby New Jersey Devils franchise (which had been the Colorado Rockies until very recently) by making a number of disparaging remarks about the team's futility. The proceeds from both the dinner and show benefited the Juvenile Diabetes Foundation.

Later, the board of governors met. Their number one priority was to discuss moving the St. Louis Blues to Saskatoon, Saskatchewan, but they decided to let the matter rest until the end of the season. On another issue, they voted 19–2 to abolish the long pants— called Cooperalls—that were being worn by only Hartford and Philadelphia (not surprisingly, these were the two dissenting votes at table), and so ended one of the league's great equipment experiments.

Meanwhile, matters got worse for the reputation of the All–Star Game when president Ziegler revealed that not only had the league not named a city for the 1984 game, but apparently none of them wanted to host it. Quebec had been awarded the honour but team president Marcel Aubut backed out, saying that his Nordiques weren't ready to take on the challenge.

Goalie John Garrett seemed to have MVP honours locked up for this game. After he'd made a few impressive saves, teammate Lanny McDonald skated by and told him he'd won the glove compartment (of the car that was given away every year to the MVP). A few more saves and McDonald was saying Garrett had the tires. In a while, Lanny was asking if he

wanted a four- or a five-speed. Then Gretzky, playing on an all-Edmonton line with Kurri and Messier, scored four goals in the third period and drove off in the car, leaving McDonald to solace the goalie by saying Gretzky had promised to let him ride in the back!

Garrett was thankful to be playing in the All–Star Game at all, since he was replacing the injured Richard Brodeur. And the only reason for that was that he had been traded just a few days before the game from Quebec to Vancouver. He had been Brodeur's backup when King Richard was felled by a Dan Daoust slapshot in a Leafs–Canucks game. Brodeur had punctured an eardrum, so Garrett not only finished that game but got to replace Brodeur in the All–Star Game too. And the only reason that happened was that Brodeur was Vancouver's sole representative so Campbells coach Roger Neilson didn't have any choice.

"The atmosphere was pretty loose in the room," Garrett said. "The guys were getting on me pretty good about how I got there, but I joked with them, telling them I was going to win the car."

And he came close to doing it, but perhaps Gretzky merely saved face for the NHL with his performance. Having Garrett win the MVP would not have bode well for the way players were selected to the teams. "Imagine," Garrett said before the game in mock earnest, "me, head-to-head against Hector Marini."

Marini was on the team as New Jersey's sole representative even though more talented right wingers (Rick Middleton and Mike Gartner) were on the sidelines.

"I came close to scoring," Marini later recalled. "I was playing on a line with Don Maloney and Darryl Sittler. I shot from the point, and I thought I'd scored, but Maloney said he tipped it in. Oh well. Playing in the game was a big thrill. I was a fringe player, and there's no way I'd be selected if they didn't have to take one [player] from each team."

Gretzky's big third period also set a number of All–Star Game records, including most goals in a game and period and most points in a period, and he tied the record for most points in a game (Gordie

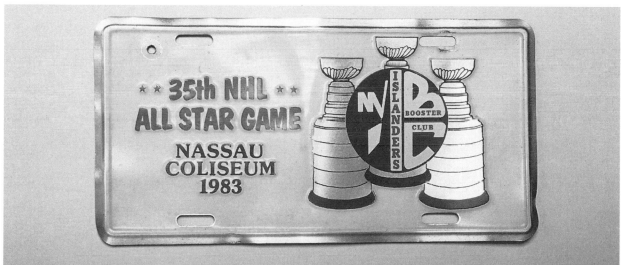

Howe, Pete Mahovlich, and Ted Lindsay had also recorded four). Said Gretzky:

"Speaking honestly, I haven't played well in All–Star Games. I guess you could say when it came to the All–Star Game, I had a bad attitude. Except, until this year, I'd managed to convince myself it was the right attitude. I convinced myself that the All–Star Game was supposed to be fun. My idea was this was the one game of the year that I didn't have to prepare to play."

That year, he changed his approach.

"I went to bed fairly early Monday. I enjoyed a very relaxing weekend at Atlantic City. I promised myself I'd prepare for this one. I had a good rest in the afternoon. I'd received so much criticism that it started to bother me. I decided I wanted to show people I could play well in this game, too.... Trouble is, I felt really lousy when I got to the rink tonight. I told Vicki [Moss, his girlfriend] I didn't feel as good as I thought I should. The last time I told her I didn't feel good before a game was just before the Philadelphia Flyers game last year."

That had been the night he scored five goals, including his 50th of the season, in his 39th game. Entering the 1983 All–Star Game, he led the league in scoring by an astronomical 52 points.

At least one other player paid a price for the Great One's success at this game, though. Gretzky scored all four of the goals that robbed Garrett of the car against Pelle Lindbergh, whose confidence was so shaken by the barrage that he couldn't regain his all–star form in the days after the game and wound up finishing the season in the minors. It would be the next season before he could re-establish the confidence required to play at the highest level.

As for the Professional Hockey Writers' Association, it added three names to its Good Guy Award (begun in 1981) by including George Gross (Toronto), Tom Fitzgerald (Boston), and Jack Dulmage (Windsor) on a plaque displayed at the U.S. Hockey Hall of Fame in Eveleth, Minnesota.

Campbell 9   Wales 3

<table>
<tr><td colspan="4">Campbell Conference All–Stars
Roger Neilson, coach (Vancouver)</td></tr>
<tr><td>3</td><td>D</td><td>Willie Huber (Detroit)</td></tr>
<tr><td>4b</td><td>D</td><td>Craig Hartsburg (Minnesota)</td></tr>
<tr><td>6</td><td>D</td><td>Bob Murray (Chicago)</td></tr>
<tr><td>7b</td><td>D</td><td>Paul Coffey (Edmonton)</td></tr>
<tr><td>8</td><td>C</td><td>Neal Broten (Minnesota)</td></tr>
<tr><td>9a</td><td>RW</td><td>Lanny McDonald (Calgary)</td></tr>
<tr><td>10</td><td>LW</td><td>Brian Sutter (St. Louis)</td></tr>
<tr><td>11b</td><td>LW</td><td>Mark Messier (Edmonton)</td></tr>
<tr><td>12</td><td>LW</td><td>Tom McCarthy (Minnesota)</td></tr>
<tr><td>16</td><td>C</td><td>Marcel Dionne (Los Angeles)</td></tr>
<tr><td>17</td><td>LW</td><td>Jari Kurri (Edmonton)</td></tr>
<tr><td>18b</td><td>C</td><td>Denis Savard (Chicago)</td></tr>
<tr><td>19b</td><td>RW</td><td>Dino Ciccarelli (Minnesota)</td></tr>
<tr><td>20a</td><td>LW</td><td>Al Secord (Chicago)</td></tr>
<tr><td>22</td><td>RW</td><td>Rick Vaive (Toronto)</td></tr>
<tr><td>24a</td><td>D</td><td>Doug Wilson (Chicago)</td></tr>
<tr><td>30a</td><td>G</td><td>Murray Bannerman (Chicago)</td></tr>
<tr><td>31</td><td>G</td><td>John Garrett (Vancouver)</td></tr>
<tr><td>44a</td><td>D</td><td>Dave Babych (Winnipeg)</td></tr>
<tr><td>99a</td><td>C</td><td>Wayne Gretzky (Edmonton)</td></tr>
</table>

<table>
<tr><td colspan="4">Wales Conference All–Stars
Al Arbour, coach (N.Y. Islanders)</td></tr>
<tr><td>1a</td><td>G</td><td>Pete Peeters (Boston)</td></tr>
<tr><td>2a</td><td>D</td><td>Mark Howe (Philadelphia)</td></tr>
<tr><td>4</td><td>D</td><td>Mike Ramsey (Buffalo)</td></tr>
<tr><td>5a</td><td>D</td><td>Denis Potvin (N.Y. Islanders)</td></tr>
<tr><td>6b</td><td>D</td><td>Rod Langway (Washington)</td></tr>
<tr><td>7b</td><td>D</td><td>Ray Bourque (Boston)</td></tr>
<tr><td>8</td><td>C</td><td>Ron Francis (Hartford)</td></tr>
<tr><td>10b</td><td>C</td><td>Barry Pederson (Boston)</td></tr>
<tr><td>11a</td><td>LW</td><td>Ryan Walter (Montreal)</td></tr>
<tr><td>12</td><td>LW</td><td>Don Maloney (N.Y. Rangers)</td></tr>
<tr><td>16b</td><td>LW</td><td>Michel Goulet (Quebec)</td></tr>
<tr><td>17</td><td>RW</td><td>Rick Kehoe (Pittsburgh)</td></tr>
<tr><td>18a</td><td>RW</td><td>Marian Stastny (Quebec)</td></tr>
<tr><td>19</td><td>C</td><td>Bryan Trottier (N.Y. Islanders)</td></tr>
<tr><td>20</td><td>C</td><td>Hector Marini (New Jersey)</td></tr>
<tr><td>22b</td><td>RW</td><td>Mike Bossy (N.Y. Islanders)</td></tr>
<tr><td>26a</td><td>C</td><td>Peter Stastny (Quebec)</td></tr>
<tr><td>27</td><td>C</td><td>Darryl Sittler (Philadelphia)</td></tr>
<tr><td>28</td><td>D</td><td>Dave Langevin (N.Y. Islanders)</td></tr>
<tr><td>31b</td><td>G</td><td>Pelle Lindbergh (Philadelphia)</td></tr>
</table>

a=selected to First All–Star Team for first half of season by Professional Hockey Writers' Association

b=selected to Second All–Star Team for first half of season by Professional Hockey Writers' Association

First Period

1. Wales: Goulet (P. Stastny) 3:41
2. Campbell: Babych (McDonald, Sutter) . . . . . 11:37(pp)
3. Wales: Bourque (unassisted) 19:01

Penalties: Sutter (CC) 6:26, Langevin (WC) 10:58

Second Period

4. Campbell: Ciccarelli (Broten, Secord) 3:01
5. Campbell: McCarthy (Ciccarelli, Murray) 14:51

Penalties: None

Third Period

6. Campbell: Gretzky (Kurri, Coffey) 6:20
7. Campbell: McDonald (Sutter, Dionne) 7:29
8. Campbell: Gretzky (Messier, Kurri) 10:31
9. Wales: Maloney (Marini) 14:04
10. Campbell: Gretzky (Wilson, Messier) 15:32
11. Campbell: Vaive (unassisted) 17:15
12. Campbell: Gretzky (Messier) 19:18

Penalties: Ramsey (WC) 3:33

Shots on Goal

Campbell	5	12	15	**32**
Wales	10	16	8	**34**

In Goal

Campbell—Bannerman/Garrett [Garrett (one goal) replaced Bannerman (2 goals) at 10:04 of 2nd period]

Wales—Peeters/Lindbergh [Lindbergh (7 goals) replaced Peeters (2 goals) at 10:04 of 2nd period]

Referee Bob Myers

Linesmen Leon Stickle and Ryan Bozak

Attendance 15,230

MVP Wayne Gretzky (Edmonton)

The All–Star Team of Injured Players

Meadowlands Arena, New Jersey, Tuesday, January 31, 1984

For Wayne Gretzky, coming into New Jersey's home arena for the All–Star Game in 1984 was fraught with anxiety. It was his second visit to the Meadowlands since he'd called the Devils a "Mickey Mouse" franchise after his Oilers hammered them 13–4 on November 19 in Edmonton (Gretzky had eight points that night). His first game back in New Jersey, just two weeks before the All–Stars would play, had been tinged with humour and venom. Fans wore Mickey Mouse ears and one group held placards to spell out "Say Cheese" when the Oilers skated out for their warmup.

Generally the diplomat off ice as well as on,

Gretzky taped a special appeal before the game requesting a liver donor for a sick infant in nearby Amherstburg. The tape was played on the giant screen above centre ice during the game in the hope that eight-month-old Eric Middleton's life could be saved. Unfortunately, all the criticism over the Mickey Mouse remarks was not balanced by praise for the generous mission that followed it.

Gretzky had begun the season with the most phenomenal point-scoring streak the league had ever seen. He scored at least one point in each of the team's first 51 games and with each game it seemed ever more certain he'd get a point in every one for

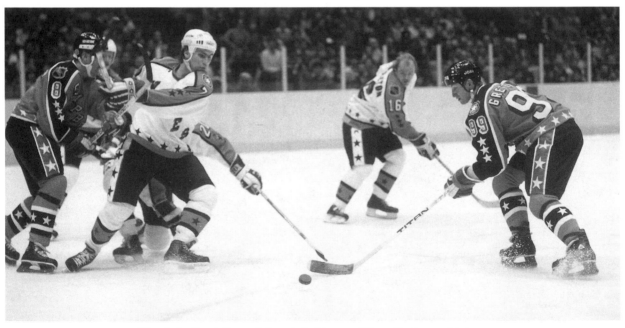

Although the Campbells scored six goals in this game, Wayne Gretzky scored just once as he watches teammate Glenn Anderson try to hold up defenceman Ray Bourque on this play.

the whole season. But he injured his shoulder toward the end of the streak, which ended in Los Angeles just before the All–Star break. After a sub-par glitter game, which he could have taken off because of the shoulder, he left New Jersey in pain.

"It's really hurting me," he said, "but I figured I came all the way down here to play in this game, and I wasn't only going to play one shift, whether I hurt my shoulder badly or not." In the end, he would miss six games before he could get back in the Edmonton lineup two weeks later.

Bernie Nicholls didn't get hurt in the game, but he, too, left New Jersey in pain, with a broken jaw. Ironically, he was playing in place of injured teammate Marcel Dionne.

"I had broken it in Calgary," Nicholls said, but doctors had given him clearance to continue to play. "Then I played in Edmonton and then in the All–Star Game without knowing it was broken. I couldn't even eat at the [All–Star] dinner. I found out after the game that it was broken."

In addition to the problems with Gretzky and Nicholls, no fewer than six players sat out the game because of injuries: Jari Kurri (strained knee), Marcel Dionne (voted to the Campbell roster, sprained ankle), Tony Tanti (cut hand), Al Jensen (Wales starting goalie, bad back), Bryan Trottier (knee surgery), and Mike Bossy (knee). And the list of replacements hardly indicated that fans would be getting an equal tradeoff in talent, mostly because coaches still had to have each team represented. Local favourite Chico Resch would be in for Jensen even though Tom Barrasso had been third in the voting for goalies, Tim Kerr for Bossy, Pierre Larouche for Trottier, Charlie Simmer for Kurri, Darcy Rota for Tanti, and Bernie Nicholls for Dionne.

In an All–Star Game first, Mark Messier played in the game despite being in the middle of a six-game suspension. (Dave Forbes had been barred from playing in the 1975 game under similar circumstances when Clarence Campbell was NHL president.) The league's executive vice-president, Bryan O'Neill, suspended Messier for six games on January 26 for a stick-swinging incident against Thomas Gradin of

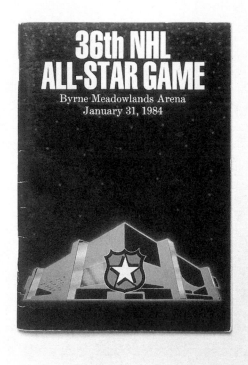

Vancouver but ruled that Messier could still play with the All–Stars even though his suspension would not end until the week after the game.

The now annual game-format discussion seemed to focus on having four All–Star teams—one for each division—play elimination games and then a final game, thus providing more bang for the buck, as it were. Though well liked, the idea never got off the ground. Still, overall the board of governors' meetings were surprisingly quiet, with only one serious and ubiquitous concern on the agenda—the Pittsburgh Penguins. While attendance throughout the league was increasing, the Pens were averaging only 5,000 fans a game, and like St. Louis the previous year, there was real concern a new home would have to be found for the team.

The annual dinner was held at the Loews Glen-Pointe Hotel and the proceeds went to the Boy Scouts of America. The emcee was Alan Thicke and entertainment was provided by John Allan Cameron and later in the evening by the Artie Shaw Orchestra.

League president John Ziegler awarded this year's Lester Patrick winner posthumously to Art Ross.

Coach Glen Sather began the game playing Rick Vaive with Wayne Gretzky and Messier but soon put Glenn Anderson between his Oilers mates after trying "Andy" with Darcy Rota and Denis Savard. Don Maloney, this year's MVP, tied the All–Star Game record for most points and most assists in a game with a goal and three helpers.

"I couldn't believe it when I won the car," he said later. "It was like being on 'The Price Is Right'.... I remember thinking after the second period, 'Boy, if I get a goal, I have a shot at winning the car.' I scored with 10 or 12 minutes left in the game, and I thought, 'Alright, I've got a pretty good chance.... But Chico Resch started making all these big saves. I figured he might end up winning."

Players on the winning team took home $1,000 while the losers got $750, and the opening faceoff was graced by the presence of Gordie Howe dropping the puck.

Wales 7   Campbell 6

Wales Conference All–Stars
Al Arbour, coach (N.Y. Islanders)

1b	G	Pete Peeters (Boston)
2	D	Joe Cirella (New Jersey)
4b	D	Rod Langway (Washington)
5a	D	Denis Potvin "C" (N.Y. Islanders)
6b	D	Phil Housley (Buffalo)
7a	D	Ray Bourque (Boston)
10	C	Barry Pederson (Boston)
11	C	Gilbert Perreault (Buffalo)
12	LW	Don Maloney (N.Y. Rangers)
14	LW	Mark Johnson (Hartford)
15a	LW	Michel Goulet (Quebec)
16b	RW	Rick Middleton (Boston)
17	C	Tim Kerr (Philadelphia)
20	D	Mike O'Connell (Boston)
23	C	Mike Bullard (Pittsburgh)
25	LW	Mats Naslund (Montreal)
26b	LW	Brian Propp (Philadelphia)
27b	C	Peter Stastny (Quebec)
28	C	Pierre Larouche (N.Y. Rangers)
30	G	Glenn Resch (New Jersey)

Campbell Conference All–Stars
Glen Sather, coach (Edmonton)

4b	D	Kevin Lowe (Edmonton)
5a	D	Rob Ramage (St. Louis)
6	D	Brad Maxwell (Minnesota)
7a	D	Paul Coffey (Edmonton)
8	RW	Glenn Anderson (Edmonton)
9	RW	Lanny McDonald (Calgary)
10	LW	Charlie Simmer (Los Angeles)
11b	LW	Mark Messier (Edmonton)
12	C	Bernie Nicholls (Los Angeles)
17	LW	Darcy Rota (Vancouver)
18	C	Denis Savard (Chicago)
19	C	Steve Yzerman (Detroit)
22b	RW	Rick Vaive (Toronto)
23	RW	Brian Bellows (Minnesota)
24b	D	Doug Wilson (Chicago)
25a	RW	John Ogrodnick (Detroit)
30a	G	Murray Bannerman (Chicago)
31b	G	Grant Fuhr (Edmonton)
44	D	Dave Babych (Winnipeg)
99a	C	Wayne Gretzky "C" (Edmonton)

a=selected to First All–Star Team for first half of season by Professional Hockey Writers' Association

b=selected to Second All–Star Team for first half of season by Professional Hockey Writers' Association

First Period

1. Wales: Cirella (P. Stastny) 8:51
2. Wales: Potvin (Kerr, Goulet) 9:30
3. Wales: Middleton (Pederson, Housley) 14:49
4. Wales: Naslund (Maloney, Potvin) 16:40
5. Wales: Larouche (Johnson, Maloney) 17:14

Penalties: Housley (WC) 17:43

Second Period

6. Campbell: Savard (Vaive, Rota) 1:23
7. Campbell: Rota (Vaive, Savard) 5:51
8. Campbell: Ogrodnick (Yzerman) 6:42
9. Wales: Larouche (Maloney, Johnson) 17:34

Penalties: None

Third Period

10. Wales: Maloney (Johnson, Cirella) 7:24
11. Campbell: Babych (Ogrodnick) 8:11
12. Campbell: Gretzky (Vaive, Simmer) 11:23
13. Campbell: Bellows (Wilson) 17:37

Penalties: Maxwell (CC) 9:04, Resch (WC) 14:19

Shots on Goal

Wales	13	11	6	**30**
Campbell	13	15	10	**38**

In Goal

Wales—Peeters/Resch [Resch (3 goals) replaced Peeters (3 goals) at 10:06 of 2nd period]

Campbell—Bannerman/Fuhr [Fuhr (2 goals) replaced Bannerman (5 goals) at 10:06 of 2nd period]

Referee Bruce Hood

Linesmen Ray Scapinello and John D'Amico

Attendance 18,939

MVP Don Maloney (N.Y. Rangers)

The Oilers Reign Supreme

Olympic Saddledome, Calgary, Tuesday, February 12, 1985

The 1985 game marked the inauguration of a new tradition, naming honourary captains for each team (in this case, Guy Lafleur and Glenn Hall) to represent their respective conferences.

Lafleur was in an unusual situation. Because he was under 35, the Canadiens would still have to protect him after putting him on the voluntary retired list just a few months before, or he could be claimed on waivers. This had already happened with Serge Savard, who had been coaxed out of retirement by Winnipeg. When the Habs wanted Savard as their general manager, they had to acquire him from the Jets for a third-round draft choice.

The league was a little quick off the mark in giving Lafleur his title as honourary captain, though. He had only retired on November 26, 1984, less than three months before, and although he stayed out of the game for four years, he was not done entirely. He came back to play for the Rangers and the Nordiques and thus became the only NHLer to play in the league *after* he'd been an honourary captain.

In other business, the league finally seemed ready

OLYMPIC SADDLEDOME
CALGARY, ALBERTA
FEBRUARY 12, 1985

to consider putting the job of voting for the starting lineups in the hands of the fans, if only because the game was getting so little media coverage that a change might stir some writers to action. The popular choice was a fan ballot system similar to that adopted by America's Big Three of sports, baseball, football, and basketball. If fans fulfilled everyone's greatest fear and stuffed the ballot boxes, then at least they would be participating in the game and seeing their favourite players, which was reason enough to implement the system.

Phil Russell of the Devils, who was in town only to attend NHL Players' Association meetings, was a last-minute replacement for Brad Marsh, who was snowed in in Toronto and was himself a fill-in for injured Philly teammate Mark Howe. Steve Payne substituted for Minnesota teammate Tony McKegney, who'd separated his shoulder in the last North Stars game before the big dance. Buffalo's Bill Hajt had also separated his shoulder and was replaced by Mike Ramsey.

The All–Star banquet was held at the Calgary Con-vention Centre and proceeds from the $250-a-plate dinner benefited the Olympic Trust of Canada and the Canadian Special Olympics. Larry Mann was the master of ceremonies and music was provided by Larry Gatlin and the Gatlin Brothers Band. In keeping with the dinner's tradition, the Lester Patrick Award was given to Jack Butterfield (president of the American Hockey League) and Arthur Wirtz (longtime owner of the Blackhawks). The Calgary hosts abandoned the black tie dress code, though, and asked everyone to wear Western garb. The results ranged from the genuinely impressive to the absurd, but one and all gamely acquiesced.

The opening faceoff was remarkable in that it was conducted by Canadian astronaut Marc Garneau using a puck he had taken to outer space. Then the players from both teams contributed vocals for the song "Tears Are Not Enough," a song written by Bryan Adams, recorded by a wide assortment of Canadian artists and produced by David Foster to help relieve the devastating Ethiopian famine. This version of the

The sensational Mario Lemieux became the first rookie to win the MVP award
when he was so honoured at the 1985 All–Star Game.

video also featured footage from the $1-a-day skate that had been held the morning of the All–Star Game. Second-intermission entertainment was provided by the Calgary Fiddlers of Mount Royal College.

The line of Lemieux–Muller–Hedberg dominated the game. Lemieux and Muller, both 19-year-old rookies, had gone one-two in the draft the previous year, while Hedberg was at the end of a glorious career that had started in Sweden and ended triumphantly in the NHL via the WHA. Lemieux was the youngest player ever to win the MVP car, and Mike Krushelnyski and Ray Bourque were selected second and third stars respectively. Mario had promised to give the car to his older brother, Alain,

who had been a less heralded NHL player. "He asked me for it," Mario revealed with a smile. In his rookie year, Lemieux was already being hailed as the next Gretzky, although at 24 the Great One still had a little hockey left in his bones. "I remember when I was 18 or 19," Gretzky recalled. "I was playing with guys 28 or 29. Now I'm 24 and playing with 18- and 19-year-olds."

The Campbells were laden with Oilers (no less than eight) and the self-made Gretzky–Kurri–Krushelnyski line was their best, although Gretzky later admitted that when he missed an open net late in the game— in dreaded Calgary, of all places—it was one of the most embarrassing moments of his career.

Wales 6   Campbell 4

Wales Conference All–Stars
Honourary Captain: Guy Lafleur
Al Arbour, coach (N.Y. Islanders)

2	D	Phil Russell (New Jersey)
3b	D	Scott Stevens (Washington)
5a	D	Rod Langway (Washington)
6	D	Mike Ramsey (Buffalo)
7a	D	Ray Bourque (Boston)
9	C	Ron Francis (Hartford)
10b	C	Bob Carpenter (Washington)
11	RW	Mike Gartner (Washington)
12b	C	Tim Kerr (Philadelphia)
15	RW	Anders Hedberg (N.Y. Rangers)
16b	LW	Michel Goulet (Quebec)
17	C	Kirk Muller (New Jersey)
19	C	Bryan Trottier (N.Y. Islanders)
21a	C	Brent Sutter (N.Y. Islanders)
22a	RW	Mike Bossy "C" (N.Y. Islanders)
24b	D	Chris Chelios (Montreal)
27a	LW	John Tonelli (N.Y. Islanders)
30a	G	Tom Barrasso (Buffalo)
31b	G	Pelle Lindbergh (Philadelphia)
66	C	Mario Lemieux (Pittsburgh)

Campbell Conference All–Stars
Honourary Captain: Glenn Hall
Glen Sather, coach (Edmonton)

2	D	Al MacInnis (Calgary)
4	D	Kevin Lowe (Edmonton)
7a	D	Paul Coffey (Edmonton)
8b	D	Randy Carlyle (Winnipeg)
9	RW	Glenn Anderson (Edmonton)
10b	C	Dale Hawerchuk (Winnipeg)
11b	LW	Brian Sutter (St. Louis)
14	RW	Miroslav Frycer (Toronto)
15b	RW	Paul MacLean (Winnipeg)
16	C	Marcel Dionne "C" (Los Angeles)
17a	RW	Jari Kurri (Edmonton)
20	C	Thomas Gradin (Vancouver)
23b	D	Paul Reinhart (Calgary)
24a	D	Doug Wilson (Chicago)
25a	LW	John Ogrodnick (Detroit)
26	C	Mike Krushelnyski (Edmonton)
31b	G	Grant Fuhr (Edmonton)
35a	G	Andy Moog (Edmonton)
44	LW	Steve Payne (Minnesota)
99a	C	Wayne Gretzky (Edmonton)

a=selected to First All–Star Team for first half of season by Professional Hockey Writers' Association

b=selected to Second All–Star Team for first half of season by Professional Hockey Writers' Association

First Period

1. Wales: Francis (Kerr) 1:40
2. Wales: Kerr (Goulet, Bourque) 5:31
3. Campbell: Dionne (Ogrodnick, MacInnis) . . . . . . 6:33(pp)
4. Campbell: Frycer (Krushelnyski, Carlyle) 16:35
Penalties: Muller (WC) 6:20

Second Period

5. Wales: Hedberg (Lemieux, Langway). 13:46
6. Wales: Lemieux (Muller, Bourque) 17:47
Penalties: None

Third Period

7. Campbell: Gretzky (Krushelnyski) 10:09
8. Wales: Lemieux (Bourque). 11:09
9. Campbell: Carlyle (Krushelnyski) 17:09
10. Wales: Gartner (Bourque). . . . . 19:51(en)
Penalties: Russell (WC) 1:52, Dionne (CC) 6:46

Shots on Goal

Wales	14	10	12	**36**
Campbell	7	10	9	**26**

In Goal

Wales—Barrasso/Lindbergh [Lindbergh (2 goals) replaced Barrasso (2 goals) at 10:49 of 2nd period]
Campbell—Moog/Fuhr [Fuhr (4 goals) replaced Moog (2 goals) at 10:49 of 2nd period]

Referee Andy van Hellemond

Linesmen Gerard Gauthier and Bob Hodges

Attendance 16,683

MVP Mario Lemieux (Pittsburgh)

38th All–Star Game

The Players
Prepare to Strike

Hartford Civic Center, Tuesday, February 4, 1986

Tim Kerr (left) and Mario Lemieux break up ice, leaving the fallen John Ogrodnick behind.

The 1986 All–Star Game was characterized by excitement and news that provided a fresh and enthusiastic atmosphere around the celebration weekend. For the first time since the 1979 Challenge Cup, fans had chosen the starting players in what was to become an annual ritual in arenas throughout the league. Balloting occurred between November 1 and December 31, 1985, and each ballot contained 96 names, 48 from each conference. There were eight names for each forward position and the goalies, 16 names for defencemen, and a line at the bottom for write-in selections. Paul Coffey led in the voting with 309,503 while teammate Wayne Gretzky was a distant second with 266,470. Incredibly, five of the six starting Campbells were from the Oilers.

But the coaches were still able to add players they needed to fill their roster. One of coach Glen Sather's additions was Denis Savard, the Blackhawk with whom Slats had engaged in a war of words during the previous spring's playoffs. Although they were still bitter enemies, it was difficult for Sather not to name Savard to the team. He was third in the league in scoring and playing with a strength and stamina he attributed to his having quit smoking. Only two rookies played in the game (Gary Suter and Wendel Clark), and they'd finished one–two in the year-end voting for the Calder Trophy. The Whalers' Sylvain Turgeon replaced teammate Ron Francis, who had a broken ankle.

like the Challenge Cup had been in 1979. The day following the game in Hartford, the formal announcement was made at the Colisée in Quebec City with both John Ziegler and Alan Eagleson on hand to give their blessings to the variation on the traditional format.

The two honourary captains, Gordie Howe and Phil Esposito, enjoy the opening faceoff, while All–Star captains Larry Robinson and Wayne Gretzky share in the good times.

Meanwhile, for the first time in many a year, the governors had tangible news to announce at the game. In supporting the application of Nordiques president Marcel Aubut, they agreed that the 1987 All–Star Game would take the form of a two-day showdown with the Soviets to be called Rendez-vous '87. It would be held during that year's Quebec Carnaval, Canadian Prime Minister Brian Mulroney would act as honourary chair, and the governors wholeheartedly endorsed the idea of a replacement

Among all the usual suggestions for a change, the only other innovation was to pit Canadian players against the best of the rest of the league now that Americans and Europeans were starting to establish themselves not just as fringe players but as regulars and, in some cases, stars. Mats Naslund, Jari Kurri, Mark Howe, Peter Stastny, Rod Langway, Petr Svoboda, and Miroslav Frycer could all have played for an international team.

Pre-Game Events

Planning to make the All–Star event more than a single game, Hartford had scheduled a multitude of tangential activities. A luncheon was held at the UConn Health Center and the All–Star Charity Dinner that night benefited that organization's Children's Cancer Fund to the tune of $100,000. Dennis Hull was the sparklingly funny emcee and Rich Little, the man of a million voices, was the guest comedian at the $250-a-plate event, where Ken Taylor, Cheryl Ladd, and Alan Thicke were among the guests.

There was also an open practice on the day of the game and the one-dollar admission proceeds were handed over to various local charities. This event turned into a public relations fiasco for the NHL, however. The league had planned to include an exciting skills competition, but unfortunately league officials neglected to inform the players. With 9,300 fans waiting for the fun to begin, the players—led by the Oilers contingent—refused to participate, citing the fact they were never consulted. Instead, they played a round of "showdown" before leaving the ice. NHL Players' Association president Bryan Trottier defended the players' sour grapes in terse and unapologetic terms: "There were some communications snags and we were concerned about injuries."

For the benefit of the Hartford fans, NHL officials held a short clinic as part of the players' workouts to demonstrate offsides and a few typical penalty calls. It had been a particularly tough season for officials to that point, with no fewer than three referees badly injured. Dave Newell hurt his rotator cuff; Terry Gregson broke his collar bone; and Don Koharski missed two months with a broken foot, all clear indications that the game is physically demanding for all the skaters out on the ice.

Pre-Game Ceremonies

Before the game, a moment of silence was observed for both Pelle Lindbergh, voted to the starting team but killed in a car crash just days before, and the seven members of the space shuttle Challenger, which had exploded shortly after takeoff the previous week. In a pre-game ceremony, Lindbergh's All-Star sweater was presented to his fiancée, and his Flyers teammates at the game had a number 1 patch sewn on their sweaters in his memory. Wayne Gretzky, ever the spokesman for hockey (and the man who'd burned Lindbergh for four goals at the 1983 All-Star Game), eloquently acknowledged the tragedy.

"We tend to think and remember often of his abilities, his games, what a great goaltender he was, and how a great hockey player is gone when you play the Flyers. Unfortunately, we also tend to forget the really important thing, which is his personality, and the outgoing, happy person he was off the ice."

Lindbergh's place was filled by the Nordiques' Mario Gosselin, who had finished second to Lindbergh in the fans' voting.

The Game

The game was broadcast by ESPN and featured a number of colourful firsts. A camera was set up inside the net to provide breathtaking angles that accented the speed of the game (and the puck), and microphones were clipped to both coaches' jackets for game action remarks. Coach Keenan grew angry when he found out that his opponent Sather wanted a water bottle kept on top of the net for his goalies, a suggestion so simple and logical one wonders in retrospect that there was ever a time when they weren't there for the goalers.

The play picked up its pace when Wendel Clark, Toronto's hard-hitting first overall draft choice, shook the cobwebs out of Mark Howe with a clean, effective hit on his first shift and later in the period nailed Bryan Trottier in similar style. On another shift, Wayne Gretzky crossed the blue line with his head down and took a solid hit from Mike Ramsey. Kevin Lowe then stepped in and took a high-sticking penalty in defence of his teammate, and all of a sudden physical play had crept into the game for the first time in decades.

Honourary captains Gordie Howe and Phil Esposito went one-on-one in a showdown contest during the first intermission, and the winner went on to face Travis Howe, Gordie's seven-year-old grandson, who was dressed in a kid-size All–Star sweater. In the second intermission, impressionist Andre-Philippe Gagnon performed a rendition of "We Are the World" to the delight of the Civic Center crowd.

The game was followed by president Ziegler's reception for the players, and the next day it was back to their home teams for everyone. The board of governors held their traditional meetings, at the Parkview Hilton, where the NHLPA also held separate discussions. The PA met to establish a battle plan for free agency, and its executive director, Alan Eagleson, warned that there would be a players' strike if the current setup was not significantly altered.

"Our first desire is to have total free agency," he said, "but that won't be achievable without a strike and may not be achievable with a strike...The owners say that if it's six years in baseball, it should be 10 years in hockey. But if the average career in hockey is five years, then a player should be able to become a free agent without compensation after five years."

The owners, of course, begged to differ.

Eagleson was also promoting the idea of handing out a lump sum payment of $250,000 for every player upon playing his 400th NHL game, a proposal that was eventually adopted and remains one of Eagleson's key initiatives as PA director.

Wales 4   Campbell 3 (OT)

Wales Conference All–Stars
Honourary Captain: Gordie Howe
Mike Keenan, coach (Philadelphia)

2	D	Mark Howe (Philadelphia)
5a	D	Rod Langway (Washington)
6	D	Mike Ramsey (Buffalo)
7a	D	Ray Bourque (Boston)
9	C	Kirk Muller (New Jersey)
11	RW	Mike Gartner (Washington)
12a	C	Tim Kerr (Philadelphia)
15	LW	Sylvain Turgeon (Hartford)
16a	LW	Michel Goulet (Quebec)
19	D	Larry Robinson "C" (Montreal)
20	C	Dave Poulin (Philadelphia)
22	RW	Mike Bossy (N.Y. Islanders)
25	C	Peter Stastny (Quebec)
26	LW	Brian Propp (Montreal)
27	LW	Mats Naslund (Montreal)
29	D	Reijo Ruotsalainen (N.Y. Rangers)
33a	G	Mario Gosselin (Quebec)
35	G	Bob Froese (Philadelphia)
61	C	Bryan Trottier (N.Y. Islanders)
66a	C	Mario Lemieux (Pittsburgh)

Campbell Conference All–Stars
Honourary Captain: Phil Esposito
Glen Sather, coach (Edmonton)

2	D	Lee Fogolin (Edmonton)
4	D	Kevin Lowe (Edmonton)
5	D	Rob Ramage (St. Louis)
7a	D	Paul Coffey (Edmonton)
9a	LW	Glenn Anderson (Edmonton)
10	C	Dale Hawerchuk (Winnipeg)
11	LW	Mark Messier (Edmonton)
12	C	Neal Broten (Minnesota)
14	RW	Tony Tanti (Vancouver)
15	LW	Wendel Clark (Toronto)
17a	RW	Jari Kurri (Edmonton)
18	RW	Dave Taylor (Los Angeles)
19	C	Denis Savard (Chicago)
20	RW	Mark Hunter (St. Louis)
21	D	Gary Suter (Calgary)
24a	D	Doug Wilson (Chicago)
25	LW	John Ogrodnick (Detroit)
31a	G	Grant Fuhr (Edmonton)
35	G	Andy Moog (Edmonton)
99a	C	Wayne Gretzky "C" (Edmonton)

a=voted to starting lineup by fan ballot

First Period

No Scoring
Penalties: Suter (CC) 0:51, Gartner (WC) 12:55

Second Period

1. Campbell: Tanti (unassisted). 7:56
2. Wales: Propp (Naslund, Bourque) 17:56
Penalties: None

Third Period

3. Wales: Stastny (Robinson, Turgeon) 4:45
4. Campbell: Gretzky (Coffey, Savard). 17:09
5. Wales: Propp (Robinson). . . . . 17:38(pp)
6. Campbell: Hawerchuk (Savard, Coffey). . . . . . . 19:17(pp)
Penalties: Lowe (CC) 6:14, Turgeon (WC) 15:22, Messier (CC) 16:31, Gartner (WC) 18:45

Overtime

7. Wales: Trottier (Bossy) 3:05
Penalties: None

Shots on Goal

Wales	8	15	9	3	**35**
Campbell	6	11	10	2	**29**

In Goal

Wales—Gosselin/Froese [Froese (2 goals) replaced Gosselin (one goal) at 11:03 of 2nd period]
Campbell—Fuhr/Moog [Moog (4 goals) replaced Fuhr (no goals) at 11:03 of 2nd period]

Referee Ron Wicks

Linesmen John D'Amico and Gord Broseker

Attendance 15,126

MVP Grant Fuhr (Edmonton)

Rendez-vous '87

The NHL gambled in 1987, hoping that the excitement of the 1979 Challenge Cup could be duplicated eight years later, hoping equally that the league's pros could beat the Soviets this time around. To reduce the possibility of an embarrassment, it was planned as a two-game set instead of a three-game series. From the start, the NHLers did nothing to improve their chances, however. The games would take place during a five-day league break, but the first

was scheduled for February 11 and most players had league games as late as the 8th—which left all of two practices for the players to get to know each other on ice. Canadian players had always been able to prepare quickly for these kinds of international games, but it was an obvious disadvantage to be going up against the thoroughly acquainted lines of the Soviets with so little prep time. Furthermore, common wisdom held that because this was an NHL team, it would be

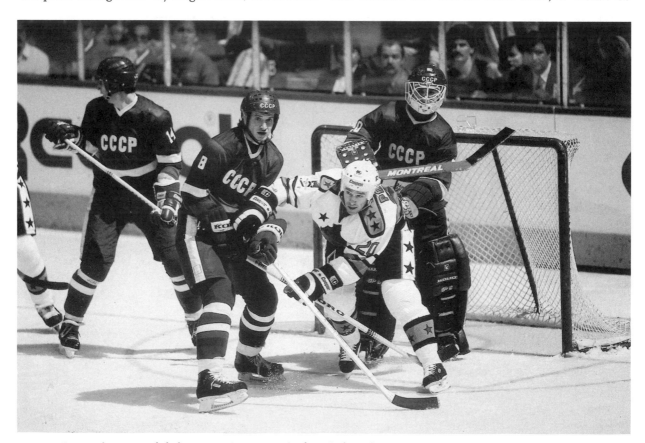

Soviet goalie Evgeny Belosheikin tries to clear Dave Poulin from the front of his crease during game one of the two-game series.

intrinsically superior to a Team Canada. But for every positive (more talent), there was a negative: more individual styles to amalgamate and adapt to in a short period of time.

In contrast, the Soviets had played together for years and their top line—the KLM troika of Krutov, Larionov, and Makarov—was at the height of its powers while their defence duo of Fetisov and Kasatonov was also in its prime. The second line consisted of Yashin, Semenov, and Svetlov with regular defencemen Pervukhin and Tatarinov. However, the Soviets were also underachieving during this period. They had lost the 1984 Canada Cup, the 1985 world championships and Isvestia tournament and, just a month before Rendez-vous, a pre-Olympic series in Calgary. In fact, they hadn't won a bona fide international competition in years.

By game day, Team NHL coach Jean Perron wasn't sure what his lines would look like. Some of his top stars were hurting coming into the series, and three of the league's finest (Mike Bossy, Paul Coffey, and Mark Howe) didn't play because of varying degrees of back injury. Mario Lemieux almost wasn't ready to play after hurting his knee on December 20. He missed 13 games, but by late January he was back in excellent form. Ray Bourque was one more on the injured list. He missed the first Rendez vous team practice because of a groin pull and Normand Rochefort of the local Nordiques was called in to suit up as a last-minute emergency fill-in, just in case.

Pre-tournament hype focused mainly on fans voting to select Mario Lemieux to the team over Wayne Gretzky despite number 99's obvious history of greatness since he'd entered the NHL seven years before. In a show of good sportsmanship, Super Mario suggested that although he had been voted to the starting position, the Great One should start at centre ice.

"I'm flattered that I got the most votes," he said, "but Gretzky is the best player in the National Hockey League, and he should be taking the opening faceoff."

Choosing the NHL team combined the best and the worst of the All–Star selection process. As in 1979, the starters were selected by fan ballot while the remaining 21 players were chosen by a committee of general managers and executives, notably Cliff Fletcher (Calgary), Serge Savard (Montreal), Bob Pulford (Chicago), Bill Torrey (N.Y. Islanders), Tommy Ivan (VP Chicago), Keith Allen (VP Philadelphia), and former coach Scotty Bowman.

An unusual sidebar to the series concerned other matters of an international nature. While the Soviets and NHLers were playing in Quebec City, the International Ice Hockey Federation was meeting in Vienna to discuss the penalties meted out to 19 Soviet and 19 Canadian junior players who had been involved in a game-ending brawl at the World Junior Championships in Piestany, Czechoslovakia, a few

Ray Bourque tries to clear the sightlines for his goalie Grant Fuhr during game two of Rendez-vous.

weeks before. When the IIHF upheld the 18-month suspensions of the 38 players without allowing an appeal, both countries rallied to support the other's claims that the penalties were severe and unwarranted and would prove ineffective. Ontario Hockey League commissioner Dave Branch called for Canada to stop playing internationally altogether, as it had in 1970.

"I see no other alternative than to withdraw," he said. "How could both countries receive the same punishment when the referee said the Russians started the whole thing?"

Furthermore, it directly affected Rendez-vous '87. Yevgeny Davidov, a Soviet national player who had been loaned to the junior team and was first off the bench to start the brawl in Piestany, was still under suspension and couldn't play in the series as a result of the banishment.

Other important international concerns were also raised and dismissed. NHL president John Ziegler suggested that Soviet players would never be able to join the North American league:

"The Soviet hockey program is designed to build an elite team, and in doing that they want their best players to play, to represent the USSR. That doesn't permit their players to come here. And they're not going to send a bad player."

Ziegler also rejected the possibility of NHLers ever playing in the Olympics, suggesting that shutting the league down would be costly and unrewarding. Of course, events have by now revealed Ziegler as zero-for-two in the prediction department.

Pre-Game Events

Thanks largely to the Quebec Carnaval that injected a spirit of joy as much as competition, this was a year of All–Star celebration. The cultural and social events planned around the five days of hockey and entertainment were the most sophisticated in All–Star Game history.

February 6–15: The Hockey Hall of Fame had transported nearly 4,000 artifacts and memorabilia to Quebec City for the duration of the Carnaval and the series. On the first day, some 60,000 people came to see the exhibits and over the course of the series that number exceeded 160,000.

February 8: Variety show by local entertainers Yvon Deschamps and Jean Lapointe.

February 9: Gourmet dinner for players and fans featuring bison steaks, numerous wines, and a wide range of international cuisine. Red Army Choir performs at the Colisée.

February 10: Business leaders luncheon with speaker Lee Iacocca and guests including Ken Taylor, Gordie Howe, and Alan Eagleson. International gala hosted by Alan Thicke and including performances by Gordon Lightfoot, among others.

February 11: Brunch and a fashion show retrospective, hosted by Mila Mulroney and featuring Pierre Cardin. Game One, Rendez-vous '87

February 12: International fashion show. Night parade featuring floats from all NHL teams through the centre of the city. Concert, featuring rock groups from Canada (Glass Tiger) and the Soviet Union (Autograph).

February 13: Game Two, Rendez-vous '87

February 15: Closing variety show featuring Quebec artists Luba, Marjo, and Sylvie Tremblay.

The traditional international exchange of sweaters
is duly followed here by Michel Goulet (left) and Alexei Kasatonov.

Game One

In game one, Team NHL executed its strategy to near perfection. It got outstanding goalkeeping from Grant Fuhr and had a 2–0 lead after two periods. The Soviets tied the game early in the third, but the NHLers were relentless. And desperate. They were also disciplined, taking only four minors and killing them all without incident. "Our plan," Perron said, "was never to get outnumbered in any zone on the ice, and to force them to the outside as much as possible." To that end, he had Langway and Green out against the KLM line all night long with the Hawerchuk line checking up front, and this fivesome made the critical difference to the outcome.

Perron's lines eventually included the Oilers trio of Gretzky–Tikkanen–Kurri; Lemieux–Goulet–Kerr (although Kerr was primarily used on the power-play); and Messier and Anderson with a number of combinations. The fourth line of Poulin–Dineen–Hawerchuk stopped the Soviets' KLM line effectively in game one, but in game two the Soviet threesome showed why many considered them, with Fetisov and Kasatonov, the best five-man unit in hockey. Newcomer Valeri Kamensky was also brilliant, and at 20 years of age was clearly a star rising on the horizon.

The Soviet referee, Sergei Morozov (who went so far as to help run the game day practice for the Soviets), called only one penalty on his own team, a bench minor, in game one. Despite the many ways Soviet hockey had become more like the Canadian game since 1972, one thing hadn't changed behind the Iron Curtain: The refereeing wasn't just poor; it was flagrantly biased.

With the clock winding down and the Soviets trying to tie the game, the team stuck with five skaters and goalie Belosheikin in his net. "I never pull my goalie," coach Viktor Tikhonov said bluntly. "I feel we would always be scored upon." Perhaps, but they also failed to tie the game. (In the case of a tie, the teams would have played a five-minute sudden-death overtime period, as was the custom in the NHL.)

Game Two

For the second game, there were a few changes to the lineups. Tomas Sandstrom had a sprained ankle and Tim Kerr a muscle pull in his leg, so both returned home and their spots were taken by Kirk Muller and Normand Rochefort. For the Soviets, Anatoly Semenov had hurt his leg sliding into the goal during game one and didn't dress for the finale.

From the opening faceoff, the Soviets showed their experience and ability to adjust. They went to the net more, they shot more, and they produced more chances to score. They also answered every NHL hit with a hit of their own and played with an intensity and passion the NHLers couldn't match because they were just a little complacent after winning game one. Defenceman Doug Wilson would admit, "I think we let them play their game a little more than the other night." The Soviets were also helped by the NHLers' inability to score around the net. Virtually every forward had a great chance but he either missed the net or was stopped by the sensational play of Belosheikin every time.

The Soviets were getting paid $80,000 for their appearance in Quebec City, while the league players added about $350,000 to their pension fund.

But perhaps the final words on the series should come from the tournament MVP, Wayne Gretzky. After game two, he exchanged sweaters with Viacheslav Fetisov, number 2 for the Soviets and future NHL nemesis, and called for a new Summit Series to revive interest on the scale of the one in 1972.

"Let's face it," Gretzky began, "people want more than two games. And they want more than Christmas tours. And when it comes to the Canada Cup, who really wants to see Canada play West Germany? People don't want to see those other countries. People want to see Canada and Russia. I'd like to see it happen before I retire."

Minutes later, he was still extolling the virtues of Rendez-vous: "That was hockey the way it is supposed to be played."

Rendez-vous '87
Le Colisée, Quebec City

Game 1 February 11
NHL All–Stars 4   USSR 3

Game 2 February 13
USSR 5   NHL All–Stars 3

NHL All–Stars
Jean Perron, coach (Montreal)
Michel Bergeron, assistant (Quebec)
Bob Johnson, assistant (Boston)

#	Pos	Player	G	A	P	Pim
3	D	Mike Ramsey (Buffalo)	0	0	0	0
4	D	Rod Langway (Washington)	0	0	0	0
5	D	Rick Green (Montreal)	0	0	0	0
6	D	Ray Bourque (Boston)	1	0	1	2
8	D	Ulf Samuelsson (Hartford)	0	0	0	0
9	LW	Glenn Anderson (Edmonton)	1	0	1	2
10	C	Dale Hawerchuk (Winnipeg)	0	1	1	2
11	C	Mark Messier (Edmonton)	1	0	1	0
14	RW	Kevin Dineen (Hartford)	1	0	1	0
15	RW	Esa Tikkanen (Edmonton)	0	1	1	2
16 c	RW	Michel Goulet (Quebec)	0	1	1	0
17	RW	Jari Kurri (Edmonton)	1	1	2	0
19	LW	Kirk Muller (New Jersey)	0	0	0	0
20	C	Dave Poulin (Philadelphia)	1	1	2	0
21 b	D	Normand Rochefort (Quebec)	0	0	0	0
24	D	Doug Wilson (Chicago)	1	1	2	0
25	D	Chris Chelios (Montreal)	0	0	0	0
28 a	RW	Tomas Sandstrom (N.Y. Rangers)	0	0	0	0
31	G	Grant Fuhr (Edmonton)	0	0	0	0
32	RW	Claude Lemieux (Montreal)	0	0	0	4
66 c	C	Mario Lemieux (Pittsburgh)	0	3	3	0
99	C	Wayne Gretzky "C" (Edmonton)	0	4	4	0

C Tim Kerr (Philadelphia) did not play
G Ron Hextall (Philadelphia) did not play
Gc Clint Malarchuk (Quebec) did not play

a played only February 11
b played only February 13
c voted to starting team by fan ballot (along with Bossy, Coffey, Howe, all of whom were injured and did not play)

	GP	Mins	W-L-T	GA	SO	Avg
Grant Fuhr	2	120	1-1-0	8	0	4.00

USSR
Victor Tikhonov, coach

#	Pos	Player	G	A	P	Pim
2	D	Viacheslav Fetisov "C" (Red Army)	0	1	1	2
4	D	Igor Stelnov (Red Army)	0	0	0	0
5	D	Vasily Pervukhin (Mos. Dynamo)	0	0	0	0
6	D	Mikhail Tatarinov (Mos. Dynamo)	0	1	1	0
7	D	Alexei Kasatonov (Red Army)	1	0	1	2
8	D	Alexei Gusarov (Red Army)	0	0	0	0
9	RW	Vladimir Krutov (Red Army)	1	0	1	2
10 b	F	Viacheslav Lavrov (SKA Leningr.)	0	0	0	0
11	C	Igor Larionov (Red Army)	0	2	2	0
12	D	Sergei Starikov (Red Army)	0	1	1	0
13	F	Valeri Kamensky (Red Army)	2	1	3	0
14	D	Zinetula Bilyaletdinov (Mos. Dynamo)	0	0	0	0
15	LW	Andrei Khomutov (Red Army)	1	2	3	0
16	RW	Sergei Svetlov (Mos. Dynamo)	0	0	0	0
18	C	Alexander Semak (Mos. Dynamo)	0	0	0	0
19 a	RW	Mikhail Varnakov (Gorky Torpedo)	0	1	1	0
20	G	Evgeny Belosheikin (Red Army)	0	0	0	0
21 b	C	Sergei Nemchinov (Soviet Wings)	0	0	0	4
22	LW	Sergei Priakhin (Soviet Wings)	0	0	0	12
24	LW	Sergei Makarov (Red Army)	0	1	1	0
27	C	Viacheslav Bykov (Red Army)	1	1	2	0
29	LW	Yuri Khmylev (Soviet Wings)	0	0	0	0
30 a	C	Anatoli Semenov (Moscow Dynamo)	2	0	2	0

1   G   Sergei Mylnikov (Traktor) did not play

a played only February 11
b played only February 13

	GP	Mins	W-L-T	GA	SO	Avg
Evgeny Belosheikin	2	120	1-1-0	7	0	3.50

Game One
NHL All–Stars 4   USSR 3

First Period

1. NHL: Kurri (Gretzky, Tikkanen) 5:23
Penalties: C. Lemieux (NHL) 10:30, Bourque (NHL) 15:34

Second Period

2. NHL: Anderson (M. Lemieux) 17:00
3. USSR: Kasatonov (Makarov) 18:42
Penalties: Hawerchuk (NHL) 12:28, USSR bench (served by Kamensky) 14:37

Third Period

4. USSR: Bykov (Khomutov, Starikov) 2:03
5. NHL: Dineen (Hawerchuk, Poulin) 7:03
6. USSR: Semenov (Tatarinov, Varnakov) 8:04
7. NHL: Poulin (M. Lemieux, Wilson) 18:45
Penalties: Tikkanen (NHL) 8:18

Shots on Goal

NHL	11	9	7	**27**
USSR	5	9	10	**24**

In Goal

NHL—Fuhr
USSR—Belosheikin

Referee Sergei Morozov

Linesmen Ray Scapinello and Ron Finn

Attendance 15,398

Game Two
USSR 5   NHL All–Stars 3

First Period

1. NHL: Messier (Kurri, Gretzky) . . . . 3:32(pp)
Penalties: Nemchinov (USSR) 3:22, Krutov (USSR) and Anderson (NHL) 9:50, C. Lemieux (NHL) 11:33, Fetisov (USSR) 17:04

Second Period

2. USSR: Kamensky (Khomutov, Bykov) 3:13
3. USSR: Krutov (Fetisov, Larionov) 5:17
4. USSR: Kamensky (unassisted) 19:41
Penalties: None

Third Period

5. NHL: Wilson (Gretzky, Goulet) . . . . 7:33(pp)
6. USSR: Semenov (Larionov) 9:19
7. USSR: Khomutov (Kamensky) 12:59
8. NHL: Bourque (M. Lemieux, Gretzky) 19:23
Penalties: Nemchinov (USSR) 6:05, Kasatonov (USSR) 11:46, Priakhin (USSR—minor, misconduct) 17:20

Shots on Goal

USSR	7	9	13	**29**
NHL	6	13	12	**31**

In Goal

USSR—Belosheikin
NHL—Fuhr

Referee Dave Newell

Linesmen Ray Scapinello and Ron Finn

Attendance 15,395

Team Canada MVP Mark Messier

Team USSR MVP Sergei Makarov

Tournament MVP Wayne Gretzky

39th All–Star Game
Mario Finds the Zone
St. Louis Arena, Tuesday, February 9, 1988

The weekend began with a celebratory meeting attended by 1,000 special invitees under the famous St. Louis Arch, but the Adam's Mark Hotel in St. Louis was headquarters for many of the events and important meetings surrounding 1988's game. The All–Star luncheon honoured the Lester Patrick winners, Keith Allen, Bob Johnson, and Fred Cusick. The evening banquet was hosted by play-by-play man Dan Kelly and TV personality Alan Thicke, with music provided by Norm Crosby and the Gatlin Brothers. The proceeds from both meals went to the Cystic Fibrosis Foundation, the Kilo Foundation, the Multiple Sclerosis Society, Cardinal Glennon Children's Hospital, and the Jesuit Program for Living and Learning.

At the NHL board of governors' meetings leading up to the game, the final approval of the sale of the L.A. Kings was granted. Bruce McNall had generally been regarded as a perfect league owner. Chairman of Numismatic Fine Arts Inc., he owned race horses and a movie company and was apparently a wealthy man who loved hockey and promised great things for southern California. Unfortunately, in a very few years, McNall was in prison serving a 70-month sentence for fraud and his fortune was revealed as a sham.

The NHL also approved Pittsburgh as host for the 1990 All–Star Game and the Penguins announced they'd invest $12 million in renovations to the Civic Arena to do so.

Although the starting lineups were selected by fan ballot, the names that went on the ballot were chosen by the Professional Hockey Writers' Association. The only substitution to the fans' stated wishes came when Al MacInnis replaced the injured Doug Wilson on the blue line for the Campbells.

Because the game was in St. Louis, the Campbells intended to have honourary co-captains, brothers Bob and Barclay Plager, against former teammate and longtime Islanders coach Al Arbour, but Barclay succumbed to brain cancer just days before the game and Bob had to do the honours alone. One of the most popular players to wear the bluenote, Barclay was famous for his good nature. "Number five in your programs; number one in your hearts," he'd say over and over during the many years of his happy St. Louis career. A moment of silence in his memory was observed prior to the opening faceoff.

The three stars of the game were Mario Lemieux, Mats Naslund, and Luc Robitaille, but this was the result of a last-minute change. The writers who choose the three stars were asked to do so early in the third period. In 1983, goalie John Garrett had been a cinch for MVP honours until Wayne Gretzky's four-goal third period forced an embarrassing but necessary change of opinion. Similarly, in 1988 Denis Savard was penned in as the third star until he set Luc Robitaille up for the game-tieing goal and it was Lucky Luc who would skate in the spotlight.

Lemieux and Naslund were nothing short of spectacular. Both set All–Star Game records, with Naslund's five assists eclipsed only by Mario's six points, including the game-winner in overtime. Both Lemieux and Gretzky were content to play against each other most of the night and showcase what was becoming the league's greatest soft rivalry. Wunderkind Gretzky was the league's prime asset and Lemieux was being hailed as the Next One, a title he tried to live up to in a clash that kept fans interested in the game.

(l-r) *Mats Naslund, Larry Robinson, Mario Lemieux, and Kevin Dineen celebrate one of Lemieux's three goals, all assisted by Naslund.*

"When I was 20," Gretzky recalled, "I came here with fire in my eyes because I wanted to show I could play with Lafleur and Bossy. I'm sure he [Mario] has fire in his eyes now."

While the Super Mario–Great One slant got plenty of press, Gretzky's concerns were more social during the time he spent in St Louis. He had recently announced his engagement to a native of the city, Janet Jones, and the couple used the trip as an opportunity to get together with her family and the brides-maids and groom's men. Affectionately referred to as Canada's Royal Wedding, the marriage was to have significant on-ice repercussions as well. This was to be Gretzky's last year with the Oilers before being traded to Bruce McNall's team in Los Angeles, Jones's current hometown while she pursued an acting career.

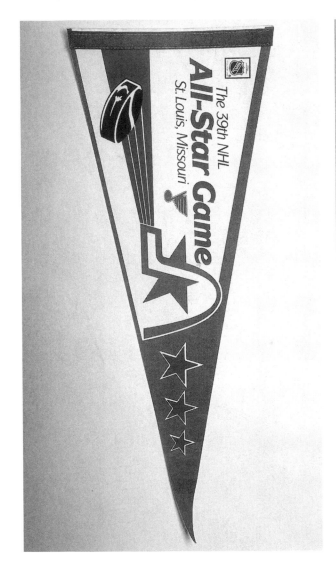

MVP Mario Lemieux tests the rear load capabilities of his new truck.

Wales 6   Campbell 5 (OT)

Wales Conference All–Stars
Honourary Captain: Al Arbour
Mike Keenan, coach (Philadelphia)

2	D	Mark Howe (Philadelphia)
5	D	Denis Potvin (N.Y. Islanders)
7a	D	Paul Coffey (Pittsburgh)
8	RW	Cam Neely (Boston)
9	C	Kirk Muller (New Jersey)
11a	RW	Kevin Dineen (Hartford)
12	RW	Mike Gartner (Washington)
15	C	Pat LaFontaine (N.Y. Islanders)
16a	LW	Michel Goulet (Quebec)
19	D	Larry Robinson (Montreal)
20	C	Dave Poulin (Philadelphia)
21	C	Christian Ruuttu (Buffalo)
25	LW	Mats Naslund (Montreal)
26	C	Peter Stastny (Quebec)
27a	G	Ron Hextall (Philadelphia)
28	RW	Tomas Sandstrom (N.Y. Rangers)
29	D	Kjell Samuelsson (Philadelphia)
33	G	Patrick Roy (Montreal)
66a	C	Mario Lemieux (Pittsburgh)
77a	D	Ray Bourque (Boston)

Campbell Conference All–Stars
Honourary Captain: Bob Plager
Glen Sather, coach (Edmonton)

2	D	Al MacInnis (Calgary)
3	D	Brad McCrimmon (Calgary)
4a	D	Kevin Lowe (Edmonton)
5	D	Rob Ramage (St. Louis)
8	C	Greg Adams (Vancouver)
9	LW	Glenn Anderson (Edmonton)
10	C	Dale Hawerchuk (Winnipeg)
11	LW	Mark Messier (Edmonton)
17a	RW	Jari Kurri (Edmonton)
18	C	Denis Savard (Chicago)
19	C	Steve Yzerman (Detroit)
20a	LW	Luc Robitaille (Los Angeles)
21	D	Gary Suter (Calgary)
23	RW	Brian Bellows (Minnesota)
24	LW	Bob Probert (Detroit)
25	C	Joe Nieuwendyk (Calgary)
30	G	Mike Vernon (Calgary)
31a	G	Grant Fuhr (Edmonton)
33	D	Al Iafrate (Toronto)
99a	C	Wayne Gretzky "C" (Edmonton)

a=voted to starting lineup by fan ballot

First Period

1. Campbell: Hawerchuk (Nieuwendyk, Bellows) 3:25
2. Wales: Sandstrom (Lemieux, Naslund) 14:45
3. Campbell: Gretzky (Probert) 18:46
Penalties: Potvin (WC) 10:11

Second Period

4. Wales: Gartner (Lemieux) 4:28
5. Wales: Stastny (Lemieux, Naslund) . . . . 10:08(pp)
6. Wales: Lemieux (Naslund) 11:34
7. Campbell: Robitaille (Savard, Lowe). 15:09
Penalties: LaFontaine (WC) 7:27, McCrimmon (CC) 8:47

Third Period

8. Campbell: Savard (Robitaille, Anderson) 5:19
9. Wales: Lemieux (Naslund, Dineen) 8:07
10. Campbell: Robitaille (Anderson, Savard) 16:28
Penalties: Bellows (CC) 2:53

Overtime

11. Wales: Lemieux (Naslund, Dineen) 1:08
Penalties: None

Shots on Goal

Wales	9	13	12	1	**35**
Campbell	14	6	10	0	**30**

In Goal

Wales—Hextall/Roy [Roy (3 goals) replaced Hextall (2 goals) at 10:08 of 2nd period]
Campbell—Fuhr/Vernon [Vernon (3 goals) replaced Fuhr (3 goals) at 10:08 of 2nd period]

Referee Denis Morel

Linesmen Kevin Collins and Randy Mitton

Attendance 17,878

MVP Mario Lemieux (Pittsburgh)

The Great One Goes Home

Northlands Coliseum, Edmonton, Tuesday, February 7, 1989

Retrospect always provides an advantage in assessing an event's importance. The 1989 All–Star Game was roundly criticised for its lack of a top rookie on either team. Missing were leading Calder candidates Joe Sakic, Brian Leetch, Tony Granato, and Pat Elynuik. Also, this year's beat-the-coach-up award went to Terry O'Reilly, who selected two of his own Bruins (Reggie Lemelin and Glen Wesley) over two superior talents, Patrick Roy and Chris Chelios.

But the game was not so much an All–Star affair as the return of Wayne Gretzky, who had been traded to Los Angeles the previous summer after winning four Stanley Cups and setting umpteen records in his nine years in Edmonton. "I know I'll be more prepared to play than I've ever been for an All–Star Game," he said on the eve of what was only his second Edmonton

Steve Yzerman, Detroit captain in perpetuity, takes a bladed check as he moves in on Reggie Lemelin.

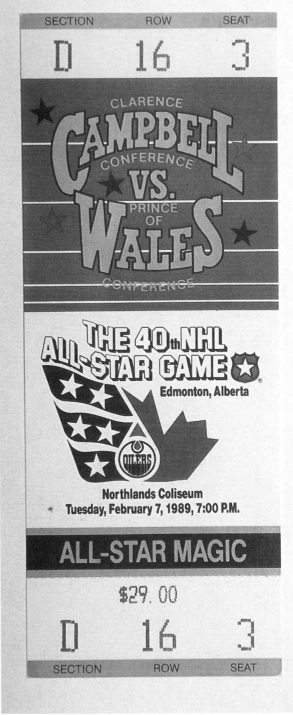

game since the trade. At the Northlands Coliseum, Oilers coach Glen Sather sat Gretzky at his old stall in the dressing room and on the ice he played number 99 with former mate Jari Kurri and current L.A. wingman Luc Robitaille. On the first shift, Gretzky set Kurri up for a goal and on the next shift he scored one himself. They dominated the game, and Gretzky's loyal fans didn't let up while he was on the ice. Inevitably, Gretzky received the car as MVP (and gave the new set of wheels to former linemate and friend, bodyguard Dave Semenko).

"Nothing against Lemieux," Kevin Lowe said later, "but there's been a lot of Mario, Mario lately. They've sort of uncrowned Wayne too early."

"Tonight was special, extra special. It was great fun," Gretzky himself said afterwards of his return. "I don't think I stopped smiling. It was a treat to play with all those guys again; it was just like old times sitting on the bench."

Old times, too, off the ice. He got to Edmonton early with his wife, Janet, and their seven-week-old daughter, Paulina, to test drive two new snowmobiles he had bought the previous winter.

Sather's other lines featured Leeman–Carson–Hull, Messier–Nieuwendyk–Mullen, and Yzerman–Nicholls–

Ciccarelli. His defence pairings included Lowe and Duchesne, Ellett and Manson, and Suter and Reinhart. Joe Nieuwendyk hadn't been invited to play, but when Denis Savard suffered ligament damage to an ankle a few days before the game, Sather chose the Flames forward as a replacement. Montreal's Mike McPhee likewise filled in for Mats Naslund after Naslund sprained his ankle in the Habs' final game leading up to the break.

Mario Lemieux had just one assist and was −4 on the night, but while he congratulated Gretzky on his return to Edmonton, he vowed next year's game, in his home rink in Pittsburgh, would be his. "I'm glad he won the MVP," Mario said. "It was his night. I'll be all right next year." There was added intensity this year, though, because Lemieux was not only leading the league in scoring, he was on pace to break Gretzky's record of 215 points. Gretzky was matter-of-fact about the possibility.

"That's what happens in this game," he said. "New people come along and break your records. I did it to guys like Trottier and Lafleur, and someday Mario will find out how it feels, too ... if he scores 93 goals and has 217 points, I'll be the first in line to shake his hand."

It was a gesture that never materialized, as Lemieux faded ever so slightly down the stretch and finished with 199 points, the closest he ever got to the magic plateau of 200.

The pre-game entertainment featured the high-kicking, balletic Shumka Dancers. Lee Greenwood and k.d. lang sang the national anthems, then two honourary captains from Edmonton, Norm Ullman and Bruce MacGregor (who had been two of Detroit's famous HUM Line with Paul Henderson) took part in the opening faceoff ceremonies.

Campbell 9   Wales 5

Campbell Conference All-Stars			Wales Conference All-Stars		
Honourary Captain: Bruce MacGregor			Honourary Captain: Norm Ullman		
Glen Sather, coach (Edmonton)			Terry O'Reilly, coach (Boston)		

2	D	Dave Ellett (Winnipeg)	1	G	Reggie Lemelin (Boston)
3	D	Dave Manson (Chicago)	3	D	Scott Stevens (Washington)
4a	D	Kevin Lowe (Edmonton)	6	D	Phil Housley (Buffalo)
7	RW	Joe Mullen (Calgary)	7a	D	Paul Coffey (Pittsburgh)
9	C	Bernie Nicholls (Los Angeles)	8a	RW	Cam Neely (Boston)
10	RW	Gary Leeman (Toronto)	11	RW	Kevin Dineen (Hartford)
11	C	Mark Messier (Edmonton)	14	RW	John MacLean (New Jersey)
12	C	Jimmy Carson (Edmonton)	15	C	Bobby Smith (Montreal)
16	RW	Brett Hull (St. Louis)	16	C	Pat LaFontaine (N.Y. Islanders)
17a	RW	Jari Kurri (Edmonton)	17	C	Mike Ridley (Washington)
19	C	Steve Yzerman (Detroit)	18	LW	Brian Mullen (N.Y. Rangers)
20	RW	Dino Ciccarelli (Minnesota)	19	D	Larry Robinson "C" (Montreal)
21	D	Gary Suter (Calgary)	22	RW	Rick Tocchet (Philadelphia)
22a	LW	Luc Robitaille (Los Angeles)	25	D	Glen Wesley (Boston)
23	D	Paul Reinhart (Vancouver)	30a	G	Sean Burke (New Jersey)
25	C	Joe Nieuwendyk (Calgary)	35	LW	Mike McPhee (Montreal)
28a	D	Steve Duchesne (Los Angeles)	44	C	Rob Brown (Pittsburgh)
30	G	Mike Vernon (Calgary)	66a	C	Mario Lemieux (Pittsburgh)
31a	G	Grant Fuhr (Edmonton)	75	C	Walt Poddubny (Quebec)
99a	C	Wayne Gretzky "C" (Los Angeles)	77a	D	Ray Bourque (Boston)

a=voted to starting lineup by fan ballot

First Period
1. Campbell: Kurri (Gretzky, Robitaille) 1:07
2. Campbell: Gretzky (Duchesne) 4:33
3. Wales: Neely (Lemieux, Stevens) . . . . 9:47(pp)
4. Wales: Poddubny (Ridley, Robinson) 10:38
Penalties: Messier (CC) 9:35

Second Period
5. Wales: Wesley (LaFontaine, B. Mullen) 3:16
6. Campbell: J. Mullen (Messier, Nieuwendyk) 7:57
7. Campbell: Yzerman (Duchesne, Ciccarelli) 17:21
8. Campbell: Leeman (Carson) 17:35
Penalties: Bourque (WC) 13:44

Third Period
9. Wales: Poddubny (Tocchet, Robinson) 4:40
10. Campbell: J. Mullen (Manson) 6:53
11. Campbell: Ridley (Bourque, Tocchet) 9:35
12. Campbell: Robitaille (Kurri, Gretzky) 12:18
13. Campbell: Carson (Leeman, Hull) 14:35

14. Campbell: Messier (Nieuwendyk, J. Mullen) 17:14
Penalties: None

Shots on Goal
Campbell	13	10	14	**37**
Wales	14	9	15	**38**

In Goal
Campbell—Fuhr/Vernon [Vernon (2 goals) replaced Fuhr (3 goals) at 9:58 of 2nd period]
Wales—Burke/Lemelin [Lemelin (6 goals) replaced Burke (3 goals) at 9:58 of 2nd period]

Referee Ron Hoggarth

Linesmen Ron Asseltine and Wayne Bonney

Attendance 17,503

MVP Wayne Gretzky (Los Angeles)

The Inaugural "Weekend"

Civic Arena, Pittsburgh, Sunday, January 21, 1990

The 1990 game was originally slated for Montreal but the Canadiens withdrew in the hope of distancing themselves as much as possible from Quebec City's superb running of Rendez-vous '87. Meanwhile, the Penguins had originally set their sights on hosting the All–Stars in 1993 and then moved their wish date up two years to 1991. When the NHL asked them to move their bid up again to the current year, Pittsburgh was only too happy to oblige.

Hosting this year's game took on new meaning when the NHL introduced two significant events to the plethora of All–Star activities, the Heroes of Hockey game (two 20-minute periods) and a skills competition among the NHLers. The competition was designed by Paul Palmer, who had produced the "Showdown" feature during intermissions on Hockey Night in Canada from 1973 to 1980, and it offered $25,000 in prize money. For the NHL All–Stars, players on the winning team now received $2,500 for wins in the skills drills—a far cry from the $500 players used to get as members of the winning side for the game itself. However, this inaugural competition was tarnished when one of the best skaters in the game, Paul Coffey, refused to take part in the speed challenge. "You can look pretty bad. It's not worth it," was all he would say on the matter.

The "Heroes" this year consisted of Wales versus Campbell alumni, an odd notion given that many of

The greatest scorers of the 1990s face off at the 1990 scorefest in Pittsburgh, a 19-goal outburst that broke all records for one game.

the players had retired by the time the conference names were introduced to the league. Future years featured alumni from the host city versus the best of the retired rest. And here again there was controversy. Gordie Howe refused to play in the Heroes of Hockey because he claimed that he had originally proposed the idea for the 1986 All–Star Game in Hartford and the league had told him it would never work.

But the NHL itself was entering a new era at that year's game, thanks to two developments during the NHL Players' Association meetings. First, it hired Bob Goodenow as its deputy to serve under Alan Eagleson until December 31, 1991, at which point he would then replace Eagleson as full-time director of the PA. Goodenow's hiring had been a long time in the making as a six-player committee headed by Kevin Dineen whittled some 300 applicants down to six before a unanimous vote chose Goodenow to succeed the Eagle. A native of Detroit, Goodenow had been captain of Harvard's hockey team in 1974 and more recently both a practising lawyer and player agent. The second important development was that as of February 4, all players' salaries would be made public, almost instantly setting up a situation where incomes would increase because of league-wide comparisons to other players with equivalent statistics or skill.

At the board of governors' meetings, there were also initial talks regarding still more expansion. The league's mandate had been to expand from 21 to 28 teams by the end of the century and now was the time to consider options. To that end, Hamilton mayor Bob Morrow flew to Pittsburgh to make his presence felt and his intentions clear.

"We're very excited about the prospects of the '90s for hockey and the National Hockey League," president Ziegler said. "We did a study over a year ago setting our goals for the next 10 years and we set some ambitious goals for growth. From the standpoint of the product on ice, I think everybody in the business recognizes it's never been better. The players are playing with a level of skill and competition

we've never had before. Financially, we've enjoyed five very solid, profitable years. We've had 10 consecutive years of breaking the all-time attendance record. We believe our television prospects continue to grow and are exciting and by being way out on the forefront of international hockey—the globalization of our sport—we have some advantages the other professional sports do not have and we hope to take advantage of that."

During the weekend's activities, L.A. general manager Rogie Vachon traded Bernie Nicholls to the Rangers for Tony Granato and Tomas Sandstrom. As he had yet to play for the Rangers, however, Nicholls

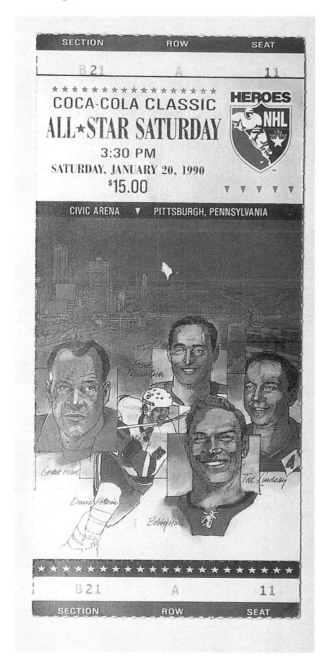

SECTION   ROW   SEAT

B 21   A   11

★ ★ ★ ★ ★ ★ ★ ★ ★ ★ ★ ★ ★ ★ ★   HEROES
COCA-COLA CLASSIC   NHL
ALL★STAR SATURDAY
3:30 PM
SATURDAY, JANUARY 20, 1990
$15.00   ▼ ▼ ▼ ▼ ▼

CIVIC ARENA ▼ PITTSBURGH, PENNSYLVANIA

★ ★ ★ ★ ★ ★ ★ ★ ★ ★ ★ ★ ★ ★ ★ ★ ★ ★ ★

B 21   A   11

SECTION   ROW   SEAT

the other no-show was Thomas Steen, whose back spasms allowed Doug Smail to participate.

On the morning of the big game, the Canadian media beat the U.S. media 6–2 in an ugly all–star tilt of their own in nearby Mount Lebanon, Pennsylvania.

In yet more significant breaks from tradition, the game was played on a Sunday afternoon instead of the usual Tuesday night to accommodate the expanded format of activities, and NBC carried the game live into the U.S. Incredibly, it was the first time a national American audience had seen either Gretzky or Lemieux play. And to augment the telecast, the game officials and both coaches were wired for sound and the network conducted interviews during stoppages in play from the players' benches, much to the chagrin of Hockey Night in Canada, which had been requesting such effects and been denied now for many years.

The All–Star Game proper was a game of records: goals scored by both teams and one team; most shots by both teams and one team; and most goals in a period. And true to his word of a year before when Gretzky took centre stage in Edmonton, Mario was truly magnificent at home in the Igloo. He tied Gretzky's record of four goals in a game (he scored three in the first—on his first three shots), and to add salt to the wound, Gretzky was on the ice for all four. Lemieux's third MVP award was also a record.

Incredibly, Gretzky was held pointless in a game that featured 19 goals, setting off another round of suggestions that the Great One was on the decline while Mario seemed destined to go beyond anywhere Gretzky had been. As small consolation, Gretzky had bettered Mario in the puck control skills showdown the day before.

"I know the feeling he had today," Gretzky said afterward of Lemieux's four-goal performance. "I went through it last year in Edmonton. The fans get behind you and you get one early and you just kind of have the puck all night, and that is what happened to him.... I'm glad he did well."

still played for the Campbell Conference instead of the Wales the next day. On the injured list, Denis Savard had to withdraw for the second successive year (he was replaced by teammate Steve Larmer), while

*Pre-game ceremonies featured banners
for every one of the league's 21 teams in the rafters.*

Wales 12   Campbell 7

Wales Conference All–Stars
Honourary Captain: Maurice Richard
Pat Burns, coach (Montreal)

2	D	Brian Leetch (N.Y. Rangers)
4	D	Kevin Hatcher (Washington)
6	D	Phil Housley (Buffalo)
7a	D	Paul Coffey (Pittsburgh)
8a	RW	Cam Neely (Boston)
9	C	Kirk Muller (New Jersey)
10	C	Ron Francis (Hartford)
16	C	Pat LaFontaine (N.Y. Islanders)
17	C	Pierre Turgeon (Buffalo)
19	C	Joe Sakic (Quebec)
22	RW	Rick Tocchet (Philadelphia)
24	D	Chris Chelios (Montreal)
25	LW	Dave Andreychuk (Buffalo)
26a	RW	Brian Propp (Philadelphia)
27	C	Shayne Corson (Montreal)
31	G	Daren Puppa (Buffalo)
33a	G	Patrick Roy (Montreal)
44	RW	Stephane Richer (Montreal)
66a	C	Mario Lemieux "C" (Pittsburgh)
77a	D	Ray Bourque (Boston)

Campbell Conference All–Stars
Honourary Captain: Alex Delvecchio
Terry Crisp, coach (Calgary)

1	G	Kirk McLean (Vancouver)
2a	D	Al MacInnis (Calgary)
4a	D	Kevin Lowe (Edmonton)
7	RW	Joe Mullen (Calgary)
9	C	Bernie Nicholls (Los Angeles)
11	C	Mark Messier (Edmonton)
12	RW	Mike Gartner (Minnesota)
14	D	Paul Cavallini (St. Louis)
16a	RW	Brett Hull (St. Louis)
17	RW	Jari Kurri (Edmonton)
19	C	Steve Yzerman (Detroit)
20a	LW	Luc Robitaille (Los Angeles)
24	D	Doug Wilson (Chicago)
25	LW	Doug Smail (Winnipeg)
26	C	Joe Nieuwendyk (Calgary)
27	RW	Steve Larmer (Chicago)
28	D	Steve Duchesne (Los Angeles)
30a	G	Mike Vernon (Calgary)
33	D	Al Iafrate (Toronto)
99	C	Wayne Gretzky "C" (Los Angeles)

a=voted to starting lineup by fan ballot

First Period

1. Wales: Lemieux (Propp, Neely) 0:21
2. Wales: Andreychuk (unassisted) 5:13
3. Wales: Turgeon (Francis) 9:22
4. Campbell: Messier (Hull, Smail) 11:01
5. Wales: Lemieux (Housley) 13:00
6. Campbell: Yzerman (unassisted) 14:31
7. Wales: Tocchet (Bourque, Muller) 16:55
8. Wales: Lemieux (Coffey) 17:37
9. Wales: Turgeon (Francis, Andreychuk) 18:52
Penalties: None

Second Period

10. Wales: Muller (Coffey, Sakic) . . . . 8:47(sh)
11. Campbell: MacInnis (Lowe) . . . . 9:03(pp)
12. Campbell: Mullen (Nicholls) 13:00
13. Wales: Corson (LaFontaine) 16:43
Penalties: Roy (WC) 7:05, Iafrate (CC) 17:28

Third Period

14. Wales: Lemieux (Neely) 1:07
15. Wales: Neely (Sakic, Hatcher) 11:20
16. Campbell: Robitaille (Yzerman, Hull) 15:09
17. Campbell: Robitaille (Hull, Yzerman) 16:11
18. Wales: Muller (Tocchet) 17:50
19. Campbell: Smail (Mullen, Nieuwendyk) 19:35
Penalties: Neely (WC) 6:17, Smail (CC) 7:33

Shots on Goal

Wales	16	15	14	**45**
Campbell	9	11	22	**42**

In Goal

Wales—Roy/Puppa [Puppa (4 goals) replaced Roy (3 goals) at 9:14 of 2nd period]
Campbell—Vernon/McLean [McLean (4 goals) replaced Vernon (8 goals) at 9:14 of 2nd period]

Referee Kerry Fraser
Linesmen Bob Hodges and Dan McCourt
Attendance 17,503
MVP Mario Lemieux (Pittsburgh)

The Alumni Seek Pride and Restitution

Chicago Stadium, Saturday, January 19, 1991

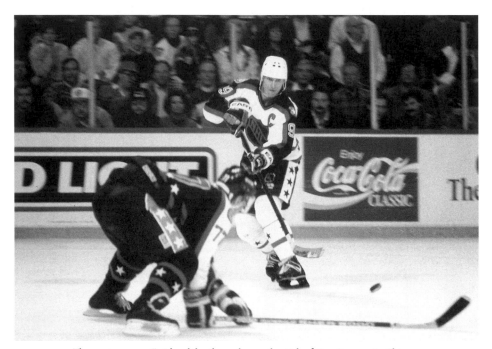

The master passer Gretzky slides the puck over the stick of Ray Bourque in Chicago.

Perhaps no coach ever so thoroughly earned the vehement wrath of so many as Mike Milbury at 1991's game when he selected enforcer Chris Nilan and checkers Brian Skrudland and Gary Galley to his Wales roster ahead of, among others, Kirk Muller and Guy Lafleur. "All I asked for was a little backchecking," Milbury explained. "That's what I tried to do by picking a few role players." Justice worked quietly to right Milbury's wrongs, though. Nilan was forced to withdraw from the game because of an ankle sprain and was replaced by Dave Christian, while Skrudland fractured his right foot and was replaced by future Hall of Famer Denis Savard. Of Milbury's choices, only Galley played. And it forced a decision. As a result of Milbury's abuse of power, the league's governors quickly decreed future teams would be picked by committee.

In a more popular move, this was the first year the NHL named two "senior" players to play in the game though they might ordinarily have been left off the roster. It was a generous way to honour their years in the league and their contributions to the game. Guy Lafleur (Wales) and Bobby Smith (Campbell) were the first two selected. (Larry Robinson had initially been asked to join the Campbells but begged for a deferral because of a sore hip.)

The skills competition offered $75,000 in prizes, triple the take from its inaugural foray the previous year. And the Heroes of Hockey game featured the heroes of the Chicago Blackhawks versus the retired best of the rest of the league. The aging Hawks were coached by Billy Reay (who had been the West Division coach the last time the All–Star Game was hosted at Chicago Stadium in 1974) and they won 3–1 on

to sue the NHL for $50 million over a pension surplus to which they felt entitled. In 1986, the NHL had taken control of $24 million in pensions. From that sum, $4 million was distributed among oldtimers while $12 million was put toward current players' pensions. The oldtimers rightfully contended that that

Rick Tocchet and Paul Coffey chat during the pre-game skate in the Wales Conference end.

goals by Cliff Korroll, Peter Marsh, and Jim Pappin before an ecstatic crowd of 18,472.

The Heroes game was boycotted by some of the greatest players of all—Gordie Howe, Bobby Orr, Ted Lindsay and Frank Mahovlich were among them— who also vociferously tried to have the game cancelled. But Bobby Hull couldn't resist playing in his old haunt in spite of the groundswell of support for the boycotters. "I spent the prime of my life here," he said joyously after receiving a tremendous standing ovation from the fans.

Still, the mood surrounding the Heroes was sombre. The NHL Alumni Association (a.k.a. "the old-timers") had decided at meetings in the Windy City

$12 million was theirs, and it was easy to understand their bitterness. Gordie Howe, an NHLer for 26 years, was currently pulling in exactly $1,200 a month from his pension, a revelation that made it only too clear how little the majority of older players was getting. Putting it bluntly, Howe said:

"Years ago, if I had picked up a shovel instead of a hockey stick, my pension would have been a hell of a lot better. We have a lot of guys who are getting the hell kicked out of them. We're fighting for them."

Unfortunately, the fight was quickly becoming two-pronged. The oldtimers had hoped to enlist the support of the current players through the NHL Players' Association, but when the old asked the young if

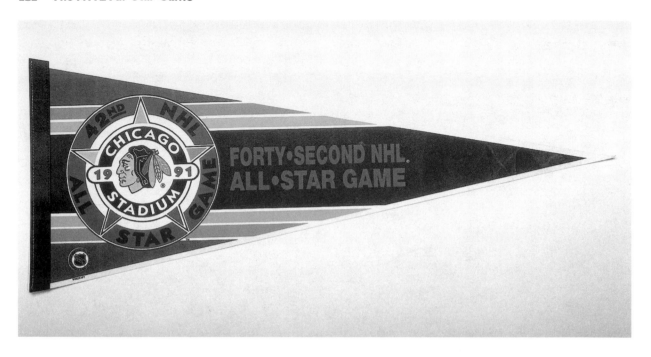

they could attend PA meetings, they were rebuffed.

"They told us it was a closed meeting and we weren't invited in," Dennis Owchar said bluntly. "We wanted their support, but now the NHLPA may be named in the lawsuit, too," which would allow the oldsters to peruse the books and find out where the pension money had gone.

Ankles were the injury of choice in 1991, as Brett Hull also had to be replaced by Adam Oates because of a badly twisted one. But most notably absent was Mario Lemieux, who had missed many weeks of play with a back problem and had yet to play with the Penguins that season.

The game was broadcast not only in the U.S. but to Allied soldiers fighting in Operation Desert Storm in the Persian Gulf (players also wore a decal on their helmets in support of them). In fact, Wayne Gretzky had called for the game to be cancelled.

"If I had any say," he opined, "I'd cancel the game on Saturday. I'd tell everybody to go home and evaluate what is going on. My grandfather fought in the First World War, so I have a right to give an opinion." (Gretzky's cousin, Kenny Hopper, was flying a mission in the Gulf as he spoke.)

Gretzky also used the All-Star Game platform to renew his own war, of sorts, on fighting.

"The image of our sport in the U.S. is just awful," he explained. "It's because we allow fighting. I'm not saying it should be done tomorrow or that I want to take away anyone's job, but I'm sick and tired of seeing a bench-clearing brawl in baseball and some announcer saying, 'It looks like a hockey game out there.' Look at Cam Neely and Mark Messier, two players who score goals but play the game hard."

The game was special for memorabilia collectors too. Upper Deck produced a special sheet of cards with six All-Stars, and only the 18,000 fans going into the building for the game received one.

That year also marked the introduction of the MAC Award (Most Assists with Children), a $10,000 donation by Ronald McDonald Children's Charities to one all-star player in honour of his dedication to children

And it was made so. Starting in 1992, a total of six goalies would play 20 minutes each in the glory game for the two teams.

Vincent Damphousse's late goal surge once again forced writers to change their choice for the MVP. They scratched Jeremy Roenick, who had played a great game for the first two periods before being eclipsed by Damphousse, whose three-goal third period gave him four for the game. He'd been playing on a line with Steve Yzerman and Adam Oates, but late in the game Muckler sent him out with Gretzky and Tomas Sandstrom to see if he could get a fifth. Muckler's other top line was an all-Kings trio of Gretzky–Robitaille–Sandstrom.

For the second straight year, Media Team Canada hammered Media Team U.S. 8–3 in the penmen's own all–star tilt.

and related charities. Of course, the money was donated to a charity of that player's choice.

At game time, Bill Ranford's appearance in the Campbell crease raised the ire of the local Chicago fans. Ranford was put on the team by his own Edmonton coach, John Muckler, who passed over Hawks goaler Ed Belfour even though Eddie the Eagle was statistically the best in the league at that point in the season. When Ranford took over for Mike Vernon halfway through the game, he was booed mercilessly. Muckler suggested a solution. "We should name three goalies [to a team] and let them play a period each."

Campbell 11   Wales 5

Campbell Conference All–Stars
Honourary Captain: Stan Mikita
John Muckler, coach (Edmonton)

1	G	Bill Ranford (Edmonton)
2a	D	Al MacInnis (Calgary)
3	D	Scott Stevens (St. Louis)
5	D	Steve Smith (Edmonton)
6	D	Phil Housley (Winnipeg)
7a	D	Chris Chelios (Chicago)
8	RW	Tomas Sandstrom (Los Angeles)
10	LW	Vincent Damphousse (Toronto)
11	C	Mark Messier (Edmonton)
12	C	Adam Oates (St. Louis)
14	RW	Theoren Fleury (Calgary)
15	C	Dave Gagner (Minnesota)
17	RW	Trevor Linden (Vancouver)
18b	C	Bobby Smith (Minnesota)
19	C	Steve Yzerman (Detroit)
20	D	Gary Suter (Calgary)
21a	LW	Luc Robitaille (Los Angeles)
27	C	Jeremy Roenick (Chicago)
28	RW	Steve Larmer (Chicago)
30a	G	Mike Vernon (Calgary)
99a	C	Wayne Gretzky "C" (Los Angeles)

Wales Conference All–Stars
Honourary Captain: Jean Béliveau
Mike Milbury, coach (Boston)

2	D	Brian Leetch (N.Y. Rangers)
4	D	Kevin Hatcher (Washington)
5	D	Uwe Krupp (Buffalo)
7a	D	Paul Coffey (Pittsburgh)
8a	RW	Cam Neely (Boston)
9	C	Darren Turcotte (N.Y. Rangers)
10b	RW	Guy Lafleur (Quebec)
11	C	John Cullen (Pittsburgh)
12	RW	Mark Recchi (Pittsburgh)
15	RW	John MacLean (New Jersey)
16	LW	Pat Verbeek (Hartford)
17	C	Pat LaFontaine (N.Y. Islanders)
18	C	Denis Savard (Montreal)
19a	C	Joe Sakic (Quebec)
22a	RW	Rick Tocchet (Philadelphia)
25	LW	Kevin Stevens (Pittsburgh)
27	RW	Dave Christian (Boston)
28	D	Garry Galley (Boston)
33a	G	Patrick Roy (Montreal)
35	G	Andy Moog (Boston)
77a	D	Ray Bourque "C" (Boston)

a=voted to starting lineup by fan ballot

b=Commissioner's selection

First Period

1. Campbell: Gagner (Roenick, Larmer) 6:17
2. Wales: LaFontaine (Turcotte) 9:14
3. Campbell: Damphousse (Oates, S. Smith) 11:36
Penalties: None

Second Period

4. Wales: LaFontaine (Hatcher) 1:33
5. Campbell: Suter (unassisted) 5:23
6. Campbell: Gretzky (Sandstrom) 9:10
7. Campbell: Oates (Yzerman) 9:48
8. Campbell: Fleury (Messier, Chelios) 14:40
9. Wales: Tocchet (Verbeek, Sakic) 15:36
10. Campbell: Roenick (S. Smith, Oates) 17:07
Penalties: None

Third Period

11. Wales: MacLean (Cullen, Bourque) . . . . 2:29(pp)
12. Campbell: Chelios (Roenick, Larmer) 5:23
13. Campbell: Damphousse (Oates, Housley) 8:54

14. Campbell: Damphousse (Housley, Oates) 11:40
15. Wales: Stevens (Tocchet) . . . . 13:56(pp)
16. Campbell: Damphousse (unassisted) 17:16
Penalties: Housley (CC) 0:57, Housley (CC) 12:26

Shots on Goal

Campbell	15	15	11	**41**
Wales	10	9	22	**41**

In Goal

Campbell—Vernon/Ranford [Ranford (3 goals) replaced Vernon (2 goals) at 9:48 of 2nd period]
Wales—Roy/Moog [Moog (6 goals) replaced Roy (5 goals) at 9:48 of 2nd period]

Referee Terry Gregson
Linesmen Jerry Pateman and Dan Schachte
Attendance 18,472
MVP Vincent Damphousse (Toronto)

Meetings Take Precedence to the Game

The Spectrum, Philadelphia, Saturday, January 18, 1992

Irony was the order of the day in Philadelphia in 1992 as the home of the Broad Street Bullies provided fans with the first-ever penalty-free All–Star classic. The game wasn't sold out—good seats were available right up to game time—and it remained close for the first half. Then a five-goal explosion by the Campbells took the score to 8–2 after two periods and left the result (of infinitesimal interest at the best of times) obvious. For the first time, both teams used three goalies, one for each period, a format that continues to this day.

The NHL and NHL Players' Association held meetings over the weekend on their collective bargaining agreement, which had expired the previous summer. To that point in the season, both sides had operated in good faith without a contract. They had not met since training camp, and rumour had it that after the All–Star break, the owners would lock out the players to force an agreement. In part, this was an aggressive tactic to break the stalemate, but it was also a defensive plan in case the players called a strike for the playoffs, when they didn't get paid but the owners made the vast majority of their annual income.

Key to the lack of agreement, of course, were free agency and salary arbitration, both of which the players felt heavily favoured the owners. Free agency didn't come early enough for the players, and arbitration was usually carried out by adjudicators affiliated with the league.

The players also met separately to discuss the impact AIDS might have on the game, particularly through fighting, though in the end doctors assured them that transmitting the HIV virus in hockey (via blood spattered during a fight, for instance) was

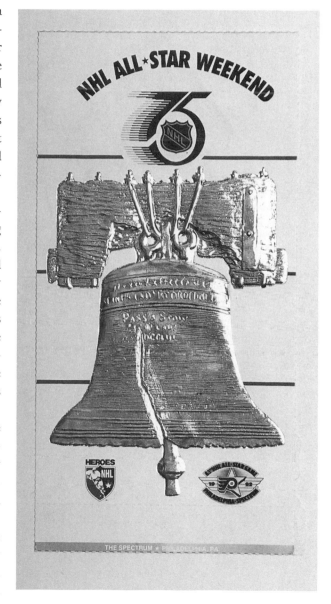

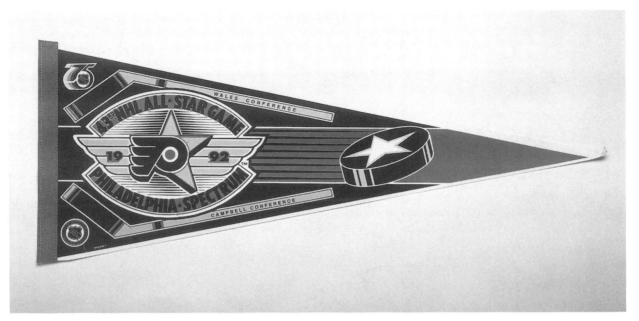

*The post-game handshakes, while genuine,
can't conjure up the feelings of celebration and devastation that they do at playoff time.*

Dave Ellett (left) and Kirk Muller check out the scoreboard during a break in action.

much more unlikely than being hit by lightning. In addition, the NHLPA had to worry about an FBI investigation into the pension fund vis-à-vis the old-timers' lawsuit against the league.

The All–Stars weekend was always good for a few trade rumours. In 1992, the main gossip centred around Paul Coffey of Pittsburgh going to the very Spectrum where the game would be played. In a humourous touch, the Flyers trainer assigned Tocchet's stall to Coffey for the All–Star Game. Pittsburgh was interested in dealing Coffey to reduce its payroll, which had swelled to $11.5 million, and it was widely believed the deal would see Rick Tocchet and cash go to the Penguins. In the end, it never materialised.

For the first time, a committee of general managers made all the additions to the teams beyond those selected by fan balloting. Meanwhile, in peripheral activity, the Canadian media clobbered the U.S. media 6–1 in their own game for the third straight year and the Flyers Heroes of Hockey defeated the NHL Selects 3–2. The Flyers' dud-studded roster included Dave "the Hammer" Schultz, Andre "Moose" Dupont, Don "Big Bird" Saleski, and "Mad Dog" Bob Kelly, a WWF gang of NHLers if ever there was one.

For the main event of the weekend, players wore replica sweaters from the first All–Star Game in 1947. The Wales wore white with a blue logo and red and blue stripes to go with red pants, the Campbells red sweaters with a white logo, blue and white stripes and blue pants. The officials also wore old-style sweaters, white with a V-neck and a small NHL logo over the heart.

The opening ceremonies featured Martha Johnson, wife of the late coach Bob Johnson, dropping the puck. She then presented team captains Gretzky and Lemieux with the same commemorative "Badger" patches that the Penguins had been wearing all season. This was followed by Celine Dion's breathtaking version of "The Star-Spangled Banner."

The top plus/minus of the day went to 40-year-old Larry Robinson, who was a +4. At the other end, Paul Coffey was on for five of the first eight Campbell goals (which perhaps contributed to scuttling any plans for a trade). Unquestionably, the stars of the game were Gretzky and wingman Brett Hull. The two combined for six points, Hull won MVP honours, and both had the time of their lives.

"I've played with Gordie, Guy, and now I got a chance to play with Brett. I've been pretty lucky to have played with some of the best right wingers in hockey," Gretzky said.

"I've said it a million times. Getting a chance to play with Wayne is something I've always wanted to do, and it was fantastic," echoed Hull in the dressing room after the game.

Having scored 86 goals the previous season, Hull was being touted as the next player likely to break Gretzky's record of 92 in a year and perhaps even to become the first century man in the game. His output declined in the second half, however, and he finished that year with 70.

And, for the second year in a row, Mario Lemieux's attendance had been in doubt. He had missed the 1991 game because of serious back problems but he played in Philadelphia despite having missed four Penguins games with a herniated disc prior to the All–Star tilt.

Again, hockey's growth in the U.S. was on everyone's mind, and again the game's greatest spokesman felt the need to address the subject of fighting if the game were to develop in the States and compete with baseball, football, and basketball.

"It is a Canadian sport and it will always be a Canadian sport," Gretzky said. "We need to grow and need the U.S. TV market. But we will not get on as long as we allow fighting."

The players didn't receive money as winners or losers in the All–Star Game. Instead, they received either special his-and-hers rings or a Tiffany-style mantle clock to honour their participation. The NHL also paid for wives or girlfriends to attend the game.

Campbell 10   Wales 6

Campbell Conference All–Stars
Honourary Captain: Lanny McDonald
Bob Gainey, coach (Minnesota)

1	G	Kirk McLean (Vancouver)
2a	D	Al MacInnis (Calgary)
4	D	Dave Ellett (Toronto)
6	D	Phil Housley (Winnipeg)
7a	D	Chris Chelios (Chicago)
10	LW	Gary Roberts (Calgary)
12	C	Adam Oates (St. Louis)
14	RW	Theoren Fleury (Calgary)
16a	RW	Brett Hull (St. Louis)
17	RW	Trevor Linden (Vancouver)
18	C	Steve Yzerman (Detroit)
19b	D	Larry Robinson (Los Angeles)
20a	LW	Luc Robitaille (Los Angeles)
21	LW	Vincent Damphousse (Edmonton)
23	LW	Brian Bellows (Minnesota)
24	D	Doug Wilson (San Jose)
25	D	Mark Tinordi (Minnesota)
27	C	Jeremy Roenick (Chicago)
30a	G	Ed Belfour (Chicago)
32	G	Tim Cheveldae (Detroit)
91	C	Sergei Fedorov (Detroit)
99a	C	Wayne Gretzky "C" (Los Angeles)

a=voted to starting lineup by fan ballot

Wales Conference All–Stars
Honourary Captain: Bobby Clarke
Scotty Bowman, coach (Pittsburgh)

1	G	Don Beaupre (Washington)
2	D	Brian Leetch (N.Y. Rangers)
4a	D	Scott Stevens (New Jersey)
5	D	Kevin Hatcher (Washington)
7a	D	Paul Coffey (Pittsburgh)
9	LW	Kirk Muller (Montreal)
11	C	Mark Messier (N.Y. Rangers)
12	RW	Owen Nolan (Quebec)
15	C	John Cullen (Hartford)
16	C	Joe Sakic (Quebec)
17	RW	Rod Brind'Amour (Philadelphia)
18	LW	Randy Burridge (Washington)
19b	C	Bryan Trottier (Pittsburgh)
20	LW	Ray Ferraro (N.Y. Islanders)
25	LW	Kevin Stevens (Pittsburgh)
28	D	Eric Desjardins (Montreal)
33a	G	Patrick Roy (Montreal)
35	G	Mike Richter (N.Y. Rangers)
66a	C	Mario Lemieux "C" (Pittsburgh)
68a	RW	Jaromir Jagr (Pittsburgh)
77a	D	Ray Bourque (Boston)
89	RW	Alexander Mogilny (Buffalo)

b=Commissioner's selection

First Period

1. Campbell: Linden (Roenick, Tinordi) 7:53
2. Wales: K. Stevens (Lemieux, Jagr) 11:20
3. Campbell: Gretzky (Hull, Robitaille) 14:56
Penalties: None

Second Period

4. Campbell: Hull (Gretzky, Robitaille) 0:42
5. Wales: S. Stevens (Mogilny, Messier) 5:37
6. Campbell: Bellows (Fedorov, MacInnis) 7:40
7. Campbell: Roenick (Ellett) 8:13
8. Campbell: Fleury (Robinson) 11:06
9. Campbell: Hull (Gretzky, Robitaille) 11:59
10. Campbell: Fleury (Damphousse, Oates) 17:33
11. Wales: Nolan (Sakic, Bourque) 19:29
Penalties: None

Third Period

12. Wales: Trottier (Hatcher) 4:03
13. Campbell: Bellows (Fedorov) 4:50
14. Wales: Mogilny (Desjardins) 5:28
15. Campbell: Roberts (Linden) 18:42
16. Wales: Burridge (Sakic, Nolan) 19:12
Penalties: None

Shots on Goal

Campbell	15	12	15	**42**
Wales	14	9	18	**41**

In Goal

Campbell—Belfour (1st period, one goal); Cheveldae (2nd period, 2 goals); McLean (3rd period, 3 goals)
Wales—Roy (1st period, 2 goals); Beaupre (2nd period, 6 goals); Richter (3rd period, 2 goals)

Referee Don Koharski
Linesmen Mark Vines and Mark Pare
Attendance 17,380
MVP Brett Hull (St. Louis)

44th All–Star Game

No Hitting, No Helmet, No Contest

Montreal Forum, Saturday, February 6, 1993

The *Club de hockey* billed this All–Star weekend as Hockey Fest '93 and provided fans with interactive games as well as many opportunities to meet their heroes. They set up a small, makeshift rink for skills competitions, clinics, and demonstrations conducted by players past and present, from Maurice Richard and Jean Béliveau to homegrown newcomer Alexandre Daigle.

The NHL Players' Association discussed licensing, drug abuse, and the arrival of the league's new commissioner, Gary Bettman, who dropped in on the meetings to introduce himself. The All–Star Game was more or less Bettman's coming out party, as he had officially taken office just a few days before, but he was stepping into a league fraught with problems. The most pressing included a collective bargaining agreement with the players and a contract with the officials' union, but he was also tinkering with computer

Double-oh, Eddie Belfour, in goal, keeps his eagle eyes on the puck during play around his net.

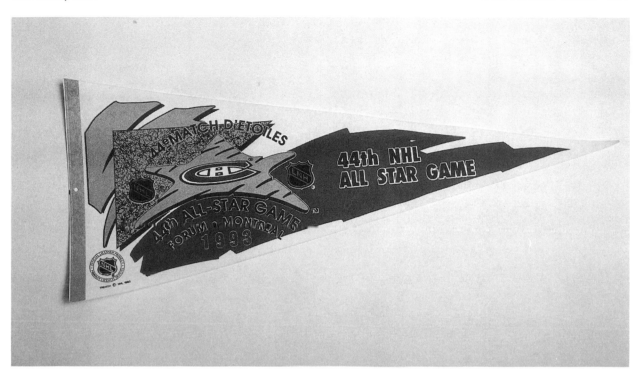

enhancement of the puck and turning the three-period game into two halves as ways to develop a base in the evasive, ever-elusive U.S. television market.

At the board of governors' meetings, the main discussions focused on realignment and the involvement of the league in the Lillehammer Olympics, but no decisions were made so that Bettman could take some time to familiarise himself with the league and its ambitions. He did meet with Gordie Howe, though, to discuss the litigation brought by the oldtimers against the NHL, and later he joined Henri Richard and Frank Mahovlich at a special unveiling of a plaque at the old Windsor Hotel in downtown Montreal where the NHL was officially formed on November 22, 1917.

Coach Mike Keenan was participating in the game under the oddest of circumstances. He'd been elected to coach the Campbell Conference because he'd been a Cup finalist with Chicago the previous spring. But on November 5 of the current season, he'd been fired by the Hawks when the team got off to a sluggish start. Thus he became the only unemployed coach ever to boss an All–Star bench. "I'm pleased and thankful to get this opportunity," he said. "I look forward to being around the Blackhawks players. I miss them." He was accompanied by two well-known coaches who acted as his assistants, Tommy Ivan and Billy Reay.

While the fans selected the starting players for both teams, a panel of general managers filled in the remaining selections on the roster. This year's executive foursome consisted of Craig Patrick (Pittsburgh), Bob Pulford (Chicago), Harry Sinden (Boston), and Glen Sather (Edmonton). Even this seemingly objective method was not without controversy, however, mostly because of the persistent rule that each team must be represented. The Ottawa Senators, for instance—some 50 points behind Vancouver in the standings—had two players going to the game (Brad Marsh and Peter Sidorkiewicz) while the Canucks had only Pavel Bure, and three of the top goalies in the game (Kirk McLean, Tom Barrasso, and Ron Hextall) were all missing from the final roster.

Rick Tocchet was named as a Pittsburgh replacement for Mario Lemieux, who was still out of the lineup with a form of Hodgkin's disease. Lemieux did accept commissioner Bettman's invitation to watch the game, though, and coach Scotty Bowman presented Mario with a Campbell team sweater at centre ice to a thunderous ovation.

In a less elevating pre-game ceremony—the last at the Forum—Jean Béliveau, Guy Lafleur, and Rocket

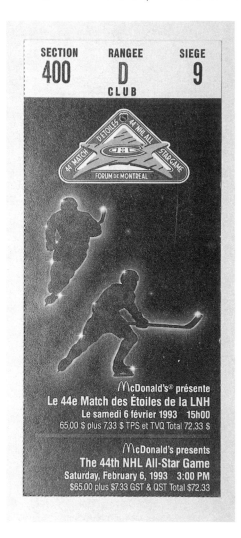

Richard came out to centre ice with the Rocket carrying the Stanley Cup. On the way, he slipped and fell and took the Cup with him, denting it in the process. The anthems didn't go a lot better when Roch Voisine butchered a line from "The Star-Spangled Banner."

Pat Falloon's dislocated shoulder gave Kelly Kisio a chance to play; Kevin Lowe replaced the injured Brian Leetch; and Mike Gartner was a late replacement for another injured star, teammate Mark Messier. Gartner was playing in his sixth glitter game and was the only man to score 30 or more goals in 15 successive seasons. Playing on a line with Adam Oates and Peter Bondra, he finished the 1993 game with four goals, five points, and a car as game MVP.

Brett Hull elected to play without a helmet, a clear indictment of just how (literally) carefree the game had become. "It's something I did for the fans," he said. "I thought the fans would appreciate a chance to see Brett Hull without a helmet." Clearly, this was not a "check your ego at the door" kind of game, but events proved he wasn't far wrong. A record 22 goals flew past the waving hands and splayed legs of the goalies, leaving more people disgusted with what the All–Star Game had turned into than impressed by the players' speed, skill, and strength. Even referee Dan Marouelli commented wryly that it was the only game he could recall in which he dropped the puck more frequently than his linesmen. (Referees were selected to All–Star Game honours on a rotating basis among those who had 10 years' experience.)

While Wayne Gretzky centred four different lines in the first period alone, he was held pointless. But this didn't come as a big surprise. He'd missed the first 39 games of the season with a herniated disc and was only now getting back into shape.

"The first eight or nine games I was trying to slowly come back," he said, "and it was going nicely. But the last four or five games have been really tough. My confidence is a little low right now."

Outpointing Gretzky was 34-year-old all–star rookie Brad Marsh, who scored midway through the third. In 1,086 regular-season games, he scored exactly 23 goals, the lowest ratio of any 1,000-game player in league history. "One day I'm going to build a bar in my house," he said. "That puck will be hanging there." (Even better, he ended up opening a bar in Ottawa's new Corel Centre and it is there that his All–Star Game puck resides.)

Prize money remained the same in 1993: $2,000 for winning players; $1,000 for losers; $2,500 for winners in the skills competition. Players on the winning team were also given a set of custom-built golf clubs.

Wales 16   Campbell 6

		Wales Conference All–Stars Honourary Captain: Henri Richard Scotty Bowman, coach (Pittsburgh)				Campbell Conference All–Stars Honourary Captain: Frank Mahovlich Mike Keenan, coach (Chicago)
1	G	Craig Billington (New Jersey)		00a	G	Ed Belfour (Chicago)
3	D	Zarley Zalapski (Hartford)		3	D	Steve Chiasson (Detroit)
4	D	Kevin Lowe (N.Y. Rangers)		5	D	Garth Butcher (St. Louis)
5	D	Scott Stevens (New Jersey)		6	D	Phil Housley (Winnipeg)
7	C	Pierre Turgeon (N.Y. Islanders)		7a	D	Chris Chelios (Chicago)
8	RW	Mark Recchi (Philadelphia)		8b	D	Randy Carlyle (Winnipeg)
9	C	Kirk Muller (Montreal)		9	RW	Mike Modano (Minnesota)
11	RW	Mike Gartner (N.Y. Rangers)		10	LW	Gary Roberts (Calgary)
12	C	Adam Oates (Boston)		11	C	Kelly Kisio (San Jose)
14b	D	Brad Marsh (Ottawa)		12a	RW	Pavel Bure (Vancouver)
16	C	Pat LaFontaine (Buffalo)		13	RW	Teemu Selanne (Winnipeg)
18	RW	Peter Bondra (Washington)		14	C	Brian Bradley (Tampa Bay)
19	C	Joe Sakic (Quebec)		16a	RW	Brett Hull (St. Louis)
22	RW	Rick Tocchet (Pittsburgh)		17	RW	Jari Kurri (Los Angeles)
25a	LW	Kevin Stevens (Pittsburgh)		19a	C	Steve Yzerman (Detroit)
28	D	Steve Duchesne (Quebec)		20	LW	Luc Robitaille (Los Angeles)
31	G	Peter Sidorkiewicz (Ottawa)		24	D	Dave Manson (Edmonton)
33a	G	Patrick Roy (Montreal)		27	C	Jeremy Roenick (Chicago)
34	D	Al Iafrate (Washington)		30	G	Mike Vernon (Calgary)
68a	RW	Jaromir Jagr (Pittsburgh)		35	G	Jon Casey (Minnesota)
77a	D	Ray Bourque (Boston)		77a	D	Paul Coffey (Detroit)
89	RW	Alexander Mogilny (Buffalo)		93	C	Doug Gilmour (Toronto)
				99	C	Wayne Gretzky "C" (Los Angeles)

a=voted to starting lineup by fan ballot   b=Commissioner's selection

First Period

1. Wales: Gartner (Oates, Lowe). 3:15
2. Wales: Gartner (Oates) 3:37
3. Wales: Bondra (Oates, Gartner) 4:23
4. Wales: Mogilny (Bourque) . . . . 11:40(pp)
5. Wales: Turgeon (Recchi) 13:05
6. Wales: Gartner (Oates, Bondra) 13:22

Penalties: Manson (CC) 11:12

Second Period

7. Wales: Tocchet (K. Stevens, Recchi) 0:19
8. Wales: Gartner (Turgeon) 3:33
9. Wales: Tocchet (S. Stevens) 4:57
10. Campbell: Roenick (Selanne) 5:52
11. Wales: Recchi (Marsh) 9:25
12. Campbell: Kisio (Roenick, Modano). 10:15
13. Wales: K. Stevens (Recchi) 14:50
14. Wales: Turgeon (Sakic, Jagr). 17:56

Penalties: None

Third Period

15. Wales: LaFontaine (Muller, Mogilny) 8:07
16. Wales: Jagr (Sakic, Turgeon). 9:08
17. Wales: Marsh (K. Stevens, Recchi). 12:52
18. Campbell: Gilmour (Coffey). 13:51
19. Wales: Turgeon (Sakic, S. Stevens) 15:51
20. Campbell: Selanne (Manson, Kurri) 17:03
21. Campbell: Bure (Kisio) 18:44
22. Campbell: Bure (unassisted). 19:31

Penalties: None

Shots on Goal

Wales	22	15	12	**49**
Campbell	11	16	14	**41**

In Goal

Wales—Roy (1st period, no goals); Sidorkiewicz (2nd period, 2 goals); Billington (3rd period, 4 goals)
Campbell—Belfour (1st period, 6 goals); Vernon (2nd period, 6 goals); Casey (3rd period, 4 goals)

Referee Dan Marouelli

Linesmen Ryan Bozak and Kevin Collins

Attendance 17,137

MVP Mike Gartner (N.Y. Rangers)

A Strike Seems Imminent

Madison Square Garden, New York, Saturday, January 22, 1994

The 1994 All–Star Game was almost forced to relocate to the Meadowlands in New Jersey the day before it was scheduled to be played. A major labour dispute left 17 of 18 unions involved in the day-to-day operations of Madison Square Garden without contracts and workers seemed unwilling to accommodate the NHL. However, a last-minute agreement ensured they would put on the game and save face for all concerned.

As usual, both the players and league officials held important meetings during the weekend, and the players were decidedly not impressed when the league suggested that a salary cap would be the basis for upcoming negotiations on a new collective bargaining agreement.

"We are not in favour of any form of a salary cap," NHL Players' Association executive director Bob Goodenow emphatically reiterated. "We reviewed the [NHL's] proposal and our reaction is that some of the major principles the league has put forth cause serious problems for us."

And that was just the tip of the bargaining iceberg. The players also wanted the Entry Draft shortened from 10 rounds to four (thus creating a huge market of young, undrafted free agent players); they wanted a cut of sweater and merchandise sales to the public; and they were relentless in their desire for greater mobility in free agency. The term "labour" was fast replacing "play" and "business" was subbing for "game" to such an extent that a confrontation

*Jeremy Roenick (left) and Teemu Selanne say a friendly hi during the Skills competition,
the now traditional prelude to the big game itself.*

between Goodenow and commissioner Gary Bettman made it clear that a strike or lockout would soon threaten the season.

For the first time, the NHL voted to resort to a shootout if the score were tied after 60 minutes and the five-minute overtime, a decision based partly on recent discussions to adopt the entertaining method of breaking a tie for the regular season. In fact, the league put together a committee of 10 general managers (Cliff Fletcher, Bill Torrey, Harry Sinden, Phil Esposito, Jim Devellano, Howard Baldwin, Barry Shenkarow, Steve Walsh, Marcel Aubut, and Michael Eisner) to examine the possibility of shootouts. Eisner, president and chairman of the Mighty Ducks, was leading the pro-shootout charge in an attempt to reach out to younger fans craving excitement. It had been used in minor pro leagues to some effect, but the NHL board of directors had steadfastly refused to alter the game in a way they found both fundamen-

tally vulgar and an unacceptable break with tradition.

The two coaches from the Stanley Cup finals represented their respective conferences and Eastern boss Jacques Demers brought along his son, Jason, as the team's stickboy. And the sweaters were different that year. The East wore a San Jose teal while the West adopted an Anaheim purple. Each player wore five different sweaters during the weekend: one went to the NHLPA, one to the team, one to the league, one to Ronald McDonald House for charity, and one was left for the player to do with as he pleased. To generate more intense competition and avoid the embarrassment of a lopsided game like the previous year's 16–6 outcome, winning players received $5,000, losers nothing.

Missing in action because of injury were Mario Lemieux (bad back and his continuing struggle with cancer), Mike Modano, Mark Howe (the commissioner's selection for the Eastern Conference; replaced

Patrick Roy makes the save as Jeremy Roenick moves in,
while Larry Murphy ties up Teemu Selanne by the side of the goal.

by Joe Mullen), Pat Lafontaine, Wendel Clark (bruised ankle; replaced by Brendan Shanahan), and Steve Yzerman. Mike Vernon was also a late scratch because of a bad left knee that wasn't healing; he was replaced by Arturs Irbe. Jaromir Jagr was in New York but pulled his groin during the fastest-skater event of the skills competition and had to withdraw from the game. Local Rangers captain Mark Messier filled in at the last minute for the young superstar being billed as "Mario Jr."

To help promote the game in the Big Apple, Eric Lindros appeared on the "David Letterman Show" and Jeremy Roenick and Adam Graves sat down on "NBC Today," Lindros and Brett Hull did the weather on "Good Morning America" the day of the game (cold and clear with a chance of flurries), and Gordie Howe appeared on the "Conan O'Brien Show." Waiting in the green room, fans on the set begged old Elbows to bodycheck them into the walls.

Alexei Yashin was the only rookie in the game but he scored twice, including the game-winner with less than four minutes to play. "It was all luck," he said later. Though scoring was down slightly from the previous year's grand mêlée, even Wayne Gretzky begged for some sort of change to create a more competitive spirit on ice. "Maybe next year in San Jose we can have Canada against an international team," he suggested.

The hardest hit of the game came in a collision between teammates Eric Lindros and Mark Recchi. Mike Richter won the MVP car on the strength of a near-perfect second period that included fine stops on Pavel Bure and Doug Gilmour and 19 of 21 in total.

1994 COCA-COLA NHL
ALL·STAR WEEKEND

MADISON SQUARE GARDEN   JANUARY 21-22, 1994

Eastern 9   Western 8

Eastern Conference All–Stars
Honourary Captain: Rod Gilbert
Jacques Demers, coach (Montreal)

2a	D	Brian Leetch (N.Y. Rangers)
3	D	Garry Galley (Philadelphia)
4	D	Scott Stevens (New Jersey)
7b	RW	Joe Mullen (Pittsburgh)
8	RW	Mark Recchi (Philadelphia)
9	LW	Adam Graves (N.Y. Rangers)
10	LW	Geoff Sanderson (Hartford)
11	C	Mark Messier (N.Y. Rangers)
12	C	Adam Oates (Boston)
17	C	Pierre Turgeon (N.Y. Islanders)
18	C	Joe Sakic (Quebec)
19	C	Brian Bradley (Tampa Bay)
20	C	Alexei Yashin (Ottawa)
22	RW	Bob Kudelski (Florida)
33a	G	Patrick Roy (Montreal)
34	D	Al Iafrate (Washington)
34	G	John Vanbiesbrouck (Florida)
35	G	Mike Richter (N.Y. Rangers)
55	D	Larry Murphy (Pittsburgh)
77a	D	Ray Bourque (Boston)
88a	C	Eric Lindros (Philadelphia)
89a	RW	Alexander Mogilny (Buffalo)

a=voted to starting lineup by fan ballot

Western Conference All–Stars
Honourary Captain: Gordie Howe
Barry Melrose, coach (Los Angeles)

2	D	Al MacInnis (Calgary)
4	D	Rob Blake (Los Angeles)
5	D	Alexei Kasatonov (Anaheim)
6	D	Sandis Ozolinsh (San Jose)
7a	D	Chris Chelios (Chicago)
9	LW	Shayne Corson (Edmonton)
10a	RW	Pavel Bure (Vancouver)
13	RW	Teemu Selanne (Winnipeg)
14	LW	Dave Andreychuk (Toronto)
16a	RW	Brett Hull (St. Louis)
18b	RW	Dave Taylor (Los Angeles)
19	LW	Brendan Shanahan (St. Louis)
25	C	Joe Nieuwendyk (Calgary)
26	RW	Russ Courtnall (Dallas)
27	C	Jeremy Roenick (Chicago)
29a	G	Felix Potvin (Toronto)
31	G	Curtis Joseph (St. Louis)
32	G	Arturs Irbe (San Jose)
77a	D	Paul Coffey (Detroit)
91	C	Sergei Fedorov (Detroit)
93	C	Doug Gilmour (Toronto)
99a	C	Wayne Gretzky "C" (Los Angeles)

b=Commissioner's selection

First Period
1. Western: Roenick (Nieuwendyk, Blake) 7:31
2. Eastern: Kudelski (Turgeon, Bourque). 9:46
3. Western: Fedorov (Bure, Ozolinsh) 10:20
4. Eastern: Lindros (unassisted) 11:00
5. Western: Shanahan (Gretzky, Hull) 13:21
6. Eastern: Yashin (Sakic, Turgeon) 14:29
7. Western: Andreychuk (MacInnis, Fedorov). 15:10
Penalties: None

Second Period
8. Eastern: Stevens (Oates, Sanderson) 10:37
9. Western: Coffey (Andreychuk, Gilmour) 12:36
10. Western: Ozolinsh (Taylor, Roenick) 14:39
11. Eastern: Messier (Mullen, Graves) 15:05
Penalties: None

Third Period
12. Western: Ozolinsh (Bure) 0:55

13. Eastern: Mullen (Graves, Messier) 1:28
14. Western: Shanahan (Gretzky, Chelios) 7:40
15. Eastern: Sakic (Turgeon, Stevens) 10:41
16. Eastern: Kudelski (Messier) 13:59
17. Eastern: Yashin (Sakic, Turgeon) 16:18
Penalties: None

Shots on Goal

Eastern	19	18	19	**56**
Western	17	21	8	**46**

In Goal
Eastern—Roy (1st period, 4 goals); Richter (2nd period, 2 goals); Vanbiesbrouck (3rd period, 2 goals)

Western—Potvin (1st period, 3 goals); Irbe (2nd period, 2 goals); Joseph (3rd period, 4 goals)

Referee Bill McCreary
Linesmen Gord Broseker and Pat Dapuzzo
Attendance 18,200
MVP Mike Richter (N.Y. Rangers)

The Glowing, All-American Puck

FleetCenter, Boston, Saturday, January 20, 1996

A glitzy, highly improbable way of allowing American fans to follow the puck made its debut at the 1996 All–Star Game. The FoxTrax puck was tailed by a blue dot and red streak when it was passed or shot, and the system required not only a special puck but also special cameras. And it proved more distracting than innovative, more controversial than clearly successful, and more an insult to hockey than a pioneering advance. After investing years of experimentation and millions of dollars, the puck eventually lost what little lustre it brought to the game. And they might have known. Its predecessor, the Fire Puck, had been used once in practice by the Minnesota North Stars. The puck glowed on TV because of a special chip in the vulcanised rubber that could be picked up by cameras, but it made an inferior puck that slowed the flow of the game.

Because of the owners' lockout during the 1994–95 season, the All-Star game set for January 1995 in San Jose had been cancelled for the first time in league history, a dubious distinction that made Boston host of the 46th version. The Sharks would have to wait another year to get their turn.

The league's governors agreed at their meetings to the sale of the Dallas Stars and allowed the transfer of Winnipeg to Phoenix for the upcoming season, the second Canadian team to go south after Quebec in the summer of 1995. Gary Bettman's financial success with the league was rewarded when the board of governors extended his contract as commissioner for another five years.

In other quarters, there were suggestions of

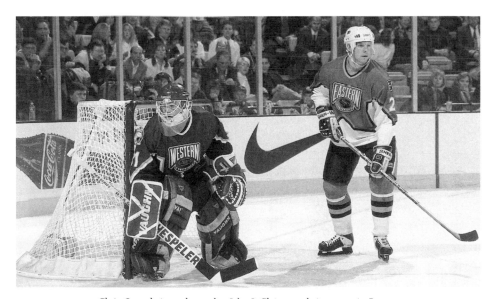

Chris Osgood, in goal, watches John LeClair swoosh in on net in Boston.

Pressure, intensity, and focus are not writ large on the faces of All–Star players, as Wayne Gretzky (top) enjoys a bench moment, while Mario Lemieux (bottom) relaxes at his pew in the dressing room.

impending tampering charges against the St. Louis Blues. Wayne Gretzky was due to become an unrestricted free agent on July 1, and he would almost certainly be traded prior to that. Blues general manager and coach Mike Keenan had been lobbying Gretzky's agent, Mike Barnett, for some time, even though number 99 was still under contract with L.A. Regardless, rumours of a trade were surfacing hourly—to New Jersey, Toronto (close to home), Detroit (where his idol, Gordie Howe, had played), and Chicago (where former Soo Greyhound teammate Craig Hartsburg was coaching).

Spurred by the suspect selections coach Mike Milbury made for the 1991 game, the practice of GMs (and not coaches) selecting the players had been followed since 1994 and the rules for voting players to the teams had become very formal. A secret panel of GMs and league officials selected the names of the players that went on the ballot fans used to cast votes and each team had at least two players on the ballot. Such were the vagaries of a 26-team league and a 96-name ballot that a number of great players—Peter Forsberg, Steve Yzerman and Grant Fuhr, for instance—were left off the card. After the fans voted the starting lineups, another anonymous committee

of GMs selected the remaining players for both sides.

And now the selection of coaches for the game changed for the first time. Before this, the two men who had been in the Stanley Cup finals the previous spring bossed the All–Star benches. In 1996, it was the two men whose teams were in first place when All–Star balloting closed. The assistants also now came from the other leaders in their respective divisions to allow greater representation and participation.

The ever more merchandise-conscious NHL debuted some new paraphernalia at the 1996 All–Star Game. Wayne Gretzky forsook his cardboard-thin Jofa helmet for a CCM model while Daniel Alfredsson showed up in a Cooper and Mats Sundin had a white Nike swoosh on his lid. And Sergei Fedorov dashed along the ice in white Nike skates.

Larry Murphy had to cut short a Las Vegas mini-vacation as a late fill-in for Gary Suter, who'd injured his knee a few days before the All–Stars got together. Yet another replacement proved to be crucial. Paul Kariya was in for injury-prone Pavel Bure, who had suffered a career-threatening knee injury (a complete tear of the anterior cruciate ligament (ACL) that cost him the rest of the season) in a game against Chicago the previous November. Playing with Brett Hull and Wayne Gretzky, Kariya stole the show with a superb pass to Hull and an even more spectacular breakaway goal of his own. Altogether, though, this was the lowest-scoring game in eight years, an indication of the end of the 1980s offense and the arrival of defensive hockey. (A tie would have led to five minutes of overtime and then a shootout, if needed.)

"There was no joking any more on our bench when the score was 4–4," Mats Sundin said of the extra intensity late in the third with the result hanging in the balance. "It was like a real game."

Eastern 5   Western 4

Eastern Conference All–Stars
Honourary Captain: Bobby Orr
Doug MacLean, coach (Florida)

2	D	Brian Leetch (N.Y. Rangers)
4a	D	Scott Stevens (New Jersey)
7	C	Pierre Turgeon (Montreal)
8	RW	Cam Neely (Boston)
10	C	Ron Francis (Pittsburgh)
11	C	Mark Messier (N.Y. Rangers)
12	RW	Peter Bondra (Washington)
14b	C	Craig MacTavish (Philadelphia)
15	RW	Daniel Alfredsson (Ottawa)
16	RW	Pat Verbeek (N.Y. Rangers)
20	LW	John LeClair (Philadelphia)
27	RW	Scott Mellanby (Florida)
30a	G	Martin Brodeur (New Jersey)
34	G	John Vanbiesbrouck (Florida)
37	D	Eric Desjardins (Philadelphia)
39	G	Dominik Hasek (Buffalo)
44	D	Roman Hamrlik (Tampa Bay)
66a	C	Mario Lemieux (Pittsburgh)
68a	RW	Jaromir Jagr (Pittsburgh)
72	D	Mathieu Schneider (N.Y. Islanders)
77a	D	Ray Bourque (Boston)
88	C	Eric Lindros (Philadelphia)
94a	LW	Brendan Shanahan (Hartford)

a=voted to starting lineup by fan ballot

Western Conference All–Stars
Honourary Captain: Glenn Hall
Scotty Bowman, coach (Detroit)

2	D	Al MacInnis (St. Louis)
4	D	Kevin Hatcher (Dallas)
5	D	Nicklas Lidstrom (Detroit)
7a	D	Chris Chelios (Chicago)
8	RW	Teemu Selanne (Winnipeg)
9	LW	Paul Kariya (Anaheim)
11	RW	Owen Nolan (San Jose)
13	C	Mats Sundin (Toronto)
14	RW	Theoren Fleury (Calgary)
16a	RW	Brett Hull (St. Louis)
18b	C	Denis Savard (Chicago)
19	C	Joe Sakic (Colorado)
21	C	Peter Forsberg (Colorado) AVS.
22	RW	Mike Gartner (Toronto)
29	G	Felix Potvin (Toronto)
30a	G	Ed Belfour (Chicago)
31	G	Chris Osgood (Detroit)
39	C	Doug Weight (Edmonton)
55	D	Larry Murphy (Toronto)
77a	D	Paul Coffey (Detroit)
89	RW	Alexander Mogilny (Vancouver)
91	C	Sergei Fedorov (Detroit)
99a	C	Wayne Gretzky "C" (Los Angeles)

b=Commissioner's selection

First Period
1. Eastern: Lindros (Leetch, LeClair) 11:05
2. Eastern: Verbeek (Lemieux, Schneider) 13:49
Penalties: (West) too many men 4:35

Second Period
3. Eastern: Jagr (Lemieux, Francis) 2:07
4. Western: Hull (Kariya, Coffey). 5:33
5. Eastern: Shanahan (Turgeon, Neely) 8:51
6. Western: Coffey (Fedorov, Mogilny) 11:42
7. Western: Kariya (Sundin) 17:47
Penalties: (East) too many men 15:14

Third Period
8. Western: Selanne (unassisted) 16:31
9. Eastern: Bourque (Verbeek, Messier) 19:22
Penalties: None

Shots on Goal

Eastern	18	15	8	**41**
Western	12	7	13	**32**

In Goal
Eastern—Brodeur (1st period, no goals); Vanbiesbrouck (2nd period, 3 goals); Hasek (3rd period, one goal)
Western—Belfour (1st period, 2 goals); Osgood (2nd period, 2 goals); Potvin (3rd period, one goal)

Referee Mark Faucette

Linesmen Ron Assel, Brad Lazarowich

Attendance 17,565

MVP Ray Bourque (Boston)

47th All–Star Game
Expansion Takes Hold
San Jose Arena, Saturday, January 18, 1997

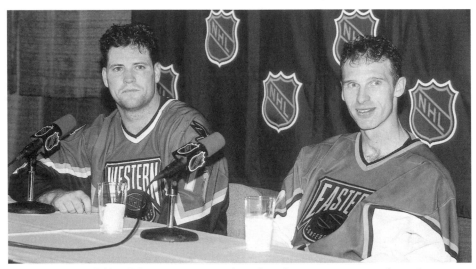

Owen Nolan (left) and the Dominator, Dominik Hasek, perform post-game press conference duties.

San Jose had been slated to host the 1995 All–Star Game when the owners' lockout disrupted the league and forced the cancellation not only of that game but much of the season. The makeup game in 1997 was rejuvenated by introducing a winner-take-all prize of $250,000 to add intensity and competition. And despite the almost total, league-wide hatred of the FoxTrax puck, it was back in use for this game.

That San Jose was even an NHL city, let alone All–Star host, spoke volumes about the league's expansion in the 1990s to places no one would have imagined a generation before. Florida, Dallas, Phoenix, and Anaheim all had teams that were selling out their arenas. But make no mistake. What the NHL of the 1990s had that the 1970s didn't was simply Wayne Gretzky, and the great western and southern expansion can be traced directly to one day, August 9, 1988, when the Great One was traded from

Edmonton's wintry, traditional climate for hockey to sunny Los Angeles.

Gretzky was the ultimate prize: a great player, a great presence, a man who dedicated himself to creating success in his new city and the U.S. at large. As soon as he joined the Kings, the Great Western Forum started to attract 16,000 fans instead of 10,000, and his popularity alone enabled the league to expand and generate interest so an entertainment empire like Disney would invest in the Mighty Ducks and Canadian owners would sell teams to American interests in places such as Colorado and Phoenix. With the new cities came new arenas in both established and new hockey centres such as San Jose. All–Star Games in the 1990s provided a showcase for franchises that hadn't hosted before and at the same time promoted new buildings. In 1996, Boston hosted the game in its new FleetCenter; this year it was the new "Shark Tank" (more formally

246

called the San Jose Arena); and the year after that it would be General Motors Place in Vancouver.

The governors also formed an expansion committee to hear proposals for what would be the final round of new entries for the millennium, which would bring the NHL to a whopping 30 teams. This group was made up of nine members: Bill Wirtz (Chicago), Harley Hotchkiss (Calgary), Jeremy Jacobs (Boston), George Gund (San Jose), Ronald Corey (Montreal), John McMullen (New Jersey), Howard Baldwin (Pittsburgh), Mike Ilitch (Detroit), and Ed Snider (Philadelphia).

And for once the regular NHL meetings themselves generated considerable interest. The league promised to renew its crackdown on stick and obstruction fouls—which it had previously initiated and then shirked—while director of officiating Bryan Lewis had his hands full with disciplinary matters. Commissioner Gary Bettman had fined Scotty Bowman $10,000 for uttering unflattering remarks to the effect that referee Terry Gregson was anti-Russian (Bowman had five Soviets on his team); Mike Milbury had apparently revived the old "doughnut" salvo at chunky official Don Koharski; and Mark Messier had

called referee Don van Massenhoven "a disgrace to the league." Bowman in particular was incensed that a player's maximum fine was just $1,000 but a coach's ten times that amount. He also renewed his call for a union of some sort.

"Coaches are on an island," he explained. "The players are in the care of the players' association. The referees also have an association. The coaches have nothing. We badly need an association to solidify as a group."

While the players were circulating at the arena, physicians were discussing concussions and other serious injuries that had become almost epidemic in the game. The names missing in action this All–Star weekend would have made perhaps the best team of all: Jaromir Jagr (ankle injury; replaced by Adam Oates), Chris Osgood (strained hamstring; replaced by Guy Hebert), Joe Sakic (replaced by Tony Granato), Peter Forsberg, Mike Modano (knee; replaced by Keith Tkachuk), Zigmund Palffy (shoulder; replaced by Scott Lachance), and Pat Lafontaine (concussion). In addition, Jason Arnott played with two newly inserted pins in his ankle and Owen Nolan had a bad shoulder he felt he could play with. But none of this phased

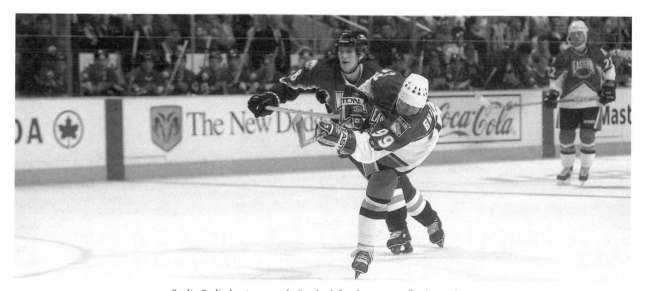

Sandis Ozolinsh tries to catch Gretzky before he can get off a decent shot.

On the positive side, Granato's participation was little short of a miracle given that he'd had brain surgery the previous year and doctors felt he'd be lucky simply to live a normal life again (at season's end, he was awarded the Masterton Trophy for his successful and remarkable comeback). This was also Larry Murphy's first All-Star Game despite having been in the league since 1981 and a consistent defenceman for his whole career.

It was the first—and last—time Wayne Gretzky and Mario Lemieux had played together since their historic combination won the Canada Cup in 1987. Just months before this All-Star Game, Lemieux had refused to play in the first World Cup (and before that the 1991 Canada Cup), and a year later he would be equally unwilling to represent Canada at the Olympic Winter Games in Nagano after he had retired in the previous summer. This time, Gretzky made a classic pass to Mario from behind the net for the East's second goal and, in fitting tribute to what Lemieux had been trumpeting for months as his last season in the league, Eastern Conference coach Doug MacLean put him out for his final shift on a line with Gretzky and Messier with Coffey and Bourque on defence, sure Hall of Famers one and all.

Bettman. "We don't like injuries," he commented. "We worry about them, but it isn't an epidemic yet. It may be an issue that superstars are being injured disproportionately."

CELEBRATING THE 1997 COCA-COLA™/NHL™ ALL-STAR WEEKEND

1997 NHL ALL ★ STAR

MAGAZINE

JANUARY 17-18, 1997

$10.00 U.S./$13.00 CANADA

71>

0 70989 36239 0

™
COOLEST GAME on earth
www.nhl.com

Eastern 11   Western 7

		Eastern				Western
2a	D	Brian Leetch (N.Y. Rangers)		2	D	Al MacInnis (St. Louis)
4	D	Scott Stevens (New Jersey)		3	D	Derian Hatcher (Dallas)
7	D	Paul Coffey (Philadelphia)		7a	D	Chris Chelios "C" (Chicago)
8	RW	Mark Recchi (Montreal)		8a	D	Sandis Ozolinsh (Colorado)
9	RW	Daniel Alfredsson (Ottawa)		9a	LW	Paul Kariya (Anaheim)
10	LW	John LeClair (Philadelphia)		10	RW	Tony Amonte (Chicago)
11	C	Mark Messier (N.Y. Rangers)		11	RW	Owen Nolan (San Jose)
12	RW	Peter Bondra (Washington)		13	C	Mats Sundin (Toronto)
15b	C	Dale Hawerchuk (Philadelphia)		14	RW	Theoren Fleury (Calgary)
16	D	Scott Lachance (N.Y. Islanders)		16a	RW	Brett Hull (St. Louis)
18	LW	Geoff Sanderson (Hartford)		17	RW	Teemu Selanne (Anaheim)
21	C	Adam Oates (Boston)		18	LW	Brendan Shanahan (Detroit)
22a	RW	Dino Ciccarelli (Tampa Bay)		19	C	Steve Yzerman (Detroit)
24	D	Robert Svehla (Florida)		20	D	Oleg Tverdovsky (Phoenix)
30	G	Martin Brodeur (New Jersey)		21b	LW	Tony Granato (San Jose)
32b	C	Dale Hunter (Washington)		22b	D	Viacheslav Fetisov (Detroit)
34a	G	John Vanbiesbrouck (Florida)		31	G	Guy Hebert (Anaheim)
39	G	Dominik Hasek (Buffalo)		33a	G	Patrick Roy (Colorado)
44	D	Kevin Hatcher (Pittsburgh)		35	G	Andy Moog (Dallas)
66	C	Mario Lemieux (Pittsburgh)		70	C	Jason Arnott (Edmonton)
77a	D	Ray Bourque (Boston)		77	LW	Keith Tkachuk (Phoenix)
88	C	Eric Lindros (Philadelphia)		80	LW	Dimitri Khristich (Los Angeles)
99a	C	Wayne Gretzky "C" (N.Y. Rangers)		96	RW	Pavel Bure (Vancouver)

a=voted to starting lineup by fan ballot — b=Commissioner's selection

First Period

1. Eastern: LeClair (Bondra, Stevens) 8:52
2. Eastern: Lemieux (Gretzky) 9:49
3. Eastern: Recchi (Messier, Alfredsson) 15:32
4. Eastern: Hawerchuk (Lindros, Coffey) 16:19
5. Western: Bure (Sundin, Amonte) 17:36
6. Western: Kariya (Bure, Ozolinsh) 18:36

Penalties: None

Second Period

7. Eastern: Recchi (Svehla, Messier) 1:56
8. Eastern: Sanderson (Lindros) 3:21
9. Western: Bure (Selanne, Fetisov) 4:40
10. Eastern: Lemieux (Svehla, Ciccarelli) 6:09
11. Eastern: Messier (K. Hatcher, Alfredsson) 8:45
12. Eastern: Recchi (Oates, Lemieux) 10:57
13. Western: Shanahan (Hull, Ozolinsh) . . . . 16:38(pp)
14. Eastern: Hawerchuk (LeClair, Stevens) 17:28
15. Western: Nolan (Fleury, Ozolinsh) 18:54

16. Western: Nolan (Amonte) 19:02

Penalties: Coffey (East) 15:37

Third Period

17. Eastern: LeClair (Bondra, Oates) 8:50
18. Western: Nolan (unassisted) 17:57

Penalties: K. Hatcher (EaC) 14:56

Shots on Goal

Eastern	15	15	11	**41**
Western	12	13	21	**46**

In Goal

Eastern—Vanbiesbrouck (1st period, 2 goals); Brodeur (2nd period, 4 goals); Hasek (3rd period, one goal)
Western—Roy (1st period, 4 goals); Moog (2nd period, 6 goals); Hebert (3rd period, one goal)

Referee Rob Shick
Linesmen Ron Asseltine, Bob Hodges, and Leon Stickle
Attendance 17,442
MVP Mark Recchi (Montreal)

A Format Fit for Nagano

General Motors Place, Vancouver, Sunday, January 18, 1998

*P*lus ça change... During the more competitive years of the All–Star Game, some of the greats didn't play because they weren't yet under contract and league rules prohibited holdouts from participating, which forced many to sign. In the late 1990s, a similar conflict was keeping players out of the game even though the prestige of the game had decreased so that they weren't about to be pressured to sign. In 1998, both Paul Kariya and Sergei Fedorov had already been chosen to play for their country at the Olympic Winter Games in Nagano a few weeks after the All–Star Game would be played but missed the game itself because of contract disputes with their respective clubs, Anaheim and Detroit.

The All–Star Game had come to reflect the multinational makeup of the 1990s NHL by adopting a new format—North America versus the World—that had been suggested before. Introduced in an attempt to increase the contest's intensity, the rationale was that the pride of birthplace might be both more symbolic and motivating than simply pitting one conference against another. In addition, the $250,000 winner-take-all prize was again up for grabs.

But the 1998 All–Star Game was doubly significant. Not only was it the annual showcase of the league's top talent, it also anticipated the NHL's full-fledged involvement in the Olympic Winter Games, where players of all nationalities from the league would go to Nagano to represent their countries.

"[Summit Series] '72 wasn't a big deal until the end," Team Canada general manager Bob Clarke explained. "It turned out to be a big deal. But this is already a big deal. A huge thing."

The Canadian Hockey Association used the All–Star

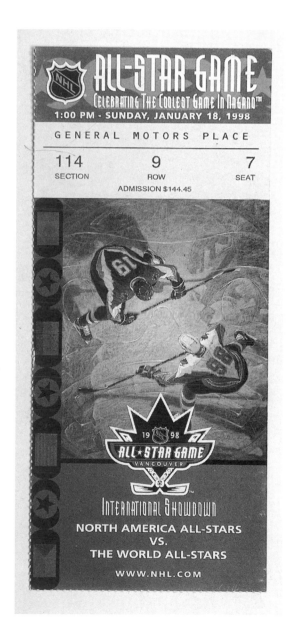

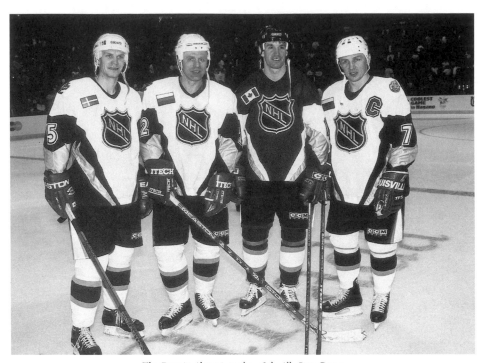

The Detroit Alumni at the 48th All–Star Game:
(l-r) Nicklas Lidstrom, Sergei Fedorov, Brendan Shanahan, and Igor Larionov.

Game to invite all 23 of its Canadian players (including the unsigned Kariya) to Vancouver to meet and prepare for the Olympics. "This is the beginning of building a team," CHA president Bob Nicholson said of the event. Rooms and beds the size of what the players could expect in Japan were constructed in a Vancouver hotel, all the players were given a video to help prepare them for the Olympics and the various adjustments they would have to make in the three days between playing their last NHL game in North America and their first Olympic game in Japan, and discussions vis-à-vis culture, jetlag, and acclimatization were incorporated into a weekend's meetings.

The weekend also celebrated the fact that this would be the first time women would play hockey at the Olympics. A Canada–U.S. exhibition game the night before the All–Star Game drew a crowd of more than 14,000, the largest ever to see a women's game up to that point.

Bob Clarke also used the assembly as a forum for trying to end NHL teams' implementation of a dreaded form of defensive hockey.

"The trap we're seeing is illegal," he said. "According to the rule book, you can't face a player and impede his progress. You can only check him if you're skating in the same direction...We have to do something. The league can't put up with this kind of crap."

The NHL also took advantage of the high profile of this year's game to announce hiring Willie O'Ree as a goodwill ambassador for the league. O'Ree had been the first black player in the NHL (in 1957), and now he'd been employed to promote racial awareness, increase the participation of minorities in hockey at the grassroots level, and act as a diplomat for the ever-increasing worldwide appeal of the sport. The All–Star Game was now televised to 170 countries—a record attraction for the NHL—and

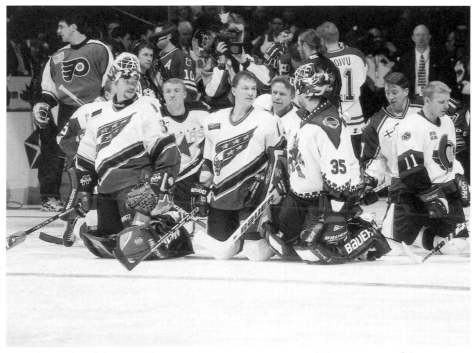

Players relax while waiting their turn during the skills competition: (l-r) John LeClair, Olaf Kolzig,
Jere Lehtinen, Peter Bondra, Viacheslav Fetisov, Nikolai Khabibulin, Jari Kurri, and Daniel Alfredsson.

broadening hockey's appeal not just to fans but aspiring players was a key element in the NHL's mandate. The governors also donated $500,000 to relief efforts in Quebec to help deal with the devastating ice storm that had crippled the province that winter.

At the board of governors' meeting, rule changes were first and foremost on the agenda. Some of the considerations involved mere tinkering, but others would have changed the game in the future entirely: making the goals bigger; eliminating the centre red line; disallowing goalies from handling the puck at all; using two referees; moving the goal line two or three feet closer to centre ice. Most contentious of all was a proposal by Dallas general manager Bob Gainey to pander to American TV: changing the length of periods to four 15-minute quarters. The idea was beyond preposterous, but it was actually discussed, in large measure because the league felt it had to do something to curry favour with U.S. networks. The

discrepancy between hockey and the other major sports in revenue in the U.S. was staggering. Networks had recently signed an eight-year deal with the NFL for $17 billion, yet the NHL was earning a comparatively minuscule $50 million per season from Fox. Ironically, the four-quarter suggestion came at the same time as concerns about ever-decreasing ice quality were being asserted. Clearly, the conflicting issues only exacerbated the league's difficulties.

Before the game, Mats Sundin was asked about the new, nationality-based format.

"I think it would be great if the World Team got ahead by a couple of goals early," he offered. "That would get the North Americans ticked off."

In fact, that's exactly what happened. Four minutes after the opening faceoff, the score was 3–0 for the World.

"We didn't want to be embarrassed, no question," North America captain Wayne Gretzky admitted later.

"There were a lot of guys on the bench who were concerned. We knew we had to buckle up."

They didn't exactly buckle up on defence but they did splurge on offence, scoring the next four goals and holding on for the win.

Teemu Selanne won the MVP truck for his hat-trick day, but the memorable efforts of Gretzky and Messier provided the most unforgettable moments of the evening, particularly in the third when the Great One sent the Moose in alone on goalie Nikolai Khabibulin with a gentle, perfect pass. Messier, celebrating his 37th birthday and skating down his favoured off wing, scored a lovely, remember-the-Oilers goal which proved to be the game-winner.

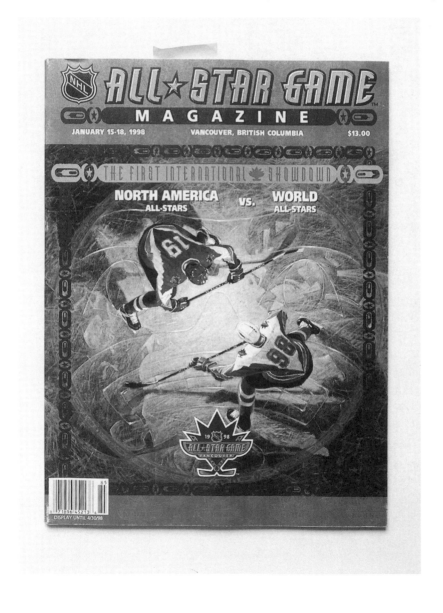

North America 8   World 7

		North America All–Stars				World All–Stars
		Honourary Captain: Yvan Cournoyer				Honourary Captain: Ken Dryden
		Jacques Lemaire, coach (New Jersey—CAN)				Ken Hitchcock, coach (Dallas—CAN)

		North America				World
2a	D	Brian Leetch (N.Y. Rangers—US)	2a	D	Viacheslav Fetisov (Detroit—Russia)
4	D	Scott Stevens (New Jersey—CAN)	5	D	Nicklas Lidstrom (Detroit—Sweden)
5	D	Darryl Sydor (Dallas—CAN)	6a	D	Sandis Ozolinsh (Colorado—Latvia)
7	D	Chris Chelios (Chicago—US)	7b	C	Igor Larionov "C" (Detroit—Russia)
8	RW	Mark Recchi (Montreal—CAN)	8a	RW	Teemu Selanne (Anaheim—Finland)
9	C	Mike Modano (Dallas—US)	9	C	Saku Koivu (Montreal—Finland)
10a	LW	John LeClair (Philadelphia—US)	10	RW	Pavel Bure (Vancouver—Russia)
11b	C	Mark Messier (Vancouver—CAN)	11	RW	Daniel Alfredsson (Ottawa—Sweden)
12	RW	Tony Amonte (Chicago—US)	12	RW	Peter Bondra (Washington—Slovakia)
14a	LW	Brendan Shanahan (Detroit—CAN)	13	C	Mats Sundin (Toronto—Sweden)
17	LW	Keith Tkachuk (Phoenix—US)	15	D	Dmitri Mironov (Anaheim—Russia)
19	C	Joe Sakic (Colorado—CAN)	16	C	Bobby Holik (New Jersey—Czech Republic)
20	G	Ed Belfour (Dallas—CAN)	17b	RW	Jari Kurri (Colorado—Finland)
22b	D	Al MacInnis (St. Louis—CAN)	18	LW	Valeri Kamensky (Colorado—Russia)
27	LW	Shayne Corson (Montreal—CAN)	21a	C	Peter Forsberg (Colorado—Sweden)
28	D	Scott Niedermayer (New Jersey—CAN)	24	RW	Zigmund Palffy (N.Y. Islanders—Slovakia)
30	G	Martin Brodeur (New Jersey—CAN)	26	RW	Jere Lehtinen (Dallas—Finland)
33a	G	Patrick Roy (Colorado—CAN)	29	D	Igor Kravchuk (Ottawa—Russia)
39	C	Doug Weight (Edmonton—US)	35	G	Nikolai Khabibulin (Phoenix—Russia)
74	RW	Theoren Fleury (Calgary—CAN)	37	G	Olaf Kolzig (Washington—Germany)
77a	D	Ray Bourque (Boston—CAN)	39a	G	Dominik Hasek (Buffalo—Czech Republic)
88a	C	Eric Lindros (Philadelphia—CAN)	56	D	Sergei Zubov (Dallas—Russia)
99	C	Wayne Gretzky "C" (N.Y. Rangers—CAN)	68a	RW	Jaromir Jagr (Pittsburgh—Czech Republic)

a=voted to starting lineup by fan ballot   b=Commissioner's selection

First Period

1. World: Selanne (Koivu) 0:53
2. World: Jagr (Bondra, Mironov) 2:15
3. World: Selanne (Lehtinen, Fetisov) 4:00
4. North America: LeClair (Gretzky, Chelios) 4:13
5. North America: Tkachuk (Fleury, Chelios) . . . . 10:50(pp)
6. North America: Niedermayer (Sakic, Recchi) 18:25
Penalties: Fetisov (W) 10:04

Second Period

7. North America: Fleury (Modano, Tkachuk) 1:53
8. World: Selanne (Lehtinen, Koivu) 7:11
9. World: Kurri (Koivu, Lehtinen) 12:36
10. North America: Lindros (Chelios, Messier) 14:46
11. North America: Amonte (Sakic, Bourque) 16:19
Penalties: Fleury (NA) 18:48

Third Period

12. North America: Tkachuk (Modano, Fleury) 1:36
13. North America: Messier (Gretzky) 4:00
14. World: Kravchuk (Sundin, Forsberg) 7:03
15. World: Larionov (Bure) 9:41
Penalties: Weight (NA) 10:32

Shots on Goal

North America	13	17	13	**43**
World	7	11	11	**29**

In Goal

North America—Roy (1st period, 3 goals); Belfour (2nd period, 2 goals); Brodeur (3rd period, 2 goals)
World—Hasek (1st period, 3 goals); Kolzig (2nd period, 3 goals); Khabibulin (3rd period, 2 goals)

Referee Paul Stewart
Linesmen Mike Cvik and Shane Heyer
Attendance 18,422
MVP Teemu Selanne (Anaheim)

The Great One Does It One Last Time

Ice Palace, Tampa Bay, Sunday, January 24, 1999

Hoping to build on the fervour created by the Nagano-bound North America versus the World format of the previous year, the NHL used the same format for Tampa Bay in 1999. But after this second year of All–Star Team selections based on place of birth, the NHL saw that while the nation-based rivalry inspired conversation and one form of competition, it still had its weaknesses. Many superior players, primarily Canadians, didn't play in the game because the North American side had too many players to choose from. For instance, Patrick Roy, Byron Dafoe, and John Vanbiesbrouck weren't selected in goal. On defence, the list of superstar non-participants grew even more impressive and included Eric Desjardins, Brian Leetch, Scott Niedermayer, Chris Chelios, Derian Hatcher, Jason York, and Adam Foote. Up front, the stars not in Tampa Bay were as good as those who were there. Among those absent were Joe Sakic, Rod Brind'Amour, Doug Weight, Michael Peca, Adam Graves, Pavel Bure, Jarome Iginla, and Brett Hull. Furthermore, although Americans had been increasingly well represented in the NHL, the quality and numbers were still nowhere near the Canadian content. In Tampa Bay, this was reflected in the fact that only five of the 25 North American players were American.

Perhaps the most interesting aspect of the game for spectators was that the format contrived to allow regular-season teammates to face each other at the All–Star Game (which had happened only twice before when the First All–Star Team played the Second All–Star Team in the 1951 and 1952 games). Several teams had two representatives, one for the World Team and one for the North Americans: Ray Bourque and Dimitri Khristich of Boston; Ron Tugnutt and Alexei Yashin of Ottawa; and three from New Jersey with Martin Brodeur and Scott Stevens facing Bobby Holik.

The NHL used the weekend to showcase its newest award, the Rocket Richard Trophy, to be given each year to the player who scored the most regular-season goals. In honour of the unveiling, Richard himself faced off the opening puck between Wayne Gretzky and Jaromir Jagr in the pre-game ceremony. The Vancouver Canucks did their part to steal the spotlight and throw their own bolts of lightning at fans by firing coach Mike Keenan and hiring Marc Crawford in a loud and long process that was the talk of Tampa Bay for the time it took to play itself out.

Once again, monetary incentive was added; the winning team received $250,000 and the losers nada. That year's North America win was particularly sweet for coach Ken Hitchcock, who had lost as the World's coach the previous year and was 0–11 in his all–star career at all levels of coaching. Happy to win one, he said after the game that, "It's too bad we can't go to Europe and give them [the World Team] a home game," which is not a bad idea for the future.

By fluke, the game was marred by some last-minute injuries that forced Toronto's Curtis Joseph, Detroit's Steve Yzerman and Florida's Viktor Kozlov to the sidelines, joining earlier no-shows Uwe Krupp (Detroit) and Kenny Jonsson (Islanders). The two Mattiases, Norstrom (L.A.) and Ohlund (Vancouver), replaced Krupp and Jonsson while Tugnutt (Ottawa) filled in for Joseph and Luc Robitaille was brought in for Stevie Y. Wendel Clark, the lone Florida player who had reason to smile during an otherwise bleak

Gretzky cradles his third MVP trophy
while representing his third team at his last All–Star Game.

Lightning season, was hugely popular with the fans as the only representative of Tampa Bay in the game.

The game produced two significant records. Arturs Irbe earned the first goalie assist in a game, and Ray Bourque's goal at 0:17 of the second was the fastest from the start of a period. For the Europeans, the line of Mats Sundin–Peter Forsberg–Markus Naslund was particularly successful, with Sundin racking up four points and losing out on the MVP car keys because of Gretzky's great—and final—performance. But Gretzky played an inspired game between linemates Mark Recchi and Theo Fleury. His five shots and 19:33 minutes of playing time were both tops on the team and he became the only player to be selected game MVP in his final year in the league. Indeed, the high-light of the game was Gretzky's phenomenal pass to Mark Recchi on a two-on-one late in the first period. Everyone knew he would pass as soon as he got the puck at centre, but he still put the puck through the World defenceman's glove and stick right onto Rec-chi's blade at the top of the blue ice—a gimme and a grand farewell in league colours for number 99.

North America 8   World 6

North America All–Stars
Ken Hitchcock, coach (Dallas—CAN)
Jim Shoenfeld, assistant coach (Phoenix—CAN)

2a	D	Al MacInnis (St. Louis—CAN)
3	D	Rob Blake (Los Angeles—CAN)
4	D	Scott Stevens (New Jersey—CAN)
5	D	Darryl Sydor (Dallas—CAN)
7	LW	Keith Tkachuk (Phoenix—US)
8	RW	Mark Recchi (Montreal—CAN)
9a	LW	Paul Kariya (Anaheim—CAN)
10	LW	John LeClair (Philadelphia—US)
12	RW	Tony Amonte (Chicago—US)
14a	LW	Brendan Shanahan (Detroit—CAN)
17	LW	Wendel Clark (Tampa Bay—CAN)
19a	C	Steve Yzerman (Detroit—CAN)
20	G	Ed Belfour (Dallas—CAN)
21	LW	Luc Robitaille (Los Angeles—CAN)
22	C	Keith Primeau (Carolina—CAN)
27	C	Mike Modano (Dallas—US)
30a	G	Martin Brodeur (New Jersey—CAN)
31	G	Ron Tugnutt (Ottawa—CAN)
44	D	Chris Pronger (St. Louis—CAN)
55	D	Larry Murphy (Detroit—CAN)
74	RW	Theoren Fleury (Calgary—CAN)
77a	D	Ray Bourque (Boston—CAN)
88	C	Eric Lindros (Philadelphia—CAN)
97	C	Jeremy Roenick (Phoenix—US)
99	C	Wayne Gretzky "C" (N.Y. Rangers—CAN)

World All–Stars
Lindy Ruff, coach (Buffalo—CAN)
Robbie Ftorek, assistant coach (New Jersey—US)

1	G	Arturs Irbe (Carolina—Latvia)
2	D	Mattias Ohlund (Vancouver—Sweden)
5a	D	Nicklas Lidstrom (Detroit—Sweden)
8a	RW	Teemu Selanne (Anaheim—Finland)
9	RW	Markus Naslund (Vancouver—Sweden)
12	RW	Peter Bondra (Washington—Czech Republic)
13	C	Mats Sundin (Toronto—Sweden)
14	D	Mattias Norstrom (Los Angeles—Sweden)
16	C	Bobby Holik (New Jersey—Czech Republic)
19	C	Alexei Yashin (Ottawa—Russia)
20	C	Marco Sturm (San Jose—Germany)
21a	C	Peter Forsberg (Colorado—Sweden)
22	D	Roman Hamrlik (Edmonton—Czech Rep.)
25	RW	Sergei Krivokrasov (Nashville—Russia)
27	D	Teppo Numminen (Phoenix—Finland)
35	G	Nikolai Khabibulin (Phoenix—Russia)
38	LW	Pavol Demitra (St. Louis—Czech Republic)
39a	G	Dominik Hasek (Buffalo—Czech Republic)
44	D	Alexei Zhitnik (Buffalo—Russia)
56	D	Sergei Zubov (Dallas—Russia)
68a	RW	Jaromir Jagr "C" (Pittsburgh—Czech Rep.)
80	LW	Dimitri Khristich (Boston—Russia)
82	C	Martin Straka (Pittsburgh—Czech Republic)

a=voted to starting lineup by fan ballot
b=Commissioner's selection

First Period

1. North America: Modano (Robitaille, Pronger) 4:09
2. World: Sturm (Forsberg, Sundin) 9:42
3. North America: Robitaille (Roenick, Clark) 10:06
4. North America: Kariya (Modano, Amonte) 16:45
5. North America: Recchi (Gretzky, Fleury) 17:18
Penalties: None

Second Period

6. North America: Bourque (Modano) 0:17
7. North America: Gretzky (Fleury, Pronger) 1:14
8. World: Selanne (Yashin, Irbe) 2:02
9. World: Demitra (Zhitnik, Sundin) 8:59
10. North America: Blake (Gretzky, Recchi) 14:23
11. World: Ohlund (Naslund, Sundin) 15:08
Penalties: None

Third Period

12. World: Sundin (Ohlund, Jagr) 2:57

13. North America: Sydor (Modano, Amonte) 4:02
14. World: Zubov (Khristich, Holik) 4:20
Penalties: MacInnis (NA) 7:22

Shots on Goal

North America	19	15	15	**49**
World	9	15	12	**36**

In Goal

North America—Brodeur (1st period, one goal); Tugnutt (2nd period, 3 goals); Belfour (3rd period, 2 goals)
World—Hasek (1st period, 4 goals); Irbe (2nd period, 3 goals); Khabibulin (3rd period, one goal)

Referee Paul Devorski
Linesmen Pierre Champoux and Brian Murphy
Attendance 19,758
MVP Wayne Gretzky (N.Y. Rangers)

50th All–Star Game

The Game
Comes Home

Air Canada Centre, Toronto, Sunday, February 6, 2000

The crowded Team World bench is all mirth and merriment during their waltz in the park at the Air Canada Centre.

Although one of the first All–Star Games had been played in 1934 at Maple Leaf Gardens and the first annual game in Toronto in 1947, the 2000 game was actually considered the 50th thanks to a few blips along the way. The first four games—in 1908, 1934, 1937, and 1939—had been benefits for individual players; no game had been played during the calendar year of 1966 when the game's scheduling changed from the start to the middle of the season; there had been no NHL All–Star Games in 1979 and 1987 when international mini-series had replaced the All–Star format; and in 1995 the game had been cancelled because of the owners' lockout. So it was that, a bit awkwardly, the year 2000 officially celebrated half a century of All–Star Games.

The Leafs had been working for years to have Toronto awarded this special game, ever since Cliff Fletcher had come to Maple Leaf Gardens. "One of the first things I did when I arrived in Toronto was ask the NHL to consider us as a future site," Fletcher said at the 1992 game in Philadelphia, when he began serious lobbying. Fletcher was a member of the NHL's Marketing and Public Relations Committee that decided on the host cities and felt confident at the time that the home of hockey would soon get the All–Star Game.

"We're looking at 1995," he said. "It'll be discussed during meetings in February and March [1992] and the league could act on it during the June draft."

However, in part because of the lockout (which pushed San Jose's successful application back a year) and in part because of uncertainty about a new home for the Leafs to replace Maple Leaf Gardens, Toronto's bid was put on hold for a few years. Finally, when Ken Dryden was hired in the summer of 1997 as team president, his renewed efforts ensured Fletcher's campaign would come to fruition.

Never before had so many important events surrounded the game, and never had they all been so well attended as in the world's hockey capital. The Canadian Hockey League's Top Prospects game was played on the Wednesday, with Team Orr beating Team Cherry

6–3; the women's national teams of Canada and the U.S. played on the Friday, with the Canadians winning 6–0; and all week long a group of amateurs took over the open-air rink at City Hall to set a world record for the longest continuous hockey game, which went almost 72 hours before they were done. The opening faceoff for the Heroes of Hockey Game and Skills Competition was taken by Ted Lindsay and Fleming Mackell, who had played in the first annual game in 1947, and that event was sold out, as was an open practice held Saturday morning. Indeed, the crowd of 19,300 fans who came just to see a practice so impressed Jaromir Jagr he suggested the All–Star Game should be played in Canada every year.

Further proof of Toronto's place as the hockey capital of the world came when it was announced that, for the first time, there would be no public sale of tickets; half would go to Leafs subscribers and half to the NHL. Tickets for subscribers ranged from $165 to $275, and only those who had had season's seats

since before 1970 need apply, such was the huge interest and devotion of season's ticket holders. The NHL's FANtasy also set records for attendance as more than 160,000 clicked the turnstiles to play games, meet the players, and participate in all aspects of the game.

For this year, the All–Star coaches were decided on the basis of teams' winning percentage on January 4, 2000, and the coach of the second-place team was named assistant. Appropriately, Pat Quinn earned the right to coach the North Americans based on his Maple Leafs' front-running position. He had last coached the All–Stars back in 1981, the longest time between coaching appearances in All–Star history. His appointment was also the first for a Leafs coach since Punch Imlach in 1968, the last year the game had been played in Toronto. And this was World Team coach Scotty Bowman's first All–Star Game in Toronto, the last of the Original Six cities he'd been in for the Stars.

Olaf Kolzig makes a stop during his 20 minutes of All–Star fame at the Air Canada Centre.

Mark Messier moves in on goal during his 14th All–Star classic (top)
while Chris Pronger moves the puck up ice with North America teammates (bottom).

But much of the hype in the days leading up to the game focused on two Czech stars. Dominik Hasek had missed most of the season with a serious groin pull but tried to come back on February 1 against Anaheim, hoping to cash in on a lucrative bonus in his contract for playing in the All–Star Game. His groin didn't react well to the Ducks test so he was replaced by Roman Turek of St. Louis. Jagr was also worried about missing the game with a thumb injury, but he was cleared by doctors to play just before the opening faceoff. Pierre Turgeon was injured and replaced by Ray Whitney for the North Americans and two World players went down, Kimmo Timonen and Peter Forsberg. Patrick Elias filled for them both and thus the World roster at 24 players was one under the North Americans' 25.

Once the starting lineups had been voted to each team by fans across the continent (with Jagr the first player to top one million votes), the roster was filled in by an anonymous group of general managers and executives. Again, the rule stipulating representation from each team hurt the game's reputation. The Flames were incensed their number one goalie Fred Brathwaite was not named, but neither was Ed Belfour of the Cup-champion Dallas Stars. Also missing from the action were Janne Niinimaa, Brian Leetch, Rod Brind'Amour, Wade Redden, Theo Fleury, Keith Tkachuk, and a host of other worthy players. The only two rookies named this year were Scott Gomez for the North Americans and Petr Buzek for the World.

Incredibly, the World Team was radically different from the previous year with 13 new faces named to the 2000 team. And history was made when both Valeri and Pavel Bure were named; it was the first time European brothers played in the game.

The game featured a complete redesign of the sweaters for both players and officials. The World Team's featured a red base with white on the upper half of the shoulders and black and grey trim, a similar stripe around the trunk of the sweater and the NHL crest off to the right. The North American version had a dark blue base and white half-shoulders with red and grey trim. Goalies wore sweaters that were slightly different from their teammates' and officials sported a large orange stripe down one side and another along the legs of their pants.

Pre-Game Ceremonies

In pre-game ceremonies, the league officially retired Wayne Gretzky's number 99. Commissioner Gary Bettman had made the historic announcement prior to the Great One's final game at Madison Square Garden, and before this All–Star Game a special number 99 banner was lifted into the rafters of the Air Canada Centre to acknowledge that a league-wide retirement of a number was being made for the first time ever. Gretzky made clear in Toronto that, with one possible exception, he would never play in an oldtimers or Heroes of Hockey game now that his NHL days were over:

> "If they ever have another All–Star Game in Edmonton, and it was the Oilers old guys versus the Heroes of Hockey, maybe I would play in that one. But that would be the only one."

The Game

Both Mark Messier and Ray Bourque each had an assist to pass Gretzky as all-time leaders in that category, but the Bures shone brightest on the night. Pavel (who was leading the league in goals and had a virtual lock on the Rocket Richard Trophy) scored three times and two of those goals were assisted by Valeri. Although the game was close after two periods, the World ended the anxiety with four third-period goals that left the outcome in no doubt.

World 9   North America 4

North America All–Stars
Pat Quinn, coach (Toronto—CAN)
Roger Neilson, assistant (Philadelphia—CAN)

2	D	Al MacInnis (St. Louis—CAN)
3	D	Scott Stevens (New Jersey—CAN)
4a	D	Rob Blake (Los Angeles—CAN)
6	D	Phil Housley (Calgary—US)
8	RW	Mark Recchi (Philadelphia—CAN)
9a	LW	Paul Kariya (Anaheim—CAN)
10	RW	Tony Amonte (Chicago—US)
11b	C	Mark Messier (Vancouver—CAN)
13	LW	Owen Nolan (San Jose—CAN)
14a	LW	Brendan Shanahan (Detroit—CAN)
15	LW	Ray Whitney (Florida—CAN)
16	LW	John LeClair (Philadelphia—US)
19a	C	Steve Yzerman (Detroit—CAN)
23	C	Scott Gomez (New Jersey—US)
24	D	Chris Chelios (Detroit—US)
27	C	Mike Modano (Dallas—US)
30	G	Martin Brodeur (New Jersey—CAN)
31a	G	Curtis Joseph (Toronto—CAN)
35	G	Mike Richter (N.Y. Rangers—US)
37	D	Eric Desjardins (Philadelphia—CAN)
44a	D	Chris Pronger (St. Louis—CAN)
77	D	Ray Bourque "C" (Boston—CAN)
88	C	Eric Lindros (Philadelphia—CAN)
91	C	Joe Sakic (Colorado—CAN)
97	C	Jeremy Roenick (Phoenix—US)

World All–Stars
Scotty Bowman, coach (Detroit—CAN)
Joel Quenneville, assistant (St. Louis—CAN)

1	G	Roman Turek (St. Louis—Czech Republic)
2	D	Petr Buzek (Atlanta—Czech Republic)
5a	D	Nicklas Lidstrom "C" (Detroit—Sweden)
8a	RW	Teemu Selanne (Anaheim—Finland)
10	RW	Pavel Bure (Florida—Russia)
13a	C	Mats Sundin (Toronto—Sweden)
14	C	Radek Bonk (Ottawa—Czech Republic)
18a	D	Sandis Ozolinsh (Colorado—Latvia)
20	RW	Valeri Bure (Calgary—Russia)
22	RW	Milan Hejduk (Colorado—Czech Republic)
23	D	Petr Svoboda (Tampa Bay—Czech Republic)
24	RW	Sami Kapanen (Carolina—Finland)
25	C	Viktor Kozlov (Florida—Russia)
26	D	Martin Rucinsky (Montreal—Czech Republic)
27	D	Teppo Numminen (Phoenix—Finland)
28	RW	Mariusz Czerkawski (N.Y. Islanders—Poland)
29	LW	Patrik Elias (New Jersey—Czech Republic)
35	G	Tommy Salo (Edmonton—Sweden)
36	D	Dmitry Yushkevich (Toronto—Russia)
37	G	Olaf Kolzig (Washington—South Africa)
38	RW	Pavol Demitra (St. Louis—Czech Republic)
56	D	Sergei Zubov (Dallas—Russia)
68a	RW	Jaromir Jagr (Pittsburgh—Czech Republic)
81	LW	Miroslav Satan (Buffalo—Czech Republic)

a=voted to starting lineup by fan ballot   b=Commissioner's selection

First Period
1. World: Demitra (Yushkevich, Elias) 3:12
2. World: Jagr (Rucinsky) 10:50
3. North America: Sakic (Whitney, Recchi) 13:56
4. World: Yushkevich (Kozlov, P. Bure) 14:35
5. North America: Roenick (Modano) 19:30
Penalties: None

Second Period
6. World: P. Bure (V. Bure) 0:33
7. World: P. Bure (V. Bure, Kozlov) 8:38
8. North America: Amonte (Modano, Bourque) 12:14
9. North America: Whitney (Desjardins, Messier) . . . 17:08
Penalties: None

Third Period
10. World: Demitra (Hejduk, Elias) 8:52
11. World: P. Bure (Lidstrom, Kozlov) 9:31

12. World: Satan (Czerkawski, Bonk) 10:51
13. World: Bonk (Jagr, Rucinsky) 19:28
Penalties: Ozolinsh (W) 5:51

Shots on Goal
World	20	13	15	**48**
North America	12	11	9	**32**

In Goal
World—Turek (1st period, 2 goals); Salo (2nd period, 2 goals); Kolzig (3rd period, no goals)

North America—Joseph (1st period, 3 goals); Brodeur (2nd period, 2 goals); Richter (3rd period, 4 goals)

Referees Kerry Fraser and Don Koharski
Linesmen Gerard Gauthier and Ray Scapinello
Attendance 19,300
MVP Pavel Bure (Florida)

All–Time
All–Star Game Register

*=All–Star Game MVP

R=rookie

- team in brackets signifies All–Star team appearance
- for 1979 (3-game Challenge Cup in New York) and 1987 (2-game Rendez-vous in Quebec City) the figure that appears after the name of the competition refers to the number of games that player participated in. For instance, "Challenge Cup (2)" means that player was in two of the three games. These totals are not included in the final line, which represents career NHL All–Star Game statistics only.
- for goalies, "nd" in the won/lost column means no decision
- Ottawa (I) refers to the original team; Ottawa (II) refers to the expansion team
- "Colorado" refers to the Rockies; "Avalanche" refers to the current Colorado franchise.

		G Mins	A W-L	P GA	Pim Avg
Sid Abel					
1949	Detroit (All–Stars)	0	0	0	0
1950	Detroit (Stanley Cup)	0	1	1	2
1951	Detroit (Second Team)	0	0	0	0
	3 games	0	1	1	2
Keith Acton					
1982	Montreal (Wales)	0	0	0	0
Greg Adams					
1988	Vancouver (Campbell)	0	0	0	0
Daniel Alfredsson					
1996	Ottawa (II) (Eastern)	0	0	0	0R
1997	Ottawa (II) (Eastern)	0	2	2	0
1998	Ottawa (II) (World)	0	0	0	0
	3 games	0	2	2	0
Keith Allen					
1954	Detroit (Stanley Cup)	0	0	0	0R
Tony Amonte					
1997	Chicago (Western)	0	2	2	0
1998	Chicago (North America)	1	0	1	0
1999	Chicago (North America)	0	2	2	0
2000	Chicago (North America)	1	0	1	0
	4 games	2	4	6	0
Glenn Anderson					
1984	Edmonton (Campbell)	0	0	0	0
1985	Edmonton (Campbell)	0	0	0	0
1986	Edmonton (Campbell)	0	0	0	0
1987	Rendez-vous (2)	1	0	1	2
1988	Edmonton (Campbell)	0	2	2	0
	4 games	0	2	2	0
Tom Anderson					
1939	N.Y. Americans (Siebert)	0	0	0	0
Dave Andreychuk					
1990	Buffalo (Wales)	1	1	2	0
1994	Toronto (Western)	1	1	2	0
	2 games	2	2	4	0
Syl Apps					
1939	Toronto (Siebert)	1	3	4	0
1947	Toronto (Stanley Cup)	1	1	2	0
	2 games	2	4	6	0
Syl Apps, Jr.					
1975	Pittsburgh (Wales)*	2	0	2	0
Al Arbour					
1969	St. Louis (West)	0	0	0	0
George Armstrong					
1956	Toronto (All–Stars)	0	0	0	0
1957	Toronto (All–Stars)	0	0	0	0
1959	Toronto (All–Stars)	0	0	0	0
1962	Toronto (Stanley Cup)	0	1	1	0
1963	Toronto (Stanley Cup)	0	1	1	0
1964	Toronto (Stanley Cup)	0	0	0	0
1968	Toronto (Stanley Cup)	0	0	0	0
	7 games	0	2	2	0
Bob Armstrong					
1960	Boston (All–Stars)	0	0	0	0
Jason Arnott					
1997	Edmonton (Western)	0	0	0	0

Larry Aurie

		G / Mins	A / W-L	P / GA	Pim / Avg
1934	Detroit (Bailey)	0	0	0	0

Don Awrey

1974	St. Louis (West)	0	1	1	0

Dave Babych

1983	Winnipeg (Campbell)	1	0	1	0
1984	Winnipeg (Campbell)	1	0	1	0
	2 games	2	0	2	0

Wayne Babych

1981	St. Louis (Campbell)	1	0	1	0

Ralph Backstrom

1958	Montreal (Stanley Cup)	0	0	0	0R
1959	Montreal (Stanley Cup)	0	1	1	0
1960	Montreal (Stanley Cup)	0	1	1	0
1962	Montreal (All–Stars)	0	0	0	0
1965	Montreal (Stanley Cup)	0	1	1	0
1967	Montreal (Stanley Cup)	0	0	0	0
	6 games	0	3	3	0

Dave Balon

1965	Montreal (Stanley Cup)	0	0	0	2
1967	Montreal (Stanley Cup)	0	0	0	0
1968	Minnesota (All–Stars)	0	0	0	0
1971	N.Y. Rangers (East)	0	1	1	0
	4 games	0	1	1	2

Murray Bannerman

1983	Chicago (Campbell)	30:04	nd	2	3.99
1984	Chicago (Campbell)	30:06	nd	5	9.97
	2 games	60:10	0-0-0	7	6.98

Bill Barber

1975	Philadelphia (Campbell)	0	0	0	0
1976	Philadelphia (Campbell)	0	0	0	2
1978	Philadelphia (Campbell)	1	0	1	0
1979	Challenge Cup (3)	0	1	1	0
1980	Philadelphia (Campbell)	0	0	0	0
1981	Philadelphia (Campbell)	1	1	2	0
1982	Philadelphia (Wales)	0	0	0	0
	6 games	2	1	3	2

Bill Barilko

1947	Toronto (Stanley Cup)	0	0	0	0
1948	Toronto (Stanley Cup)	0	0	0	0
1949	Toronto (Stanley Cup)	1	0	1	0
	3 games	1	0	1	0

Norm Barnes

1980	Philadelphia (Campbell)	0	0	0	0R

Tom Barrasso

1985	Buffalo (Wales)	30:49	nd	2	3.89

Marty Barry

1937	Detroit (Morenz)	1	1	2	0

Andy Bathgate

1957	N.Y. Rangers (All–Stars)	1	1	2	0
1958	N.Y. Rangers (All–Stars)	2	0	2	0
1959	N.Y. Rangers (All–Stars)	0	0	0	2
1960	N.Y. Rangers (All–Stars)	0	0	0	0
1961	N.Y. Rangers (All–Stars)	0	1	1	0
1962	N.Y. Rangers (All–Stars)	0	0	0	0
1963	N.Y. Rangers (All–Stars)	0	0	0	0
1964	Toronto (Stanley Cup)	0	1	1	2
	8 games	3	3	6	4

Bobby Bauer

1939	Boston (Siebert)	1	1	2	0
1947	Boston (All–Stars)	0	0	0	2
	2 games	1	1	2	2

Gary Bauman

1967	Montreal (Stanley Cup)	20:00	nd	0	0.00R

Bobby Baun

		G / Mins	A / W-L	P / GA	Pim / Avg
1962	Toronto (Stanley Cup)	0	0	0	2
1963	Toronto (Stanley Cup)	0	1	1	2
1964	Toronto (Stanley Cup)	0	0	0	4
1965	Toronto (All–Stars)	0	1	1	0
1968	Oakland (All–Stars)	0	0	0	0
	5 games	0	2	2	8

Don Beaupre

1981	Minnesota (Wales)	31:43	L	2	3.78R
1992	Washington (Wales)	20:00	L	6	18.00
	2 games	51:43	0-2-0	8	9.28

Barry Beck

1978	Colorado (Campbell)	0	0	0	0R
1979	Challenge Cup (3)	0	1	1	2
1982	N.Y. Rangers (Wales)	0	1	1	0
	2 games	0	1	1	0

Ed Belfour

1992	Chicago (Campbell)	20:00	nd	1	3.00
1993	Chicago (Campbell)	20:00	nd	6	18.00
1996	Chicago (Western)	20:00	nd	2	6.00
1998	Dallas (North America)	20:00	nd	2	6.00
1999	Dallas (North America)	20:00	nd	2	6.00
	5 games	100:00	0-0-0	13	7.80

Jean Béliveau

1953	Montreal (Stanley Cup)	0	1	1	0R
1954	Montreal (All–Stars)	0	1	1	0
1955	Montreal (All–Stars)	0	1	1	0
1956	Montreal (Stanley Cup)	0	0	0	4
1957	Montreal (Stanley Cup)	0	0	0	0
1958	Montreal (Stanley Cup)	0	0	0	0
1959	Montreal (Stanley Cup)	2	0	2	0
1960	Montreal (Stanley Cup)	0	0	0	0
1963	Montreal (All–Stars)	0	0	0	0
1964	Montreal (All–Stars)*	1	0	1	0
1965	Montreal (Stanley Cup)	1	0	1	2
1968	Montreal (All–Stars)	0	0	0	0
1969	Montreal (East)	0	0	0	0
	13 games	4	3	7	6

Brian Bellows

1984	Minnesota (Campbell)	1	0	1	0
1988	Minnesota (Campbell)	0	1	1	2
1992	Minnesota (Campbell)	2	0	2	0
	3 games	3	1	4	2

Curt Bennett

1975	Atlanta (Campbell)	0	0	0	0
1976	Atlanta (Campbell)	1	0	1	0
	2 games	1	0	1	0

Doug Bentley

1947	Chicago (All–Stars)	1	0	1	0
1948	Chicago (All–Stars)	0	1	1	0
1949	Chicago (All–Stars)	1	0	1	0
1950	Chicago (All–Stars)	0	0	0	2
1951	Chicago (First)	0	0	0	0
	5 games	2	1	3	2

Max Bentley

1947	Chicago (All–Stars)	1	0	1	1
1948	Toronto (Stanley Cup)	1	0	1	0
1949	Toronto (Stanley Cup)	0	0	0	0
1951	Toronto (Second)	0	1	1	0
	4 games	2	1	3	0

Red Berenson

1965	Montreal (Stanley Cup)	0	0	0	0
1969	St. Louis (West)	1	1	2	0
1970	St. Louis (West)	0	1	1	0
1971	St. Louis (West)	0	0	0	0
1972	Detroit (East)	0	0	0	0
1974	Detroit (East)	0	1	1	2
	6 games	1	3	4	2

	G	A	P	Pim
	Mins	W-L	GA	Avg
Gary Bergman				
1973 Detroit (East)	0	0	0	2
Bob Berry				
1973 Los Angeles (West)	0	0	0	0
1974 Los Angeles (West)	1	0	1	0
2 games	1	0	1	0
Craig Billington				
1993 New Jersey (Wales)	20:00	nd	4	12.00
Steve Black				
1950 Detroit (Stanley Cup)	0	0	0	0
Tom Bladon				
1977 Philadelphia (Campbell)	0	0	0	0
1978 Philadelphia (Campbell)	0	0	0	0
2 games	0	0	0	0
Andy Blair				
1934 Toronto (Bailey)	1	2	3	0
Rob Blake				
1994 Los Angeles (Western)	0	1	1	0
1999 Los Angeles (North America)	1	0	1	0
2000 Los Angeles (North America)	0	0	0	0
3 games	1	1	2	0
Toe Blake				
1937 Montreal (Morenz)	0	1	1	0
1939 Montreal (Siebert)	0	0	0	0
2 games	0	1	1	0
Russ Blinco				
1937 Maroons (Morenz)	0	1	1	0
Gus Bodnar				
1951 Chicago (First)	0	0	0	0
Garth Boesch				
1948 Toronto (Stanley Cup)	0	0	0	0
1949 Toronto (Stanley Cup)	0	0	0	2
2 games	0	0	0	2
Leo Boivin				
1961 Boston (All-Stars)	0	0	0	0
1962 Boston (All-Stars)	0	0	0	2
1964 Boston (All Stars)	1	0	1	0
3 games	1	0	1	2
Ivan Boldirev				
1978 Chicago (Campbell)	0	0	0	0
Buzz Boll				
1934 Toronto (Bailey)	0	0	0	0R
Hugh Bolton				
1956 Toronto (All-Stars)	0	0	0	0
Peter Bondra				
1993 Washington (Wales)	1	1	2	0
1996 Washington (Eastern)	0	0	0	0
1997 Washington (Eastern)	0	2	2	0
1998 Washington (World)	0	1	1	0
1999 Washington (World)	0	0	0	0
5 games	1	4	5	0
Marcel Bonin				
1954 Detroit (Stanley Cup)	0	0	0	6
1957 Montreal (Stanley Cup)	0	1	1	0
1958 Montreal (Stanley Cup)	0	0	0	0
1959 Montreal (Stanley Cup)	0	1	1	0
1960 Montreal (Stanley Cup)	0	0	0	0
5 games	0	2	2	6
Radek Bonk				
2000 Ottawa (World)	1	1	2	0

	G	A	P	Pim
	Mins	W-L	GA	Avg
Mike Bossy				
1978 N.Y. Islanders (Campbell)	0	0	0	0R
1979 Challenge Cup (3)	2	2	4	0
1980 N.Y. Islanders (Campbell)	0	0	0	0
1981 N.Y. Islanders (Campbell)	0	1	1	0
1982 N.Y. Islanders (Wales)*	2	0	2	0
1983 N.Y. Islanders (Wales)	0	0	0	0
1985 N.Y. Islanders (Wales)	0	0	0	0
1986 N.Y. Islanders (Wales)	0	1	1	0
7 games	2	2	4	0
Butch Bouchard				
1947 Montreal (All-Stars)	0	0	0	2
1948 Montreal (All-Stars)	0	0	0	4
1950 Montreal (All-Stars)	0	0	0	0
1951 Montreal (Second)	0	0	0	0
1952 Montreal (Second)	0	0	0	2
1953 Montreal (Stanley Cup)	0	0	0	0
6 games	0	0	0	8
Frank Boucher				
1937 N.Y. Rangers (Morenz)	0	0	0	0
Andre Boudrias				
1967 Montreal (Stanley Cup)	0	0	0	0R
Bob Bourne				
1981 N.Y. Islanders (Campbell)	0	0	0	2
Ray Bourque				
1981 Boston (Wales)	0	0	0	0
1982 Boston (Wales)	1	0	1	0
1983 Boston (Wales)	1	0	1	0
1984 Boston (Wales)	0	0	0	0
1985 Boston (Wales)	0	1	1	0
1986 Boston (Wales)	0	1	1	0
1987 Rendez-vous (2)	1	0	1	2
1988 Boston (Wales)	0	0	0	0
1989 Boston (Wales)	0	1	1	2
1990 Boston (Wales)	0	1	1	0
1991 Boston (Wales)	0	1	1	0
1992 Boston (Wales)	0	1	1	0
1993 Boston (Wales)	0	1	1	0
1994 Boston (Eastern)	0	1	1	0
1996 Boston (Eastern)*	1	0	1	0
1997 Boston (Eastern)	0	0	0	0
1998 Boston (North America)	0	1	1	0
1999 Boston (North America)	1	0	1	0
2000 Boston (North America)	0	1	1	0
18 games	4	13	17	2
Johnny Bower				
1961 Toronto (All-Stars)	30:00	W	1	2.00
1962 Toronto (Stanley Cup)	60:00	W	1	1.00
1963 Toronto (Stanley Cup)	40:00	nd	2	3.00
1964 Toronto (Stanley Cup)	29:43	nd	0	0.00
4 games	159:43	2-0-0	4	1.50
Brian Bradley				
1993 Tampa Bay (Campbell)	0	0	0	0
1994 Tampa Bay (Eastern)	0	0	0	0
2 games	0	0	0	0
Carl Brewer				
1959 Toronto (All-Stars)	0	0	0	0
1962 Toronto (Stanley Cup)	0	0	0	4
1964 Toronto (Stanley Cup)	0	0	0	0
1970 Detroit (East)	0	1	1	0
4 games	0	1	1	4
Frank Brimsek				
1939 Boston (Siebert)	60:00	W	2	2.00
1947 Boston (All-Stars)	29:00	W	0	0.00
1948 Boston (All-Stars)	30:00	W	1	2.00
3 games	119:00	3-0-0	3	1.51
Rod Brind'Amour				
1992 Philadelphia (Wales)	0	0	0	0

	G	A	P	Pim
	Mins	W–L	GA	Avg
Turk Broda				
1947 Toronto (Stanley Cup)	60:00	L	4	4.00
1948 Toronto (Stanley Cup)	60:00	L	3	3.00
1949 Toronto (Stanley Cup)	60:00	L	3	3.00
1950 Toronto (All–Stars)	28:48	nd	4	8.33
4 games	208:48	0-3-0	14	4.02
Martin Brodeur				
1996 New Jersey (Eastern)	20:00	nd	0	0.00
1997 New Jersey (Eastern)	20:00	W	4	12.00
1998 New Jersey (North America)	20:00	W	2	6.00
1999 New Jersey (North America)	20:00	nd	1	3.00
2000 New Jersey (North America)	20:00	L	2	6.00
5 games	100:00	2-1-0	9	5.40
Neal Broten				
1983 Minnesota (Campbell)	0	1	1	0
1986 Minnesota (Campbell)	0	0	0	0
2 games	0	1	1	0
Rob Brown				
1989 Pittsburgh (Wales)	0	0	0	0
Johnny Bucyk				
1955 Detroit (Stanley Cup)	0	0	0	2R
1963 Boston (All–Stars)	0	1	1	0
1964 Boston (All–Stars)	0	1	1	0
1965 Boston (All–Stars)	1	0	1	0
1968 Boston (All–Stars)	0	0	0	0
1970 Boston (East)	0	1	1	0
1971 Boston (East)	0	0	0	2
7 games	1	3	4	4
Mike Bullard				
1984 Pittsburgh (Wales)	0	0	0	0
Hy Buller				
1952 N.Y. Rangers (Second)	0	1	1	2
Pavel Bure				
1993 Vancouver (Campbell)	2	0	2	0
1994 Vancouver (Western)	0	2	2	0
1997 Vancouver (Western)	2	1	3	0
1998 Vancouver (World)	0	1	1	0
2000 Florida (World)*	3	1	4	0
5 games	7	5	12	0
Valeri Bure				
2000 Calgary (World)	0	2	2	0
Sean Burke				
1989 New Jersey (Wales)	29:58	nd	3	6.01
Randy Burridge				
1992 Washington (Wales)	1	0	1	0
Dave Burrows				
1974 Pittsburgh (West)	0	0	0	0
1976 Pittsburgh (Wales)	0	0	0	0
1980 Toronto (Wales)	0	0	0	0
3 games	0	0	0	0
Walt Buswell				
1937 Montreal (Morenz)	0	0	0	0
1939 Montreal (Siebert)	0	0	0	0
2 games	0	0	0	0
Garth Butcher				
1993 St. Louis (Campbell)	0	0	0	0
Petr Buzek				
2000 Atlanta (World)	0	0	0	0
Wayne Carleton				
1968 Toronto (Stanley Cup)	0	2	2	0R
Randy Carlyle				
1981 Pittsburgh (Wales)	0	0	0	0
1982 Pittsburgh (Wales)	0	1	1	0
1985 Winnipeg (Campbell)	1	1	2	0
1993 Winnipeg (Campbell)	0	0	0	0
4 games	1	2	3	0
Bob Carpenter				
1985 Washington (Wales)	0	0	0	0

	G	A	P	Pim
	Mins	W–L	GA	Avg
Jimmy Carson				
1989 Edmonton (Campbell)	1	1	2	0
Joe Carveth				
1950 Detroit (Stanley Cup)	0	0	0	0
Jon Casey				
1993 Minnesota (Campbell)	20:00	nd	4	12.00
Wayne Cashman				
1974 Boston (East)	0	0	0	0
Paul Cavallini				
1990 St. Louis (Campbell)	0	0	0	0
Art Chapman				
1937 N.Y. Americans (Morenz)	0	1	1	0
Guy Charron				
1977 Washington (Wales)	0	0	0	0
Gerry Cheevers				
1969 Boston (East)	20:00	nd	1	3.00
1979 Challenge Cup (1)	60:00	L	6	6.00
Chris Chelios				
1985 Montreal (Wales)	0	0	0	0R
1987 Rendez-vous (2)	0	0	0	0
1990 Montreal (Wales)	0	0	0	0
1991 Chicago (Campbell)	1	1	2	0
1992 Chicago (Campbell)	0	0	0	0
1993 Chicago (Campbell)	0	0	0	0
1994 Chicago (Western)	0	1	1	0
1996 Chicago (Western)	0	0	0	0
1997 Chicago (Western)	0	0	0	0
1998 Chicago (North America)	0	3	3	0
2000 Detroit (North America)	0	0	0	0
10 games	1	5	6	0
Tim Cheveldae				
1992 Detroit (Campbell)	20:00	1-0-0	2	6.00
Real Chevrefils				
1955 Detroit (Stanley Cup)	0	0	0	0
1957 Boston (All–Stars)	0	1	1	2
2 games	0	1	1	2
Steve Chiasson				
1993 Detroit (Campbell)	0	0	0	0
Dave Christian				
1991 Boston (Wales)	0	0	0	0
Dino Ciccarelli				
1982 Minnesota (Campbell)	0	1	1	0
1983 Minnesota (Campbell)	1	1	2	0
1989 Minnesota (Campbell)	0	1	1	0
1997 Tampa Bay (Eastern)	0	1	1	0
4 games	1	4	5	0
Joe Cirella				
1984 New Jersey (Wales)	1	1	2	0
King Clancy				
1934 Toronto (Bailey)	0	0	0	0
1937 Maroons (Morenz)	0	0	0	0
2 games	0	0	0	0
Dit Clapper				
1937 Boston (Morenz)	1	0	1	0
1939 Boston (Siebert)	0	0	0	0
2 games	1	0	1	0
Wendel Clark				
1986 Toronto (Campbell)	0	0	0	0R
1999 Tampa Bay (North America)	0	1	1	0
2 games	0	1	1	0

	G	A	P	Pim
	Mins	W–L	GA	Avg

Bobby Clarke

		G	A	P	Pim
1970	Philadelphia (West)	0	0	0	0R
1971	Philadelphia (West)	0	0	0	0
1972	Philadelphia (West)	0	0	0	0
1973	Philadelphia (West)	0	1	1	0
1974	Philadelphia (West)	0	1	1	0
1975	Philadelphia (Campbell)	0	0	0	2
1977	Philadelphia (Campbell)	0	0	0	0
1978	Philadelphia (Campbell)	0	1	1	0
1979	Challenge Cup (3)	0	1	1	0
	8 games	0	3	3	2

Bill Clement

		G	A	P	Pim
1976	Washington (Wales)	0	0	0	0
1978	Atlanta (Campbell)	0	0	0	0
	2 games	0	0	0	0

Real Cloutier

		G	A	P	Pim
1980	Quebec (Wales)	1	1	2	0

Paul Coffey

		G	A	P	Pim
1982	Edmonton (Campbell)	0	1	1	0
1983	Edmonton (Campbell)	0	1	1	0
1984	Edmonton (Campbell)	0	0	0	0
1985	Edmonton (Campbell)	0	0	0	0
1986	Edmonton (Campbell)	0	2	2	0
1988	Pittsburgh (Wales)	0	0	0	0
1989	Pittsburgh (Wales)	0	0	0	0
1990	Pittsburgh (Wales)	0	2	2	0
1991	Pittsburgh (Wales)	0	0	0	0
1992	Pittsburgh (Wales)	0	0	0	0
1993	Detroit (Campbell)	0	1	1	0
1994	Detroit (Western)	1	0	1	0
1996	Detroit (Western)	1	1	2	0
1997	Philadelphia (Eastern)	0	1	1	2
	14 games	2	9	11	2

Neil Colville

		G	A	P	Pim
1939	N.Y. Rangers (Siebert)	0	0	0	0
1948	N.Y. Rangers (All–Stars)	0	0	0	0
	2 games	0	0	0	0

Brian Conacher

		G	A	P	Pim
1968	Toronto (Stanley Cup)	0	0	0	0

Charlie Conacher

		G	A	P	Pim
1934	Toronto (Bailey)	0	0	0	0
1937	Toronto (Morenz)	1	1	2	0
	2 games	1	1	2	0

Lionel Conacher

		G	A	P	Pim
1934	Chicago (Bailey)	0	0	0	0

Roy Conacher

		G	A	P	Pim
1949	Chicago (All–Stars)	0	0	0	0

Bill Cook

		G	A	P	Pim
1934	N.Y. Rangers (Bailey)	0	0	0	0

Norm Corcoran

		G	A	P	Pim
1955	Detroit (Stanley Cup)	0	0	0	4

Shayne Corson

		G	A	P	Pim
1990	Montreal (Wales)	1	0	1	0
1994	Edmonton (Western)	0	0	0	0
1998	Montreal (North America)	0	0	0	0
	3 games	1	0	1	0

Les Costello

		G	A	P	Pim
1948	Toronto (Stanley Cup)	0	1	1	0R

Baldy Cotton

		G	A	P	Pim
1934	Toronto (Bailey)	1	0	1	0

Art Coulter

		G	A	P	Pim
1939	N.Y. Rangers (Siebert)	0	1	1	0

Yvan Cournoyer

		G	A	P	Pim
1967	Montreal (Stanley Cup)	0	0	0	0
1971	Montreal (East)	1	0	1	0
1972	Montreal (East)	0	0	0	0
1973	Montreal (East)	0	0	0	0
1974	Montreal (East)	1	1	2	0
1978	Montreal (Wales)	0	0	0	0
	6 games	2	1	3	0

Russ Courtnall

		G	A	P	Pim
1994	Dallas (Western)	0	0	0	0

Gerry Couture

		G	A	P	Pim
1950	Detroit (Stanley Cup)	0	0	0	2

Dave Creighton

		G	A	P	Pim
1952	Boston (First)	0	1	1	0
1956	N.Y. Rangers (All–Stars)	0	0	0	0
	2 games	0	1	1	0

Wilf Cude

		Mins	W–L	GA	Avg
1937	Montreal (Morenz)	60:00	T	6	6.00
1939	Montreal (Siebert)	60:00	L	5	5.00
	2 games	120:00	0–2–0	11	5.50

John Cullen

		G	A	P	Pim
1991	Pittsburgh (Wales)	0	1	1	0
1992	Hartford (Wales)	0	0	0	0
	2 games	0	1	1	0

Floyd Curry

		G	A	P	Pim
1951	Montreal (Second)	0	0	0	2
1952	Montreal (Second)	0	0	0	0
1953	Montreal (Stanley Cup)	0	0	0	0
1956	Montreal (Stanley Cup)	0	0	0	0
1957	Montreal (Stanley Cup)	0	0	0	0
	5 games	0	0	0	2

Ian Cushenan

		G	A	P	Pim
1958	Montreal (Stanley Cup)	0	0	0	0

Mariusz Czerkawski

		G	A	P	Pim
2000	N.Y. Islanders (World)	0	1	1	0

Bob Dailey

		G	A	P	Pim
1978	Philadelphia (Campbell)	0	0	0	2
1981	Philadelphia (Campbell)	0	0	0	0
	2 games	0	0	0	2

Vincent Damphousse

		G	A	P	Pim
1991	Toronto (Campbell)*	4	0	4	0
1992	Edmonton (Campbell)	0	1	1	0
	2 games	4	1	5	0

Lorne Davis

		G	A	P	Pim
1953	Montreal (Stanley Cup)	0	0	0	0R

Bobby Dawes

		G	A	P	Pim
1949	Toronto (Stanley Cup)	0	0	0	0R

Happy Day

		G	A	P	Pim
1934	Toronto (Bailey)	1	0	1	0
1937	N.Y. Americans (Morenz)	0	0	0	0
	2 games	1	0	1	0

Alex Delvecchio

		G	A	P	Pim
1953	Detroit (All–Stars)	1	0	1	0
1954	Detroit (Stanley Cup)	1	0	1	0
1955	Detroit (Stanley Cup)	0	1	1	0
1956	Detroit (All–Stars)	0	0	0	0
1957	Detroit (All–Stars)	0	0	0	0
1958	Detroit (All–Stars)	0	0	0	0
1959	Detroit (All–Stars)	0	0	0	0
1961	Detroit (All–Stars)	1	1	2	0
1962	Detroit (All–Stars)	0	1	1	0
1963	Detroit (All–Stars)	0	0	0	0
1964	Detroit (All–Stars)	0	0	0	0
1965	Detroit (All–Stars)	0	0	0	0
1967	Detroit (All–Stars)	0	0	0	0
	13 games	3	3	6	0

		G / Mins	A / W-L	P / GA	Pim / Avg
Pavol Demitra					
1999	St. Louis (World)	1	0	1	0
2000	St. Louis (World)	2	0	2	0
	2 games	3	0	3	0
Eric Desjardins					
1992	Montreal (Wales)	0	1	1	0
1996	Philadelphia (Eastern)	0	0	0	0
2000	Philadelphia (North America)	0	1	1	0
	3 games	0	2	2	0
Gerry Desjardins					
1977	Buffalo (Wales)	28:33	1-0-0	2	4.20
Al Dewsbury					
1951	Chicago (First)	0	0	0	0
Cecil Dillon					
1937	N.Y. Rangers (Morenz)	1	1	2	0
Kevin Dineen					
1987	Rendez-vous (2)	1	0	1	0
1988	Hartford (Wales)	0	2	2	0
1989	Hartford (Wales)	0	0	0	0
	2 games	0	2	2	0
Bill Dineen					
1954	Detroit (Stanley Cup)	0	0	0	2
1955	Detroit (Stanley Cup)	0	0	0	0
	2 games	0	0	0	2
Michel Dion					
1982	Pittsburgh (Wales)	30:23	nd	2	3.95
Marcel Dionne					
1975	Detroit (Wales)	0	0	0	0
1976	Los Angeles (Wales)	1	0	1	0
1977	Los Angeles (Wales)	0	2	2	0
1978	Los Angeles (Wales)	0	1	1	0
1979	Challenge Cup (2)	0	1	1	0
1980	Los Angeles (Wales)	0	0	0	0
1981	Los Angeles (Wales)	0	0	0	0
1983	Los Angeles (Campbell)	0	1	1	0
1985	Los Angeles (Campbell)	1	0	1	2
	8 games	2	4	6	2
Ken Doraty					
1934	Toronto (Bailey)	1	1	2	0
Gary Dornhoefer					
1973	Philadelphia (West)	0	0	0	0
1977	Philadelphia (Campbell)	0	1	1	2
	2 games	0	1	1	2
Kent Douglas					
1962	Toronto (Stanley Cup)	0	1	1	0R
1963	Toronto (Stanley Cup)	0	0	0	0
1964	Toronto (Stanley Cup)	1	0	1	4
	3 games	1	1	2	4
Gord Drillon					
1939	Toronto (Siebert)	0	0	0	0
Polly Drouin					
1939	Montreal (Siebert)	0	1	1	0
Dave Dryden					
1974	Buffalo (East)	29:37	0-1-0	5	10.13
Ken Dryden					
1972	Montreal (East)	30:24	nd	2	3.95R
1975	Montreal (Wales)	29:21	nd	0	0.00
1976	Montreal (Wales)	29:34	nd	1	2.03
1977	Montreal (Wales)	31:27	nd	1	1.91
1978	Montreal (Wales)	29:26	nd	2	4.08
1979	Challenge Cup (2)	120:00	1-1-0	7	3.50
	5 games	150:12	0-0-0	6	2.40
Steve Duchesne					
1989	Los Angeles (Campbell)	0	2	2	0
1990	Los Angeles (Campbell)	0	0	0	0
1993	Quebec (Wales)	0	0	0	0
	3 games	0	2	2	0
Dick Duff					
1956	Toronto (All–Stars)	0	0	0	0
1957	Toronto (All–Stars)	0	0	0	0
1958	Toronto (All–Stars)	0	0	0	2
1962	Toronto (Stanley Cup)	1	0	1	0
1963	Toronto (Stanley Cup)	0	0	0	2
1965	Montreal (Stanley Cup)	0	1	1	0
1967	Montreal (Stanley Cup)	0	0	0	0
	7 games	1	1	2	4
Ron Duguay					
1982	N.Y. Rangers (Wales)	0	0	0	0
Woody Dumart					
1947	Boston (All–Stars)	0	0	0	0
1948	Boston (All–Stars)	1	0	1	0
	2 games	1	0	1	0
Denis Dupere					
1975	Washington (Wales)	0	1	1	0
Andre Dupont					
1976	Philadelphia (Campbell)	0	1	1	0
Bill Durnan					
1947	Montreal (All–Stars)	31:00	nd	3	5.81
1948	Montreal (All–Stars)	30:00	nd	0	0.00
1949	Montreal (All–Stars)	29:30	nd	1	2.03
	3 games	90:30	0-0-0	4	2.65
Red Dutton					
1934	N.Y. Americans (Bailey)	0	0	0	0
Tim Ecclestone					
1971	St. Louis (West)	0	0	0	0
Frank Eddolls					
1951	N.Y. Rangers (First)	0	0	0	2
Don Edwards					
1980	Buffalo (Wales)	29:27	nd	2	4.07
1982	Buffalo (Wales)	29:37	W	0	0.00
	2 games	59:04	1-0-0	2	2.03
Pat Egan					
1949	N.Y. Rangers (All–Stars)	0	0	0	2
Gerry Ehman					
1964	Toronto (Stanley Cup)	0	1	1	0
Patrick Elias					
2000	New Jersey (World)	0	2	2	0
Dave Ellett					
1989	Winnipeg (Campbell)	0	0	0	0
1992	Toronto (Campbell)	0	1	1	0
	2 games	0	1	1	0
Ron Ellis					
1964	Toronto (Stanley Cup)	0	0	0	0R
1965	Toronto (All–Stars)	0	0	0	2
1968	Toronto (Stanley Cup)	1	0	1	0
1970	Toronto (East)	0	0	0	0
	4 games	1	0	1	2
Rolie Eriksson					
1978	Minnesota (Campbell)	0	0	0	0
Phil Esposito					
1969	Boston (East)	0	0	0	0
1970	Boston (East)	0	0	0	0
1971	Boston (East)	0	0	0	0
1972	Boston (East)	1	0	1	2
1973	Boston (East)	0	1	1	0
1974	Boston (East)	0	0	0	0
1975	Boston (Wales)	1	0	1	0
1977	N.Y. Rangers (Campbell)	1	0	1	0
1978	N.Y. Rangers (Campbell)	0	0	0	0
1980	N.Y. Rangers (Campbell)	0	1	1	0
	10 games	3	2	5	2

		G	A	P	Pim
		Mins	W–L	GA	Avg

Tony Esposito

		G/Mins	A/W–L	P/GA	Pim/Avg
1970	Chicago (East)	30:23	nd	0	0.00R
1971	Chicago (West)	30:41	W	1	1.96
1972	Chicago (West)	30:24	nd	1	1.97
1973	Chicago (West)	29:16	nd	1	2.05
1974	Chicago (West)	30:01	W	2	4.00
1980	Chicago (Campbell)	15:10	nd	2	7.91
	6 games	165:55	2-0-0	7	2.53

Jack Evans

1961	Chicago (Stanley Cup)	0	0	0	0
1962	Chicago (All–Stars)	0	0	0	0
	2 games	0	0	0	0

Bill Ezinicki

1947	Toronto (Stanley Cup)	1	1	2	6
1948	Toronto (Stanley Cup)	0	0	0	2
	2 games	1	1	2	8

Bernie Federko

1980	St. Louis (Campbell)	0	1	1	0
1981	St. Louis (Campbell)	0	1	1	0
	2 games	0	2	2	0

Sergei Fedorov

1992	Detroit (Campbell)	0	2	2	0
1994	Detroit (Western)	1	1	2	0
1996	Detroit (Western)	0	1	1	0
	3 games	1	4	5	0

John Ferguson

1965	Montreal (Stanley Cup)	0	0	0	2
1967	Montreal (Stanley Cup)	2	0	2	2
	2 games	2	0	2	4

Ray Ferraro

| 1992 | N.Y. Islanders (Wales) | 0 | 0 | 0 | 0 |

Viacheslav Fetisov

1997	Detroit (Western)	0	1	1	0
1998	Detroit (World)	0	1	1	2
	2 games	0	2	2	2

Frank Finnigan

| 1934 | Ottawa (I) (Bailey) | 1 | 0 | 1 | 0 |

Fern Flaman

1952	Toronto (Second)	0	0	0	0
1955	Boston (All–Stars)	0	0	0	2
1956	Boston (All–Stars)	0	0	0	2
1957	Boston (All–Stars)	0	0	0	4
1958	Boston (All–Stars)	0	0	0	0
1959	Boston (All–Stars)	0	0	0	0
	6 games	0	0	0	8

Reggie Fleming

| 1961 | Chicago (Stanley Cup) | 0 | 0 | 0 | 0 |

Bill Flett

| 1971 | Los Angeles (West) | 0 | 1 | 1 | 0 |

Theoren Fleury

1991	Calgary (Campbell)	1	0	1	0
1992	Calgary (Campbell)	2	0	2	0
1996	Calgary (Western)	0	0	0	0
1997	Calgary (Western)	0	1	1	0
1998	Calgary (North America)	1	2	3	2
1999	Calgary (North America)	0	2	2	0
	6 games	4	5	9	2

Lee Fogolin

1950	Detroit (Stanley Cup)	0	0	0	0
1951	Chicago (First)	0	0	0	0
	2 games	0	0	0	0

Lee Fogolin, Jr.

| 1986 | Edmonton (Campbell) | 0 | 0 | 0 | 0 |

Peter Forsberg

1996	Avalanche (Western)	0	0	0	0
1998	Avalanche (World)	0	1	1	0
1999	Avalanche (World)	0	1	1	0
	3 games	0	2	2	0

Ron Francis

		G/Mins	A/W–L	P/GA	Pim/Avg
1983	Hartford (Wales)	0	0	0	0
1985	Hartford (Wales)	1	0	1	0
1990	Hartford (Wales)	0	2	2	0
]996	Pittsburgh (Eastern)	0	1	1	0
	4 games	1	3	4	0

Bob Froese

| 1986 | Philadelphia (Wales) | 32:02 | 1-0-0 | 2 | 3.75 |

Miroslav Frycer

| 1985 | Toronto (Campbell) | 1 | 0 | 1 | 0 |

Grant Fuhr

1982	Edmonton (Campbell)	30:23	nd	2	3.95R
1984	Edmonton (Campbell)	29:20	L	2	4.09
1985	Edmonton (Campbell)	28:35	L	4	8.40
1986	Edmonton (Campbell)*	31:03	nd	0	0.00
1987	Rendez-vous (2)	120:00	1-1-0	8	4.00
1988	Edmonton (Campbell)	30:08	nd	3	5.97
1989	Edmonton (Campbell)	29:58	nd	3	6.01
	6 games	179:27	0-2-0	13	4.35

Bill Gadsby

1953	Chicago (All–Stars)	0	0	0	0
1954	Chicago (All–Stars)	0	1	1	0
1956	N.Y. Rangers (All–Stars)	0	0	0	0
1957	N.Y. Rangers (All–Stars)	0	0	0	0
1958	N.Y. Rangers (All–Stars)	0	0	0	0
1959	N.Y. Rangers (All–Stars)	0	0	0	0
1960	N.Y. Rangers (All–Stars)	0	0	0	2
1965	Detroit (All–Stars)	0	1	1	2
	8 games	0	2	2	4

Dave Gagner

| 1991 | Minnesota (Campbell) | 1 | 0 | 1 | 0 |

Johnny Gagnon

1937	Montreal (Morenz)	2	1	3	0
1939	Montreal (Siebert)	0	0	0	0
	2 games	2	1	3	0

Bob Gainey

1977	Montreal (Wales)	0	1	1	0
1978	Montreal (Wales)	0	0	0	0
1979	Challenge Cup (3)	1	0	1	0
1980	Montreal (Wales)	0	0	0	0
1981	Montreal (Wales)	0	0	0	0
	4 games	0	1	1	0

Garry Galley

1991	Boston (Wales)	0	0	0	0
1994	Philadelphia (Eastern)	0	0	0	0
	2 games	0	0	0	0

Bruce Gamble

| 1968 | Toronto (Stanley Cup) | 40:00 | 0-0-0 | 2 | 3.00 |

Dick Gamble

| 1953 | Montreal (Stanley Cup) | 0 | 0 | 0 | 0 |

Chuck Gardiner

| 1934 | Chicago (Bailey) | 60:00 | 0-1-0 | 7 | 7.00 |

Cal Gardner

1948	Toronto (Stanley Cup)	0	0	0	0
1949	Toronto (Stanley Cup)	0	1	1	0
	2 games	0	1	1	0

Danny Gare

1980	Buffalo (Wales)	0	0	0	0
1981	Buffalo (Wales)	0	0	0	0
	2 games	0	0	0	0

John Garrett

| 1983 | Vancouver (Campbell) | 29:56 | 1-0-0 | 1 | 2.00 |

		G	A	P	Pim
		Mins	W–L	GA	Avg

Mike Gartner

Year	Team	G	A	P	Pim
1981	Washington (Campbell)	0	0	0	0
1985	Washington (Wales)	1	0	1	0
1986	Washington (Wales)	0	0	0	4
1988	Washington (Wales)	1	0	1	0
1990	Minnesota (Campbell)	0	0	0	0
1993	N.Y. Rangers (Wales)*	4	1	5	0
1996	Toronto (Western)	0	0	0	0
	7 games	6	1	7	4

George Gee

Year	Team	G	A	P	Pim
1950	Detroit (Stanley Cup)	0	0	0	0

Bernie Geoffrion

Year	Team	G	A	P	Pim
1952	Montreal (Second)	0	0	0	0
1953	Montreal (Stanley Cup)	0	0	0	0
1954	Montreal (All–Stars)	0	0	0	0
1955	Montreal (All–Stars)	0	0	0	2
1956	Montreal (Stanley Cup)	0	0	0	0
1958	Montreal (Stanley Cup)	1	0	1	0
1959	Montreal (Stanley Cup)	0	1	1	0
1960	Montreal (Stanley Cup)	0	0	0	0
1961	Montreal (All–Stars)	0	0	0	0
1962	Montreal (All–Stars)	0	0	0	0
1963	Montreal (All–Stars)	0	1	1	0
	11 games	1	2	3	2

Ray Getliffe

Year	Team	G	A	P	Pim
1939	Montreal (Siebert)	0	1	1	0

Ed Giacomin

Year	Team	Mins	W–L	GA	Avg
1967	N.Y. Rangers (All–Stars)	30:00	nd	1	2.00
1968	N.Y. Rangers (All–Stars)	20:00	nd	1	3.00
1969	N.Y. Rangers (East)	40:00	T	2	3.00
1970	N.Y. Rangers (East)	29:37	W	1	2.03
1971	N.Y. Rangers (East)	30:41	L	2	3.91
1973	N.Y. Rangers (East)	30:44	W	3	5.86
	6 games	181:02	2-1-1	10	3.31

Barry Gibbs

Year	Team	G	A	P	Pim
1973	Minnesota (West)	0	0	0	0

Gilles Gilbert

Year	Team	Mins	W–L	GA	Avg
1974	Boston (East)	29:59	nd	1	2.00

Rod Gilbert

Year	Team	G	A	P	Pim
1964	N.Y. Rangers (All–Stars)	0	0	0	0
1965	N.Y. Rangers (All–Stars)	0	0	0	0
1967	N.Y. Rangers (All–Stars)	0	0	0	0
1969	N.Y. Rangers (East)	0	1	1	0
1970	N.Y. Rangers (East)	0	0	0	0
1972	N.Y. Rangers (East)	0	1	1	0
1975	N.Y. Rangers (Campbell)	0	0	0	0
1977	N.Y. Rangers (Campbell)	0	1	1	0
	8 games	0	3	3	0

Clark Gillies

Year	Team	G	A	P	Pim
1978	N.Y. Islanders (Campbell)	0	0	0	2
1979	Challenge Cup (3)	1	2	3	2

Doug Gilmour

Year	Team	G	A	P	Pim
1993	Toronto (Campbell)	1	0	1	0
1994	Toronto (Western)	0	1	1	0
	2 games	1	1	2	0

Warren Godfrey

Year	Team	G	A	P	Pim
1955	Detroit (Stanley Cup)	0	0	0	0

Bob Goldham

Year	Team	G	A	P	Pim
1947	Toronto (Stanley Cup)	0	0	0	0
1949	Chicago (All–Stars)	1	1	2	0
1950	Detroit (Stanley Cup)	0	0	0	0
1952	Detroit (First)	0	0	0	0
1954	Detroit (Stanley Cup)	0	0	0	0
1955	Detroit (Stanley Cup)	0	1	1	0
	6 games	1	2	3	0

Bill Goldsworthy

Year	Team	G	A	P	Pim
1970	Minnesota (West)	0	0	0	0
1972	Minnesota (West)	0	0	0	0
1974	Minnesota (West)	0	0	0	0
1976	Minnesota (Campbell)	0	0	0	0
	4 games	0	0	0	0

Scott Gomez

Year	Team	G	A	P	Pim
2000	New Jersey (North America)	0	0	0	0R

Ebbie Goodfellow

Year	Team	G	A	P	Pim
1937	Detroit (Morenz)	0	0	0	0
1939	Detroit (Siebert)	0	0	0	2
	2 games	0	0	0	2

Butch Goring

Year	Team	G	A	P	Pim
1980	Los Angeles (Wales)	0	1	1	0

Mario Gosselin

Year	Team	Mins	W–L	GA	Avg
1986	Quebec (Wales)	31:03	0-0-0	1	1.93

Johnny Gottselig

Year	Team	G	A	P	Pim
1937	Chicago (Morenz)	1	1	2	0
1939	Chicago (Siebert)	1	2	3	0
	2 games	2	3	5	0

Michel Goulet

Year	Team	G	A	P	Pim
1983	Quebec (Wales)	1	0	1	0
1984	Quebec (Wales)	0	1	1	0
1985	Quebec (Wales)	0	1	1	0
1986	Quebec (Wales)	0	0	0	0
1987	Rendez-vous (2)	0	1	1	0
1988	Quebec (Wales)	0	0	0	0
	5 games	1	2	3	0

Red Goupille

Year	Team	G	A	P	Pim
1939	Montreal (Siebert)	0	0	0	2

Phil Goyette

Year	Team	G	A	P	Pim
1957	Montreal (Stanley Cup)	0	0	0	0R
1958	Montreal (Stanley Cup)	0	0	0	0
1959	Montreal (Stanley Cup)	0	0	0	0
1961	Montreal (All–Stars)	0	0	0	2
	4 games	0	0	0	2

Thomas Gradin

Year	Team	G	A	P	Pim
1985	Vancouver (Campbell)	0	0	0	0

Tony Granato

Year	Team	G	A	P	Pim
1997	San Jose (Western)	0	0	0	0

Danny Grant

Year	Team	G	A	P	Pim
1969	Minnesota (West)	0	1	1	0
1970	Minnesota (West)	0	0	0	0
1971	Minnesota (West)	0	0	0	0
	3 games	0	1	1	0

Adam Graves

Year	Team	G	A	P	Pim
1994	N.Y. Rangers (Eastern)	0	2	2	0

Rick Green

Year	Team	G	A	P	Pim
1987	Rendez-vous (2)	0	0	0	0

Ted Green

Year	Team	G	A	P	Pim
1965	Boston (All–Stars)	0	0	0	0
1969	Boston (East)	0	0	0	0
	2 games	0	0	0	0

Ron Greschner

Year	Team	G	A	P	Pim
1980	N.Y. Rangers (Campbell)	0	0	0	0

Wayne Gretzky

Year	Team	G	A	P	Pim
1980	Edmonton (Campbell)	0	0	0	0
1981	Edmonton (Campbell)	0	1	1	0
1982	Edmonton (Campbell)	1	0	1	0
1983	Edmonton (Campbell)*	4	0	4	0
1984	Edmonton (Campbell)	1	0	1	0
1985	Edmonton (Campbell)	1	0	1	0
1986	Edmonton (Campbell)	1	0	1	0
1987	Rendez-vous (2)	0	4	4	0
1988	Edmonton (Campbell)	1	0	1	0
1989	Los Angeles (Campbell)*	1	2	3	0
1990	Los Angeles (Campbell)	0	0	0	0
1991	Los Angeles (Campbell)	1	0	1	0
1992	Los Angeles (Campbell)	1	2	3	0

		G	A	P	Pim
		Mins	W-L	GA	Avg
1993	Los Angeles (Campbell)	0	0	0	0
1994	Los Angeles (Western)	0	2	2	0
1996	Los Angeles (Western)	0	0	0	0
1997	N.Y. Rangers (Eastern)	0	1	1	0
1998	N.Y. Rangers (North America)	0	2	2	0
1999	N.Y. Rangers (North America)*	1	2	3	0
	18 games	13	12	25	0

Jocelyn Guevremont

1974	Vancouver (East)	0	0	0	0

Vic Hadfield

1965	N.Y. Rangers (All–Stars)	0	0	0	0
1972	N.Y. Rangers (East)	0	0	0	2
	2 games	0	0	0	2

George Hainsworth

1934	Toronto (Bailey)	60:00	1-0-0	3	3.00

Glenn Hall

1955	Detroit (Stanley Cup)	60:00	W	1	1.00R
1956	Detroit (All–Stars)	29:30	nd	0	0.00
1957	Detroit (All–Stars)	60:00	W	3	3.00
1958	Chicago (All–Stars)	60:00	L	6	6.00
1960	Chicago (All–Stars)	60:00	W	1	1.00
1961	Chicago (Stanley Cup)	60:00	L	3	3.00
1962	Chicago (All–Stars)	20:00	nd	0	0.00
1963	Chicago (All–Stars)	31:03	nd	2	3.86
1964	Chicago (All–Stars)	29:43	nd	0	0.00
1965	Chicago (All–Stars)	60:00	W	2	2.00
1967	Chicago (All Stars)	30:00	L	2	4.00
1968	St. Louis (All–Stars)	20:00	L	1	3.00
1969	St. Louis (West)	20:00	nd	1	3.00
	13 games	540:16	4-4-0	22	2.44

Murray Hall

1961	Chicago (Stanley Cup)	0	0	0	0R

Ted Hampson

1969	Oakland (West)	0	0	0	0

Roman Hamrlik

1996	Tampa Bay (Eastern)	0	0	0	0
1999	Edmonton (World)	0	0	0	0
	2 games	0	0	0	0

Glen Harmon

1949	Montreal (All–Stars)	0	0	0	2
1950	Montreal (All–Stars)	0	0	0	0
	2 games	0	0	0	2

Terry Harper

1965	Montreal (Stanley Cup)	0	0	0	0
1967	Montreal (Stanley Cup)	0	1	1	0
1973	Los Angeles (West)	1	1	2	0
1975	Los Angeles (Wales)	0	0	0	2
	4 games	1	2	3	2

Billy Harris

1958	Toronto (All–Stars)	0	1	1	0
1962	Toronto (Stanley Cup)	0	0	0	0
1963	Toronto (Stanley Cup)	0	0	0	0
1964	Toronto (Stanley Cup)	0	0	0	0
	4 games	0	1	1	0

Billy Harris

1976	N.Y. Islanders (Campbell)	0	2	2	0

Ted Harris

1965	Montreal (Stanley Cup)	0	0	0	4
1967	Montreal (Stanley Cup)	0	0	0	0
1969	Montreal (East)	0	1	1	0
1971	Minnesota (West)	0	0	0	2
1972	Minnesota (West)	0	0	0	0
	5 games	0	1	1	6

Craig Hartsburg

1980	Minnesota (Wales)	1	0	1	2R
1982	Minnesota (Campbell)	0	0	0	2
1983	Minnesota (Campbell)	0	0	0	0
	3 games	1	0	1	4

Doug Harvey

		G	A	P	Pim
		Mins	W-L	GA	Avg
1951	Montreal (Second)	0	0	0	0
1952	Montreal (First)	0	0	0	0
1953	Montreal (Stanley Cup)	0	1	1	0
1954	Montreal (All–Stars)	0	0	0	0
1955	Montreal (All–Stars)	1	0	1	2
1956	Montreal (Stanley Cup)	0	1	1	0
1957	Montreal (Stanley Cup)	0	0	0	2
1958	Montreal (Stanley Cup)	0	1	1	2
1959	Montreal (Stanley Cup)	0	3	3	0
1960	Montreal (Stanley Cup)	0	0	0	2
1961	N.Y. Rangers (All–Stars)	0	0	0	0
1962	N.Y. Rangers (All–Stars)	0	0	0	0
1969	St. Louis (West)	0	1	1	2
	13 games	1	7	8	10

Dominik Hasek

1996	Buffalo (Eastern)	20:00	W	1	3.00
1997	Buffalo (Eastern)	20:00	nd	1	3.00
1998	Buffalo (World)	20:00	nd	3	9.00
1999	Buffalo (World)	20:00	nd	4	12.00
	4 games	80:00	1-0-0	9	6.75

Derian Hatcher

1997	Dallas (Western)	0	0	0	0

Kevin Hatcher

1990	Washington (Wales)	0	1	1	0
1991	Washington (Wales)	0	1	1	0
1992	Washington (Wales)	0	1	1	0
1996	Dallas (Western)	0	0	0	0
1997	Pittsburgh (Eastern)	0	1	1	2
	5 games	0	4	4	2

Dale Hawerchuk

1982	Winnipeg (Campbell)	0	0	0	2R
1985	Winnipeg (Campbell)	0	0	0	0
1986	Winnipeg (Campbell)	1	0	1	0
1987	Rendez-vous (2)	0	1	1	2
1988	Winnipeg (Campbell)	1	0	1	0
1997	Philadelphia (Eastern)	2	0	2	0
	5 games	4	0	4	2

Bill Hay

1960	Chicago (All–Stars)	0	0	0	0
1961	Chicago (Stanley Cup)	0	0	0	2
	2 games	0	0	0	2

Paul Haynes

1937	Montreal (Morenz)	1	0	1	0
1939	Montreal (Siebert)	0	0	0	0
	2 games	1	0	1	0

Andy Hebenton

1960	N.Y. Rangers (All–Stars)	1	0	1	0

Guy Hebert

1997	Anaheim (Western)	20:00	nd	1	3.00

Anders Hedberg

1979	Challenge Cup (2)	0	0	0	0
1985	N.Y. Rangers (Wales)	1	0	1	0

Milan Hejduk

2000	Avalanche (World)	0	1	1	0

Paul Henderson

1972	Toronto (East)	0	0	0	0
1973	Toronto (East)	1	0	1	0
	2 games	1	0	1	0

Camille Henry

1958	N.Y. Rangers (All–Stars)	0	1	1	2
1963	N.Y. Rangers (All–Stars)	0	1	1	0
1964	N.Y. Rangers (All–Stars)	0	0	0	0
	3 games	0	2	2	2

Sugar Jim Henry

1952	Boston (Second)	29:57	nd	1	2.00

			G	A	P	Pim
			Mins	W–L	GA	Avg
Wally Hergesheimer						
1953	N.Y. Rangers (All–Stars)		2	0	2	0
1956	Chicago (All–Stars)		0	0	0	0
	2 games		2	0	2	0
Dennis Hextall						
1974	Minnesota (West)		0	0	0	2
1975	Minnesota (Campbell)		0	0	0	0
	2 games		0	0	0	2
Ron Hextall						
1988	Philadelphia (Wales)		30:08	nd	2	3.98
Bill Hicke						
1959	Montreal (Stanley Cup)		0	2	2	0R
1960	Montreal (Stanley Cup)		0	0	0	2
1969	Oakland (West)		0	0	0	0
	3 games		0	2	2	2
Larry Hillman						
1955	Detroit (Stanley Cup)		0	0	0	0R
1962	Toronto (Stanley Cup)		0	0	0	0
1963	Toronto (Stanley Cup)		0	0	0	0
1964	Toronto (Stanley Cup)		0	0	0	0
1968	Toronto (Stanley Cup)		0	2	2	0
	5 games		0	2	2	0
Normie Himes						
1934	N.Y. Americans (Bailey)		0	0	0	0
Charlie Hodge						
1964	Montreal (All–Stars)		30:17	W	2	1.98
1965	Montreal (Stanley Cup)		29:14	L	4	8.21
1967	Montreal (Stanley Cup)		40:00	W	0	0.00
	3 games		99:31	2-1-0	6	3.60
*2 pim in 1964						
Ken Hodge						
1971	Boston (East)		0	0	0	0
1973	Boston (East)		0	1	1	2
1974	Boston (East)		0	0	0	0
	3 games		0	1	1	2
Bobby Holik						
1998	New Jersey (World)		0	0	0	0
1999	New Jersey (World)		0	1	1	0
	2 games		0	1	1	0
Gord Hollingworth						
1955	Detroit (Stanley Cup)		0	0	0	4
Paul Holmgren						
1981	Philadelphia (Campbell)		0	1	1	0
Red Horner						
1934	Toronto (Bailey)		0	0	0	0
1937	Toronto (Morenz)		0	0	0	2
	2 games		0	0	0	2
Tim Horton						
1954	Toronto (All–Stars)		0	0	0	2
1961	Toronto (All–Stars)		0	0	0	0
1962	Toronto (Stanley Cup)		0	0	0	0
1963	Toronto (Stanley Cup)		0	0	0	4
1964	Toronto (Stanley Cup)		0	0	0	0
1968	Toronto (Stanley Cup)		0	0	0	0
1969	Toronto (East)		0	0	0	4
	7 games		0	0	0	10
Bronco Horvath						
1960	Boston (All–Stars)		0	0	0	0
1961	Chicago (Stanley Cup)		0	0	0	0
	2 games		0	0	0	0
Phil Housley						
1984	Buffalo (Wales)		0	1	1	2
1989	Buffalo (Wales)		0	0	0	0
1990	Buffalo (Wales)		0	1	1	0
1991	Winnipeg (Campbell)		0	2	2	4
1992	Winnipeg (Campbell)		0	0	0	0
1993	Winnipeg (Campbell)		0	0	0	0
2000	Calgary (North America)		0	0	0	0
	7 games		0	4	4	6

			G	A	P	Pim
			Mins	W–L	GA	Avg
Gordie Howe						
1948	Detroit (All–Stars)		0	0	0	5
1949	Detroit (All–Stars)		0	0	0	2
1950	Detroit (Stanley Cup)		1	1	2	0
1951	Detroit (First)		1	0	1	2
1952	Detroit (First)		0	0	0	2
1953	Detroit (All–Stars)		0	0	0	2
1954	Detroit (Stanley Cup)		1	0	1	0
1955	Detroit (Stanley Cup)		1	1	2	0
1957	Detroit (All–Stars)		1	0	1	4
1958	Detroit (All–Stars)		0	0	0	0
1959	Detroit (All–Stars)		0	0	0	0
1960	Detroit (All–Stars)		0	0	0	0
1961	Detroit (All–Stars)		1	1	2	0
1962	Detroit (All–Stars)		1	0	1	4
1963	Detroit (All–Stars)		0	1	1	0
1964	Detroit (All–Stars)		0	1	1	0
1965	Detroit (All–Stars)*		2	2	4	0
1967	Detroit (All–Stars)		0	0	0	0
1968	Detroit (All–Stars)		0	1	1	4
1969	Detroit (East)		0	0	0	0
1970	Detroit (East)		1	0	1	0
1971	Detroit (East)		0	0	0	0
1980	Hartford (Wales)		0	1	1	0
	23 games		10	9	19	25
Mark Howe						
1981	Hartford (Wales)		0	1	1	0
1983	Philadelphia (Wales)		0	0	0	0
1986	Philadelphia (Wales)		0	0	0	0
1988	Philadelphia (Wales)		0	0	0	0
	4 games		0	1	1	0
Syd Howe						
1939	Detroit (Siebert)		0	0	0	0
Harry Howell						
1954	N.Y. Rangers (All–Stars)		0	0	0	4
1963	N.Y. Rangers (All–Stars)		0	0	0	2
1964	N.Y. Rangers (All–Stars)		0	1	1	4
1965	N.Y. Rangers (All–Stars)		0	0	0	4
1967	N.Y. Rangers (All–Stars)		0	0	0	2
1968	N.Y. Rangers (All–Stars)		0	0	0	2
1970	Oakland (West)		0	0	0	0
	7 games		0	1	1	18
Willie Huber						
1983	Detroit (Campbell)		0	0	0	0
Bobby Hull						
1960	Chicago (All–Stars)		0	0	0	2
1961	Chicago (Stanley Cup)		0	1	1	2
1962	Chicago (All–Stars)		0	0	0	0
1963	Chicago (All–Stars)		1	0	1	2
1964	Chicago (All–Stars)		0	1	1	0
1965	Chicago (All–Stars)		1	1	2	0
1967	Chicago (All–Stars)		0	0	0	0
1968	Chicago (All–Stars)		0	1	1	0
1969	Chicago (East)		0	0	0	0
1970	Chicago (East)*		1	1	2	0
1971	Chicago (West)*		1	0	1	2
1972	Chicago (West)		1	0	1	0
	12 games		5	5	10	8
Brett Hull						
1989	St. Louis (Campbell)		0	1	1	0
1990	St. Louis (Campbell)		0	3	3	0
1992	St. Louis (Campbell)*		2	1	3	0
1993	St. Louis (Campbell)		0	0	0	0
1994	St. Louis (Western)		0	1	1	0
1996	St. Louis (Western)		1	0	1	0
1997	St. Louis (Western)		0	1	1	0
	7 games		3	7	10	0

	G	A	P	Pim
	Mins	W–L	GA	Avg

Dennis Hull
	G	A	P	Pim
1969 Chicago (East)	0	0	0	0
1971 Chicago (West)	0	0	0	0
1972 Chicago (West)	0	1	1	0
1973 Chicago (West)	0	1	1	0
1974 Chicago (West)	0	0	0	0
5 games	0	2	2	0

Dale Hunter
	G	A	P	Pim
1997 Washington (Eastern)	0	0	0	0

Mark Hunter
	G	A	P	Pim
1986 St. Louis (Campbell)	0	0	0	0

Al Iafrate
	G	A	P	Pim
1988 Toronto (Campbell)	0	0	0	0
1990 Toronto (Campbell)	0	0	0	2
1993 Washington (Wales)	0	0	0	0
1994 Washington (Eastern)	0	0	0	0
4 games	0	0	0	2

Arturs Irbe
	Mins	W–L	GA	Avg
1994 San Jose (Western)	20:00	nd	2	6.00
1999 Carolina (World)	20:00	L	3	9.00
2 games	40:00	0-1-0	5	7.50
*one assist in 1999

Harvey Jackson
	G	A	P	Pim
1934 Toronto (Bailey)	2	1	3	0
1937 Toronto (Morenz)	0	0	0	0
1939 N.Y. Americans (Siebert)	0	0	0	2
3 games	2	1	3	2

Jaromir Jagr
	G	A	P	Pim
1992 Pittsburgh (Wales)	0	1	1	0
1993 Pittsburgh (Wales)	1	1	2	0
1996 Pittsburgh (Eastern)	1	0	1	0
1998 Pittsburgh (World)	1	0	1	0
1999 Pittsburgh (World)	0	1	1	0
2000 Pittsburgh (World)	1	1	2	0
6 games	4	4	8	0

Doug Jarrett
	G	A	P	Pim
1975 Chicago (Campbell)	0	0	0	0

Ching Johnson
	G	A	P	Pim
1934 N.Y. Rangers (Bailey)	0	0	0	0

Mark Johnson
	G	A	P	Pim
1984 Hartford (Wales)	0	3	3	0

Tom Johnson
	G	A	P	Pim
1952 Montreal (Second)	0	0	0	0
1953 Montreal (Stanley Cup)	0	0	0	0
1956 Montreal (Stanley Cup)	0	0	0	0
1957 Montreal (Stanley Cup)	0	1	1	2
1958 Montreal (Stanley Cup)	0	0	0	0
1959 Montreal (Stanley Cup)	0	1	1	0
1960 Montreal (Stanley Cup)	0	0	0	2
1963 Boston (All–Stars)	0	0	0	0
8 games	0	2	2	4

Joey Johnston
	G	A	P	Pim
1973 California (West)	0	0	0	0
1974 California (West)	0	0	0	0
1975 California (Wales)	0	1	1	0
3 games	0	1	1	0

Eddie Johnstone
	G	A	P	Pim
1981 N.Y. Rangers (Campbell)	0	2	2	0

Aurel Joliat
	G	A	P	Pim
1934 Montreal (Bailey)	0	1	1	0
1937 Montreal (Morenz)	0	0	0	0
2 games	0	1	1	0

Kenny Jonsson
	G	A	P	Pim
1999 N.Y. Islanders (World)	0	0	0	0

Curtis Joseph
	Mins	W–L	GA	Avg
1994 St. Louis (Western)	19:00	0-1-0	4	12.63
2000 Toronto (North America)	20:00	nd	3	12.00
2 games	39:00	0-1-0	7	10.77

Bill Juzda
	G	A	P	Pim
1948 Toronto (Stanley Cup)	0	0	0	2
1949 Toronto (Stanley Cup)	0	0	0	0
2 games	0	0	0	2

Valeri Kamensky
	G	A	P	Pim
1998 Avalanche (World)	0	0	0	0

Sami Kapanen
	G	A	P	Pim
2000 Carolina (World)	0	0	0	0

Paul Kariya
	G	A	P	Pim
1996 Anaheim (Western)	1	1	2	0
1997 Anaheim (Western)	1	0	1	0
1999 Anaheim (North America)	1	0	1	0
2000 Anaheim (North America)	0	0	0	0
4 games	3	1	4	0

Alexei Kasatonov
	G	A	P	Pim
1994 Anaheim (Western)	0	0	0	0

Rick Kehoe
	G	A	P	Pim
1981 Pittsburgh (Wales)	0	1	1	0
1983 Pittsburgh (Wales)	0	0	0	0
2 games	0	1	1	0

Red Kelly
	G	A	P	Pim
1950 Detroit (Stanley Cup)	0	2	2	0
1951 Detroit (First)	0	0	0	0
1952 Detroit (First)	0	0	0	0
1953 Detroit (All–Stars)	0	2	2	5
1954 Detroit (Stanley Cup)	0	1	1	0
1955 Detroit (Stanley Cup)	0	0	0	0
1956 Detroit (All–Stars)	0	0	0	0
1957 Detroit (All–Stars)	1	0	1	0
1958 Detroit (All–Stars)	0	0	0	0
1960 Toronto (All–Stars)	0	1	1	0
1962 Toronto (Stanley Cup)	0	0	0	2
1963 Toronto (Stanley Cup)	0	1	1	0
12 games	1	7	8	7

Ted Kennedy
	G	A	P	Pim
1947 Toronto (Stanley Cup)	0	0	0	0
1948 Toronto (Stanley Cup)	0	0	0	0
1949 Toronto (Stanley Cup)	0	0	0	0
1950 Toronto (All–Stars)	0	0	0	0
1951 Toronto (Second)	0	0	0	0
1954 Toronto (All–Stars)	0	1	1	0
6 games	0	1	1	0

Dave Keon
	G	A	P	Pim
1962 Toronto (Stanley Cup)	0	1	1	0
1963 Toronto (Stanley Cup)	0	1	1	0
1964 Toronto (Stanley Cup)	0	0	0	0
1967 Toronto (All–Stars)	0	0	0	0
1968 Toronto (Stanley Cup)	0	0	0	0
1970 Toronto (East)	0	0	0	0
1971 Toronto (East)	0	0	0	0
1973 Toronto (East)	0	0	0	0
8 games	0	2	2	0

Tim Kerr
	G	A	P	Pim
1984 Philadelphia (Wales)	0	1	1	0
1985 Philadelphia (Wales)	1	1	2	0
1986 Philadelphia (Wales)	0	0	0	0
3 games	1	2	3	0

Nikolai Khabibulin
	Mins	W–L	GA	Avg
1998 Phoenix (World)	20:00	L	2	6.00
1999 Phoenix (World)	20:00	nd	1	3.00
2 games	40:00	0-1-0	3	4.50

Dimitri Khristich
	G	A	P	Pim
1997 Los Angeles (Western)	0	0	0	0
1999 Boston (World)	0	1	1	0
2 games	0	1	1	0

Hec Kilrea
	G	A	P	Pim
1934 Toronto (Bailey)	1	1	2	0

Kelly Kisio
	G	A	P	Pim
1993 San Jose (Campbell)	1	1	2	0

		G	A	P	Pim
		Mins	W–L	GA	Avg
Joe Klukay					
1947	Toronto (Stanley Cup)	0	0	0	0
1948	Toronto (Stanley Cup)	0	0	0	0
1949	Toronto (Stanley Cup)	0	0	0	0
	3 games	0	0	0	0
Saku Koivu					
1998	Montreal (World)	0	3	3	0
Olaf Kolzig					
1998	Washington (World)	20:00	nd	3	9.00
2000	Washington (World)	20:00	nd	0	0.00
	2 games	40:00	0–0–0	3	4.50
Jerry Korab					
1975	Buffalo (Wales)	0	0	0	2
1976	Buffalo (Wales)	0	0	0	0
	2 games	0	0	0	2
Viktor Kozlov					
1999	Florida (World)	0	0	0	0
2000	Florida (World)	0	3	3	0
	2 games	0	3	3	0
Igor Kravchuk					
1998	Ottawa (II) (World)	1	0	1	0
Sergei Krivokrasov					
1999	Nashville (World)	0	0	0	0
Uwe Krupp					
1991	Buffalo (Wales)	0	0	0	0
1999	Detroit (World)	0	0	0	0
	2 games	0	0	0	0
Mike Krushelnyski					
1985	Edmonton (Campbell)	0	3	3	0
Bob Kudelski					
1994	Florida (Eastern)	2	0	2	0
Jari Kurri					
1983	Edmonton (Campbell)	0	2	2	0
1985	Edmonton (Campbell)	0	0	0	0
1986	Edmonton (Campbell)	0	0	0	0
1987	Rendez-vous (2)	1	1	2	0
1988	Edmonton (Campbell)	0	0	0	0
1989	Edmonton (Campbell)	1	1	2	0
1990	Edmonton (Campbell)	0	0	0	0
1993	Los Angeles (Campbell)	0	1	1	0
1998	Avalanche (World)	1	0	1	0
	8 games	2	4	6	0
Leo Labine					
1955	Boston (All–Stars)	0	0	0	0
1956	Boston (All–Stars)	0	0	0	2
	2 games	0	0	0	2
Elmer Lach					
1948	Montreal (All–Stars)	0	1	1	0
1952	Montreal (First)	0	0	0	2
1953	Montreal (Stanley Cup)	0	0	0	0
	3 games	0	1	1	2
Scott Lachance					
1997	N.Y. Islanders (Eastern)	0	0	0	0
Guy Lafleur					
1975	Montreal (Wales)	0	3	3	0
1976	Montreal (Wales)	1	2	3	0
1977	Montreal (Wales)	0	1	1	0
1978	Montreal (Wales)	0	0	0	0
1979	Challenge Cup (3)	1	2	3	0
1980	Montreal (Wales)	0	1	1	0
1991	Quebec (Wales)	0	0	0	0
	6 games	1	7	8	0
Pat LaFontaine					
1988	N.Y. Islanders (Wales)	0	0	0	2
1989	N.Y. Islanders (Wales)	0	1	1	0
1990	N.Y. Islanders (Wales)	0	1	1	0
1991	N.Y. Islanders (Wales)	2	0	2	0
1993	Buffalo (Wales)	1	0	1	0
	5 games	3	2	5	2
Dave Langevin					
1983	N.Y. Islanders (Wales)	0	0	0	2
Al Langlois					
1959	Montreal (Stanley Cup)	0	0	0	0
1960	Montreal (Stanley Cup)	0	0	0	0
	2 games	0	0	0	0
Rod Langway					
1981	Montreal (Wales)	0	0	0	0
1982	Montreal (Wales)	0	0	0	0
1983	Washington (Wales)	0	0	0	0
1984	Washington (Wales)	0	0	0	0
1985	Washington (Wales)	0	1	1	0
1986	Washington (Wales)	0	0	0	0
1987	Rendez-vous (2)	0	0	0	0
	6 games	0	1	1	0
Jacques Laperrière					
1964	Montreal (All–Stars)	0	1	1	2
1965	Montreal (Stanley Cup)	1	0	1	0
1967	Montreal (Stanley Cup)	0	0	0	0
1968	Montreal (All–Stars)	0	0	0	0
1970	Montreal (East)	1	0	1	0
	5 games	2	1	3	2
Guy Lapointe					
1973	Montreal (East)	0	1	1	0
1975	Montreal (Wales)	0	0	0	0
1976	Montreal (Wales)	0	1	1	0
1977	Montreal (Wales)	0	0	0	4
1979	Challenge Cup (1)	0	0	0	0
	4 games	0	2	2	4
Edgar Laprade					
1947	N.Y. Rangers (All–Stars)	0	1	1	0
1948	N.Y. Rangers (All–Stars)	0	0	0	0
1949	N.Y. Rangers (All–Stars)	0	1	1	0
1950	N.Y. Rangers (All–Stars)	0	0	0	0
	4 games	0	2	2	0
Igor Larionov					
1998	Detroit (World)	1	0	1	0
Steve Larmer					
1990	Chicago (Campbell)	0	0	0	0
1991	Chicago (Campbell)	0	2	2	0
	2 games	0	2	2	0
Claude Larose					
1965	Montreal (Stanley Cup)	0	1	1	2
1967	Montreal (Stanley Cup)	0	1	1	0
1969	Minnesota (West)	1	0	1	0
1970	Minnesota (West)	0	0	0	0
	4 games	1	2	3	2
Pierre Larouche					
1976	Pittsburgh (Wales)	0	1	1	0
1984	N.Y. Rangers (Wales)	2	0	2	0
	2 games	2	1	3	0
Reed Larson					
1978	Detroit (Wales)	0	0	0	0R
1980	Detroit (Wales)	1	0	1	0
1981	Detroit (Wales)	0	0	0	0
	3 games	1	0	1	0
Reggie Leach					
1976	Philadelphia (Campbell)	0	0	0	0
1980	Philadelphia (Campbell)*	1	1	2	0
	2 games	1	1	2	0
Jackie LeClair					
1956	Montreal (Stanley Cup)	0	0	0	0
John LeClair					
1996	Philadelphia (Eastern)	0	1	1	0
1997	Philadelphia (Eastern)	2	1	3	0
1998	Philadelphia (North America)	1	0	1	0
1999	Philadelphia (North America)	0	0	0	0
2000	Philadelphia (North America)	0	0	0	0
	5 games	3	2	5	0

| | G | A | P | Pim |
| | Mins | W-L | GA | Avg |

Gary Leeman

	G	A	P	Pim
1989 Toronto (Campbell)	1	1	2	0

Brian Leetch

	G	A	P	Pim
1990 N.Y. Rangers (Wales)	0	0	0	0
1991 N.Y. Rangers (Wales)	0	0	0	0
1992 N.Y. Rangers (Wales)	0	0	0	0
1994 N.Y. Rangers (Eastern)	0	0	0	0
1996 N.Y. Rangers (Eastern)	0	1	1	0
1997 N.Y. Rangers (Eastern)	0	0	0	0
6 games	0	1	1	0

Jere Lehtinen

	G	A	P	Pim
1998 Dallas (World)	0	3	3	0

Jacques Lemaire

	G	A	P	Pim
1970 Montreal (East)	0	1	1	0
1973 Montreal (East)	1	0	1	0
2 games	1	1	2	0

Reggie Lemelin

	Mins	W-L	GA	Avg
1989 Boston (Wales)	30:02	0-1-0	6	11.99

Claude Lemieux

	G	A	P	Pim
1987 Rendez-vous (2)	0	0	0	4

Mario Lemieux

	G	A	P	Pim
1985 Pittsburgh (Wales)*	2	1	3	0R
1986 Pittsburgh (Wales)	0	0	0	0
1987 Rendez-vous (2)	0	3	3	0
1988 Pittsburgh (Wales)*	3	3	6	0
1989 Pittsburgh (Wales)	0	1	1	0
1990 Pittsburgh (Wales)*	4	0	4	0
1992 Pittsburgh (Wales)	0	1	1	0
1996 Pittsburgh (Eastern)	0	2	2	0
1997 Pittsburgh (Eastern)	2	1	3	0
8 games	11	9	20	0

Pit Lepine

	G	A	P	Pim
1937 Montreal (Morenz)	1	0	1	0

Mario Lessard

	Mins	W-L	GA	Avg
1981 Los Angeles (Wales)	28:17	nd	2	4.24

Tony Leswick

	G	A	P	Pim
1947 N.Y. Rangers (All-Stars)	0	0	0	2
1948 N.Y. Rangers (All-Stars)	0	0	0	0
1949 N.Y. Rangers (All-Stars)	0	0	0	0
1950 N.Y. Rangers (All-Stars)	0	0	0	4
1952 Detroit (First)	0	0	0	0
1954 Detroit (Stanley Cup)	0	0	0	0
6 games	0	0	0	6

Don Lever

	G	A	P	Pim
1982 Colorado (Campbell)	0	0	0	0

Alex Levinsky

	G	A	P	Pim
1934 Toronto (Bailey)	0	0	0	0

Danny Lewicki

	G	A	P	Pim
1955 N.Y. Rangers (All-Stars)	0	0	0	0

Herbie Lewis

	G	A	P	Pim
1934 Detroit (Bailey)	0	0	0	0

Nick Libett

	G	A	P	Pim
1977 Detroit (Wales)	0	0	0	0

Nicklas Lidstrom

	G	A	P	Pim
1996 Detroit (Eastern)	0	0	0	0
1998 Detroit (World)	0	0	0	0
1999 Detroit (World)	0	0	0	0
2000 Detroit (World)	0	1	1	0
4 games	0	1	1	0

Pelle Lindbergh

	Mins	W-L	GA	Avg
1983 Philadelphia (Wales)	29:56	L	7	14.03R
1985 Philadelphia (Wales)	29:11	W	2	4.11
2 games	59:07	1-1-0	9	9.13

Trevor Linden

	G	A	P	Pim
1991 Vancouver (Campbell)	0	0	0	0
1992 Vancouver (Campbell)	1	1	2	0
2 games	1	1	2	0

| | G | A | P | Pim |
| | Mins | W-L | GA | Avg |

Lars Lindgren

	G	A	P	Pim
1980 Vancouver (Campbell)	0	0	0	0

Eric Lindros

	G	A	P	Pim
1994 Philadelphia (Eastern)	1	0	1	0
1996 Philadelphia (Eastern)	1	0	1	0
1997 Philadelphia (Eastern)	0	2	2	0
1998 Philadelphia (North America)	1	0	1	0
1999 Philadelphia (North America)	0	0	0	0
2000 Philadelphia (North America)	0	0	0	0
6 games	3	2	5	0

Ted Lindsay

	G	A	P	Pim
1947 Detroit (All-Stars)	0	0	0	0
1948 Detroit (All-Stars)	1	0	1	0
1949 Detroit (All-Stars)	0	0	0	0
1950 Detroit (Stanley Cup)	3	1	4	0
1951 Detroit (First)	0	1	1	4
1952 Detroit (First)	0	0	0	0
1953 Detroit (All-Stars)	0	0	0	2
1954 Detroit (Stanley Cup)	0	1	1	2
1955 Detroit (Stanley Cup)	0	2	2	0
1956 Detroit (All-Stars)	1	0	1	0
1957 Detroit (All-Stars)	0	0	0	0
11 games	5	5	10	8

Ed Litzenberger

	G	A	P	Pim
1955 Chicago (All-Stars)	0	0	0	0
1957 Chicago (All-Stars)	0	2	2	0
1958 Chicago (All-Stars)	0	1	1	0
1959 Chicago (All-Stars)	0	1	1	0
1962 Toronto (Stanley Cup)	0	0	0	0
1963 Toronto (Stanley Cup)	1	1	2	0
6 games	1	5	6	0

Mike Liut

	Mins	W-L	GA	Avg
1981 St. Louis (Campbell)*	31:43	1-0-0	0	0.00

Ross Lonsberry

	G	A	P	Pim
1972 Los Angeles (West)	0	0	0	0

Rod Lorrain

	G	A	P	Pim
1939 Montreal (Siebert)	0	1	1	0

Kevin Lowe

	G	A	P	Pim
1984 Edmonton (Campbell)	0	0	0	0
1985 Edmonton (Campbell)	0	0	0	0
1986 Edmonton (Campbell)	0	0	0	2
1988 Edmonton (Campbell)	0	1	1	0
1989 Edmonton (Campbell)	0	0	0	0
1990 Edmonton (Campbell)	0	1	1	0
1993 N.Y. Rangers (Wales)	0	1	1	0
7 games	0	3	3	2

Don Luce

	G	A	P	Pim
1975 Buffalo (Wales)	1	0	1	2

Morris Lukowich

	G	A	P	Pim
1980 Winnipeg (Campbell)	0	0	0	0
1981 Winnipeg (Campbell)	0	0	0	0
2 games	0	0	0	0

Harry Lumley

	Mins	W-L	GA	Avg
1951 Chicago (First)	30:52	T	1	1.97
1954 Toronto (All-Stars)	30:59	nd	2	3.87
1955 Toronto (All-Stars)	32:10	L	2	3.73
3 games	93:41	0-1-1	5	3.20

Vic Lynn

	G	A	P	Pim
1947 Toronto (Stanley Cup)	0	0	0	7
1948 Toronto (Stanley Cup)	0	0	0	0
1949 Toronto (Stanley Cup)	0	0	0	0
3 games	0	0	0	7

Tom Lysiak

	G	A	P	Pim
1975 Atlanta (Campbell)	0	0	0	0
1976 Atlanta (Campbell)	0	0	0	0
1977 Atlanta (Campbell)	0	0	0	0
3 games	0	0	0	0

	G	A	P	Pim
	Mins	W–L	GA	Avg

Al MacAdam

		G	A	P	Pim
1976	California (Wales)	1	1	2	0
1977	Cleveland (Wales)	0	0	0	0
	2 games	1	1	2	0

Blair MacDonald

		G	A	P	Pim
1980	Edmonton (Campbell)	0	0	0	0

Lowell MacDonald

		G	A	P	Pim
1973	Pittsburgh (West)	0	1	1	0
1974	Pittsburgh (West)	1	1	2	0
	2 games	1	2	3	0

Al MacInnis

		G	A	P	Pim
1985	Calgary (Campbell)	0	1	1	0
1988	Calgary (Campbell)	0	0	0	0
1990	Calgary (Campbell)	1	0	1	0
1991	Calgary (Campbell)	0	0	0	0
1992	Calgary (Campbell)	0	1	1	0
1994	Calgary (Campbell)	0	1	1	0
1996	St. Louis (Western)	0	0	0	0
1997	St. Louis (Western)	0	0	0	0
1999	St. Louis (North America)	0	0	0	2
2000	St. Louis (North America)	0	0	0	0
	10 games	1	3	4	2

Calum MacKay

		G	A	P	Pim
1953	Montreal (Stanley Cup)	0	0	0	0

Fleming Mackell

		G	A	P	Pim
1947	Toronto (Stanley Cup)	0	0	0	0R
1948	Toronto (Stanley Cup)	0	0	0	0
1949	Toronto (Stanley Cup)	0	0	0	0
1954	Boston (All–Stars)	0	0	0	2
	4 games	0	0	0	2

John MacLean

		G	A	P	Pim
1989	New Jersey (Wales)	0	0	0	0
1991	New Jersey (Wales)	1	0	1	0
	2 games	1	0	1	0

Paul MacLean

		G	A	P	Pim
1985	Winnipeg (Campbell)	0	0	0	0

Rick MacLeish

		G	A	P	Pim
1976	Philadelphia (Campbell)	0	0	0	0
1977	Philadelphia (Campbell)	1	0	1	0
1980	Philadelphia (Campbell)	0	1	1	0
	3 games	1	1	2	0

John MacMillan

		G	A	P	Pim
1962	Toronto (Stanley Cup)	0	0	0	0
1963	Toronto (Stanley Cup)	0	0	0	0
	2 games	0	0	0	0

Bud MacPherson

		G	A	P	Pim
1953	Montreal (Stanley Cup)	0	0	0	2

Craig MacTavish

		G	A	P	Pim
1996	Philadelphia (Eastern)	0	0	0	0

Keith Magnuson

		G	A	P	Pim
1971	Chicago (West)	0	0	0	2
1972	Chicago (West)	0	0	0	0
	2 games	0	0	0	2

Frank Mahovlich

		G	A	P	Pim
1959	Toronto (All–Stars)	0	0	0	0
1960	Toronto (All–Stars)	1	0	1	0
1961	Toronto (All–Stars)	0	0	0	6
1962	Toronto (Stanley Cup)	1	0	1	0
1963	Toronto (Stanley Cup)*	2	1	3	0
1964	Toronto (Stanley Cup)	0	1	1	0
1965	Toronto (All–Stars)	0	0	0	0
1967	Toronto (All–Stars)	0	0	0	0
1968	Toronto (Stanley Cup)	0	2	2	0
1969	Detroit (East)*	2	0	2	0
1970	Detroit (East)	0	0	0	0
1971	Montreal (East)	0	0	0	2
1972	Montreal (East)	0	0	0	0
1973	Montreal (East)	1	1	2	0
1974	Montreal (East)	1	0	1	0
	15 games	8	5	13	8

Pete Mahovlich

		G	A	P	Pim
1971	Montreal (East)	0	0	0	0
1976	Montreal (Wales)*	1	3	4	0
	2 games	1	3	4	0

Chico Maki

		G	A	P	Pim
1961	Chicago (Stanley Cup)	0	0	0	0R
1971	Chicago (West)	1	0	1	0
1972	Chicago (West)	0	1	1	0
	3 games	1	1	2	0

Dan Maloney

		G	A	P	Pim
1976	Detroit (Wales)	1	1	2	0

Don Maloney

		G	A	P	Pim
1983	N.Y. Rangers (Wales)	1	0	1	0
1984	N.Y. Rangers (Wales)*	1	3	4	0
	2 games	2	3	5	0

Randy Manery

		G	A	P	Pim
1973	Atlanta (West)	0	0	0	0R

Bob Manno

		G	A	P	Pim
1982	Toronto (Campbell)	0	0	0	0

Dave Manson

		G	A	P	Pim
1989	Chicago (Campbell)	0	1	1	0
1993	Edmonton (Campbell)	0	1	1	2
	2 games	0	2	2	2

Georges Mantha

		G	A	P	Pim
1937	Montreal (Morenz)	0	1	1	0
1939	Montreal (Siebert)	0	1	1	0
	2 games	0	2	2	0

Mush March

		G	A	P	Pim
1937	Chicago (Morenz)	0	0	0	0

Don Marcotte

		G	A	P	Pim
1979	Challenge Cup (1)	0	0	0	2

Hector Marini

		G	A	P	Pim
1983	New Jersey (Wales)	0	1	1	0

John Marks

		G	A	P	Pim
1976	Chicago (Campbell)	0	0	0	2

Gilles Marotte

		G	A	P	Pim
1973	Los Angeles (West)	0	0	0	0

Brad Marsh

		G	A	P	Pim
1993	Ottawa (II) (Wales)	1	1	2	0

Don Marshall

		G	A	P	Pim
1956	Montreal (Stanley Cup)	0	0	0	0
1957	Montreal (Stanley Cup)	0	0	0	0
1958	Montreal (Stanley Cup)	1	1	2	0
1959	Montreal (Stanley Cup)	0	0	0	0
1960	Montreal (Stanley Cup)	0	0	0	0
1961	Montreal (All–Stars)	0	0	0	0
1968	N.Y. Rangers (All–Stars)	0	0	0	0
	7 games	1	1	2	0

Frank Martin

		G	A	P	Pim
1955	Chicago (All–Stars)	0	0	0	0

Pit Martin

		G	A	P	Pim
1971	Chicago (West)	0	0	0	0
1972	Chicago (West)	0	1	1	0
1973	Chicago (West)	1	0	1	0
1974	Chicago (West)	1	0	1	2
	4 games	2	1	3	2

Rick Martin

		G	A	P	Pim
1972	Buffalo (East)	0	0	0	0R
1973	Buffalo (East)	0	0	0	0
1974	Buffalo (East)	0	0	0	0
1975	Buffalo (Wales)	0	1	1	0
1976	Buffalo (Wales)	1	2	3	0
1977	Buffalo (Wales)*	2	0	2	0
1978	Buffalo (Wales)	1	0	1	0
	7 games	4	3	7	0

	G	A	P	Pim
	Mins	W–L	GA	Avg

Dennis Maruk
	G	A	P	Pim
1978 Cleveland (Wales)	0	0	0	0
1982 Washington (Wales)	0	1	1	0
2 games	0	1	1	0

Frank Mathers
1948 Toronto (Stanley Cup)	0	0	0	0R

Brad Maxwell
1984 Minnesota (Campbell)	0	0	0	2

Eddie Mazur
1953 Montreal (Stanley Cup)	0	0	0	0R

Kevin McCarthy
1981 Vancouver (Campbell)	0	0	0	0

Tom McCarthy
1983 Minnesota (Campbell)	1	0	1	0

John McCormack
1953 Montreal (Stanley Cup)	0	0	0	0

Brad McCrimmon
1988 Calgary (Campbell)	0	0	0	2

Ab McDonald
1958 Montreal (Stanley Cup)	1	0	1	0R
1959 Montreal (Stanley Cup)	1	0	1	0
1961 Chicago (Stanley Cup)	0	0	0	0
1969 St. Louis (West)	0	0	0	0
1970 St. Louis (West)	0	0	0	0
5 games	2	0	2	0

Lanny McDonald
1977 Toronto (Wales)	2	0	2	0
1978 Toronto (Wales)	0	0	0	2
1979 Challenge Cup (3)	0	0	0	2
1983 Calgary (Campbell)	1	1	2	0
1984 Calgary (Campbell)	0	0	0	0
4 games	3	1	4	2

Al McDonough
1974 Atlanta (West)	1	0	1	0

Mike McEwen
1980 Colorado (Campbell)	0	1	1	0

Jim McFadden
1950 Detroit (Stanley Cup)	0	0	0	0

Don McKenney
1957 Boston (All–Stars)	0	0	0	0
1958 Boston (All–Stars)	0	0	0	0
1959 Boston (All–Stars)	1	0	1	0
1960 Boston (All–Stars)	0	0	0	0
1961 Boston (All–Stars)	1	0	1	2
1962 Boston (All–Stars)	0	0	0	2
1964 Toronto (Stanley Cup)	0	0	0	0
7 games	2	0	2	4

Jim McKenny
1974 Toronto (East)	0	0	0	0

John McKenzie
1970 Boston (East)	0	1	1	0
1972 Boston (East)	1	0	1	0
2 games	1	1	2	0

Kirk McLean
1990 Vancouver (Campbell)	30:46	nd	4	7.80
1992 Vancouver (Campbell)	20:00	nd	3	9.00
2 games	50:46	0-0-0	7	8.27

Peter McNab
1977 Boston (Wales)	0	1	1	0

Gerry McNeil
1951 Montreal (Second)	30:32	T	1	1.97
1952 Montreal (Second)	30:03	T	0	0.00
1953 Montreal (Stanley Cup)	60:00	L	2	2.00
3 games	120:35	0-1-2	3	1.49

Mike McPhee
1989 Montreal (Wales)	0	0	0	0

	G	A	P	Pim
	Mins	W–L	GA	Avg

Howie Meeker
1947 Toronto (Stanley Cup)	0	0	0	0
1948 Toronto (Stanley Cup)	0	0	0	0
1949 Toronto (Stanley Cup)	0	0	0	2
3 games	0	0	0	2

Paul Meger
1951 Montreal (Second)	0	0	0	0
1952 Montreal (Second)	0	0	0	0
1953 Montreal (Stanley Cup)	0	0	0	2
3 games	0	0	0	2

Scott Mellanby
1996 Florida (Eastern)	0	0	0	0

Gerry Melnyk
1961 Chicago (Stanley Cup)	0	0	0	0

Gilles Meloche
1980 Minnesota (Wales)	30:33	W	1	1.96
1982 Minnesota (Campbell)	29:37	L	2	4.05
2 games	60:10	1-1-0	3	2.99

Mark Messier
1982 Edmonton (Campbell)	0	0	0	0
1983 Edmonton (Campbell)	0	3	3	0
1984 Edmonton (Campbell)	0	0	0	0
1986 Edmonton (Campbell)	0	0	0	2
1987 Rendez-vous (2)	1	0	1	0
1988 Edmonton (Campbell)	0	0	0	0
1989 Edmonton (Campbell)	1	1	2	2
1990 Edmonton (Campbell)	1	0	1	0
1991 Edmonton (Campbell)	0	1	1	0
1992 N.Y. Rangers (Wales)	0	1	1	0
1994 N.Y. Rangers (Eastern)	1	2	3	0
1996 N.Y. Rangers (Eastern)	0	1	1	0
1997 N.Y. Rangers (Eastern)	1	2	3	0
1998 Vancouver (North America)	1	1	2	0
2000 Vancouver (North America)	0	1	1	0
14 games	5	13	18	4

Don Metz
1947 Toronto (Stanley Cup)	0	0	0	0

Nick Mickoski
1956 Chicago (All-Stars)	0	0	0	0

Rick Middleton
1981 Boston (Wales)	0	0	0	0
1982 Boston (Wales)	0	1	1	0
1984 Boston (Wales)	1	0	1	0
3 games	1	1	2	0

Rudy Migay
1957 Toronto (All-Stars)	0	1	1	2

Stan Mikita
1964 Chicago (All-Stars)	0	0	0	2
1967 Chicago (All Stars)	0	0	0	0
1968 Chicago (All-Stars)	1	1	2	0
1969 Chicago (East)	0	0	0	0
1971 Chicago (West)	0	0	0	0
1972 Chicago (West)	0	0	0	0
1973 Chicago (West)	0	1	1	0
1974 Chicago (West)	1	2	3	0
1975 Chicago (Campbell)	0	0	0	0
9 games	2	4	6	2

Dmitri Mironov
1998 Anaheim (World)	0	1	1	0

Mike Modano
1993 Minnesota (Campbell)	0	1	1	0
1998 Dallas (North America)	0	2	2	0
1999 Dallas (North America)	1	3	4	0
2000 Dallas (North America)	0	2	2	0
4 games	1	8	9	0

Alexander Mogilny

		G	A	P	Pim
		Mins	W-L	GA	Avg
1992	Buffalo (Wales)	1	1	2	0
1993	Buffalo (Wales)	1	1	2	0
1994	Buffalo (Eastern)	0	0	0	0
1996	Vancouver (Western)	0	1	1	0
	4 games	2	3	5	0

Doug Mohns

1954	Boston (All–Stars)	1	0	1	2
1958	Boston (All–Stars)	0	0	0	2
1959	Boston (All–Stars)	0	0	0	0
1961	Boston (All–Stars)	0	0	0	0
1962	Boston (All–Stars)	0	0	0	2
1965	Chicago (All–Stars)	0	0	0	0
1972	Minnesota (West)	0	0	0	2
	7 games	1	0	1	8

Armand Mondou

1939	Montreal (Siebert)	0	0	0	0

Andy Moog

1985	Edmonton (Campbell)	30:49	nd	2	3.89
1986	Edmonton (Campbell)	32:02	L	4	7.49
1991	Boston (Wales)	30:12	L	6	11.92
1997	Dallas (Western)	20:00	L	6	18.00
	4 games	113:03	0-3-0	18	9.55

Dickie Moore

1953	Montreal (Stanley Cup)	0	0	0	0
1956	Montreal (Stanley Cup)	0	0	0	0
1957	Montreal (Stanley Cup)	0	1	1	0
1958	Montreal (Stanley Cup)	0	3	3	0
1959	Montreal (Stanley Cup)	1	1	2	0
1960	Montreal (Stanley Cup)	0	0	0	0
	6 games	1	5	6	0

Howie Morenz

1934	Montreal (Bailey)	1	0	1	0

Jim Morrison

1955	Toronto (All–Stars)	0	0	0	2
1956	Toronto (All–Stars)	0	0	0	0
1957	Toronto (All–Stars)	0	1	1	0
	3 games	0	1	1	2

Gus Mortson

1947	Toronto (Stanley Cup)	0	0	0	6
1948	Toronto (Stanley Cup)	0	0	0	5
1950	Toronto (All–Stars)	0	0	0	0
1951	Toronto (Second)	0	1	1	0
1952	Toronto (First)	0	0	0	0
1953	Chicago (All–Stars)	0	0	0	2
1954	Chicago (All–Stars)	1	0	1	4
1956	Chicago (All–Stars)	0	1	1	4
	8 games	1	2	3	21

Ken Mosdell

1951	Montreal (Second)	1	0	1	0
1952	Montreal (Second)	0	0	0	0
1953	Montreal (Stanley Cup)	0	0	0	2
1954	Montreal (All–Stars)	0	0	0	0
1955	Montreal (All–Stars)	0	0	0	0
	5 games	1	0	1	2

Bill Mosienko

1947	Chicago (All–Stars)	0	0	0	0
1949	Chicago (All–Stars)	0	0	0	0
1950	Chicago (All–Stars)	0	0	0	0
1952	Chicago (First)	0	1	1	0
1953	Chicago (All–Stars)	0	0	0	0
	5 games	0	1	1	0

Brian Mullen

1989	N.Y. Rangers (Wales)	0	1	1	0

Joe Mullen

1989	Calgary (Campbell)	2	1	3	0
1990	Calgary (Campbell)	1	1	2	0
1994	Pittsburgh (Eastern)	1	1	2	0
	3 games	4	3	7	0

Kirk Muller

		G	A	P	Pim
		Mins	W-L	GA	Avg
1985	New Jersey (Wales)	0	1	1	2R
1986	New Jersey (Wales)	0	0	0	0
1987	Rendez-vous (2)	0	0	0	0
1988	New Jersey (Wales)	0	0	0	0
1990	New Jersey (Wales)	2	1	3	0
1992	Montreal (Wales)	0	0	0	0
1993	Montreal (Wales)	0	1	1	0
	6 games	2	3	5	2

Bob Murdoch

1975	Los Angeles (Wales)	0	1	1	0

Don Murdoch

1977	N.Y. Rangers (Campbell)	0	0	0	0R

Larry Murphy

1994	Pittsburgh (Eastern)	0	0	0	0
1996	Toronto (Western)	0	0	0	0
1999	Detroit (North America)	0	0	0	0
	2 games	0	0	0	0

Mike Murphy

1980	Los Angeles (Wales)	0	1	1	0

Ron Murphy

1961	Chicago (Stanley Cup)	0	0	0	0

Bob Murray

1981	Chicago (Campbell)	0	0	0	0
1983	Chicago (Campbell)	0	1	1	0
	2 games	0	1	1	0

Markus Naslund

1999	Vancouver (World)	0	1	1	0

Mats Naslund

1984	Montreal (Wales)	1	0	1	0
1986	Montreal (Wales)	0	1	1	0
1988	Montreal (Wales)	0	5	5	0
	3 games	1	6	7	0

Cam Neely

1988	Boston (Wales)	0	0	0	0
1989	Boston (Wales)	1	0	1	0
1990	Boston (Wales)	1	2	3	2
1991	Boston (Wales)	0	0	0	0
1996	Boston (Eastern)	0	1	1	0
	5 games	2	3	5	2

Jim Neilson

1967	N.Y. Rangers (All–Stars)	0	0	0	0
1971	N.Y. Rangers (East)	0	0	0	0
	2 games	0	0	0	0

Eric Nesterenko

1961	Chicago (Stanley Cup)	1	0	1	6
1965	Chicago (All–Stars)	0	0	0	0
	2 games	1	0	1	6

Bob Nevin

1962	Toronto (Stanley Cup)	0	0	0	2
1963	Toronto (Stanley Cup)	0	0	0	0
1967	N.Y. Rangers (All–Stars)	0	0	0	0
1969	N.Y. Rangers (East)	1	0	1	0
	4 games	1	0	1	2

Bernie Nicholls

1984	Los Angeles (Campbell)	0	0	0	0
1989	Los Angeles (Campbell)	0	0	0	0
1990	Los Angeles (Campbell)	0	1	1	0
	3 games	0	1	1	0

Scott Niedermayer

1998	New Jersey (North America)	1	0	1	0

Joe Nieuwendyk

1988	Calgary (Campbell)	0	1	1	0R
1989	Calgary (Campbell)	0	2	2	0
1990	Calgary (Campbell)	0	1	1	0
1994	Calgary (Western)	0	1	1	0
	4 games	0	5	5	0

		G	A	P	Pim
		Mins	W-L	GA	Avg

Kent Nilsson

		G	A	P	Pim
1980	Atlanta (Campbell)	1	0	1	0
1981	Calgary (Campbell)	1	0	1	0
	2 games	2	0	2	0

Ulf Nilsson

		G	A	P	Pim
1979	Challenge Cup (2)	0	0	0	0

Owen Nolan

		G	A	P	Pim
1992	Quebec (Wales)	1	1	2	0
1996	San Jose (Western)	0	0	0	0
1997	San Jose (Western)	3	0	3	0
2000	San Jose (North America)	0	0	0	0
	4 games	4	1	5	0

Simon Nôlet

		G	A	P	Pim
1972	Philadelphia (West)	1	0	1	0
1975	Kansas City (Campbell)	0	0	0	0
	2 games	1	0	1	0

Baldy Northcott

		G	A	P	Pim
1937	Maroons (Morenz)	0	0	0	0

Teppo Numminen

		G	A	P	Pim
1999	Phoenix (World)	0	0	0	0
2000	Phoenix (World)	0	0	0	0
	2 games	0	0	0	0

Bob Nystrom

		G	A	P	Pim
1977	N.Y. Islanders (Campbell)	0	1	1	0

Adam Oates

		G	A	P	Pim
1991	St. Louis (Campbell)	1	4	5	0
1992	St. Louis (Campbell)	0	1	1	0
1993	Boston (Wales)	0	4	4	0
1994	Boston (Eastern)	0	1	1	0
1997	Boston (Eastern)	0	2	2	0
	5 games	1	12	13	0

Mike O'Connell

		G	A	P	Pim
1984	Boston (Wales)	0	0	0	0

Buddy O'Connor

		G	A	P	Pim
1949	N.Y. Rangers (All–Stars)	0	0	0	0

John Ogrodnick

		G	A	P	Pim
1981	Detroit (Wales)	1	0	1	0
1982	Detroit (Campbell)	0	0	0	0
1984	Detroit (Campbell)	1	1	2	0
1985	Detroit (Campbell)	0	1	1	0
1986	Detroit (Campbell)	0	0	0	0
	5 games	2	2	4	0

Mattias Ohlund

		G	A	P	Pim
1999	Vancouver (World)	1	1	2	0

Murray Oliver

		G	A	P	Pim
1963	Boston (All–Stars)	0	1	1	0
1964	Boston (All–stars)	1	1	2	2
1965	Boston (All–stars)	0	2	2	0
1967	Boston (All–Stars)	0	0	0	0
1968	Toronto (Stanley Cup)	1	0	1	0
	5 games	2	4	6	2

Bert Olmstead

		G	A	P	Pim
1953	Montreal (Stanley Cup)	0	0	0	5
1956	Montreal (Stanley Cup)	0	1	1	0
1957	Montreal (Stanley Cup)	1	0	1	2
1959	Toronto (All–Stars)	0	0	0	0
	4 games	1	1	2	7

Terry O'Reilly

		G	A	P	Pim
1975	Boston (Wales)	1	1	2	0
1978	Boston (Wales)	0	1	1	0
	2 games	1	2	3	0

Bobby Orr

		G	A	P	Pim
1968	Boston (All–Stars)	0	1	1	0
1969	Boston (East)	0	0	0	0
1970	Boston (East)	0	0	0	0
1971	Boston (East)	0	0	0	0
1972	Boston (East)*	0	1	1	0
1973	Boston (East)	0	0	0	2
1975	Boston (Wales)	1	0	1	0
	7 games	1	2	3	2

Chris Osgood

		Mins	W-L	GA	Avg
1996	Detroit (Western)	20:00	nd	2	6.00

Danny O'Shea

		G	A	P	Pim
1969	Minnesota (West)	0	1	1	0R
1970	Minnesota (West)	0	0	0	0
	2 games	0	1	1	0

Sandis Ozolinsh

		G	A	P	Pim
1994	San Jose (Western)	2	1	3	0
1997	Avalanche (Western)	0	3	3	0
1998	Avalanche (World)	0	0	0	0
2000	Avalanche (World)	0	0	0	2
	4 games	2	4	6	2

Wilf Paiement

		G	A	P	Pim
1976	Kansas City (Campbell)	0	0	0	0
1977	Colorado (Campbell)	0	0	0	2
1978	Colorado (Campbell)	0	0	0	0
	3 games	0	0	0	2

Zigmund Palffy

		G	A	P	Pim
1998	N.Y. Islanders (World)	0	0	0	0

Jim Pappin

		G	A	P	Pim
1964	Toronto (Stanley Cup)	1	0	1	0
1968	Toronto (Stanley Cup)	0	0	0	0
1973	Chicago (West)	0	1	1	0
1974	Chicago (West)	0	1	1	0
1975	Chicago (Campbell)	0	0	0	0
	5 games	1	2	3	0

Bernie Parent

		Mins	W-L	GA	Avg
1969	Philadelphia (West)	20:00	nd	0	0.00
1970	Philadelphia (West)	29:37	L	4	8.10
1974	Philadelphia (West)	29:59	nd	2	4.00
1975	Philadelphia (Campbell)	29:17	L	3	6.15
1977	Philadelphia (Campbell)	31:27	nd	1	1.91
	5 games	140:20	0-2-0	10	4.28

J.P. Parise

		G	A	P	Pim
1970	Minnesota (West)	0	0	0	0
1973	Minnesota (West)	0	0	0	0
	2 games	0	0	0	0

Brad Park

		G	A	P	Pim
1970	N.Y. Rangers (East)	0	0	0	2
1971	N.Y. Rangers (East)	0	0	0	0
1972	N.Y. Rangers (East)	0	1	1	0
1973	N.Y. Rangers (East)	0	1	1	0
1974	N.Y. Rangers (East)	0	0	0	0
1975	N.Y. Rangers (Campbell)	0	0	0	0
1976	Boston (Wales)	1	0	1	0
1977	Boston (Wales)	0	0	0	0
1978	Boston (Wales)	0	1	1	0
	9 games	1	3	4	2

Marty Pavelich

		G	A	P	Pim
1950	Detroit (Stanley Cup)	1	1	2	0
1952	Detroit (First)	1	0	1	2
1954	Detroit (Stanley Cup)	0	0	0	0
1955	Detroit (Stanley Cup)	0	0	0	0
	4 games	2	1	3	0

Steve Payne

		G	A	P	Pim
1980	Minnesota (Wales)	1	1	2	0
1985	Minnesota (Campbell)	0	0	0	0
	2 games	1	1	2	0

			G	A	P	Pim
			Mins	W-L	GA	Avg
Barry Pederson						
1983	Boston (Wales)		0	0	0	0
1984	Boston (Wales)		0	1	1	0
	2 games		0	1	1	0
Pete Peeters						
1980	**Philadelphia (Campbell)**		**44:50**	**L**	**4**	**5.35**
1981	**Philadelphia (Campbell)**		**28:17**	**nd**	**1**	**2.12**
1983	**Boston (Wales)**		**30:04**	**nd**	**2**	**3.99**
1984	**Boston (Wales)**		**30:06**	**nd**	**3**	**5.98**
	4 games		**133:17**	**0-1-0**	**10**	**4.50**
Johnny Peirson						
1950	Boston (All–Stars)		0	1	1	0
1951	Boston (First)		1	0	1	0
	2 games		1	1	2	0
Gilbert Perreault						
1971	Buffalo (East)		0	0	0	0R
1972	Buffalo (East)		0	0	0	0
1977	Buffalo (Wales)		0	1	1	0
1978	Buffalo (Wales)		1	0	1	0
1979	Challenge Cup (3)		1	1	2	2
1980	Buffalo (Wales)		0	1	1	0
1984	Buffalo (Wales)		0	0	0	0
	6 games		1	2	3	0
Jim Peters						
1950	Detroit (Stanley Cup)		1	1	2	0
Noel Picard						
1969	St. Louis (West)		0	2	2	0
Robert Picard						
1980	Washington (Campbell)		0	0	0	0
1981	Toronto (Wales)		0	0	0	0
	2 games		0	0	0	0
Pierre Pilote						
1960	Chicago (All–Stars)		0	1	1	2
1961	Chicago (Stanley Cup)		0	1	1	2
1962	Chicago (All–Stars)		0	1	1	0
1963	Chicago (All–Stars)		0	0	0	0
1964	Chicago (All–Stars)		0	0	0	2
1965	Chicago (All–Stars)		0	0	0	0
1967	Chicago (All–Stars)		0	0	0	0
1968	Chicago (All–Stars)		0	0	0	0
	8 games		0	3	3	6
Barclay Plager						
1970	St. Louis (West)		0	0	0	0
1971	St. Louis (West)		0	0	0	0
1973	St. Louis (West)		0	0	0	0
1974	St. Louis (West)		0	1	1	2
	4 games		0	1	1	2
Jacques Plante						
1956	**Montreal (Stanley Cup)**		**60:00**	**T**	**1**	**1.00**
1957	**Montreal (Stanley Cup)**		**60:00**	**L**	**5**	**5.00**
1958	**Montreal (Stanley Cup)**		**60:00**	**W**	**3**	**3.00**
1959	**Montreal (Stanley Cup)**		**60:00**	**W**	**1**	**1.00**
1960	**Montreal (Stanley Cup)**		**60:00**	**L**	**2**	**2.00**
1962	**Montreal (All–Stars)**		**20:00**	**L**	**4**	**12.00**
1969	**St. Louis (West)**		**20:00**	**T**	**2**	**6.00**
1970	**St. Louis (West)**		**30:23**	**nd**	**0**	**0.00**
	8 games		**370:23**	**2-3-2**	**18**	**2.92**
Walt Poddubny						
1989	Quebec (Wales)		2	0	2	0
Bud Poile						
1947	Toronto (Stanley Cup)		0	0	0	0
1948	Chicago (All–Stars)		0	0	0	0
	2 games		0	0	0	0
Don Poile						
1954	Detroit (Stanley Cup)		0	0	0	0R

			G	A	P	Pim
			Mins	W-L	GA	Avg
Greg Polis						
1971	Pittsburgh (West)		0	0	0	0R
1972	Pittsburgh (West)		0	0	0	0
1973	Pittsburgh (West)*		2	0	2	0
	3 games		2	0	2	0
Denis Potvin						
1974	N.Y. Islanders (East)		1	0	1	0R
1975	N.Y. Islanders (Campbell)		1	0	1	0
1976	N.Y. Islanders (Campbell)		1	1	2	0
1977	N.Y. Islanders (Campbell)		0	2	2	2
1978	N.Y. Islanders (Campbell)		1	0	1	0
1979	Challenge Cup (1)		0	0	0	0
1981	N.Y. Islanders (Campbell)		0	0	0	0
1983	N.Y. Islanders (Wales)		0	0	0	0
1984	N.Y. Islanders (Wales)		1	1	2	0
1988	N.Y. Islanders (Wales)		0	0	0	2
	9 games		5	4	9	4
Felix Potvin						
1994	**Toronto (Western)**		**20:00**	**nd**	**3**	**9.00**
1996	**Toronto (Western)**		**20:00**	**L**	**1**	**3.00**
	2 games		**40:00**	**0-1-0**	**4**	**6.00**
Dave Poulin						
1986	Philadelphia (Wales)		0	0	0	0
1987	Rendez-vous (2)		1	1	2	0
1988	Philadelphia (Wales)		0	0	0	0
	2 games		0	0	0	0
Tracy Pratt						
1975	Vancouver (Campbell)		0	0	0	0
Dean Prentice						
1957	N.Y. Rangers (All–Stars)		1	2	3	0
1961	N.Y. Rangers (All–Stars)		0	0	0	0
1963	Boston (All–Stars)		0	0	0	0
1970	Pittsburgh (West)		1	0	1	0
	4 games		2	2	4	0
Noel Price						
1967	Montreal (Stanley Cup)		0	0	0	0
Joe Primeau						
1934	Toronto (Bailey)		0	1	1	0
Keith Primeau						
1999	Carolina (North America)		0	0	0	0
Bob Probert						
1988	Detroit (Campbell)		0	1	1	0
Chris Pronger						
1999	St. Louis (North America)		0	2	2	0
2000	St. Louis (North America)		0	0	0	0
	2 games		0	2	2	0
Andre Pronovost						
1957	Montreal (Stanley Cup)		0	0	0	0
1958	Montreal (Stanley Cup)		0	0	0	0
1959	Montreal (Stanley Cup)		1	0	1	0
1960	Montreal (Stanley Cup)		0	1	1	0
	4 games		1	1	2	0
Jean Pronovost						
1975	Pittsburgh (Wales)		0	0	0	0
1976	Pittsburgh (Wales)		0	0	0	0
1977	Pittsburgh (Wales)		0	0	0	0
1978	Pittsburgh (Wales)		0	0	0	0
	4 games		0	0	0	0

Marcel Pronovost

		G	A	P	Pim
		Mins	W–L	GA	Avg
1950	Detroit (Stanley Cup)	0	0	0	2R
1954	Detroit (Stanley Cup)	0	0	0	0
1955	Detroit (Stanley Cup)	0	0	0	0
1957	Detroit (All–Stars)	0	0	0	0
1958	Detroit (All–Stars)	0	0	0	0
1959	Detroit (All–Stars)	0	0	0	0
1960	Detroit (All–Stars)	0	0	0	0
1961	Detroit (All–Stars)	0	1	1	0
1963	Detroit (All–Stars)	1	0	1	2
1965	Detroit (All–Stars)	0	0	0	2
1968	Toronto (Stanley Cup)	0	0	0	0
	11 games	1	1	2	6

Brian Propp

1980	Philadelphia (Campbell)	1	0	1	0R
1982	Philadelphia (Wales)	0	0	0	0
1984	Philadelphia (Wales)	0	0	0	0
1986	Philadelphia (Wales)	2	0	2	0
1990	Philadelphia (Wales)	0	1	1	0
	5 games	3	1	4	0

Claude Provost

1956	Montreal (Stanley Cup)	0	0	0	0
1957	Montreal (Stanley Cup)	0	0	0	0
1958	Montreal (Stanley Cup)	0	2	2	2
1959	Montreal (Stanley Cup)	0	0	0	0
1960	Montreal (Stanley Cup)	1	0	1	0
1961	Montreal (All–Stars)	0	0	0	0
1962	Montreal (All–Stars)	0	0	0	0
1963	Montreal (All–Stars)	0	0	0	0
1964	Montreal (All Stars)	0	0	0	2
1965	Montreal (Stanley Cup)	0	0	0	0
1967	Montreal (Stanley Cup)	0	0	0	0
	11 games	1	2	3	4

Metro Prystai

1950	Detroit (Stanley Cup)	1	2	3	0
1953	Detroit (All–Stars)	0	0	0	0
1954	Detroit (Stanley Cup)	0	0	0	0
	3 games	1	2	3	0

Bob Pulford

1958	Toronto (All–Stars)	1	1	2	0
1960	Toronto (All–Stars)	0	0	0	0
1962	Toronto (Stanley Cup)	1	0	1	0
1963	Toronto (Stanley Cup)	0	0	0	0
1964	Toronto (Stanley Cup)	0	0	0	0
1968	Toronto (Stanley Cup)	0	0	0	0
	6 games	2	1	3	0

Daren Puppa

1990	Buffalo (Wales)	30:46	nd	4	7.80

Bill Quackenbush

1947	Detroit (All–Stars)	0	0	0	0
1948	Detroit (All–Stars)	0	0	0	0
1949	Boston (All–Stars)	0	1	1	0
1950	Boston (All–Stars)	0	0	0	0
1951	Boston (First)	0	0	0	0
1952	Boston (First)	0	0	0	0
1953	Boston (All–Stars)	0	0	0	0
1954	Boston (All–Stars)	0	0	0	0
	8 games	0	1	1	0

Don Raleigh

1951	N.Y. Rangers (First)	0	1	1	2
1954	N.Y. Rangers (All–Stars)	0	0	0	0
	2 games	0	1	1	2

Rob Ramage

1981	Colorado (Campbell)	0	0	0	0
1984	St. Louis (Campbell)	0	0	0	0
1986	St. Louis (Campbell)	0	0	0	0
1988	St. Louis (Campbell)	0	0	0	0
	4 games	0	0	0	0

Craig Ramsay

1976	Buffalo (Wales)	0	0	0	0

Mike Ramsey

		G	A	P	Pim
		Mins	W–L	GA	Avg
1982	Buffalo (Wales)	0	0	0	0
1983	Buffalo (Wales)	0	0	0	2
1985	Buffalo (Wales)	0	0	0	0
1986	Buffalo (Wales)	0	0	0	0
1987	Rendez–vous (2)	0	0	0	0
	4 games	0	0	0	2

Bill Ranford

1991	Edmonton (Campbell)	30:12	1-0-0	3	5.96

Jean Ratelle

1970	N.Y. Rangers (East)	0	0	0	0
1971	N.Y. Rangers (East)	0	0	0	0
1972	N.Y. Rangers (East)	1	0	1	0
1973	N.Y. Rangers (East)	0	0	0	0
1980	Boston (Wales)	0	1	1	0
	5 games	1	1	2	0

Pekka Rautakallio

1982	Calgary (Campbell)	0	0	0	0

Charlie Rayner

1949	N.Y. Rangers (All–Stars)	30:30	W	0	0.00
1950	N.Y. Rangers (All–Stars)	31:12	L	3	5.77
1951	N.Y. Rangers (Second)	29:28	nd	1	2.04
	3 games	91:10	1-1-0	4	2.63

Ken Reardon

1947	Montreal (All–Stars)	0	1	1	7
1948	Montreal (All–Stars)	0	0	0	2
1949	Montreal (All–Stars)	0	0	0	0
	3 games	0	1	1	9

Billy Reay

1952	Montreal (Second)	0	0	0	0

Mark Recchi

1991	Pittsburgh (Wales)	0	0	0	0
1993	Philadelphia (Wales)	1	4	5	0
1994	Philadelphia (Eastern)	0	0	0	0
1997	Montreal (Eastern)*	3	0	3	0
1998	Montreal (North America)	0	1	1	0
1999	Montreal (North America)	1	1	2	0
2000	Philadelphia (North America)	0	1	1	0
	7 games	5	7	12	0

Mickey Redmond

1974	Detroit (East)	1	0	1	0

Earl Reibel

1954	Detroit (Stanley Cup)	0	2	2	0
1955	Detroit (Stanley Cup)	2	1	3	0
	2 games	2	3	5	0

Paul Reinhart

1985	Calgary (Campbell)	0	0	0	0
1989	Vancouver (Campbell)	0	0	0	0
	2 games	0	0	0	0

Leo Reise, Jr.

1950	Detroit (Stanley Cup)	0	0	0	0
1951	Detroit (Second)	0	0	0	0
1952	N.Y. Rangers (First)	0	0	0	0
1953	N.Y. Rangers (All–Stars)	0	0	0	0
	4 games	0	0	0	0

Chico Resch

1976	N.Y. Islanders (Campbell)	29:18	nd	3	6.14
1977	N.Y. Islanders (Campbell)	28:33	L	3	6.30
1984	New Jersey (Wales)	29:54	W	3	6.02
	3 games	87:45	1-1-0	9	6.15

*2 pim in 1984

	G	A	P	Pim
	Mins	W-L	GA	Avg

Henri Richard

		G	A	P	Pim
1956	Montreal (Stanley Cup)	0	0	0	0
1957	Montreal (Stanley Cup)	0	1	1	0
1958	Montreal (Stanley Cup)	1	2	3	0
1959	Montreal (Stanley Cup)	1	1	2	0
1960	Montreal (Stanley Cup)	0	0	0	0
1961	Montreal (All–Stars)	0	0	0	2
1963	Montreal (All–Stars)	1	0	1	0
1965	Montreal (Stanley Cup)	0	0	0	0
1967	Montreal (Stanley Cup)*	1	1	2	2
1974	Montreal (East)	0	0	0	0
	10 games	4	5	9	4

Maurice Richard

		G	A	P	Pim
1947	Montreal (All–Stars)	1	1	2	0
1948	Montreal (All–Stars)	0	1	1	0
1949	Montreal (All–Stars)	0	0	0	2
1950	Montreal (All–Stars)	0	0	0	2
1951	Montreal (Second)	0	0	0	0
1952	Montreal (Second)	1	0	1	2
1953	Montreal (Stanley Cup)	1	0	1	2
1954	Montreal (All–Stars)	0	0	0	0
1955	Montreal (All–Stars)	0	0	0	0
1956	Montreal (Stanley Cup)	1	0	1	0
1957	Montreal (Stanley Cup)	1	0	1	0
1958	Montreal (Stanley Cup)	2	0	2	0
1959	Montreal (Stanley Cup)	0	0	0	0
	13 games	7	2	9	8

Stephane Richer

		G	A	P	Pim
1990	Montreal (Wales)	0	0	0	0

Mike Richter

		Mins	W-L	GA	Avg
1992	N.Y. Rangers (Wales)	20:00	nd	2	6.00
1994	N.Y. Rangers (Eastern)*	20:00	nd	2	6.00
2000	N.Y. Rangers (North America)	20:00	nd	4	12.00
	3 games	60:00	0-0-0	8	8.00

Mike Ridley

		G	A	P	Pim
1989	Washington (Wales)	1	1	2	0

René Robert

		G	A	P	Pim
1973	Buffalo (East)	1	0	1	0
1975	Buffalo (Wales)	0	1	1	0
	2 games	1	1	2	0

Doug Roberts

		G	A	P	Pim
1971	California (West)	0	0	0	0

Gary Roberts

		G	A	P	Pim
1992	Calgary (Campbell)	1	0	1	0
1993	Calgary (Campbell)	0	0	0	0
	2 games	1	0	1	0

Jim Roberts

		G	A	P	Pim
1965	Montreal (Stanley Cup)	0	0	0	0
1969	St. Louis (West)	1	0	1	0
1970	St. Louis (West)	0	0	0	0
	3 games	1	0	1	0

Earl Robinson

		G	A	P	Pim
1937	Maroons (Morenz)	0	0	0	0
1939	Montreal (Siebert)	1	0	1	0
	2 games	1	0	1	0

Larry Robinson

		G	A	P	Pim
1974	Montreal (East)	0	0	0	0
1976	Montreal (Wales)	0	0	0	0
1977	Montreal (Wales)	0	2	2	0
1978	Montreal (Wales)	0	1	1	0
1979	Challenge Cup (3)	1	0	1	0
1980	Montreal (Wales)	1	0	1	0
1982	Montreal (Wales)	0	1	1	0
1986	Montreal (Wales)	0	2	2	0
1988	Montreal (Wales)	0	0	0	0
1989	Montreal (Wales)	0	2	2	0
1992	Los Angeles (Campbell)	0	1	1	0
	10 games	1	9	10	0

Luc Robitaille

		G	A	P	Pim
1988	Los Angeles (Campbell)	2	1	3	0
1989	Los Angeles (Campbell)	1	1	2	0
1990	Los Angeles (Campbell)	2	0	2	0
1991	Los Angeles (Campbell)	0	0	0	0
1992	Los Angeles (Campbell)	0	3	3	0
1993	Los Angeles (Campbell)	0	0	0	0
1999	Los Angeles (North America)	1	1	2	0
	7 games	6	6	12	0

Leon Rochefort

		G	A	P	Pim
1968	Philadelphia (All–Stars)	0	0	0	0

Normand Rochefort

		G	A	P	Pim
1987	Rendez-vous (1)	0	0	0	0

Jeremy Roenick

		G	A	P	Pim
1991	Chicago (Campbell)	1	2	3	0
1992	Chicago (Campbell)	1	1	2	0
1993	Chicago (Campbell)	1	1	2	0
1994	Chicago (Western)	1	1	2	0
1999	Phoenix (North America)	0	1	1	0
2000	Phoenix (North America)	1	0	1	0
	6 games	5	6	11	0

Mike Rogers

		G	A	P	Pim
1981	Hartford (Wales)	0	0	0	0

Al Rollins

		Mins	W-L	GA	Avg
1954	Chicago (All–Stars)	29:01	0-0-1	0	0.00

Paul Ronty

		G	A	P	Pim
1949	Boston (All–Stars)	1	0	1	0
1950	Boston (All–Stars)	0	0	0	0
1953	N.Y. Rangers (All–Stars)	0	1	1	0
1954	N.Y. Rangers (All–Stars)	0	0	0	0
	4 games	1	1	2	0

Darcy Rota

		G	A	P	Pim
1984	Vancouver (Campbell)	1	1	2	0

Bobby Rousseau

		G	A	P	Pim
1965	Montreal (Stanley Cup)	0	1	1	0
1967	Montreal (Stanley Cup)	0	2	2	0
1969	Montreal (East)	0	1	1	0
	3 games	0	4	4	0

Patrick Roy

		Mins	W-L	GA	Avg
1988	Montreal (Wales)	29:52	W	3	6.03
1990	Montreal (Wales)	29:14	W	3	6.16
1991	Montreal (Wales)	29:48	nd	5	10.07
1992	Montreal (Wales)	20:00	nd	2	6.00
1993	Montreal (Wales)	20:00	nd	0	0.00
1994	Montreal (Eastern)	20:00	nd	4	12.00
1997	Avalanche (North America)	20:00	nd	4	12.00
1998	Avalanche (North America)	20:00	nd	3	9.00
	8 games	188:54	2-0-0	24	7.62

*2 pim in 1990

Martin Rucinsky

		G	A	P	Pim
2000	Montreal (World)	0	2	2	0

Reijo Ruotsalainen

		G	A	P	Pim
1986	N.Y. Rangers (Wales)	0	0	0	0

Duane Rupp

		G	A	P	Pim
1968	Toronto (Stanley Cup)	0	1	1	0

Phil Russell

		G	A	P	Pim
1976	Chicago (Campbell)	0	0	0	0
1977	Chicago (Campbell)	0	0	0	2
1985	New Jersey (Wales)	0	0	0	2
	3 games	0	0	0	4

Christian Ruuttu

		G	A	P	Pim
1988	Buffalo (Wales)	0	0	0	0

Gary Sabourin

		G	A	P	Pim
1970	St. Louis (West)	0	0	0	0
1971	St. Louis (West)	0	0	0	0
	2 games	0	0	0	0

	G	A	P	Pim
	Mins	W-L	GA	Avg

Joe Sakic

	G	A	P	Pim
1990 Quebec (Wales)	0	2	2	0
1991 Quebec (Wales)	0	1	1	0
1992 Quebec (Wales)	0	2	2	0
1993 Quebec (Wales)	0	3	3	0
1994 Quebec (Eastern)	1	2	3	0
1996 Avalanche (Western)	0	0	0	0
1998 Avalanche (North America)	0	2	2	0
2000 Avalanche (North America)	1	0	1	0
8 games	2	12	14	0

Borje Salming

	G	A	P	Pim
1976 Toronto (Wales)	0	0	0	0
1977 Toronto (Wales)	0	0	0	2
1978 Toronto (Wales)	0	1	1	2
1979 Challenge Cup (3)	0	0	0	2
3 games	0	1	1	4

Tommy Salo

	Mins	W-L	GA	Avg
2000 Edmonton (World)	20:00	W	2	6.00

Kjell Samuelsson

	G	A	P	Pim
1988 Philadelphia (Wales)	0	0	0	0

Ulf Samuelsson

	G	A	P	Pim
1987 Rendez-vous (2)	0	0	0	0

Geoff Sanderson

	G	A	P	Pim
1994 Hartford (Eastern)	0	1	1	0
1997 Hartford (Eastern)	1	0	1	0
2 games	1	1	2	0

Ed Sandford

	G	A	P	Pim
1951 Boston (First)	0	0	0	0
1952 Boston (First)	0	0	0	2
1953 Boston (All-Stars)	0	0	0	0
1954 Boston (All-Stars)	0	0	0	2
1955 Detroit (Stanley Cup)	0	0	0	0
5 games	0	0	0	4

Charlie Sands

	G	A	P	Pim
1934 Toronto (Bailey)	0	0	0	0R

Tomas Sandstrom

	G	A	P	Pim
1987 Rendez-vous (1)	0	0	0	0
1988 N.Y. Rangers (Wales)	1	0	1	0
1991 Los Angeles (Campbell)	0	1	1	0
2 games	1	1	2	0

Miroslav Satan

	G	A	P	Pim
2000 Buffalo (World)	1	0	1	0

Denis Savard

	G	A	P	Pim
1982 Chicago (Campbell)	0	0	0	0
1983 Chicago (Campbell)	0	0	0	0
1984 Chicago (Campbell)	1	1	2	0
1986 Chicago (Campbell)	0	2	2	0
1988 Chicago (Campbell)	1	2	3	0
1991 Montreal (Wales)	0	0	0	0
1996 Chicago (Western)	0	0	0	0
7 games	2	5	7	0

Serge Savard

	G	A	P	Pim
1970 Montreal (East)	0	0	0	0
1973 Montreal (East)	0	1	1	0
1977 Montreal (Wales)	0	0	0	0
1978 Montreal (Wales)	0	0	0	0
1979 Challenge Cup (3)	0	0	0	0
4 games	0	1	1	0

Terry Sawchuk

	Mins	W-L	GA	Avg
1950 Detroit (Stanley Cup)	60:00	W	1	1.00R
1951 Detroit (First)	29:28	nd	1	2.04
1952 Detroit (First)	60:00	T	1	1.00
1953 Detroit (All-Stars)	60:00	W	1	1.00
1954 Detroit (Stanley Cup)	60:00	T	2	2.00
1955 Boston (All-Stars)	27:50	nd	1	2.16
1956 Boston (All-Stars)	30:30	T	0	0.00
1959 Detroit (All-Stars)	60:00	L	6	6.00
1963 Detroit (All-Stars)	28:57	T	1	2.07
1964 Toronto (Stanley Cup)	30:17	L	3	5.94
1968 Los Angeles (All-Stars)	20:00	L	2	6.00
11 games	467:02	2-2-4	19	2.44

Ken Schinkel

	G	A	P	Pim
1968 Pittsburgh (All-Stars)	0	0	0	0
1969 Pittsburgh (West)	0	0	0	0
2 games	0	0	0	0

Bobby Schmautz

	G	A	P	Pim
1973 Vancouver (East)	1	0	1	0
1974 Vancouver (East)	0	0	0	0
2 games	1	0	1	0

Milt Schmidt

	G	A	P	Pim
1947 Boston (All-Stars)	0	1	1	2
1948 Boston (All-Stars)	0	0	0	0
1951 Boston (First)	0	1	1	0
1952 Boston (Second)	0	0	0	0
4 games	0	2	2	2

Mathieu Schneider

	G	A	P	Pim
1996 N.Y. Islanders (Eastern)	0	1	1	0

Jim Schoenfeld

	G	A	P	Pim
1977 Buffalo (Wales)	0	0	0	0
1980 Buffalo (Wales)	0	0	0	0
2 games	0	0	0	0

Sweeney Schriner

	G	A	P	Pim
1937 N.Y. Americans (Morenz)	1	0	1	0

Al Secord

	G	A	P	Pim
1982 Chicago (Campbell)	0	0	0	0
1983 Chicago (Campbell)	0	1	1	0
2 games	0	1	1	0

Earl Seibert

	G	A	P	Pim
1939 Chicago (Siebert)	1	0	1	0

Rod Seiling

	G	A	P	Pim
1972 N.Y. Rangers (East)	0	1	1	0

Teemu Selanne

	G	A	P	Pim
1993 Winnipeg (Campbell)	1	1	2	0R
1994 Winnipeg (Western)	0	0	0	0
1996 Winnipeg (Western)	1	0	1	0
1997 Anaheim (Western)	0	1	1	0
1998 Anaheim (World)	3	0	3	0
1999 Anaheim (World)	1	0	1	0
2000 Anaheim (World)	0	0	0	0
7 games	6	2	8	0

Eddie Shack

	G	A	P	Pim
1962 Toronto (Stanley Cup)*	1	0	1	4
1963 Toronto (Stanley Cup)	0	0	0	0
1964 Toronto (Stanley Cup)	0	0	0	0
3 games	1	0	1	4

Brendan Shanahan

	G	A	P	Pim
1994 St. Louis (Western)	2	0	2	0
1996 Hartford (Eastern)	1	0	1	0
1997 Detroit (Western)	1	0	1	0
1998 Detroit (North America)	0	0	0	0
1999 Detroit (North America)	0	0	0	0
2000 Detroit (North America)	0	0	0	0
6 games	4	0	4	0

Greg Sheppard

	G	A	P	Pim
1976 Boston (Wales)	0	0	0	0

Al Shields

	G	A	P	Pim
1934 Ottawa (I) (Bailey)	0	0	0	0

| | G | A | P | Pim |
	Mins	W-L	GA	Avg
Eddie Shore				
1934　Boston (Bailey)	0	0	0	0
1937　Boston (Morenz)	0	1	1	0
1939　Boston (Siebert)	1	0	1	0
3 games	1	1	2	0
Steve Shutt				
1976　Montreal (Wales)	0	0	0	0
1978　Montreal (Wales)	0	1	1	0
1979　Challenge Cup (2)	0	1	1	0
1981　Montreal (Wales)	0	0	0	0
3 games	0	1	1	0
Peter Sidorkiewicz				
1993　Ottawa (II) (Wales)	20:00	1-0-0	2	6.00
Babe Siebert				
1937　Montreal (Morenz)	1	1	2	0
Charlie Simmer				
1981　Los Angeles (Wales)	0	0	0	0
1984　Los Angeles (Campbell)	0	1	1	0
2 games	0	1	1	0
Don Simmons				
1963　Toronto (Stanley Cup)	20:00	0-0-1	1	3.00
Reg Sinclair				
1951　N.Y. Rangers (First)	0	0	0	0
1952　Detroit (First)	0	0	0	0
2 games	0	0	0	0
Bob Sirois				
1978　Washington (Wales)	0	0	0	0
Darryl Sittler				
1975　Toronto (Wales)	1	1	2	0
1978　Toronto (Wales)	1	0	1	0
1979　Challenge Cup (3)	0	1	1	0
1980　Toronto (Wales)	0	1	1	0
1983　Philadelphia (Wales)	0	0	0	0
4 games	2	2	4	0
Glen Skov				
1954　Detroit (Stanley Cup)	0	0	0	0
Tod Sloan				
1951　Toronto (Second)	1	1	2	2
1952　Toronto (Second)	0	0	0	0
1956　Toronto (All-Stars)	0	0	0	0
3 games	1	1	2	2
Doug Smail				
1990　Winnipeg (Campbell)	1	1	2	2
Al Smith				
1968　Toronto (Stanley Cup)	20:00	1-0-0	1	3.00R
*did not play in the NHL in 1967–68				
Billy Smith				
1978　N.Y. Islanders (Campbell)	29:26	nd	0	0.00
*2 pim in 1978				
Bobby Smith				
1981　Minnesota (Wales)	0	0	0	0
1982　Minnesota (Campbell)	0	0	0	0
1989　Montreal (Wales)	0	0	0	0
1991　Minnesota (Campbell)	0	0	0	0
4 games	0	0	0	0
Dallas Smith				
1971　Boston (East)	0	1	1	0
1972　Boston (East)	0	1	1	0
1973　Boston (East)	0	0	0	0
1974　Boston (East)	0	0	0	0
4 games	0	2	2	0
Gary Smith				
1975　Vancouver (Campbell)	30:43	nd	4	7.81
Hooley Smith				
1934　Maroons (Bailey)	0	0	0	0
Sid Smith				
1949　Toronto (Stanley Cup)	0	0	0	2
1950　Toronto (All-Stars)	1	0	1	0
1951　Toronto (Second)	0	0	0	0
1952　Toronto (Second)	0	0	0	0
1953　Toronto (All-Stars)	0	0	0	2
1954　Toronto (All-Stars)	0	0	0	0
1955　Toronto (All-Stars)	0	1	1	0
7 games	1	1	2	4
Steve Smith				
1991　Edmonton (Campbell)	0	2	2	0
Stan Smrke				
1957　Montreal (Stanley Cup)	1	0	1	0R
Harold Snepsts				
1977　Vancouver (Campbell)	0	0	0	0
1982　Vancouver (Campbell)	0	0	0	0
2 games	0	0	0	0
Ron Stackhouse				
1980　Pittsburgh (Wales)	1	0	1	0
Allan Stanley				
1955　Chicago (All-Stars)	0	0	0	2
1957　Boston (All-Stars)	1	0	1	0
1960　Toronto (All-Stars)	0	0	0	0
1962　Toronto (Stanley Cup)	0	1	1	0
1963　Toronto (Stanley Cup)	0	0	0	4
1967　Toronto (All-Stars)	0	0	0	0
1968　Toronto (Stanley Cup)	1	0	1	0
7 games	2	1	3	6
Wally Stanowski				
1947　Toronto (Stanley Cup)	0	0	0	0
Pat Stapleton				
1967　Chicago (All-Stars)	0	0	0	0
1969　Chicago (East)	0	1	1	0
1971　Chicago (West)	0	0	0	2
1972　Chicago (West)	0	0	0	0
4 games	0	1	1	2
Vic Stasiuk				
1960　Boston (All-Stars)	0	0	0	0
Marian Stastny				
1983　Quebec (Wales)	0	0	0	0
Peter Stastny				
1981　Quebec (Wales)	0	0	0	0R
1982　Quebec (Wales)	0	1	1	0
1983　Quebec (Wales)	0	1	1	0
1984　Quebec (Wales)	0	1	1	0
1986　Quebec (Wales)	1	0	1	0
1988　Quebec (Wales)	1	0	1	0
6 games	2	3	5	0
Pete Stemkowski				
1968　Toronto (Stanley Cup)	1	1	2	2
Wayne Stephenson				
1976　Philadelphia (Campbell)	30:42	L	4	7.82
1978　Philadelphia (Campbell)	34:29	L	3	5.22
2 games	65:11	0-2-0	7	6.44
Kevin Stevens				
1991　Pittsburgh (Wales)	1	0	1	0
1992　Pittsburgh (Wales)	1	0	1	0
1993　Pittsburgh (Wales)	1	2	3	0
3 games	3	2	5	0

	G	A	P	Pim
	Mins	W–L	GA	Avg

Scott Stevens

	G	A	P	Pim
1985 Washington (Wales)	0	0	0	0
1989 Washington (Wales)	0	1	1	0
1991 St. Louis (Campbell)	0	0	0	0
1992 New Jersey (Wales)	1	0	1	0
1993 New Jersey (Wales)	0	2	2	0
1994 New Jersey (Eastern)	1	1	2	0
1996 New Jersey (Eastern)	0	0	0	0
1997 New Jersey (Eastern)	0	2	2	0
1998 New Jersey (North America)	0	0	0	0
1999 New Jersey (North America)	0	0	0	0
2000 New Jersey (North America)	0	0	0	0
11 games	2	6	8	0

Gaye Stewart

	G	A	P	Pim
1947 Toronto (Stanley Cup)	0	0	0	0
1948 Chicago (All–Stars)	1	0	1	0
1950 Detroit (Stanley Cup)	0	0	0	2
1951 N.Y. Rangers (First)	0	1	1	0
4 games	1	1	2	2

Jack Stewart

	G	A	P	Pim
1947 Detroit (All–Stars)	0	0	0	0
1948 Detroit (All–Stars)	0	0	0	2
1949 Detroit (All–Stars)	0	0	0	0
1950 Chicago (All–Stars)	0	0	0	0
4 games	0	0	0	2

Nels Stewart

	G	A	P	Pim
1934 Boston (Bailey)	1	1	2	0

Ron Stewart

	G	A	P	Pim
1955 Toronto (All–Stars)	0	0	0	2
1962 Toronto (Stanley Cup)	0	1	1	0
1963 Toronto (Stanley Cup)	0	0	0	0
1964 Toronto (Stanley Cup)	0	0	0	2
4 games	0	1	1	4

Dollard St. Laurent

	G	A	P	Pim
1953 Montreal (Stanley Cup)	0	0	0	2
1956 Montreal (Stanley Cup)	0	0	0	0
1957 Montreal (Stanley Cup)	0	0	0	0
1958 Chicago (All–Stars)	0	0	0	0
1961 Chicago (Stanley Cup)	0	0	0	0
5 games	0	0	0	2

Frank St. Marseille

	G	A	P	Pim
1970 St. Louis (West)	0	0	0	2

Blaine Stoughton

	G	A	P	Pim
1982 Hartford (Wales)	0	0	0	2

Martin Straka

	G	A	P	Pim
1999 Pittsburgh (World)	0	0	0	0

Marco Sturm

	G	A	P	Pim
1999 San Jose (World)	1	0	1	0

Red Sullivan

	G	A	P	Pim
1955 Chicago (All–Stars)	0	0	0	0
1956 Chicago (All–Stars)	0	0	0	2
1958 N.Y. Rangers (All–Stars)	0	1	1	0
1959 N.Y. Rangers (All–Stars)	0	0	0	0
1960 N.Y. Rangers (All–Stars)	0	1	1	2
5 games	0	2	2	4

Mats Sundin

	G	A	P	Pim
1996 Toronto (Western)	0	1	1	0
1997 Toronto (Western)	0	1	1	0
1998 Toronto (World)	0	1	1	0
1999 Toronto (World)	1	3	4	0
2000 Toronto (World)	0	0	0	0
5 games	1	6	7	0

Gary Suter

	G	A	P	Pim
1986 Calgary (Campbell)	0	0	0	2R
1988 Calgary (Campbell)	0	0	0	0
1989 Calgary (Campbell)	0	0	0	0
1991 Calgary (Campbell)	1	0	1	0
4 games	1	0	1	2

Brent Sutter

	G	A	P	Pim
1985 N.Y. Islanders (Wales)	0	0	0	0

Brian Sutter

	G	A	P	Pim
1982 St. Louis (Campbell)	0	1	1	0
1983 St. Louis (Campbell)	0	2	2	2
1985 St. Louis (Campbell)	0	0	0	0
3 games	0	3	3	2

Robert Svehla

	G	A	P	Pim
1997 Florida (Eastern)	0	2	2	0

Petr Svoboda

	G	A	P	Pim
2000 Tampa Bay (World)	0	0	0	0

Darryl Sydor

	G	A	P	Pim
1998 Dallas (North America)	0	0	0	0
1999 Dallas (North America)	1	0	1	0
2 games	1	0	1	0

Jean-Guy Talbot

	G	A	P	Pim
1956 Montreal (Stanley Cup)	0	0	0	0
1957 Montreal (Stanley Cup)	0	0	0	4
1958 Montreal (Stanley Cup)	0	1	1	0
1960 Montreal (Stanley Cup)	0	0	0	2
1962 Montreal (All–Stars)	0	0	0	0
1965 Montreal (Stanley Cup)	0	0	0	0
1967 Montreal (Stanley Cup)	0	0	0	0
7 games	0	1	1	6

Dale Tallon

	G	A	P	Pim
1971 Vancouver (East)	0	0	0	0R
1972 Vancouver (East)	0	0	0	0
2 games	0	0	0	0

Tony Tanti

	G	A	P	Pim
1986 Vancouver (Campbell)	1	0	1	0

Marc Tardif

	G	A	P	Pim
1982 Quebec (Wales)	1	0	1	4

Dave Taylor

	G	A	P	Pim
1981 Los Angeles (Wales)	0	0	0	0
1982 Los Angeles (Campbell)	0	0	0	0
1986 Los Angeles (Campbell)	0	0	0	0
1994 Los Angeles (Western)	0	1	1	0
4 games	0	1	1	0

Wayne Thomas

	Mins	W–L	GA	Avg
1976 Toronto (Wales)	30:26	1-0-0	4	7.89

Tiny Thompson

	Mins	W–L	GA	Avg
1937 Boston (Morenz)	60:00	1-0-0	5	5.00

Bill Thoms

	G	A	P	Pim
1934 Toronto (Bailey)	0	1	1	0

Jim Thomson

	G	A	P	Pim
1947 Toronto (Stanley Cup)	0	0	0	0
1948 Toronto (Stanley Cup)	0	0	0	0
1949 Toronto (Stanley Cup)	0	0	0	4
1950 Toronto (All–Stars)	0	0	0	0
1951 Toronto (Second)	0	0	0	0
1952 Toronto (Second)	0	0	0	6
1953 Toronto (All–Stars)	0	0	0	0
7 games	0	0	0	10

Esa Tikkanen

	G	A	P	Pim
1987 Rendez-vous (2)	0	1	1	2

Ray Timgren

	G	A	P	Pim
1949 Toronto (Stanley Cup)	0	0	0	0

Mark Tinordi

	G	A	P	Pim
1992 Minnesota (Campbell)	0	1	1	0

Keith Tkachuk

	G	A	P	Pim
1997 Phoenix (Western)	0	0	0	0
1998 Phoenix (North America)	2	1	3	0
1999 Phoenix (North America)	0	0	0	0
3 games	2	1	3	0

Walt Tkaczuk

	G	A	P	Pim
1970 N.Y. Rangers (East)	1	0	1	0

		G	A	P	Pim
		Mins	W-L	GA	Avg

Rick Tocchet

		G	A	P	Pim
1989	Philadelphia (Wales)	0	2	2	0
1990	Philadelphia (Wales)	1	1	2	0
1991	Philadelphia (Wales)	1	1	2	0
1993	Pittsburgh (Wales)	2	0	2	0
	4 games	4	4	8	0

John Tonelli

1982	N.Y. Islanders (Wales)	0	1	1	0
1985	N.Y. Islanders (Wales)	0	0	0	0
	2 games	0	1	1	0

Jerry Toppazzini

1955	Detroit (Stanley Cup)	0	0	0	0
1958	Boston (All-Stars)	0	1	1	0
1959	Boston (All-Stars)	0	0	0	0
	3 games	0	1	1	0

Gilles Tremblay

1965	Montreal (Stanley Cup)	0	0	0	0
1967	Montreal (Stanley Cup)	0	0	0	0
	2 games	0	0	0	0

J.C. Tremblay

1959	Montreal (Stanley Cup)	0	0	0	2R
1965	Montreal (Stanley Cup)	0	0	0	0
1967	Montreal (Stanley Cup)	0	0	0	0
1968	Montreal (All-Stars)	0	1	1	0
1969	Montreal (East)	0	0	0	0
1971	Montreal (East)	0	0	0	0
1972	Montreal (East)	0	1	1	2
	7 games	0	2	2	4

Bryan Trottier

1976	N.Y. Islanders (Campbell)	0	2	2	0R
1978	N.Y. Islanders (Campbell)	0	0	0	0
1979	Challenge Cup (3)	1	1	2	2
1980	N.Y. Islanders (Campbell)	0	0	0	0
1982	N.Y. Islanders (Wales)	0	0	0	0
1983	N.Y. Islanders (Wales)	0	0	0	0
1985	N.Y. Islanders (Wales)	0	0	0	0
1986	N.Y. Islanders (Wales)	1	0	1	0
1992	Pittsburgh (Wales)	1	0	1	0
	8 games	2	2	4	0

Dave Trottier

1937	Maroons (Morenz)	0	0	0	0

Louis Trudel

1939	Montreal (Siebert)	1	0	1	0

Ron Tugnutt

1999	Ottawa (II) (North America)	20:00	W	3	9.00

Roman Turek

2000	St. Louis (World)	20:00	nd	2	6.00

Darren Turcotte

1991	N.Y. Rangers (Wales)	0	1	1	0

Pierre Turgeon

1990	Buffalo (Wales)	2	0	2	0
1993	N.Y. Islanders (Wales)	3	2	5	0
1994	N.Y. Islanders (Eastern)	0	4	4	0
1996	Montreal (Eastern)	0	1	1	0
	4 games	5	7	12	0

Sylvain Turgeon

1986	Hartford (Wales)	0	1	1	2

Ian Turnbull

1977	Toronto (Wales)	0	0	0	0

Bob Turner

1956	Montreal (Stanley Cup)	0	0	0	0
1957	Montreal (Stanley Cup)	0	0	0	0
1958	Montreal (Stanley Cup)	0	0	0	2
1959	Montreal (Stanley Cup)	0	0	0	2
1960	Montreal (Stanley Cup)	0	0	0	0
1961	Chicago (Stanley Cup)	0	0	0	0
	6 games	0	0	0	4

Oleg Tverdovsky

1997	Phoenix (Western)	0	0	0	0

Norm Ullman

		G	A	P	Pim
1955	Detroit (Stanley Cup)	0	0	0	0R
1960	Detroit (All-Stars)	0	0	0	0
1961	Detroit (All-Stars)	0	2	2	0
1962	Detroit (All-Stars)	0	0	0	0
1963	Detroit (All-Stars)	0	0	0	0
1964	Detroit (All-Stars)	0	0	0	0
1965	Detroit (All-Stars)	1	1	2	0
1967	Detroit (All-Stars)	0	0	0	0
1968	Detroit (All-Stars)	1	0	1	0
1969	Toronto (East)	0	1	1	0
1974	Toronto (East)	0	2	2	0
	11 games	2	6	8	0

Garry Unger

1972	St. Louis (West)	0	0	0	0
1973	St. Louis (West)	0	0	0	0
1974	St. Louis (West)*	1	1	2	0
1975	St. Louis (Campbell)	0	1	1	0
1976	St. Louis (Campbell)	0	1	1	0
1977	St. Louis (Campbell)	0	0	0	0
1978	St. Louis (Campbell)	0	0	0	0
	7 games	1	3	4	0

Rogie Vachon

1973	Los Angeles (West)	30:44	L	4	7.81
1975	Los Angeles (Wales)	29:21	W	1	2.04
1978	Los Angeles (Wales)	34:29	W	0	0.00
	3 games	94:34	2-1-0	5	3.17

Carol Vadnais

1969	Oakland (West)	0	0	0	2
1970	Oakland (West)	0	0	0	0
1972	California (West)	0	0	0	0
1975	Boston (Wales)	0	1	1	0
1976	N.Y. Rangers (Campbell)	0	0	0	0
1978	N.Y. Rangers (Campbell)	0	0	0	2
	6 games	0	1	1	4

Eric Vail

1977	Atlanta (Campbell)	1	0	1	0

Rick Vaive

1982	Toronto (Campbell)	1	0	1	0
1983	Toronto (Campbell)	1	0	1	0
1984	Toronto (Campbell)	0	3	3	0
	3 games	2	3	5	0

John Vanbiesbrouck

1994	Florida (Eastern)	20:00	W	2	6.00
1996	Florida (Eastern)	20:00	nd	3	9.00
1997	Florida (Eastern)	20:00	nd	2	6.00
	3 games	60:00	1-0-0	7	7.00

Ed Van Impe

1969	Philadelphia (West)	0	0	0	0
1974	Philadelphia (West)	0	0	0	0
1975	Philadelphia (Campbell)	0	0	0	0
	3 games	0	0	0	0

Elmer Vasko

1961	Chicago (Stanley Cup)	0	0	0	2
1963	Chicago (All-Stars)	0	0	0	0
1964	Chicago (All-Stars)	0	0	0	0
1969	Minnesota (West)	0	0	0	0R
	4 games	0	0	0	2

Pat Verbeek

1991	Hartford (Wales)	0	1	1	0
1996	N.Y. Rangers (Eastern)	1	1	2	0
	2 games	1	2	3	0

Mike Vernon

1988	Calgary (Campbell)	31:00	L	3	5.81
1989	Calgary (Campbell)	30:02	W	2	4.00
1990	Calgary (Campbell)	29:14	L	8	16.42
1991	Calgary (Campbell)	29:48	nd	2	4.03
1993	Calgary (Campbell)	20:00	L	6	18.00
	5 games	140:04	1-3-0	21	9.00

	G	A	P	Pim
	Mins	W–L	GA	Avg

Dennis Ververgaert

1976	Vancouver (Campbell)	2	0	2	0
1978	Vancouver (Campbell)	0	0	0	0
	2 games	2	0	2	0

Steve Vickers

1975	N.Y. Rangers (Campbell)	0	0	0	2
1976	N.Y. Rangers (Campbell)	1	0	1	0
	2 games	1	0	1	2

Gilles Villemure

1971	N.Y. Rangers (East)	29:19	nd	0	0.00
1972	N.Y. Rangers (East)	29:36	W	0	0.00
1973	N.Y. Rangers (East)	29:16	nd	1	2.05
	3 games	88:11	1-0-0	1	0.68

Ernie Wakely

1971	St. Louis (East)	29:19	0-0-0	0	0.00

Ryan Walter

1983	Montreal (Wales)	0	0	0	0

Mike Walton

1968	Toronto (Stanley Cup)	0	0	0	2

Jimmy Ward

1934	Maroons (Bailey)	0	1	1	0
1937	Maroons (Morenz)	0	1	1	0
	2 games	0	2	2	0

Grant Warwick

1947	N.Y. Rangers (All–Stars)	1	0	1	0

Harry Watson

1947	Toronto (Stanley Cup)	1	2	3	0
1948	Toronto (Stanley Cup)	0	0	0	0
1949	Toronto (Stanley Cup)	0	1	1	0
1951	Toronto (Second)	0	1	1	0
1952	Toronto (Second)	0	0	0	0
1953	Toronto (All–Stars)	0	0	0	0
1955	Chicago (All–Stars)	0	0	0	0
	7 games	1	4	5	0

Jim Watson

1975	Philadelphia (Campbell)	0	0	0	2
1976	Philadelphia (Campbell)	0	0	0	0
1977	Philadelphia (Campbell)	0	0	0	0
1978	Philadelphia (Campbell)	0	0	0	0
1980	Philadelphia (Campbell)	0	0	0	0
	5 games	0	0	0	2

Joe Watson

1974	Philadelphia (West)	0	0	0	0
1977	Philadelphia (Campbell)	0	0	0	2
	2 games	0	0	0	2

Doug Weight

1996	Edmonton (Western)	0	0	0	0
1998	Edmonton (North America)	0	0	0	2
	2 games	0	0	0	2

Cy Wentworth

1937	Maroons (Morenz)	0	0	0	0
1939	Montreal (Siebert)	0	0	0	2
	2 games	0	0	0	2

Glen Wesley

1989	Boston (Wales)	1	0	1	0

Ed Westfall

1971	Boston (East)	0	0	0	0
1973	N.Y. Islanders (East)	0	0	0	0
1974	N.Y. Islanders (East)	0	0	0	0
1975	N.Y. Islanders (Campbell)	0	0	0	0
	4 games	0	0	0	0

Ken Wharram

1961	Chicago (Stanley Cup)	0	0	0	0
1968	Chicago (All–Stars)	1	0	1	0
	2 games	1	0	1	0

	G	A	P	Pim
	Mins	W–L	GA	Avg

Bill White

1969	Los Angeles (West)	0	0	0	4
1970	Los Angeles (West)	0	0	0	0
1971	Chicago (West)	0	0	0	0
1972	Chicago (West)	0	0	0	4
1973	Chicago (West)	0	0	0	2
1974	Chicago (West)	0	2	2	0
	6 games	0	2	2	10

Ray Whitney

2000	Florida (North America)	1	1	2	0

Dave Williams

1981	Vancouver (Campbell)	0	0	0	2

Behn Wilson

1981	Philadelphia (Campbell)	1	0	1	0

Doug Wilson

1982	Chicago (Campbell)	0	0	0	0
1983	Chicago (Campbell)	0	1	1	0
1984	Chicago (Campbell)	0	1	1	0
1985	Chicago (Campbell)	0	0	0	0
1986	Chicago (Campbell)	0	0	0	0
1987	Rendez-vous (2)	1	1	2	0
1990	Chicago (Campbell)	0	0	0	0
1992	San Jose (Campbell)	0	0	0	0
	7 games	0	2	2	0

Johnny Wilson

1954	Detroit (Stanley Cup)	0	0	0	0
1956	Chicago (All–Stars)	0	0	0	0
	2 games	0	0	0	0

Benny Woit

1954	Detroit (Stanley Cup)	0	0	0	2

Gump Worsley

1961	N.Y. Rangers (All–Stars)	30:00	nd	0	0.00
1962	N.Y. Rangers (All–Stars)	20:00	nd	0	0.00
1965	Montreal (All–Stars)	30:46	nd	1	1.95
1972	Minnesota (West)	29:36	L	2	4.05
	4 games	110:22	0-1-0	3	1.63

Bob Woytowich

1970	Pittsburgh (West)	0	1	1	4

Alexei Yashin

1994	Ottawa (II) (Eastern)	2	0	2	0R
1999	Ottawa (II) (World)	0	1	1	0
	2 games	2	1	3	0

Doug Young

1939	Montreal (Siebert)	0	0	0	0

Tim Young

1977	Minnesota (Campbell)	0	0	0	0

Dmitry Yushkevich

2000	Toronto (World)	1	1	2	0

Steve Yzerman

1984	Detroit (Campbell)	0	1	1	0R
1988	Detroit (Campbell)	0	0	0	0
1989	Detroit (Campbell)	1	0	1	0
1990	Detroit (Campbell)	1	2	3	0
1991	Detroit (Campbell)	0	1	1	0
1992	Detroit (Campbell)	0	0	0	0
1993	Detroit (Campbell)	0	0	0	0
1997	Detroit (Western)	0	0	0	0
1999	Detroit (North America)	0	0	0	0
2000	Detroit (North America)	0	0	0	0
	10 games	2	4	6	0

Zarley Zalapski

1993	Hartford (Wales)	0	0	0	0

Alexei Zhitnik

1999	Buffalo (World)	0	1	1	0

Sergei Zubov

1998	Dallas (World)	0	0	0	0
1999	Dallas (World)	1	0	1	0
2000	Dallas (World)	0	0	0	0
	3 games	1	0	1	0

All–Star Game Coaching Register

Sid Abel

1961	Detroit (All–Stars)	W
1963	Detroit (All–Stars)	T
1964	Detroit (All–Stars)	W
1967	Detroit (All–Stars)	L
	4 games	2-1-1

Jack Adams

1937	Detroit (All–Stars)	W (1-0-0)

Al Arbour

1980	N.Y. Islanders (Campbell)	L
1982	N.Y. Islanders (Wales)	W
1983	N.Y. Islanders (Wales)	L
1984	N.Y. Islanders (Wales)	W
1985	N.Y. Islanders (Wales)	W
	5 games	3-2-0

Toe Blake

1956	Montreal (Stanley Cup)	T
1957	Montreal (Stanley Cup)	L
1958	Montreal (Stanley Cup)	W
1959	Montreal (Stanley Cup)	W
1960	Montreal (Stanley Cup)	L
1965	Montreal (Stanley Cup)	L
1967	Montreal (Stanley Cup)	W
1968	Montreal (All–Stars)	L
1969	Montreal (East)	T
	9 games	3-4-2

Scotty Bowman

1969	St. Louis (West)	T
1970	St. Louis (West)	L
1971	St. Louis (West)	W
1974	Montreal (East)	L
1977	Montreal (Wales)	W
1978	Montreal (Wales)	W
1980	Buffalo (Wales)	W
1981	Buffalo (Wales)	L
1992	Pittsburgh (Wales)	L
1993	Pittsburgh (Wales)	W
1996	Detroit (Western)	L
2000	Detroit (World)	W
	12 games	6-5-1

Pat Burns

1990	Montreal (Wales)	W (1-0-0)

King Clancy

1954	Toronto (All–Stars)	T (0-0-1)

Terry Crisp

1990	Calgary (Campbell)	L (0-1-0)

Happy Day

1947	Toronto (Stanley Cup)	L
1948	Toronto (Stanley Cup)	L
1949	Toronto (Stanley Cup)	L
	3 games	0-3-0

Jacques Demers

1994	Montreal (Eastern)	W (1-0-0)

Bob Gainey

1992	Minnesota (Campbell)	W (1-0-0)

Bep Guidolin

1975	Kansas City (Wales)	W (1-0-0)

Cecil Hart

1937	Montreal (Morenz)	L (0-1-0)

Ken Hitchcock

1997	Dallas (Western)	L
1998	Dallas (World)	L
1999	Dallas (North America)	W
	3 games	1-2-0

Punch Imlach

1959	Toronto (All–Stars)	L
1960	Toronto (All–Stars)	W
1962	Toronto (Stanley Cup)	W
1963	Toronto (Stanley Cup)	T
1964	Toronto (Stanley Cup)	L
1968	Toronto (Stanley Cup)	W
	6 games	3-2-1

Dick Irvin

1934	Toronto (Bailey)	W
1947	Montreal (All–Stars)	W
1951	Montreal (Second)	L
1952	Montreal (Second)	T
1953	Montreal (Stanley Cup)	L
1955	Chicago (All–Stars)	L
	6 games	2-2-2

Tommy Ivan

1948	Detroit (All–Stars)	W
1949	Detroit (All–Stars)	W
1950	Detroit (Stanley Cup)	W
1952	Detroit (First)	T
	4 games	3-0-1

Tom Johnson

1973	Boston (East)	W (1-0-0)

Mike Keenan

1986	Philadelphia (Wales)	W
1988	Philadelphia (Wales)	W
1993	Chicago (Campbell)	L
	3 games	2-1-0

Jacques Lemaire

1998	New Jersey (N. America)	W (1-0-0)

Pit Lepine

1939	Montreal (Siebert)	L (0-1-0)

Doug MacLean

1996	Florida (Eastern)	W
1997	Florida (Eastern)	W
	2 games	2-0-0

Al MacNeil

1972	Montreal (Eastern)	W (1-0-0)

Barry Melrose

1994	Los Angeles (Western)	L (0-1-0)

Mike Milbury

1991	Boston (Wales)	L (0-1-0)

John Muckler

1991	Edmonton (Campbell)	W (1-0-0)

Roger Neilson

1983	Vancouver (Campbell)	W (1-0-0)

Terry O'Reilly

1989	Boston (Wales)	L (0-1-0)

Lester Patrick

1934	N.Y. Rangers (All–Stars)	L (0-1-0)

Lynn Patrick

1950	Boston (All–Stars)	L
1953	Boston (All–Stars)	W
	2 games	1-1-0

Rudy Pilous

1961	Chicago (Stanley Cup)	L
1962	Chicago (All–Stars)	L
	2 games	0-2-0

Joe Primeau

1951	Toronto (First)	T (0-0-1)

Pat Quinn

1981	Philadelphia (Campbell)	W
2000	Toronto (North America)	L
	2 games	1-1-0

Billy Reay

1965	Chicago (All–Stars)	W
1972	Chicago (West)	L
1973	Chicago (West)	L
1974	Chicago (West)	W
	4 games	2-2-0

Art Ross

1939	Boston (All–Stars)	W (1-0-0)

Claude Ruel

1970	Montreal (East)	W (1-0-0)

Lindy Ruff

1999	Buffalo (World)	L (0-1-0)

Glen Sather

1984	Edmonton (Campbell)	L
1985	Edmonton (Campbell)	L
1986	Edmonton (Campbell)	L
1988	Edmonton (Campbell)	L
1989	Edmonton (Campbell)	W
	5 games	1-4-0

Milt Schmidt

1957	Boston (All–Stars)	W
1958	Boston (All–Stars)	L
	2 games	1-1-0

Fred Shero

1975	Philadelphia (Campbell)	L
1976	Philadelphia (Campbell)	L
1977	Philadelphia (Campbell)	L
1978	Philadelphia (Campbell)	L
	4 games	0-4-0

Harry Sinden

1971	Boston (East)	L (0-1-0)

Jimmy Skinner

1954	Detroit (Stanley Cup)	T
1955	Detroit (Stanley Cup)	W
1956	Detroit (All–Stars)	T
	3 games	1-0-2

Floyd Smith

1976	Buffalo (Wales)	W (1-0-0)

Glen Sonmor

1982	Minnesota (Campbell)	L (0-1-0)

All–Star Game Officials' Register

Neil Armstrong
1960 L
1961 L
1963 L
1964 L
1965 L
1967 L
1969 L
1971 L
1973 L
1976 L

John Ashley
1964 L
1969 R

Ron Asseltine
1989 L
1996 L
1997 L

Sammy Babcock
1948 L
1951 L
1953 L

Claude Bechard
1970 L
1972 L
1975 L

Wayne Bonney
1989 L

Ryan Bozak
1983 L
1993 L

Gord Broseker
1986 L
1994 L

Vern Buffey
1967 R

Brent Casselman
1968 L

Bill Chadwick
1948 R
1949 R
1951 R
1952 R
1954 R

Pierre Champoux
1999 L

Jim Christison
1981 L

King Clancy
1939 R
1947 R

Kevin Collins
1988 L
1993 L

Mike Cvik
1998 L

Eusebe Daignault
1937 L

John D'Amico
1971 L
1973 L
1976 L
1978 L
1980 L
1984 L
1986 L

Pat Dapuzzo
1994 L

Doug Davies
1953 L
1956 L
1957 L

Paul Devorski
1999 R

Mark Faucette
1996 R

Ron Finn
1977 L
1982 L

Bob Frampton
1959 L

Kerry Fraser
1990 R
2000 R

Bill Friday
1968 R
1971 R

Gerard Gauthier
1981 L
1985 L
2000 L

Lloyd Gilmour
1973 R
1976 R

George Gravel
1950 R

Terry Gregson
1991 R

Wally Harris
1975 R
1982 R

George Hayes
1950 L
1952 L
1954 L
1955 L
1958 L
1959 L
1960 L
1961 L

Bobby Hewitson
1934 R

Shane Heyer
1998 L

Bob Hodges
1985 L
1990 L
1997 L

Ron Hoggarth
1989 R

Bruce Hood
1972 R
1977 R
1978 R
1984 R

Mickey Ion
1937 R

Swede Knox
1982 L

Don Koharski
1992 R
2000 R

Brad Lazarowich
1996 L

Bryan Lewis
1981 R

Mush March
1948 L

Dan Marouelli
1993 R

Dan McCourt
1990 L

Bill McCreary
1994 R

Ed Mepham
1947 L
1949 L

Randy Mitton
1988 L

Denis Morel
1988 R

William Morrison
1951 L
1955 L
1957 L
1958 L

Brian Murphy
1999 L

Bob Myers
1983 R

Dave Newell
1980 R

Will Norris
1974 L

Mark Pare
1992 L

Jerry Pateman
1991 L

Matt Pavelich
1962 L
1963 L
1964 L
1965 L
1967 L
1969 L
1970 L
1972 L
1974 L
1977 L

Eddie Powers
1958 R
1960 R
1962 R

Jim Primeau
1947 L
1949 L

Bill Roberts
1956 L

Mike Rodden
1934 R

Ray Scapinello
1980 L
1984 L
2000 L

Dan Schachte
1991 L

Pat Shetler
1968 L

Rob Shick
1997 R

Art Skov
1965 R
1970 R
1974 R

Bill Stewart
1939 R

Paul Stewart
1998 R

Leon Stickle
1975 L
1978 L
1983 L
1997 L

Red Storey
1953 R
1956 R
1957 R

Frank Udvari
1955 R
1959 R
1961 R
1963 R

Andy van Hellemond
1985 R

Mark Vines
1992 L

Ron Wicks
1962 L
1986 R

Doug Young
1950 L
1952 L
1954 L

All–Star Teams
1930–2000

(* indicates rookie)

1930–31
First Team
Chuck Gardiner, goal (Chicago)
Eddie Shore, defence (Boston)
King Clancy, defence (Toronto)
Howie Morenz, centre (Montreal)
Bill Cook, right wing (N.Y. Rangers)
Aurel Joliat, left wing (Montreal)
Lester Patrick, coach (N.Y. Rangers)
Second Team
Tiny Thompson, goal (Boston)
Sylvio Mantha, defence (Montreal)
Ivan Johnson, defence (N.Y. Rangers)
Frank Boucher, centre (N.Y. Rangers)
Dit Clapper, right wing (Boston)
Bun Cook, left wing (N.Y. Rangers)
Dick Irvin, coach (Chicago)

1931–32
First Team
Chuck Gardiner, goal (Chicago)
Eddie Shore, defence (Boston)
Ivan Johnson, defence (N.Y. Rangers)
Howie Morenz, centre (Montreal)
Bill Cook, right wing (N.Y. Rangers)
Harvey Jackson, left wing (Toronto)
Lester Patrick, coach (N.Y. Rangers)
Second Team
Roy Worters, goal (N.Y. Americans)
Sylvio Mantha, defence (Montreal)
King Clancy, defence (Toronto)
Hooley Smith, centre (Maroons)
Charlie Conacher, right wing (Toronto)
Aurel Joliat, left wing (Montreal)
Dick Irvin, coach (Toronto)

1932–33
First Team
John Ross Roach, goal (Detroit)
Eddie Shore, defence (Boston)
Ivan Johnson, defence (N.Y. Rangers)
Frank Boucher, centre (N.Y. Rangers)
Bill Cook, right wing (N.Y. Rangers)
Baldy Northcott, left wing (Maroons)
Lester Patrick, coach (N.Y. Rangers)

Second Team
Chuck Gardiner, goal (Chicago)
King Clancy, defence (Toronto)
Lionel Conacher, defence (Maroons)
Howie Morenz, centre (Montreal)
Charlie Conacher, right wing (Toronto)
Harvey Jackson, left wing (Toronto)
Dick Irvin, coach (Toronto)

1933–34
First Team
Chuck Gardiner, goal (Chicago)
King Clancy, defence (Toronto)
Lionel Conacher, defence (Chicago)
Frank Boucher, centre (N.Y. Rangers)
Charlie Conacher, right wing (Toronto)
Harvey Jackson, left wing (Toronto)
Lester Patrick, coach (N.Y. Rangers)
Second Team
Roy Worters, goal (N.Y. Americans)
Eddie Shore, defence (Boston)
Ivan Johnson, defence (N.Y. Rangers)
Joe Primeau, centre (Toronto)
Bill Cook, right wing (N.Y. Rangers)
Aurel Joliat, left wing (Montreal)
Dick Irvin, coach (Toronto)

1934–35
First Team
Lorne Chabot, goal (Chicago)
Eddie Shore, defence (Boston)
Earl Seibert, defence (N.Y. Rangers)
Frank Boucher, centre (N.Y. Rangers)
Charlie Conacher, right wing (Toronto)
Harvey Jackson, left wing (Toronto)
Lester Patrick, coach (N.Y. Rangers)
Second Team
Tiny Thompson, goal (Boston)
Cy Wentworth, defence (Maroons)
Art Coulter, defence (Chicago)
Cooney Weiland, centre (Detroit)
Dit Clapper, right wing (Boston)
Aurel Joliat, left wing (Montreal)
Dick Irvin, coach (Toronto)

1935–36
First Team
Tiny Thompson, goal (Boston)
Eddie Shore, defence (Boston)
Babe Siebert, defence (Boston)
Hooley Smith, centre (Maroons)
Charlie Conacher, right wing (Toronto)
Sweeney Schriner, left wing (N.Y. Americans)
Lester Patrick, coach (N.Y. Rangers)
Second Team
Wilf Cude, goal (Montreal)
Earl Seibert, defence (Chicago)
Ebbie Goodfellow, defence (Detroit)
Bill Thoms, centre (Toronto)
Cecil Dillon, right wing (N.Y. Rangers)
Paul Thompson, left wing (Chicago)
Tommy Gorman, coach (Maroons)

1936–37
First Team
Normie Smith, goal (Detroit)
Babe Siebert, defence (Montreal)
Ebbie Goodfellow, defence (Detroit)
Marty Barry, centre (Detroit)
Larry Aurie, right wing (Detroit)
Harvey Jackson, left wing (Toronto)
Jack Adams, coach (Detroit)
Second Team
Wilf Cude, goal (Montreal)
Earl Seibert, defence (Chicago)
Lionel Conacher, defence (Maroons)
Art Chapman, centre (N.Y. Americans)
Cecil Dillon, right wing (N.Y. Rangers)
Sweeney Schriner, left wing (N.Y. Americans)
Cecil Hart, coach (Montreal)

1937–38
First Team
Tiny Thompson, goal (Boston)
Eddie Shore, defence (Boston)
Babe Siebert, defence (Montreal)
Bill Cowley, centre (Boston)
Cecil Dillon, right wing (N.Y. Rangers)*
Gord Drillon, right wing (Toronto)*
Paul Thompson, left wing (Chicago)
Lester Patrick, coach (N.Y. Rangers)
* tied

Second Team

Dave Kerr, goal (N.Y. Rangers)
Art Coulter, defence (N.Y. Rangers)
Earl Seibert, defence (Chicago)
Syl Apps, centre (Toronto)
Toe Blake, left wing (Montreal)
Art Ross, coach (Boston)

1938–39
First Team

Frank Brimsek, goal (Boston)
Eddie Shore, defence (Boston)
Dit Clapper, defence (Boston)
Syl Apps, centre (Toronto)
Gord Drillon, right wing (Toronto)
Toe Blake, left wing (Montreal)
Art Ross, coach (Boston)

Second Team

Earl Robertson, goal (N.Y. Americans)
Earl Seibert, defence (Chicago)
Art Coulter, defence (N.Y. Rangers)
Neil Colville, centre (N.Y. Rangers)
Bobby Bauer, right wing (Boston)
Johnny Gottselig, left wing (Chicago)
Red Dutton, coach (N.Y. Americans)

1939–40
First Team

Dave Kerr, goal (N.Y. Rangers)
Dit Clapper, defence (Boston)
Ebbie Goodfellow, defence (Detroit)
Milt Schmidt, centre (Boston)
Bryan Hextall, right wing (N.Y. Rangers)
Toe Blake, left wing (Montreal)
Paul Thompson, coach (Chicago)

Second Team

Frank Brimsek, goal (Boston)
Art Coulter, defence (N.Y. Rangers)
Earl Seibert, defence (Chicago)
Neil Colville, centre (N.Y. Rangers)
Bobby Bauer, right wing (Boston)
Woody Dumart, left wing (Boston)
Frank Boucher, coach (N.Y. Rangers)

1940–41
First Team

Turk Broda, goal (Toronto)
Dit Clapper, defence (Boston)
Wally Stanowski, defence (Toronto)
Bill Cowley, centre (Boston)
Bryan Hextall, right wing (N.Y. Rangers)
Sweeney Schriner, left wing (Toronto)
Cooney Weiland, coach (Boston)

Second Team

Frank Brimsek, goal (Boston)
Earl Seibert, defence (Chicago)
Ott Heller, defence (N.Y. Rangers)
Syl Apps, centre (Toronto)
Bobby Bauer, right wing (Boston)
Woody Dumart, left wing (Boston)
Dick Irvin, coach (Montreal)

1941–42
First Team

Frank Brimsek, goal (Boston)
Earl Seibert, defence (Chicago)
Tom Anderson, defence (Brooklyn)
Syl Apps, centre (Toronto)
Bryan Hextall, right wing (N.Y. Rangers)
Lynn Patrick, left wing (N.Y. Rangers)
Frank Boucher, coach (N.Y. Rangers)

Second Team

Turk Broda, goal (Toronto)
Pat Egan, defence (Brooklyn)
Bucko McDonald, defence (Toronto)
Phil Watson, centre (N.Y. Rangers)
Gord Drillon, right wing (Toronto)
Sid Abel, left wing (Detroit)
Paul Thompson, coach (Chicago)

1942–43
First Team

Johnny Mowers, goal (Detroit)
Earl Seibert, defence (Chicago)
Jack Stewart, defence (Detroit)
Bill Cowley, centre (Boston)
Lorne Carr, right wing (Toronto)
Doug Bentley, left wing (Chicago)
Jack Adams, coach (Detroit)

Second Team

Frank Brimsek, goal (Boston)
Jack Crawford, defence (Boston)
Flash Hollett, defence (Boston)
Syl Apps, centre (Toronto)
Bryan Hextall, right wing (N.Y. Rangers)
Lynn Patrick, left wing (N.Y. Rangers)
Art Ross, coach (Boston)

1943–44
First Team

Bill Durnan, goal (Montreal)
Earl Seibert, defence (Chicago)
Babe Pratt, defence (Toronto)
Bill Cowley, centre (Boston)
Lorne Carr, right wing (Toronto)
Doug Bentley, left wing (Chicago)
Dick Irvin, coach (Montreal)

Second Team

Paul Bibeault, goal (Toronto)
Butch Bouchard, defence (Montreal)
Dit Clapper, defence (Boston)
Elmer Lach, centre (Montreal)
Maurice Richard, right wing (Montreal)
Herb Cain, left wing (Boston)
Happy Day, coach (Toronto)

1944–45
First Team

Bill Durnan, goal (Montreal)
Butch Bouchard, defence (Montreal)
Flash Hollett, defence (Detroit)
Elmer Lach, centre (Montreal)
Maurice Richard, right wing (Montreal)
Toe Blake, left wing (Montreal)
Dick Irvin, coach (Montreal)

Second Team

Mike Karakas, goal (Chicago)
Glen Harmon, defence (Montreal)
Babe Pratt, defence (Toronto)
Bill Cowley, centre (Boston)
Bill Mosienko, right wing (Chicago)
Syd Howe, left wing (Detroit)
Jack Adams, coach (Detroit)

1945–46
First Team

Bill Durnan, goal (Montreal)
Jack Crawford, defence (Boston)
Butch Bouchard, defence (Montreal)
Max Bentley, centre (Chicago)
Maurice Richard, right wing (Montreal)
Gaye Stewart, left wing (Toronto)
Dick Irvin, coach (Montreal)

Second Team

Frank Brimsek, goal (Boston)
Ken Reardon, defence (Montreal)
Jack Stewart, defence (Detroit)
Elmer Lach, centre (Montreal)
Bill Mosienko, right wing (Chicago)
Toe Blake, left wing (Montreal)
Johnny Gottselig, coach (Chicago)

1946–47
First Team

Bill Durnan, goal (Montreal)
Ken Reardon, defence (Montreal)
Butch Bouchard, defence (Montreal)
Milt Schmidt, centre (Boston)
Maurice Richard, right wing (Montreal)
Doug Bentley, left wing (Chicago)

Second Team

Frank Brimsek, goal (Boston)
Jack Stewart, defence (Detroit)
Bill Quackenbush, defence (Detroit)
Max Bentley, centre (Chicago)
Bobby Bauer, right wing (Boston)
Woody Dumart, left wing (Boston)

1947–48
First Team

Turk Broda, goal (Toronto)
Bill Quackenbush, defence (Detroit)
Jack Stewart, defence (Detroit)
Elmer Lach, centre (Montreal)
Maurice Richard, right wing (Montreal)
Ted Lindsay, left wing (Detroit)

Second Team
Frank Brimsek, goal (Boston)
Ken Reardon, defence (Montreal)
Neil Colville, defence (N.Y. Rangers)
Buddy O'Connor, centre (N.Y. Rangers)
Bud Poile, right wing (Chicago)
Gaye Stewart, left wing (Chicago)

1948–49
First Team
Bill Durnan, goal (Montreal)
Bill Quackenbush, defence (Detroit)
Jack Stewart, defence (Detroit)
Sid Abel, centre (Detroit)
Maurice Richard, right wing (Montreal)
Roy Conacher, left wing (Chicago)
Second Team
Chuck Rayner, goal (N.Y. Rangers)
Glen Harmon, defence (Montreal)
Ken Reardon, defence (Montreal)
Doug Bentley, centre (Chicago)
Gordie Howe, right wing (Detroit)
Ted Lindsay, left wing (Detroit)

1949–50
First Team
Bill Durnan, goal (Montreal)
Gus Mortson, defence (Toronto)
Ken Reardon, defence (Montreal)
Sid Abel, centre (Detroit)
Maurice Richard, right wing (Montreal)
Ted Lindsay, left wing (Detroit)
Second Team
Chuck Rayner, goal (N.Y. Rangers)
Leo Reise, Jr., defence (Detroit)
Red Kelly, defence (Detroit)
Ted Kennedy, centre (Toronto)
Gordie Howe, right wing (Detroit)
Tony Leswick, left wing (N.Y. Rangers)

1950–51
First Team
Terry Sawchuk, goal (Detroit)
Red Kelly, defence (Detroit)
Bill Quackenbush, defence (Boston)
Milt Schmidt, centre (Boston)
Gordie Howe, right wing (Detroit)
Ted Lindsay, left wing (Detroit)
Second Team
Chuck Rayner, goal (N.Y. Rangers)
Jim Thomson, defence (Toronto)
Leo Reise, Jr., defence (Detroit)
Sid Abel, centre (Detroit)*
Ted Kennedy, centre (Toronto)*
Maurice Richard, right wing (Montreal)
Sid Smith, left wing (Toronto)
*tied

1951–52
First Team
Terry Sawchuk, goal (Detroit)
Red Kelly, defence (Detroit)
Doug Harvey, defence (Montreal)
Elmer Lach, centre (Montreal)
Gordie Howe, right wing (Detroit)
Ted Lindsay, left wing (Detroit)
Second Team
Sugar Jim Henry, goal (Boston)
Hy Buller, defence (N.Y. Rangers)
Jim Thomson, defence (Toronto)
Milt Schmidt, centre (Boston)
Maurice Richard, right wing (Montreal)
Sid Smith, left wing (Toronto)

1952–53
First Team
Terry Sawchuk, goal (Detroit)
Red Kelly, defence (Detroit)
Doug Harvey, defence (Montreal)
Fleming Mackell, centre (Boston)
Gordie Howe, right wing (Detroit)
Ted Lindsay, left wing (Detroit)
Second Team
Gerry McNeil, goal (Montreal)
Bill Quackenbush, defence (Boston)
Bill Gadsby, defence (Chicago)
Alex Delvecchio, centre (Detroit)
Maurice Richard, right wing (Montreal)
Bert Olmstead, left wing (Montreal)

1953–54
First Team
Harry Lumley, goal (Toronto)
Red Kelly, defence (Detroit)
Doug Harvey, defence (Montreal)
Ken Mosdell, centre (Montreal)
Gordie Howe, right wing (Detroit)
Ted Lindsay, left wing (Detroit)
Second Team
Terry Sawchuk, goal (Detroit)
Bill Gadsby, defence (Chicago)
Tim Horton, defence (Toronto)
Ted Kennedy, centre (Toronto)
Maurice Richard, right wing (Montreal)
Ed Sandford, left wing (Boston)

1954–55
First Team
Harry Lumley, goal (Toronto)
Doug Harvey, defence (Montreal)
Red Kelly, defence (Detroit)
Jean Béliveau, centre (Montreal)
Maurice Richard, right wing (Montreal)
Sid Smith, left wing (Toronto)

Second Team
Terry Sawchuk, goal (Detroit)
Bob Goldham, defence (Detroit)
Fern Flaman, defence (Boston)
Ken Mosdell, centre (Montreal)
Bernie Geoffrion, right wing (Montreal)
Danny Lewicki, left wing (N.Y. Rangers)

1955–56
First Team
Jacques Plante, goal (Montreal)
Doug Harvey, defence (Montreal)
Bill Gadsby, defence (N.Y. Rangers)
Jean Béliveau, centre (Montreal)
Maurice Richard, right wing (Montreal)
Ted Lindsay, left wing (Detroit)
Second Team
Glenn Hall, goal (Detroit)
Red Kelly, defence (Detroit)
Tom Johnson, defence (Montreal)
Tod Sloan, centre (Toronto)
Gordie Howe, right wing (Detroit)
Bert Olmstead, left wing (Montreal)

1956–57
First Team
Glenn Hall, goal (Detroit)
Doug Harvey, defence (Montreal)
Red Kelly, defence (Detroit)
Jean Béliveau, centre (Montreal)
Gordie Howe, right wing (Detroit)
Ted Lindsay, left wing (Detroit)
Second Team
Jacques Plante, goal (Montreal)
Fern Flaman, defence (Boston)
Bill Gadsby, defence (N.Y. Rangers)
Ed Litzenberger, centre (Chicago)
Maurice Richard, right wing (Montreal)
Real Chevrefils, left wing (Boston)

1957–58
First Team
Glenn Hall, goal (Chicago)
Doug Harvey, defence (Montreal)
Bill Gadsby, defence (N.Y. Rangers)
Henri Richard, centre (Montreal)
Gordie Howe, right wing (Detroit)
Dickie Moore, left wing (Montreal)
Second Team
Jacques Plante, goal (Montreal)
Fern Flaman, defence (Boston)
Marcel Pronovost, defence (Detroit)
Jean Béliveau, centre (Montreal)
Andy Bathgate, right wing (N.Y. Rangers)
Camille Henry, left wing (N.Y. Rangers)

1958–59
First Team

Jacques Plante, goal (Montreal)
Tom Johnson, defence (Montreal)
Bill Gadsby, defence (N.Y. Rangers)
Jean Béliveau, centre (Montreal)
Andy Bathgate, right wing (N.Y. Rangers)
Dickie Moore, left wing (Montreal)

Second Team

Terry Sawchuk, goal (Detroit)
Marcel Pronovost, defence (Detroit)
Doug Harvey, defence (Montreal)
Henri Richard, centre (Montreal)
Gordie Howe, right wing (Detroit)
Alex Delvecchio, left wing (Detroit)

1959–60
First Team

Glenn Hall, goal (Chicago)
Doug Harvey, defence (Montreal)
Marcel Pronovost, defence (Detroit)
Jean Béliveau, centre (Montreal)
Gordie Howe, right wing (Detroit)
Bobby Hull, left wing (Chicago)

Second Team

Jacques Plante, goal (Montreal)
Allan Stanley, defence (Toronto)
Pierre Pilote, defence (Chicago)
Bronco Horvath, centre (Boston)
Bernie Geoffrion, right wing (Montreal)
Dean Prentice, left wing (N.Y. Rangers)

1960–61
First Team

Johnny Bower, goal (Toronto)
Doug Harvey, defence (Montreal)
Marcel Pronovost, defence (Detroit)
Jean Béliveau, centre (Montreal)
Bernie Geoffrion, right wing (Montreal)
Frank Mahovlich, left wing (Toronto)

Second Team

Glenn Hall, goal (Chicago)
Allan Stanley, defence (Toronto)
Pierre Pilote, defence (Chicago)
Henri Richard, centre (Montreal)
Gordie Howe, right wing (Detroit)
Dickie Moore, left wing (Montreal)

1961–62
First Team

Jacques Plante, goal (Montreal)
Doug Harvey, defence (N.Y. Rangers)
Jean-Guy Talbot, defence (N.Y. Rangers)
Stan Mikita, centre (Chicago)
Andy Bathgate, right wing (N.Y. Rangers)
Bobby Hull, left wing (Chicago)

Second Team

Glenn Hall, goal (Chicago)
Carl Brewer, defence (Toronto)
Pierre Pilote, defence (Chicago)
Dave Keon, centre (Toronto)
Gordie Howe, right wing (Detroit)
Frank Mahovlich, left wing (Toronto)

1962–63
First Team

Glenn Hall, goal (Chicago)
Pierre Pilote, defence (Chicago)
Carl Brewer, defence (Toronto)
Stan Mikita, centre (Chicago)
Gordie Howe, right wing (Detroit)
Frank Mahovlich, left wing (Toronto)

Second Team

Terry Sawchuk, goal (Detroit)
Tim Horton, defence (Toronto)
Elmer Vasko, defence (Chicago)
Henri Richard, centre (Montreal)
Andy Bathgate, right wing (N.Y. Rangers)
Bobby Hull, left wing (Chicago)

1963–64
First Team

Glenn Hall, goal (Chicago)
Pierre Pilote, defence (Chicago)
Tim Horton, defence (Toronto)
Stan Mikita, centre (Chicago)
Ken Wharram, right wing (Chicago)
Bobby Hull, left wing (Chicago)

Second Team

Charlie Hodge, goal (Montreal)
Elmer Vasko, defence (Chicago)
Jacques Laperrière, defence (Montreal)
Jean Béliveau, centre (Montreal)
Gordie Howe, right wing (Detroit)
Frank Mahovlich, left wing (Toronto)

1964–65
First Team

Roger Crozier, goal (Detroit)
Pierre Pilote, defence (Chicago)
Jacques Laperrière, defence (Montreal)
Norm Ullman, centre (Detroit)
Claude Provost, right wing (Montreal)
Bobby Hull, left wing (Chicago)

Second Team

Charlie Hodge, goal (Montreal)
Bill Gadsby, defence (Detroit)
Carl Brewer, defence (Toronto)
Stan Mikita, centre (Chicago)
Gordie Howe, right wing (Detroit)
Frank Mahovlich, left wing (Toronto)

1965–66
First Team

Glenn Hall, goal (Chicago)
Jacques Laperrière, defence (Montreal)
Pierre Pilote, defence (Chicago)
Stan Mikita, centre (Chicago)
Gordie Howe, right wing (Detroit)
Bobby Hull, left wing (Chicago)

Second Team

Gump Worsley, goal (Montreal)
Allan Stanley, defence (Toronto)
Pat Stapleton, defence (Chicago)
Jean Béliveau, centre (Montreal)
Bobby Rousseau, right wing (Montreal)
Frank Mahovlich, left wing (Toronto)

1966–67
First Team

Ed Giacomin, goal (N.Y. Rangers)
Pierre Pilote, defence (Chicago)
Harry Howell, defence (N.Y. Rangers)
Stan Mikita, centre (Chicago)
Ken Wharram, right wing (Chicago)
Bobby Hull, left wing (Chicago)

Second Team

Glenn Hall, goal (Chicago)
Tim Horton, defence (Toronto)
Bobby Orr, defence (Boston)
Norm Ullman, centre (Detroit)
Gordie Howe, right wing (Detroit)
Don Marshall, left wing (N.Y. Rangers)

1967–68
First Team

Gump Worsley, goal (Montreal)
Bobby Orr, defence (Boston)
Tim Horton, defence (Toronto)
Stan Mikita, centre (Chicago)
Gordie Howe, right wing (Detroit)
Bobby Hull, left wing (Chicago)

Second Team

Ed Giacomin, goal (N.Y. Rangers)
J.C. Tremblay, defence (Montreal)
Jim Neilson, defence (N.Y. Rangers)
Phil Esposito, centre (Boston)
Rod Gilbert, right wing (N.Y. Rangers)
Johnny Bucyk, left wing (Boston)

1968–69
First Team

Glenn Hall, goal (St. Louis)
Bobby Orr, defence (Boston)
Tim Horton, defence (Toronto)
Phil Esposito, centre (Boston)
Gordie Howe, right wing (Detroit)
Bobby Hull, left wing (Chicago)

Second Team

Ed Giacomin, goal (N.Y. Rangers)
Ted Green, defence (Boston)
Ted Harris, defence (Montreal)
Jean Béliveau, centre (Montreal)
Yvan Cournoyer, right wing (Montreal)
Frank Mahovlich, left wing (Detroit)

1969–70
First Team

Tony Esposito, goal (Chicago)
Bobby Orr, defence (Boston)
Brad Park, defence (N.Y. Rangers)
Phil Esposito, centre (Boston)
Gordie Howe, right wing (Detroit)
Bobby Hull, left wing (Chicago)

Second Team

Ed Giacomin, goal (N.Y. Rangers)
Carl Brewer, defence (Detroit)
Jacques Laperrière, defence (Montreal)
Stan Mikita, centre (Chicago)
John McKenzie, right wing (Boston)
Frank Mahovlich, left wing (Detroit)

1970–71
First Team

Ed Giacomin, goal (N.Y. Rangers)
Bobby Orr, defence (Boston)
J.C. Tremblay, defence (Montreal)
Phil Esposito, centre (Boston)
Ken Hodge, right wing (Boston)
Johnny Bucyk, left wing (Boston)

Second Team

Jacques Plante, goal (Toronto)
Brad Park, defence (N.Y. Rangers)
Pat Stapleton, defence (Chicago)
Dave Keon, centre (Toronto)
Yvan Cournoyer, right wing (Montreal)
Bobby Hull, left wing (Chicago)

1971–72
First Team

Tony Esposito, goal (Chicago)
Bobby Orr, defence (Boston)
Brad Park, defence (N.Y. Rangers)
Phil Esposito, centre (Boston)
Rod Gilbert, right wing (N.Y. Rangers)
Bobby Hull, left wing (Chicago)

Second Team

Ken Dryden, goal (Montreal)
Bill White, defence (Chicago)
Pat Stapleton, defence (Chicago)
Jean Ratelle, centre (N.Y. Rangers)
Yvan Cournoyer, right wing (Montreal)
Vic Hadfield, left wing (N.Y. Rangers)

1972–73
First Team

Ken Dryden, goal (Montreal)
Bobby Orr, defence (Boston)
Guy Lapointe, defence (Montreal)
Phil Esposito, centre (Boston)
Mickey Redmond, right wing (Detroit)
Frank Mahovlich, left wing (Montreal)

Second Team

Tony Esposito, goal (Chicago)
Brad Park, defence (N.Y. Rangers)
Bill White, defence (Chicago)
Bobby Clarke, centre (Philadelphia)
Yvan Cournoyer, right wing (Montreal)
Dennis Hull, left wing (Chicago)

1973–74
First Team

Bernie Parent, goal (Philadelphia)
Bobby Orr, defence (Boston)
Brad Park, defence (N.Y. Rangers)
Phil Esposito, centre (Boston)
Ken Hodge, right wing (Boston)
Rick Martin, left wing (Buffalo)

Second Team

Tony Esposito, goal (Chicago)
Bill White, defence (Chicago)
Barry Ashbee, defence (Philadelphia)
Bobby Clarke, centre (Philadelphia)
Mickey Redmond, right wing (Detroit)
Wayne Cashman, left wing (Boston)

1974–75
First Team

Bernie Parent, goal (Philadelphia)
Bobby Orr, defence (Boston)
Denis Potvin, defence (N.Y. Islanders)
Bobby Clarke, centre (Philadelphia)
Guy Lafleur, right wing (Montreal)
Rick Martin, left wing (Buffalo)

Second Team

Rogie Vachon, goal (Los Angeles)
Guy Lapointe, defence (Montreal)
Borje Salming, defence (Toronto)
Phil Esposito, centre (Boston)
René Robert, right wing (Buffalo)
Steve Vickers, left wing (N.Y. Rangers)

1975–76
First Team

Ken Dryden, goal (Montreal)
Denis Potvin, defence (N.Y. Islanders)
Brad Park, defence (Boston)
Bobby Clarke, centre (Philadelphia)
Guy Lafleur, right wing (Montreal)
Bill Barber, left wing (Philadelphia)

Second Team

Glenn Resch, goal (N.Y. Islanders)
Borje Salming, defence (Toronto)
Guy Lapointe, defence (Montreal)
Gil Perreault, centre (Buffalo)
Reggie Leach, right wing (Philadelphia)
Rick Martin, left wing (Buffalo)

1976–77
First Team

Ken Dryden, goal (Montreal)
Larry Robinson, defence (Montreal)
Borje Salming, defence (Toronto)
Marcel Dionne, centre (Los Angeles)
Guy Lafleur, right wing (Montreal)
Steve Shutt, left wing (Montreal)

Second Team

Rogie Vachon, goal (Los Angeles)
Denis Potvin, defence (N.Y. Islanders)
Guy Lapointe, defence (Montreal)
Gil Perreault, centre (Buffalo)
Lanny McDonald, right wing (Toronto)
Rick Martin, left wing (Buffalo)

1977–78
First Team

Ken Dryden, goal (Montreal)
Denis Potvin, defence (N.Y. Islanders)
Brad Park, defence (Boston)
Bryan Trottier, centre (N.Y. Islanders)
Guy Lafleur, right wing (Montreal)
Clark Gillies, left wing (N.Y. Islanders)

Second Team

Don Edwards, goal (Buffalo)
Larry Robinson, defence (Montreal)
Borje Salming, defence (Toronto)
Darryl Sittler, centre (Toronto)
Mike Bossy, right wing (N.Y. Islanders)
Steve Shutt, left wing (Montreal)

1978–79
First Team

Ken Dryden, goal (Montreal)
Denis Potvin, defence (N.Y. Islanders)
Larry Robinson, defence (Montreal)
Bryan Trottier, centre (N.Y. Islanders)
Guy Lafleur, right wing (Montreal)
Clark Gillies, left wing (N.Y. Islanders)

Second Team

Glenn Resch, goal (N.Y. Islanders)
Borje Salming, defence (Toronto)
Serge Savard, defence (Montreal)
Marcel Dionne, centre (Los Angeles)
Mike Bossy, right wing (N.Y. Islanders)
Bill Barber, left wing (Philadelphia)

1979–80
First Team
Tony Esposito, goal (Chicago)
Larry Robinson, defence (Montreal)
Ray Bourque, defence (Boston)
Marcel Dionne, centre (Los Angeles)
Guy Lafleur, right wing (Montreal)
Charlie Simmer, left wing (Los Angeles)
Second Team
Don Edwards, goal (Buffalo)
Borje Salming, defence (Toronto)
Jim Schoenfeld, defence (Buffalo)
Wayne Gretzky, centre (Edmonton)
Danny Gare, right wing (Buffalo)
Steve Shutt, left wing (Montreal)

1980–81
First Team
Mike Liut, goal (St. Louis)
Denis Potvin, defence (N.Y. Islanders)
Randy Carlyle, defence (Pittsburgh)
Wayne Gretzky, centre (Edmonton)
Mike Bossy, right wing (N.Y. Islanders)
Charlie Simmer, left wing (Los Angeles)
Second Team
Mario Lessard, goal (Los Angeles)
Larry Robinson, defence (Montreal)
Ray Bourque, defence (Boston)
Marcel Dionne, centre (Los Angeles)
Dave Taylor, right wing (Los Angeles)
Bill Barber, left wing (Philadelphia)

1981–82
First Team
Billy Smith, goal (N.Y. Islanders)
Doug Wilson, defence (Chicago)
Ray Bourque, defence (Boston)
Wayne Gretzky, centre (Edmonton)
Mike Bossy, right wing (N.Y. Islanders)
Mark Messier, left wing (Edmonton)
Second Team
Grant Fuhr, goal (Edmonton)
Paul Coffey, defence (Edmonton)
Brian Engblom, defence (Montreal)
Bryan Trottier, centre (N.Y. Islanders)
Rick Middleton, right wing (Boston)
John Tonelli, left wing (N.Y. Islanders)

1982–83
First Team
Pete Peeters, goal (Boston)
Mark Howe, defence (Philadelphia)
Rod Langway, defence (Washington)
Wayne Gretzky, centre (Edmonton)
Mike Bossy, right wing (N.Y. Islanders)
Mark Messier, left wing (Edmonton)

Second Team
Rollie Melanson, goal (N.Y. Islanders)
Ray Bourque, defence (Boston)
Paul Coffey, defence (Edmonton)
Denis Savard, centre (Chicago)
Lanny McDonald, right wing (Calgary)
Michel Goulet, left wing (Quebec)

1983–84
First Team
Tom Barrasso, goal (Buffalo)
Rod Langway, defence (Washington)
Ray Bourque, defence (Boton)
Wayne Gretzky, centre (Edmonton)
Mike Bossy, right wing (N.Y. Islanders)
Michel Goulet, left wing (Quebec)
Second Team
Pat Riggin, goal (Washington)
Paul Coffey, defence (Edmonton)
Denis Potvin, defence (N.Y. Islanders)
Bryan Trottier, centre (N.Y. Islanders)
Jari Kurri, right wing (Edmonton)
Mark Messier, left wing (Edmonton)

1984–85
First Team
Pelle Lindbergh, goal (Philadelphia)
Paul Coffey, defence (Edmonton)
Ray Bourque, defence (Boston)
Wayne Gretzky, centre (Edmonton)
Jari Kurri, right wing (Edmonton)
John Ogrodnick, left wing (Detroit)
Second Team
Tom Barrasso, goal (Buffalo)
Rod Langway, defence (Washington)
Doug Wilson, defence (Chicago)
Dale Hawerchuk, centre (Winnipeg)
Mike Bossy, right wing (N.Y. Islanders)
John Tonelli, left wing (N.Y. Islanders)

1985–86
First Team
John Vanbiesbrouck, goal (N.Y. Rangers)
Paul Coffey, defence (Edmonton)
Mark Howe, defence (Philadelphia)
Wayne Gretzky, centre (Edmonton)
Mike Bossy, right wing (N.Y. Islanders)
Michel Goulet, left wing (Quebec)
Second Team
Bob Froese, goal (Philadelphia)
Larry Robinson, defence (Montreal)
Ray Bourque, defence (Boston)
Mario Lemieux, centre (Pittsburgh)
Jari Kurri, right wing (Edmonton)
Mats Naslund, left wing (Montreal)

1986–87
First Team
Ron Hextall, goal (Philadelphia)
Ray Bourque, defence (Boston)
Mark Howe, defence (Philadelphia)
Wayne Gretzky, centre (Edmonton)
Jari Kurri, right wing (Edmonton)
Michel Goulet, left wing (Quebec)
Second Team
Mike Liut, goal (Hartford)
Larry Murphy, defence (Washington)
Al MacInnis, defence (Calgary)
Mario Lemieux, centre (Pittsburgh)
Tim Kerr, right wing (Philadelphia)
Luc Robitaille, left wing (Los Angeles)

1987–88
First Team
Grant Fuhr, goal (Edmonton)
Ray Bourque, defence (Boston)
Scott Stevens, defence (Washington)
Mario Lemieux, centre (Pittsburgh)
Hakan Loob, right wing (Calgary)
Luc Robitaille, left wing (Los Angeles)
Second Team
Patrick Roy, goal (Montreal)
Gary Suter, defence (Calgary)
Brad McCrimmon, defence (Calgary)
Wayne Gretzky, centre (Edmonton)
Cam Neely, right wing (Boston)
Michel Goulet, left wing (Quebec)

1988–89
First Team
Patrick Roy, goal (Montreal)
Chris Chelios, defence (Montreal)
Paul Coffey, defence (Pittsburgh)
Mario Lemieux, centre (Pittsburgh)
Joe Mullen, right wing (Calgary)
Luc Robitaille, left wing (Los Angeles)
Second Team
Mike Vernon, goal (Calgary)
Al MacInnis, defence (Calgary)
Ray Bourque, defence (Boston)
Wayne Gretzky, centre (Los Angeles)
Jari Kurri, right wing (Edmonton)
Gerard Gallant, left wing (Detroit)

1989–90
First Team
Patrick Roy, goal (Montreal)
Ray Bourque, defence (Boston)
Al MacInnis, defence (Calgary)
Mark Messier, centre (Edmonton)
Brett Hull, right wing (St. Louis)
Luc Robitaille, left wing (Los Angeles)

Second Team
Daren Puppa, goal (Buffalo)
Paul Coffey, defence (Pittsburgh)
Doug Wilson, defence (Chicago)
Wayne Gretzky, centre (Los Angeles)
Cam Neely, right wing (Boston)
Brian Bellows, left wing (Minnesota)

1990–91
First Team
Ed Belfour, goal (Chicago)
Ray Bourque, defence (Boston)
Al MacInnis, defence (Calgary)
Wayne Gretzky, centre (Los Angeles)
Brett Hull, right wing (St. Louis)
Luc Robitaille, left wing (Los Angeles)
Second Team
Patrick Roy, goal (Montreal)
Chris Chelios, defence (Chicago)
Brian Leetch, defence (N.Y. Rangers)
Adam Oates, centre (St. Louis)
Cam Neely, right wing (Boston)
Kevin Stevens, left wing (Pittsburgh)

1991–92
First Team
Patrick Roy, goal (Montreal)
Brian Leetch, defence (N.Y. Rangers)
Ray Bourque, defence (Boston)
Mark Messier, centre (N.Y. Rangers)
Brett Hull, right wing (St. Louis)
Kevin Stevens, left wing (Pittsburgh)
Second Team
Kirk McLean, goal (Vancouver)
Phil Housley, defence (Winnipeg)
Scott Stevens, defence (New Jersey)
Mario Lemieux, centre (Pittsburgh)
Mark Recchi, right wing (Pittsburgh/Philadelphia)
Luc Robitaille, left wing (Los Angeles)

1992–93
First Team
Ed Belfour, goal (Chicago)
Chris Chelios, defence (Chicago)
Ray Bourque, defence (Boston)
Mario Lemieux, centre (Pittsburgh)
Teemu Selanne, right wing (Winnipeg)
Luc Robitaille, left wing (Los Angeles)
Second Team
Tom Barrasso, goal (Pittsburgh)
Larry Murphy, defence (Pittsburgh)
Al Iafrate, defence (Washington)
Pat LaFontaine, centre (Buffalo)
Alexander Mogilny, right wing (Buffalo)
Kevin Stevens, left wing (Pittsburgh)

1993–94
First Team
Dominik Hasek, goal (Buffalo)
Ray Bourque, defence (Boston)
Scott Stevens, defence (New Jersey)
Sergei Fedorov, centre (Detroit)
Pavel Bure, right wing (Vancouver)
Brendan Shanahan, left wing (St. Louis)
Second Team
John Vanbiesbrouck, goal (Florida)
Al MacInnis, defence (Calgary)
Brian Leetch, defence (N.Y. Rangers)
Wayne Gretzky, centre (Los Aneles)
Cam Neely, right wing (Boston)
Adam Graves, left wing (N.Y. Rangers)

1994–95
First Team
Dominik Hasek, goal (Buffalo)
Paul Coffey, defence (Detroit)
Chris Chelios, defence (Chicago)
Eric Lindros, centre (Philadelphia)
Jaromir Jagr, right wing (Pittsburgh)
John LeClair, left wing (Montreal/Philadelphia)
Second Team
Ed Belfour, goal (Chicago)
Ray Bourque, defence (Boston)
Larry Murphy, defence (Pittsburgh)
Alexei Zhamnov, centre (Winnipeg)
Theoren Fleury, right wing (Calgary)
Keith Tkachuk, left wing (Winnipeg)

1995–96
First Team
Jim Carey, goal (Washington)
Chris Chelios, defence (Chicago)
Ray Bourque, defence (Boston)
Mario Lemieux, centre (Pittsburgh)
Jaromir Jagr, right wing (Pittsburgh)
Paul Kariya, left wing (Anaheim)
Second Team
Chris Osgood, goal (Detroit)
Vladimir Konstantinov, defence (Detroit)
Brian Leetch, defence (N.Y. Rangers)
Eric Lindros, centre (Philadelphia)
Alexander Mogilny, right wing (Vancouver)
John LeClair, left wing (Philadelphia)

1996–97
First Team
Dominik Hasek, goal (Buffalo)
Brian Leetch, defence (N.Y. Rangers)
Sandis Ozolinsh, defence (Avalanche)
Mario Lemieux, centre (Pittsburgh)
Teemu Selanne, right wing (Anaheim)
Paul Kariya, left wing (Anaheim)

Second Team
Martin Brodeur, goal (New Jersey)
Chris Chelios, defence (Chicago)
Scott Stevens, defence (New Jersey)
Wayne Gretzky, centre (N.Y. Rangers)
Jaromir Jagr, right wing (Pittsburgh)
John LeClair, left wing (Philadelphia)

1997–98
First Team
Dominik Hasek, goal (Buffalo)
Nicklas Lidstrom, defence (Detroit)
Rob Blake, defence (Los Angeles)
Peter Forsberg, centre (Avalanche)
Jaromir Jagr, right wing (Pittsburgh)
John LeClair, left wing (Philadelphia)
Second Team
Martin Brodeur, goal (New Jersey)
Chris Pronger, defence (St. Louis)
Scott Niedermayer, defence (New Jersey)
Wayne Gretzky, centre (N.Y. Rangers)
Teemu Selanne, right wing (Anaheim)
Keith Tkachuk, left wing (Phoenix)

1998–99
First Team
Dominik Hasek, goal (Buffalo)
Al MacInnis, defence (St. Louis)
Nicklas Lidstrom, defence (Detroit)
Peter Forsberg, centre (Avalanche)
Jaromir Jagr, right wing (Pittsburgh)
Paul Kariya, left wing (Anaheim)
Second Team
Byron Dafoe, goal (Boston)
Ray Bourque, defence (Boston)
Eric Desjardins, defence (Philadelphia)
Alexei Yashin, centre (Ottawa)
Teemu Selanne, right wing (Anaheim)
John LeClair, left wing (Philadelphia)

1999–2000
First Team
Olaf Kolzig, goal (Washington)
Chris Pronger, defence (St. Louis)
Nicklas Lidstrom, defence (Detroit)
Steve Yzerman, centre (Detroit)
Jaromir Jagr, right wing (Pittsburgh)
Brendan Shanahan, left wing (Detroit)
Second Team
Roman Turek, goal (St. Louis)
Rob Blake, defence (Los Angeles)
Eric Desjardins, defence (Philadelphia)
Mike Modano, centre (Dallas)
Pavel Bure, right wing (Florida)
Paul Kariya, left wing (Anaheim)

All–Star
Game Records

TEAM	GP	W	L	T
NHL All–Stars	22	11	8	3
Wales Conference All–Stars	17	12	5	0
Campbell Conference All–Stars	17	5	12	0
Montreal Canadiens	9	3	5	1
Toronto Maple Leafs	8	3	4	1
Eastern All–Stars	6	3	2	1
Western All–Stars	6	2	3	1
East Division All–Stars	3	3	0	0
Detroit Red Wings	3	2	0	1
West Division All–Stars	3	0	3	0
North America All–Stars	3	2	1	0
World All–Stars	3	1	2	0
First All–Stars	2	0	0	2
Second All–Stars	2	0	0	2
Chicago Blackhawks	1	0	1	0
Montreal All–Stars	1	0	1	0

All Goals Records

MOST GOALS, BOTH TEAMS, ONE GAME

22	Wales 16, Campbell 6, February 6, 1993 at Montreal
19	Wales 12, Campbell 7, January 21, 1990 at Pittsburgh
18	Eastern 11, Western 7, January 18, 1997 at San Jose

MOST GOALS, ONE TEAM, ONE GAME

16	Wales, February 6, 1993 at Montreal
12	Wales, January 21, 1990 at Pittsburgh
11	Eastern, January 18, 1997 at San Jose
11	Campbell, January 19, 1991 at Chicago

FEWEST GOALS, BOTH TEAMS, ONE GAME

2	NHL All–Stars 1, Montreal 1, October 9, 1956 at Montreal
3	West 2, East 1, January 19, 1971 at Boston
3	Montreal 3, NHL All–Stars 0, January 18, 1967 at Montreal
3	NHL All–Stars 2, Montreal 1, October 1, 1960 at Montreal

MOST GOALS, BOTH TEAMS, ONE PERIOD

10	Eastern 6, Western 4, 2nd period, January 18, 1997 at San Jose
9	Wales 7, Campbell 2, 1st period, January 21, 1990 at Pittsburgh

MOST GOALS, ONE TEAM, ONE PERIOD

7	Wales, 1st period, January 21, 1990 at Pittsburgh
6	Campbell, 3rd period, February 8, 1983 at Long Island
6	Campbell, 2nd period, January 18, 1992 at Philadelphia
6	Wales, 1st period, February 6, 1993 at Montreal
6	Wales, 2nd period, February 6, 1993 at Montreal
6	Eastern, 2nd period, January 18, 1997 at San Jose

Shots Records

MOST SHOTS, BOTH TEAMS, ONE GAME

102	Eastern 56, Western 46, January 22, 1994 at New York
90	Wales 49, Campbell 41, February 6, 1993 at Montreal
87	Western 46, Eastern 41, January 18, 1997 at San Jose
87	Wales 45, Campbell 42, January 21, 1990 at Pittsburgh

FEWEST SHOTS, BOTH TEAMS, ONE GAME

52	Wales 40, Campbell 12, January 24, 1978 at Buffalo
53	NHL All–Stars 27, Montreal 26, October 1, 1960 at Montreal
55	West 28, East 27, January 19, 1971 at Boston
55	NHL All–Stars 28, Montreal 27, October 9, 1956 at Montreal

MOST SHOTS, ONE TEAM, ONE GAME

56	Eastern, January 22, 1994 at New York
49	Wales, February 6, 1993 at Montreal
48	World, February 6, 2000 at Toronto
46	Western, January 18, 1997 at San Jose
46	Western, January 22, 1994 at New York

FEWEST SHOTS, ONE TEAM, ONE GAME

12	Campbell, January 24, 1978 at Buffalo
17	West, January 20, 1970 at St. Louis
23	Chicago, October 7, 1961 at Chicago

MOST SHOTS, BOTH TEAMS, ONE PERIOD

39	Western 21, Eastern 18, 2nd period, January 22, 1994 at New York
36	Eastern 19, Western 17, 1st period, January 22, 1994 at New York
	Campbell 22, Wales 14, 3rd period, January 21, 1990 at Pittsburgh

FEWEST SHOTS, BOTH TEAMS, ONE PERIOD

9	Wales 5, Campbell 4, 2nd period, February 5, 1980 at Detroit
9	West 7, East 2, 3rd period, January 19, 1971 at Boston
13	Wales 7 Campbell 6, 3rd period, February 9, 1982 at Washington

MOST SHOTS, ONE TEAM, ONE PERIOD

22	Wales, 1st period, February 6, 1993 at Montreal
	Wales, 3rd period, January 19, 1991 at Chicago
	Campbell, 3rd period, January 21, 1990 at Pittsburgh

FEWEST SHOTS, ONE TEAM, ONE PERIOD

2	Campbell, 2nd period, January 24, 1978 at Buffalo
	East, 3rd period, January 19, 1971 at Boston
3	Campbell, 3rd period, January 24, 1978 at Buffalo

MOST POWER-PLAY GOALS, BOTH TEAMS, ONE GAME

3	Montreal 2, NHL All–Stars 1, October 4, 1958 at Montreal
	Detroit 2, NHL All–Stars 1, October 2, 1954 at Detroit
	NHL All–Stars 2, Montreal 1, October 3, 1953 at Montreal

MOST POWER-PLAY GOALS, BOTH TEAMS, ONE PERIOD

2	All–Stars 1, Montreal 1, 3rd period, October 4, 1958 at Montreal
	All–Stars 1, Toronto 1, 1st period, October 6, 1962 at Toronto
	Wales 1, Campbell 1, 3rd period, February 4, 1986 at Hartford

MOST POWER-PLAY GOALS, ONE TEAM, ONE GAME

2	All–Stars, October 3, 1953 at Montreal
	Detroit, October 2, 1954 at Detroit
	Montreal, October 4, 1958 at Montreal
	All–Stars, October 5, 1963 at Toronto
	Wales, January 19, 1991 at Chicago

MOST POWER-PLAY GOALS, ONE TEAM, ONE PERIOD

2	All–Stars, 1st period, October 3, 1953 at Montreal
	Detroit, 1st period, October 2, 1954 at Detroit
	All–Stars, 1st period, October 5, 1963 at Toronto
	Wales, 3rd period, January 19, 1991 at Chicago

SHORT-HANDED GOALS

No team or player has ever scored more than one short-handed goal in a period or game. In fact, only nine such goals have been scored in All–Star Game history:

Ted Lindsay, October 8, 1950 at Detroit
Allan Stanley, October 5, 1957 at Montreal
Don Marshall, October 4, 1958 at Montreal
Andy Hebenton, October 1, 1960 at Montreal
Gordie Howe, October 20, 1965 at Montreal
Stan Mikita, January 16, 1968 at Toronto
Garry Unger, January 29, 1974 at Chicago
Bill Barber, February 10, 1981 at Los Angeles
Kirk Muller, January 21, 1990 at Pittsburgh

EMPTY-NET GOALS

NHL All–Stars, Alex Delvecchio (unassisted) 19:27, October 3, 1953 at Montreal
Detroit, Earl Reibel (Goldham, Lindsay) 19:33, October 2, 1955 at Detroit
Wales, Mike Gartner (Bourque) 19:51, February 12, 1985 at Calgary

EXTRA-ATTACKER GOALS

Only once has a goal been scored in All–Star play with the goalie out for an extra attacker, February 4, 1986, Dale Hawerchuk

PULLING THE GOALIE

Montreal pulled McNeil, October 3, 1953 at Montreal
NHL All–Stars pulled Sawchuk, October 2, 1955 at Detroit
West pulled Worsley, January 25, 1972 at Minnesota
West pulled Vachon, January 30, 1973 at New York
East pulled Dryden, January 29, 1974 at Chicago
Campbell pulled Stephenson, January 20, 1976 at Philadelphia
Campbell pulled Resch, January 25, 1977 at Vancouver
Campbell pulled Fuhr, January 31, 1984 at New Jersey
Campbell pulled Fuhr, February 12, 1985 at Calgary
Campbell pulled Moog, February 4, 1986 at Hartford (successful)
Western pulled Joseph, January 22, 1994 at New York

OVERTIME GOALS

Wales, Perreault (Shutt, Salming) 3:55, January 24, 1978 at Buffalo
Wales, Trottier (Bossy) 3:05, February 4, 1986 at Hartford
Wales, Lemieux (Naslund, Dineen) 1:08, February 9, 1988 at St. Louis

Speed Records

FASTEST TWO GOALS, BOTH TEAMS, FROM START OF GAME

37 seconds   Jacques Laperrière (East) at 0:20
             Dean Prentice (West) at 0:37
             January 20, 1970 at St. Louis

FASTEST TWO GOALS, ONE TEAM, FROM START OF GAME

2:15   Teemu Selanne (World) at 0:53
             Jaromir Jagr (World) at 2:15
             January 18, 1998 at Vancouver

FASTEST TWO GOALS, ONE PLAYER, FROM START OF GAME

3:37   Mike Gartner (Wales) scored at 3:15 and
             3:37, February 6, 1993 at Montreal

4:00   Teemu Selanne (World) scored at 0:53 and 4:00, January 18, 1998
             at Vancouver

FASTEST TWO GOALS, ONE PLAYER

8 seconds   Owen Nolan (Western) scored at 18:54 and 19:02, 2nd period,
             January 18, 1997 at San Jose

10 seconds   Dennis Ververgaert (Campbell) scored at 4:33 and 4:43, 3rd
             period, January 20, 1976 at Philadelphia

FASTEST TWO GOALS, BOTH TEAMS

13 seconds   Teemu Selanne (World) scored at 4:00 and John LeClair (North
             America) at 4:13, 1st period, January 18, 1998 at Vancouver

FASTEST THREE GOALS, ONE TEAM

1:08   Mike Gartner (Wales) at 3:15
             Mike Gartner (Wales) at 3:37
             Peter Bondra (Wales) at 4:23
             1st period, February 6, 1993 at Montreal

1:32   Ron Stackhouse (Wales) at 11:40
             Craig Hartsburg (Wales) at 12:40
             Reed Larson (Wales) at 13:12
             3rd period, February 5, 1980 at Detroit

FASTEST THREE GOALS, BOTH TEAMS

1:14   Bob Kudelski (Eastern) at 9:46
             Sergei Fedorov (Western) at 10:20
             Eric Lindros (Eastern) at 11:00
             1st period, January 22, 1994 at New York

1:25   Bryan Trottier (Wales) at 4:03
             Brian Bellows (Campbell) at 4:50
             Alexander Mogilny (Wales) at 5:28
             3rd period, January 18, 1992 at Philadelphia

FASTEST FOUR GOALS, BOTH TEAMS

2:24   Brendan Shanahan (Western) at 16:38
             Dale Hawerchuk (Eastern) at 17:28
             Owen Nolan (Western) at 18:54
             Owen Nolan (Western) at 19:02
             2nd period, January 18, 1997 at San Jose

3:04   Mark Recchi (Eastern) at 15:32
             Dale Hawerchuk (Eastern) at 16:19
             Pavel Bure (Western) at 17:36
             Paul Kariya (Western) at 18:36
             1st period, January 18, 1997 at San Jose

3:20   Teemu Selanne (World) at 0:53
             Jaromir Jagr (World) at 2:15
             Teemu Selanne (World) at 4:00
             John LeClair (North America) at 4:13
             1st period, January 18, 1998 at Vancouver

FASTEST FOUR GOALS, ONE TEAM

4:19   Brian Bellows (Campbell) at 7:40
             Jeremy Roenick (Campbell) at 8:13
             Theoren Fleury (Campbell) at 11:06
             Brett Hull (Campbell) at 11:59
             2nd period, January 18, 1992 at Philadelphia

4:26   Ron Stackhouse (Wales) at 11:40
             Craig Hartsburg (Wales) at 12:40
             Reed Larson (Wales) at 13:12
             Real Cloutier (Wales) at 16:06
             3rd period, February 5, 1980 at Detroit

Individual Records—Career

MOST GAMES PLAYED

23	Gordie Howe (1948 to 1980)
18	Wayne Gretzky (1980 to 1999)
	Ray Bourque (1981 to 2000)

MOST CONSECUTIVE GAMES PLAYED

18	Wayne Gretzky (1980 to 1999)
	Ray Bourque (1981 to 2000)
15	Frank Mahovlich (1960 to 1974)

MOST GOALS

13	Wayne Gretzky
11	Mario Lemieux
10	Gordie Howe

MOST ASSISTS

13	Mark Messier
	Ray Bourque
12	Wayne Gretzky
	Adam Oates
	Joe Sakic
10	Paul Coffey

MOST POINTS

25	Wayne Gretzky
20	Mario Lemieux
19	Gordie Howe

MOST PENALTY MINUTES

27	Gordie Howe
21	Gus Mortson
16	Harry Howell

MOST POWER-PLAY GOALS

6	Gordie Howe
3	Bobby Hull
2	Maurice Richard

Individual Records—One Game
MOST GOALS (all hat tricks)

4   Mike Gartner (Wales), February 6, 1993 at Montreal
Vincent Damphousse (Campbell), January 19, 1991 at Chicago
Mario Lemieux (Wales), January 21, 1990 at Pittsburgh
Wayne Gretzky (Campbell), February 8, 1983 at Long Island

3   Pavel Bure (World), February 6, 2000 at Toronto
Teemu Selanne (World), January 18, 1998 at Vancouver
Owen Nolan (Western), January 18, 1997 at San Jose
Mark Recchi (Eastern), January 18, 1997 at San Jose
Pierre Turgeon (Wales), February 6, 1993 at Montreal
Mario Lemieux (Wales), February 9, 1988 at St. Louis
Ted Lindsay (Detroit), October 8, 1950 at Detroit

MOST ASSISTS

5   Mats Naslund (Wales), February 9, 1988 at St. Louis
4   Pierre Turgeon (Eastern), January 22, 1994 at New York
Adam Oates (Wales), February 6, 1993 at Montreal
Mark Recchi (Wales), February 6, 1993 at Montreal
Adam Oates (Campbell), January 19, 1991 at Chicago
Ray Bourque (Wales), February 12, 1985 at Calgary

MOST POINTS

6   Mario Lemieux (Wales—3 goals, 3 assists), February 9, 1988
at St. Louis

5   Mike Gartner (Wales—4 goals, one assist), February 6, 1993
at Montreal
Mark Recchi (Wales—one goal, 4 assists), February 6, 1993
at Montreal
Pierre Turgeon (Wales—3 goals, 2 assists), February 6, 1993
at Montreal
Adam Oates (Campbell—one goal, 4 assists), January 19, 1991
at Chicago
Mats Naslund (Wales—5 assists), February 9, 1988 at St. Louis

Individual Records—Period
MOST GOALS

4   Wayne Gretzky (Campbell), 3rd period, February 8, 1983
at Long Island

3   Mike Gartner (Wales), 1st period, February 6, 1993 at Montreal
Vincent Damphousse (Campbell), 3rd period, January 19, 1991
at Chicago
Mario Lemieux (Wales), 1st period, January 21, 1990 at Pittsburgh

MOST ASSISTS

4   Adam Oates (Wales), 1st period, February 6, 1993 at Montreal
3   Mark Messier (Campbell), 3rd period, February 8, 1983
at Long Island

MOST POINTS

4   Mike Gartner (Wales—3 goals, one assist), 1st period, February 6,
1993 at Montreal
Adam Oates (Wales—4 assists), 1st period, February 6, 1993
at Montreal
Wayne Gretzky (Campbell—4 goals), 3rd period, February 8, 1983
at Long Island

MOST POWER-PLAY GOALS, INDIVIDUAL, ONE PERIOD & GAME

2   Wally Hergesheimer (All-Stars), 1st period, October 3, 1953
at Montreal

All Speed Records—Individual
FASTEST GOAL FROM START OF A GAME

19 seconds   Ted Lindsay (Detroit), October 8, 1950 at Detroit
20 seconds   Jacques Laperrière (East), January 20, 1970 at St. Louis
21 seconds   Mario Lemieux (Wales), January 21, 1990 at Pittsburgh

FASTEST GOAL FROM START OF A PERIOD (other than first)

19 seconds   Rick Tocchet (Wales), 2nd period, February 6, 1993 at Montreal

ALL GOALTENDER RECORDS
MOST GAMES PLAYED, CAREER

13	Glenn Hall (1955 to 1969)
11	Terry Sawchuk (1950 to 1968)
8	Patrick Roy (1988 to 1998)
	Jacques Plante (1956 to 1970)

MOST CONSECUTIVE GAMES PLAYED

9	Glenn Hall (1960 to 1969)
7	Terry Sawchuk (1950 to 1956)

MOST MINUTES PLAYED, CAREER

540	Glenn Hall
467	Terry Sawchuk
370	Jacques Plante

MOST GOALS ALLOWED, CAREER

24	Patrick Roy
22	Glenn Hall
21	Mike Vernon

MOST GOALS ALLOWED, ONE APPEARANCE

8   Mike Vernon (Campbell) played 29:14, January 21, 1990 at Pittsburgh
7   Pelle Lindbergh (Wales) played 29:56, February 8, 1983 at Long Island
6   Andy Moog (Western) played 20:00, January 18, 1997 at San Jose
Mike Vernon (Campbell) played 20:00, February 6, 1993 at Montreal
Ed Belfour (Campbell) played 20:00, February 6, 1993 at Montreal
Don Beaupre (Wales) played 20:00, January 18, 1992 at Philadelphia
Reggie Lemelin (Wales) played 30:02, February 7, 1989 at Edmonton
Andy Moog (Wales) played 30:12, January 19, 1991 at Chicago

BEST GOALS AGAINST AVERAGE

0.68	Gilles Villemure
1.50	Johnny Bower
1.51	Frank Brimsek

GOALIE SHUTOUTS

Charlie Hodge and Gary Bauman shared a shutout, Montreal, January 18, 1967
Montreal 3   NHL All-Stars 0

GOALIE ASSISTS

1   Arturs Irbe (World) 1999

GOALIE PENALTY MINUTES

2   Glenn Resch (Wales) 1984

Billy Smith (Campbell) 1978

Charlie Hodge (Montreal) 1964

YOUNGEST TO PLAY IN AN ALL–STAR GAME

Fleming Mackell (1947)*	18 years, 5 months, 13 days
Larry Hillman (1955)*	18 years, 6 months, 27 days
Steve Yzerman (1984)	18 years, 8 months, 22 days
Kirk Muller (1985)	19 years, 4 days
Wayne Gretzky (1980)	19 years, 10 days

OLDEST TO PLAY IN AN ALL–STAR GAME

Gordie Howe (1980)	51 years, 10 months, 5 days
Doug Harvey (1969)	44 years, 1 month, 2 days
Gump Worsley (1972)	42 years, 8 months, 11 days
Allan Stanley (1968)*	41 years, 10 months, 15 days
Jacques Plante (1970)	41 years, 3 days

*played as a member of Cup-winning team

Photo Credits

Dave Sandford/Hockey Hall of Fame
 p. 3 (all), 9 (all right), 16 (top), 17, 34, 45
 (top), 46, 50, 56, 85, 90, 99, 104, 111, 112,
 115, 116, 122 (both), 128 (bottom), 129 (bottom), 132, 134, 139 (top), 148 (both), 150,
 152, 157, 164, 165, 169, 170, 172, 173, 179
 (both), 183, 184 (bottom), 187, 188, 194, 195,
 202, 208 (both), 212 (both), 213, 216, 217,
 222, 223, 225, 226 (top), 231, 232 (both), 236,
 239, 243 (both), 248, 249, 251, 252, 253, 254,
 258, 260, 261, 262 (both) 263

Turofsky Collection-Imperial Oil/HHOF
 p. 5 (right), 6 (both), 8 (both), 9 (left), 21, 22,
 23, 31, 32, 38, 41 (both), 42 (bottom), 60, 62,
 68, 72

London Life-Portnoy Collection/HHOF
 p. 138, 139 (bottom)

HHOF
 p. 1, 2 (right), 5 (left), 11, 13 (all), 15, 16 (bottom), 24, 33, 42 (top), 49, 52, 55, 118, 163

Graphic Artists/HHOF
 p. 80 (both), 81, 83, 84, 88, 89, 102, 103, 108

O-Pee-Chee/HHOF
 p.189

Doug MacLellan/HHOF
 p. 211, 226 (bottom), 227, 230, 237, 238

Dave Dahms/Ed Moffatt
 p. 26, 28 (all), 29 (all), 37, 76 (both), 124,
 125, 126, 127 (both), 128 (top), 129 (top),
 131, 133, 135

Denis Brodeur
 p. 137

Bruce Bennett Studios
 p. 142, 154, 155, 156, 168, 174, 175, 177, 182,
 184 (top), 192, 193, 198, 199, 201, 207, 209,
 215, 218, 220, 221, 246, 247

Montreal Gazette
 p. 45 (bottom), 65, 94, 97, 98

Vancouver Sun
 p. 147 (both)

AP/Wide World Photos
 p. 44, 110, 114, 143, 151

Corbis/Bettman
 p. 75, 119, 120, 121

Canapress
 p. 257

Brian Babineau/Sports Action
 p. 241

Steve Babineau/Sports Action
 p. 242 (both)

Acknowledgements

The author would like to thank numbers of people who have been helpful in one way or another in getting this book from idea to bound volume to bookstore. First, to everyone at the Hockey Hall of Fame for their ongoing help and support, notably governor Phil Pritchard, who maintains a high level of energy even though the big four-oh beckons; Craig Campbell, Resource Centre guru and goaler extraordinaire with or without contacts; Darren Boyko, point man for the IIHF with a decent slapper if given time; Izak Westgate for key photo eye-dees, last minute; Tyler Wolosewich, the kindest, most patient metal-head in the city; Peter Jagla, a first rate person, a second rate pool player. To photographer Dave Sandford (SI cover boy), for expert images and going beyond the call of duty for this and other projects. And many thanks for various helps and friendships too from Jacqueline Boughazale, Marilyn Robbins, and Margaret Lockhart. To Ken Dryden, Tom Anselmi, Pat Park, and Casey Vanden Heuvel at the ACC for help and encouragement. To Benny Ercolani and David Keon at the NHL. To everyone at HarperCollins for their superior efforts in producing the book, especially Don Loney, Roy Nicol, Alan Jones, Nicole Langlois, and e-editor Sheila Wawanash. To my agent, Dean Cooke, and his associate Suzanne Brandreth, for helping me along with this and other projects over the last year. To Denis Brodeur, Phil Norton, Dave Dahms, Ed Moffatt, Bruce Bennett, and Donald Bowden for photographic assistance of the first order. To Greg Innis and Paul Patskou for numbers, names, and helpful phone calls along the way. To Dr. Hugh Smythe, Mr. Frank Selke, and Miss Joyce Bailey, for taking me to those precious games oh so many years ago. To Jon Redfern, inspector Billy Yamamoto, Jeff Davis, Geri Dasgupta, and Jack David for tons of this and that and what have you. To Zack, first-rounder in 2016, Liz, Ian, and Emily, and of course my mom, C.M., who still has three years to go before her upgrade.